MOSAIC

MOSAIC

A CHRONICLE OF FIVE GENERATIONS

DIANE ARMSTRONG

ST. MARTIN'S GRIFFIN
NEW YORK

www.stmartins.com

Library of Congress Cataloging-in-Publication Data

Armstrong, Diane, 1939–
    Mosaic : a chronicle of five generations / Diane Armstrong.—1st St. Martin's Griffin ed.
      p. cm.
    Originally published: Milsons Point, NSW : Random House, 1998.
    Includes bibliographical references.
    ISBN 0-312-27455-6 (hc)
    ISBN 0-312-30510-9 (pbk)
    1. Armstrong, Diane, 1939–. 2. Baldinger family. 3. Jews—Poland—Biography.
4. Holocaust, Jewish (1939–1945)—Poland—Personal narratives. 5. Holocaust survivors—Australia—Biography. 6. Australia—Biography. 7. Poland—Biography. I. Title.

DS135.P63 A123 2001
940.53'18'0922438—dc21
                                                  2001034904

First published in Australia by Random House Australia Pty Ltd.

First St. Martin's Griffin Edition: September 2002

10 9 8 7 6 5 4 3 2 1

To the memory of my parents, Bronia and Henry Boguslawski. Their courage was a blazing torch which lit up my life, and their love, strength and optimism have been a lifelong inspiration.

And to Michael, Jonathan and Justine. Having you in my life has been the greatest gift.

ACKNOWLEDGEMENTS

Words can't express my gratitude to my son Jonathan for his enthusiastic involvement in this book. His gentle but determined reminders spurred me on to keep writing at times when the going was tough and it would have been easier to put it off. My moment of truth came when he said, 'Mum, if you don't write this book I'll be devastated.' That's when I understood how important this family history was to him, and realised that I had to put everything else aside and write it.

My husband Michael has held my hand every step of this exciting journey, as he has throughout our married life. His boundless faith in me and in this project, together with his steady flow of humour and cappuccinos, have sustained me over the past few years. *Mosaic* has been greatly enriched by his impeccable literary taste and his reminders to concentrate on the story.

My daughter Justine gave me the confidence to take the first vital step, and made my emotional pilgrimage to Poland and Ukraine more meaningful by sharing it. Thanks to her, I became more attuned to the roles of the women I was writing about.

Susan, my new daughter, has given me her whole-hearted support every step of the way, and been unstinting in her help. Her reading of the manuscript was sensitive and meticulous, her comments were perceptive, and our frequent 'cuppas' together have been a joy.

While collecting information for Mosaic, I've come to admire the strength, intelligence and resilience of my remarkable relatives without whose help this book could not have been written. Sadly, many of the aunts and uncles whose stories form such a large part of this book, have not lived to see it completed. Aunty Lunia, Aunty Andzia, and Hela and Jozek Kwasniewski in Israel, Uncle Izio in California, Uncle Marcel in Paris and Maryla Spyra in London have all died in the past few years, as has my cousin Adam in Philadelphia.

I owe a huge debt to my cousin Wanda Matt whose humour, wisdom and insight have lightened my task. My cousin Krysia Ginzig and Aunty Slawa Szymanska have been extraordinarily patient and willing to answer endless questions, search for information and provide photographs. I'm very grateful to Jako Baldinger and Edith Baldinger, Aline Baldinger-Achour and Danielle Kertudo in Paris; Lee Zaks, Tamara Zahavi, Max Matt and Marian and Kristine Keren in the US, and to Fred and Phyllis Ross for their warmth and support. My thanks also to Shirley Hill and Gertrude Spira in England; Dov Spira, Rozia Johannes, Jozef Spira, Gabris Kling and Anne Bennett in Israel; Mario Szymanski and Lola Nowicka in Poland, and Michelle Blutman, Rywka Liberow, Anita Frydman and John Birner in Melbourne.

The following people have helped me so much along the way: Leon Plager and Zygmunt Lainer in Ukraine, and Tadeusz Dziekonski and Anna Hriniewicz in Poland. And Father Roman Soszynski whom I can never thank enough.

Writing a book is a long and solitary task but my wonderful friends kept my spirits up with their steadfast affection, support and understanding. I'm particularly grateful to Raymonde Raiz for her generous heart and readiness to help, Dasia Black

Gutman for her encouragement and illuminating comments, and Carole Solomon for her empathy. Trevor Wise helped with the glossary, Betty Harding sent me encouraging notes and prayed for me, and Sarah Billington gave me ideas for the cover.

I'm very fortunate in having Selwa Anthony as my agent. I appreciate her unbounded faith in *Mosaic* and value her enthusiasm, professionalism and dedication more than I can say.

The support I've had from the team at Random House has been overwhelming. I'd like to thank Linda Funnell, Jane Palfreyman, Margaret Sullivan and Juliet Rogers. With her sensitive heart and gentle touch, Julia Stiles was an ideal editor. Thanks also to Helen Davis-Miller and Kim Swivel.

I'm grateful to Dina Abramovich at the YIVO Institute for Jewish Research in New York, and to Professor Anna Wierzbicka and Mary Besemeres of the Australian National University for translations of Adam Mickiewicz's 'The Song Survives'.

Finally, my thanks go to the Literature Board of the Australia Council for the grant which gave me important moral as well financial support.

THE SONG SURVIVES

Flames may consume a priceless work of art,
Thieves plunder coffers full of gleaming jewels.
Only a melody lives on
And weaves among the throng.
If callous souls don't moisten it with tears
Or nourish it with hope,
It will float to the hills and soar to the spires
And from its eyrie sing of bygone days
Like a lark that flees a flame-draped building
and clings to the rooftop.
When the roof crumbles, it flies to the woods
Above ruins and tombs,
And warbles its lament to all who pass.

From 'Konrad Wallenrod' by Adam Mickiewicz; translated by
Diane Armstrong.

CONTENTS

Author's note on Polish proper names

There are many name changes throughout this narrative.

In surnames ending in 'ski' the feminine form changes to 'ska', e.g. Mr Boguslawski but Mrs Boguslawska. The feminine form of some surnames ending with a consonant end in 'owa', e.g. Mr Bogdan but Mrs Bogdanowa.

Polish first names ending in 'a' change to 'u' when the person is being addressed. So when someone is speaking to Lunia, for example, they address her as 'Luniu'.

In Polish, the affectionate diminutive form of a name is often used, so my father, for example, who was given the name Hirsh, came to be called Hesiu.

Another reason for name changes is that Jews with distinctly Jewish names often changed them to avoid discrimination and persecution. That's why my father changed his name to Henryk, whose diminutive form is Henek. In Australia, however, he became known as Henry.

Poland in 1939

BALDINGER/SPIRA FAMILY TREE
AND BRATTER/GOLDMAN FAMILY TREE

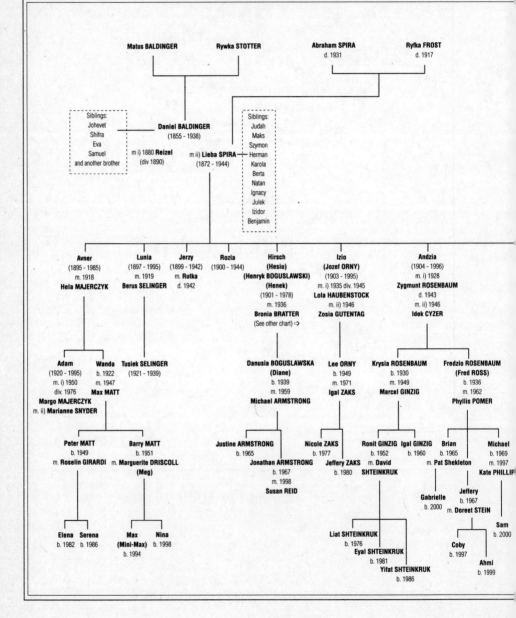

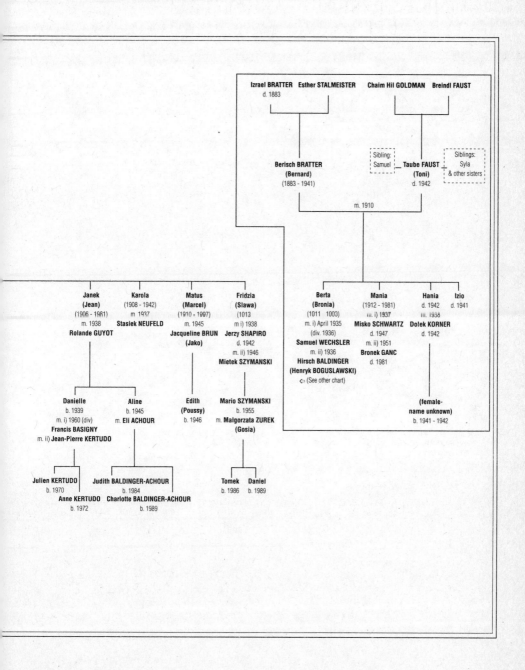

Izrael BRATTER   Esther STALMEISTER   Chaim Hil GOLDMAN   Breindl FAUST
     d. 1883

                    Berisch BRATTER   Sibling: Taube FAUST   Siblings:
                      (Bernard)   Samuel   (Toni)   Syla
                     (1883 - 1941)   d. 1942   & other sisters

                                    m. 1910

Janek   Karola   Matus   Fridzia   Berta   Mania   Hania   Izio
(Jean)   (1908 - 1942)   (Marcel)   (Slawa)   (Bronia)   (1912 - 1981) d. 1942   d. 1941
(1906 - 1981) m 1937   (1910 - 1997) (1013   (1011 1003)   iii. i) 1937   iii. 1938
m. 1938   Stasiek NEUFELD m. 1945   m i) 1938   m. i) April 1935 Misko SCHWARTZ Dolek KORNER
Rolande GUYOT   Jacqueline BRUN Jerzy SHAPIRO (div. 1936)   d. 1947   d. 1942
                               (Jako)   d. 1942   Samuel WECHSLER m. ii) 1951
                                              m. ii) 1946   m. ii) 1936   Bronek GANC
                                              Mietek SZYMANSKI Hirsch BALDINGER d. 1981
                                                             (Henryk BOGUSLAWSKI)
                                                             ↪ (See other chart)

Danielle   Aline   Edith   Mario SZYMANSKI   (female-
b. 1939   b. 1945   (Poussy)   b. 1955   name unknown)
m. i) 1960 (div) m. Eli ACHOUR b. 1946   m. Malgorzata ZUREK   b. 1941 - 1942
Francis BASIGNY   (Gosia)
m. ii) Jean-Pierre KERTUDO

Julien KERTUDO Judith BALDINGER-ACHOUR   Tomek   Daniel
b. 1970   b. 1984   b. 1986 b. 1989
Anne KERTUDO   Charlotte BALDINGER-ACHOUR
b. 1972   b. 1989

PROLOGUE

On a hazy summer's day in 1990, when the air quivered and the cobblestones sizzled beneath my feet, I wandered around Krakow's Kazimierz district with my cousin Mario. As we explored narrow lanes and discovered traces of long-forgotten buildings, the past seeped out of the worn paving stones, weathered gates and twisted alleyways. Around each corner I expected to see shadowy figures in long black coats entering prayer houses, and to hear horse carriages clattering along narrow streets.

I don't know what made me pause in front of a large white building with a stark facade. Above the entrance, two deeply recessed windows stared down at the street like knowing eyes in an ancient face. According to the plaque on the wall, this was Ajzyk's Synagogue, which was being restored. Even today this building stands out from its surroundings like a duchess at a fish market, so I could imagine what a sensation it must have created three hundred years ago when it towered over the huddle of wretched dwellings that surrounded it.

When we pushed open the oak door to look inside, acrid fumes of new paint bit my throat. The late afternoon sun slanted into the spacious prayer hall, lighting up its vaulted ceiling and newly plastered walls with a warm glow. A paint-splashed ladder stood against one wall, beside two buckets stuffed with rags. The building was deserted.

As we turned to leave, a hum of murmuring voices resounded across the room, stronger and more insistent all the time. Mario and I looked at each other. So the synagogue was not empty after all. A group of people must have gathered to pray upstairs.

The scent of newly sawn wood rose from the floorboards as we sprinted up the stairs two at a time, eager to find out who they were. I flung open the door, imagining heads turning towards us in surprise.

We stood in an empty, silent room.

There was no-one in the building, no-one in the grounds, no-one anywhere in the street. My skin prickled as I stood surrounded by white silence, grappling with thoughts too strange to comprehend. How to make sense of those murmuring voices we both had heard, that rhythmic chanting of Jews at prayer, those cadences which were to haunt me for months to come.

After returning to Sydney, I dreamed one night I was in Krakow once again. Searching in one bookshop after another, I asked each bookseller the same question. 'Do you have a book about the Jews of Kazimierz?' And at each store I received the same reply. 'There is no such book.'

Before the words had evaporated into the warm night air, I sat bolt upright as the meaning of that dream became clear. The book I'd searched for in my dream didn't exist because I hadn't written it yet. It was my own book I was looking for, and the voices that I'd heard that day in Ajzyk's Synagogue were the voices of my ancestors clamouring to be heard.

PART ONE

CHAPTER 1

Clouds scudded across a glowering sky and rustling leaves dropped off the chestnut trees that autumn day in 1890 when Daniel Baldinger trod the narrow alleys of Krakow's Jewish district, wondering how to break the news to his wife Reizel.

Lost in thought, he crossed Meiselsa Street, past prayer houses where bearded men in wide velour hats and long black coats walked brim to brim. Above narrow doorways, signs in Yiddish advertised Susser Brothers' wines, Pischinger's chocolate, Blawat's accessories and Rosenberg's tailoring. In the marketplace on Plac Estery, housewives in long skirts and silk wigs peered at cheeses, squeezed chickens and poked tomatoes on the stalls. Not far from barefoot peasant women in flowered kerchiefs holding up plump chickens, fishmongers pulled slippery carp out of wooden barrels as big as wells. Sharp eyed and sharp mannered, they pretended to curse the shoppers who bought fish from their rivals. 'Your arm should drop off when you carry it home, God forbid! Onions should sprout from your navel!' they shouted.

A lad in a fraying jacket swung past Daniel with his basket heaped with crusty salt-spangled bagels. An apple-cheeked woman had to swerve to avoid dropping her tray of pears scented with cinnamon and cloves. 'Spiced pears! Sweeter than your mother's love!' she called in a piping voice. A flustered matron, her silken wig awry, hurriedly selected carrots for the *tzimmes* and onion for the carp. 'Are you late for this Sabbath or early for the next?' the stallholder laughed.

Normally Daniel would have stopped to breathe in the country smell of white farm cheeses and pats of glistening butter, but today he walked past them, hardly noticing. Soon the stallholders would fold up their stands, the storekeepers would pull down their wooden shutters, and peace would fall like a velvet mantle over the noisy streets of Kazimierz. Inside every home freshly scrubbed faces would sit expectantly around lighted candles and braided *challahs*, ready to share the Almighty's gift of the Sabbath. Daniel's face grew sombre. Inside every home except his.

Amid the bustle of the marketplace, he exuded an aura of dignity, a solitary figure in a well-cut overcoat and homburg hat, his neatly trimmed beard streaked with grey. Daniel had the penetrating gaze of those who see beyond appearances, and the commanding presence of a man who knows himself and seeks no man's favours.

On his way home to face the most distressing decision of his life, my grandfather Daniel Baldinger is unaware that a shadowy figure is pursuing him through the crowd, dogging his footsteps, craning to catch every nuance of his expression. I am the invisible stalker, weaving a bridge between my grandfather and myself, between past and present, to piece together fragments of lives that ended before mine began. All my life my father told me about this patriarch whom he venerated and admired. Just, tolerant, understanding and wise. All my life I've accepted this image without questioning, but now I'm embarking on a journey into the past to meet the grandfather I never knew.

Daniel turned into the narrow alley which sunlight rarely warmed and reverently touched the *mezuzah* affixed to the right hand side of his front door jamb where a tiny scroll of parchment was inscribed with the main tenets of Jewish faith. But he needed no *mezuzah* to remind him of the glory of God. God's commandments were inscribed in his heart.

As soon as she heard Daniel close the front door, Reizel's heart hammered beneath her high-necked blouse. She took a deep breath, smoothed down her long skirt and gripped the well-worn oak table where they had shared so many meals. One thousand times that day her mind had churned over what her fate would be, and now that the moment had arrived, her mouth felt as dry as if it were Yom Kippur. Outside, a pewter sky hung low over a grey, cold city, but her cheeks burned and her hands were clammy.

The compassionate gaze in her husband's deep-set eyes told her the answer before he spoke. She stiffened and looked away. 'I'll provide well for you,' he said, hoping that the gentleness of his voice would soften the blow. 'You'll have a house and your own business, you'll want for nothing.' But his words didn't comfort her because the only thing she wanted in all the world was to stay with him.

Daniel and his wife had been married for ten years. Or more exactly, one hundred and twenty months, because their life together had been measured out in her menstrual cycles. Daniel was thirty-five, and with every passing year he seemed to hear God reproaching him. 'I can't live without children,' he told her. 'In return for the gift of life, a man must leave another generation to replace him. I want to have sons so that I can teach them to worship the Almighty and study the Torah. If I can't *doven in shule* beside my sons, I won't have fulfilled my duty to God,' he explained.

Reizel rarely argued with her husband, but this time her future was at stake. 'Perhaps Almighty God, blessed be His name, didn't intend us to have children,' she replied, tight-lipped. Daniel shook his head. A couple must have children.

7

Go forth and multiply, that's what the Almighty had instructed Adam and Eve. And the Gemara said that a man must have sons to say the Kaddish prayer for him after he dies so that his soul can find eternal peace.

Divorce among orthodox Jews was very rare in 1890. As couples didn't marry for love, they didn't separate when love was gone. Marriages were arranged, expectations were low, and eventually most husbands and wives came to appreciate each other's good qualities. Divorce, however, was permitted in certain circumstances and childlessness was one of them. Daniel's spiritual adviser, the Sanzer Rebbe, whom he consulted about the major dilemmas in his life, had told him that if a husband and wife have been married for ten years and have no offspring, they are permitted to separate so that both can remarry and have children. My grandfather must have been extraordinarily determined, because as well as Reizel and his parents-in-law, even his own parents opposed his decision.

'Divorce!' His mother-in-law had been aghast. 'What has poor Reizel done to deserve this terrible fate? Who will marry a woman cast off by her husband after ten years? What's to become of her?'

Daniel looked troubled. 'This is no reflection on Reizel,' he pointed out. 'Our holy books have said that there's no disgrace in divorce if a couple separate because they are childless.'

Reizel's relatives stirred the pot. 'What's the world coming to when a man can cast off a wife after ten years? Mark my words, he'll look for some young *maidl* somewhere,' one aunt sneered. 'You'll see, younger is better! So that's how our sages are applying their learning, encouraging men to forsake their wives when they become bored with them.'

Their rancour was understandable. Although the rabbis permitted a childless couple to divorce, they didn't demand it. According to my father, his father's choice was all the more remarkable since he loved his first wife, but his yearning for children overshadowed everything else in his life.

Although Daniel was born in the village of Lukowice, his parents later moved to nearby Nowy Sacz, a pretty mountain town south of Krakow, where Jewish tailors, bakers, butchers, cobblers and merchants lived and worked in dim workshops around the town square. Behind the square flowed the Dunajec River, where on hot summer days boys splashed beneath the bridge and lazed in the shade of the willow trees.

Ever since the first partition of Poland in 1772, the south-eastern part of the country had been named Galicia and had become part of the Austro-Hungarian Empire. So many Jews had settled in Galicia that it was said that even the Vistula River murmured in Yiddish. German was the official language and Vienna was the centre of the world. After completing his training as a gasfitter in Vienna, Daniel had moved to Kazimierz, the Jewish quarter of Krakow. A good tradesman with a sound business sense, he built up a successful business at a time when plumbing was in its infancy. At the age of thirty-five, he was financially secure and highly respected in the community. But without children to glorify the Almighty and ensure immortality, what was the point of such success?

The days hung heavily on Daniel and his wife until the time came to mount the well-worn stairs to the rabbi's house. Silently they sat side by side in a room where squeaking floorboards were piled with fraying books and dusty scrolls while the old scribe with a black skull cap on his head scraped on a piece of parchment with a goose quill.

When the bill of divorce was completed, the white-bearded rabbi placed it into Reizel's trembling hands and pronounced that as they were now divorced, they must never again live under the same roof and were both free to remarry after three months. I can imagine how slowly and heavily Reizel descended the stairs to begin her empty life.

After setting her up in a little dairy on Wawrzynska Street where she sold milk, eggs and butter in the front room and lived in the back, Daniel started looking for a second wife who would give him the sons he yearned for.

He didn't have long to wait. A man of exemplary character and good income who is in search of a wife rarely lacks offers, and the eager *shadchens* of Galicia soon started poring over their lists of marriageable girls. In the doorways and market-places, synagogues and *shtibls*, tongues wagged overtime. 'Have you heard? Daniel Baldinger is looking for another wife. He's a good match even though he's divorced. They say he's doing very well, laying those gas pipes of his.'

But before any of them had time to submit their candidates, a china merchant came to see Daniel. He was a stout man with dancing eyes and a tar-black beard that bristled with a life of its own. The purposeful gleam in his eye revealed that he hadn't come to sell cups and saucers. 'I've come on an important errand, Mr Baldinger. You're looking for a wife and, believe me, I know just the one. I do business with a merchant in Szczakowa called Abraham Spira who has a marriageable daughter,' he said, stroking his wiry beard. 'It's a good family, the father is rich, and the daughter is hardworking and modest. You'll get a handsome dowry and a good wife, God willing. And she's a *sheine maidl*, too, *khanaynahora*, may the evil eye not touch her.' The merchant looked at Daniel and moistened his full lips.

Daniel liked a pretty face and admired modest, industrious women. He also admired learning, and what he found out about this family's antecedents aroused his interest. Abraham Spira was descended from Nathan Nata Spira, a famous seventeenth century Jewish philosopher whose commentaries on the mystical texts of the Kabbala had become classics. He believed that the secrets of the universe could be unravelled by mathematical calculations. Abraham Spira was also said to have been descended from the great sixteenth century rabbi Moses Isserles of Krakow.

Although this impressive lineage undoubtedly whetted Daniel's interest in the prospective bride, not much linked Abraham Spira spiritually with his ancestor. Abraham was a despot who disciplined his nine sons like a general. An aristocratic looking man whose fine face was framed by a neatly trimmed beard of soft grey hair, he was a progressive Jew. He chose well-cut suits made of the finest materials and didn't want his wife Ryfka to wear a wig like other orthodox Jewish matrons of the time.

Abraham had remarkable business acumen. Long before department stores were introduced into Poland, he founded an emporium in Szczakowa, a small railway junction north of Krakow where trains converged from Austria, Prussia and Russia. This store stocked everything under one roof, from curtains, tables and washing boards, to wheels of Swiss cheese and women's corsets.

Spira's store was the wonder of the region. People used to marvel that you could go in there naked, destitute and hungry, and come out clothed, fed and equipped for life. Abraham's persuasive staff made sure that many customers left with considerably more than they'd intended to buy. Soldiers were sometimes persuaded that brassieres were double purses, and simple country women were talked into buying dresses three sizes too big for them. 'That dress makes you look like Queen Jadwiga, it fits you like a glove,' salesmen would gush, bunching folds of loose material behind the woman's back. 'Wojtek won't be able to take his eyes off you at church on Sunday!'

All the twelve Spira children worked in the store while Ryfka sat placidly behind the counter, taking the money. The sons, who were confident and good-looking, flirted with the wives and daughters of the district officials over their ribbons and laces and, according to gossip, occasionally augmented their income by taking money out of the till.

Leonora, the oldest of the three Spira daughters, who came to be called Lieba, worked so hard in her parents' store that one customer thought she was a hired help. 'Why are you killing yourself for your employers? I've watched you slaving here from morning till night,' the woman remarked. 'It's not right. Don't let them take advantage of you like that!'

The girl looked down, her fair complexion flushing with embarrassment. 'I'm Lieba Spira. My father owns the store,' she replied, and turned away from the woman's shocked expression.

At a time when there was no shortage of willing country girls to work in town in exchange for a few *groschen*, food and a corner to sleep, the Spiras' acquaintances muttered that it was preposterous that Lieba should be a drudge in her parents' store. But some people are destined for a life of unremitting toil and that turned out to be my grandmother Lieba's destiny.

When Abraham Spira made inquiries about the prospective bridegroom, he found out that although Daniel Baldinger wasn't educated, he was respected in Kazimierz as a devout and honest man. He was pleased to see that, like him, Daniel wore well-cut suits and trimmed his beard, unlike those Chassids, whom he regarded as fanatics. With his knack for sizing people up, Abraham saw that this was a decent man on whom you could depend. The betrothal contract was soon drawn up.

Tongues wagged when news got around that Lieba Spira

was to marry a man who was neither young, handsome nor educated. And when they heard the scandal about his first wife, the neighbourhood gossips shook their heads in horror. Old Spira must have lost his mind. Fancy marrying a young *maidl* to a tradesman already advanced in years, and a divorced one at that. With all his money, why didn't Abraham Spira get his daughter a doctor or lawyer, or at least a scholar?

Neither Lieba nor her mother had any say in the matter. By now Ryfka Spira had become resigned to the fact that her autocratic husband always got his way. She was an energetic woman with deep-set eyes in a bony face. Daniel was pleased that his prospective bride had a softer, prettier face than her mother, and a rounded figure that looked promisingly fertile.

Lieba, on the other hand, was bitterly disappointed with her father's choice. At thirty-five, Daniel was almost twice her age. He was too old, too stern-looking and too serious. She had dreamed of falling in love with someone young and handsome, but instead of a glass slipper she was getting a second-hand shoe. Pouring out her heart to her younger sister Berta, she sobbed, 'It's awful to have to marry an old man who's been married before. I don't love Mr Baldinger and never will. I don't want to marry him, but what can I do? Father will never change his mind.' In their family, Abraham's word was law. Lieba wasn't rebellious enough to defy him, and besides, she had no money of her own and nowhere to go.

When Daniel arrived in Szczakowa for his wedding, his father-in-law, who was only fifteen years his senior, strolled beside him along Jagiellonska Street, the dusty main street of this country town, where artisans plied their trade in poky rooms. There was the tailor, the shoe maker and the apothecary

13

whose wooden drawers smelled of cloves, powder and mush-rooms. As in most little towns in Poland, over one third of Szczakowa's residents were Jews, and most of them were merchants, tradesmen, craftsmen, millers, innkeepers and retailers.

The Spiras lived on Parkowa Street, a wide tree-lined street facing the sand dunes. Unlike Daniel, who lived mod-estly, his future in-laws lived in fine style in their large one-storey house. Their table always overflowed with food and the ornately carved Biedemeier sideboard displayed Sevres porcelain.

On the Saturday morning before the wedding, when he was about to leave for synagogue to read from the Torah, Daniel was astonished to find that his future father-in-law had left home without him. An impatient man who waited for no-one, Abraham had donned his black patent leather shoes and silk top hat, and strode to synagogue alone. The synagogue was around the corner from the Spiras' house, in Kilinskiego Street, where the boughs of old chestnut trees formed a dense canopy overhead. Next door to the synagogue was the *mikveh*, the ritual bathhouse where women immersed themselves in a pool of natural water after menstruating or before their wedding, to cleanse and purify their bodies.

The following day Lieba wore a long lace veil fastened with a garland of flowers when she stood beneath the *chuppah* beside her bridegroom. 'Behold thou art consecrated unto me, according to the laws of Abraham and Moses,' Daniel repeated after the rabbi, while Ryfka pulled back her daughter's veil and placed the goblet of wine against her trembling lips.

After the rabbi had blessed the newly-weds and read out the marriage contract, Daniel stamped on the glass goblet to crush it, in commemoration of the destruction of the Temple in Jerusalem. Ryfka dabbed her eyes as she looked at her comely, fresh-faced daughter. Mr Baldinger certainly did look old, but he seemed kind and gentle. She sighed and hoped that she'd done the right thing, giving in to Abraham on this, as in everything else in their life.

After the wedding festivities were over, Lieba bade a tearful farewell to her large family to whom she was devoted. She had spent very little time with her bridegroom before the wedding and dreaded having to live with this solemn stranger. She felt that her dreams had been shattered just like the glass her new husband had crushed under the *chuppah* with his patent leather shoe.

After the friendly forests and big skies of Szczakowa, Lieba felt miserable in the big city with its hard-eyed strangers and supercilious buildings. Entombed in her silent flat at 19 Miodowa Street, she missed the resinous smell of pine needles, the undulating stretches of biscuit-coloured sand and the hubbub of her large family.

Her new home, which Daniel had bought with her oldest brother Judah and his wife Hania, was a handsome stone-faced corner house which stands there to this day. It faced the carved, colonnaded facade of the newly built progressive temple whose walls jutted out so that the rumbling horse waggons had to swing out sharply when they turned the corner.

Miodowa Street was one of the boundaries of the Jewish district of Kazimierz. The Jews had been confined to this district after being expelled from Krakow in 1497 after a succession of pogroms. Although some had gravitated back to the city, it wasn't until the new Austro-Hungarian constitution of 1867 that they were officially permitted to live wherever they chose. Wags used to joke that the only successful campaign in the revolution of 1848 was the march of the Jews from Kazimierz to Krakow. Like many others, Daniel took advantage of the liberal decree and moved to the outer edge of Kazimierz, closer to the city.

Feeling sorry for the young girl he'd placed in a city cage, Daniel told her stories every night to cheer her up. He told long complicated stories about rabbis with magical powers who could see into people's hearts, and sages who could see into the future. Although Daniel wasn't talkative, he was a compelling storyteller who kept his new wife enthralled with his inexhaustible tales.

'In the village of Lizhensk there lived a poor tailor called Moishe-Yudl,' one story began. 'Moishe-Yudl had eleven children, a wife and a mother-in-law, and they all lived together in one tiny room with all their chickens. The children screamed, the women fought, and the hens squawked. Moishe-Yudl was a patient and pious man, but he couldn't stand this commotion, so one day he set off to see his rebbe for advice.'

While he talked, Lieba noticed that her husband's neat ears lay flat against his finely shaped head and that, beneath his jutting brow, his intense dark eyes looked kindly into hers. Like a child listening to a fairy tale, she moved closer not to miss a single word. 'After hearing the poor tailor's story, the sage said, "Moishe-Yudl, buy a goat and keep it inside your home. Come back to see me in one week's time." The tailor was horrified but you can't argue with the rebbe. So he trudged home and got a goat as the rebbe advised.'

Lieba's eyes were round with astonishment. How could a wise man suggest such a thing? Surely he'd misunderstood the poor man's predicament? Eleven children in one room with chickens, and now a goat! But Daniel just smiled and continued his story.

'When Moishe-Yudl added the goat to his tiny hut, life became unbearable because now the goat was running riot as well. It was chewing up his cloth, unravelling the thread, upsetting his wife's saucepans and eating their food.

'Moishe-Yudl could hardly wait for the week to pass. When he came back to see the rebbe a week later, his hair was wild, his face was wrinkled, and his body sagged. "Oy *vey iz mir*! My life is not worth living," he lamented. "I can't work, my wife cries all day, my mother-in-law doesn't stop cursing me, and the house, may heaven forgive me, is like a pigsty. Rebbe, what shall I do?"'

Lieba's brown eyes were glued to Daniel's face. '"Moishe-Yudl, get rid of that goat and come back in a week's time," the rebbe ordered. This time when the tailor came back he had a big smile on his face and two plump chickens for the rebbe. "Rebbe, may the Almighty bless your wisdom, I got rid of the goat, and for the past week, life has been wonderful. Now all I have at home is just my wife, my mother-in-law, the chickens and the eleven children!"'

Lieba laughed and clapped her hands with delight, but in years to come, there must have been times when she thought that only by getting a goat would her own household seem more tolerable.

Gradually she came to like the serious stranger she had married. Although she would have preferred a livelier companion, Daniel was gentle and never broke his word. As he was more devout than her father, she had to observe more religious and dietary rules; but, accustomed to doing whatever was expected of her, she ran the household exactly as he wished.

Daniel also realised that his wife was a treasure. Lieba was energetic, efficient and frugal, had good business sense and did her best to please him. The furniture gleamed, the silver sparkled, and every Friday night when he sat down to a dinner of rich chicken broth with flat white beans that melted in his mouth, succulent beef brisket and apple strudl with the finest pastry he'd ever tasted, he thanked the Almighty not only for the gift of the Sabbath but also for sending him such a devoted, competent wife.

In fact, their life together would have been very pleasant were it not for one major problem. Children, the main goal of this union, failed to arrive. Month after long month, the tension between them grew. Doubts which neither dared articulate began to gnaw at them both. Each time Lieba discovered the relentless red stain, the spectre of Daniel's first wife haunted her. He had divorced Reizel because she'd been unable to bear children. Was that also to be her fate? Initially she hadn't wanted to marry him, but now she couldn't bear to be abandoned.

One day Lieba climbed the stairs, shoulders slumped, to confide in Hania, her brother Judah's wife. 'If I can't have children, I hope a carriage runs me down in the street,' she blurted. 'Daniel divorced his first wife because she was barren. I couldn't bear it if he divorced me,' she sobbed.

Her sister-in-law clucked her tongue. 'It isn't right to divorce a woman because she's barren,' she commented. 'Maybe Daniel is the one who can't have children. After all, he didn't have children with his first wife either.'

But Lieba shook her head. 'I'm sure it's my fault,' she sighed.

Every evening, after Daniel had finished his bookkeeping, Lieba watched the precise way he placed a sheet of carbon paper on top of his metal paper press to produce copies of accounts and receipts. As he worked he spoke little, but he felt increasingly uneasy. Perhaps God had intended him to be childless after all.

In 1894, four years after they had stood under the *chuppah*, Daniel couldn't wait any longer. Like Moishe-Yudl in his story, he went on pilgrimage to see his rebbe. Unlike rabbis, who were scholars trained to interpret Jewish laws, the rebbes were sages whom Chassidic Jews consulted whenever they had serious problems. Even though my grandfather didn't belong to this ultraorthodox sect, throughout his life he consulted the Sanzer Rebbe just as his own father had done.

With his devoutness on one hand, and his assimilated appearance on the other, Daniel stood at the crossroads of the traditional and progressive world. Unlike the Chassids who left their beards uncut, wore big black hats and long black coats, and displayed their prayer fringes outside their clothes, my grandfther trimmed his beard, wore European clothes and kept the prayer fringes out of sight.

Unlike most other Chassidic rebbes who lived in luxury, the Sanzer Rebbe was modest and unassuming, and that's probably what appealed to my grandfather. It was to Nowy Sacz that Daniel came on pilgrimage over the Tatra mountains at the age of forty to ask the Sanzer Rebbe's advice about the problem which had now obsessed him for fourteen years. There was an aura of piety in the austere book-filled room where Aron Halberstamm, the Sanzer Rebbe, held his court. After praying with the other worshippers, Daniel asked the Rebbe for his blessing so that he would have a son. Aron Halberstamm had piercing pale blue eyes and a grey beard that hung over his chest in two V's like a Biblical prophet. When he looked at someone he seemed to be able to see inside their soul. 'You will have a son,' the sage told Daniel. 'Call him Avner, after the son of King David.'

Soon after this visit, Lieba realised with mounting excitement that the crimson stain which she dreaded so much had not appeared that month. She said nothing until she was absolutely certain. Telling good news too soon was a sure way of alerting malicious spirits which might, God forbid, cause a miscarriage. But when there was no longer any doubt, Lieba told Daniel the news he'd waited so long to hear. Looking at her flushed, smooth face and shining brown eyes, Daniel was filled with joy. 'The Almighty has answered my prayers,' he said.

He knew that the child would be a son.

CHAPTER 2

When his longed-for son was born in 1895, my grandfather called him Avner, just as the rebbe had instructed. For Daniel, the birth of Avner was a sign of divine blessing. When on the eighth day the *mohel* performed the ritual circumcision which symbolises the Jews' covenant with God, Daniel resolved to consecrate his son to the service of the Almighty. He carried little Avner tenderly to synagogue wrapped in his prayer shawl and, from the moment the baby was able to lisp out his first words, taught him to say Hebrew prayers.

Avner did seemed blessed. A remarkable child with eyes like dark blue pools in a triangular little face, he had an astonishing memory and a precocious mind. He would become a rabbi. In a patient but determined manner that brooked no opposition, Daniel taught his little son that from the moment his eyes opened in the morning, he must remember that he owed his life and everything in it to God. To praise the Almighty, Avner had to wash his hands before saying his prayers, to wear his *tzitzis*, or prayer fringes, if he walked further than four kubits, and to say a blessing whenever he saw a rainbow.

Every morning before dawn, Daniel woke the warm, sleepy child and took him to synagogue for morning prayers. As they crossed Miodowa Street, Avner dragged his feet, looking back at the pretty carvings and recessed windows of the important-

21

looking building his father called 'The Temple'. Dew still glistened on the cobblestones and the city was just beginning to stir. Horses' hooves echoed in the streets as carters bent under bags of coal, blocks of ice, and freshly baked bread.

Sometimes the child stared at water carriers in soft cloth caps trotting along the pavement to balance the buckets suspended from a pole across their shoulders. As father and son turned the corner into Kupa Street, they passed men in wide-brimmed hats and black coats which brushed the dusty ground as they walked.

Inside the spartan prayer house called Chevre Tilem, where worshippers cloaked in prayer shawls swayed back and forth in prayer, Daniel held Avner's little hand in his and basked in the admiration of the bearded faces around him. On the way home Avner quickened his step, longing for his breakfast of crisp kaiser rolls and poppy-seed sticks which the baker's boy delivered each morning.

Impatient for his God-given son to begin learning the sacred language of the Torah, Daniel sent him to *cheder* at Chevre Tilem when he was three years old. Most boys were enrolled at four or five, but Daniel couldn't wait for Avner's rabbinical training to begin.

Cheder was the place where childhood ended. At this religious day school, Jewish boys learned Hebrew and studied the Torah. No coloured pictures, childish stories or lively games relieved the tedium of this dour classroom where Avner had to memorise words he didn't understand, learn hundreds of rules and write strange squiggles.

Avner was too small to see over the top of his wooden desk and fidgeted on his hard chair. Whenever he tried to scramble down to go to the lavatory, the *melamed's* harsh voice told him that he'd already been. For six days a week he had to learn confusing rules and endless prayers. Whenever he stared at the shaft of light slanting in through the grimy windows, the teacher cuffed his ears or swished the birch cane against his little stockinged legs.

Daniel didn't encourage Avner to complain about *cheder*. He must value learning and respect his teachers. When Avner said that he wished he could play in the courtyard with the other children instead of learning Hebrew, Daniel looked into the child's miserable face and shook his head reproachfully. 'I give you the opportunity of studying, and all you want to do is waste time!' It never occurred to him that his three-year-old might not share his enthusiasm for religious learning.

Daniel's every waking thought was taken up with educating Avner, but it bothered him that the noisy, idle boys in their building might undermine his mission. One evening after he'd finished writing accounts in his neat, elongated hand, he looked pensive. 'The child doesn't have suitable companions,' he told Lieba. 'Those empty-headed little larrikins around here could be a bad influence on him.'

Lieba could only shake her head at her husband's notions of turning a small child into an old scholar. Her father had been a strict disciplinarian but her brothers had been allowed to play and kick balls in the sand dunes and forests of Szczakowa. 'Little boys need to run and play,' she protested, but Daniel said that Avner was meant for higher things. Time was precious and must be used wisely.

When an apartment became vacant in their house, a tall thin Chassid in his wide-brimmed hat and long coat came to inspect it. The house was a handsome two-storey building whose apartments overlooked a large central yard which was the communal playground, laundry and meeting place for the tenants and their children. As they hung eiderdowns over their railings to air, or looped their rugs on wooden stands and battered them with flat bamboo beaters, housewives with kerchiefs tied low over their foreheads called out to each other, gossiping over the day's events in Yiddish.

'Did you hear, Yentel's Taubele refuses to marry the rabbi's youngest son, she says she'd rather die, may God forgive the expression.'

The woman's hand flew to her cheek. '*Oy gewalt!*' she lamented. 'What's the world coming to? When my sisters and I were at home, our father—may his dear soul rest in peace—chose our husbands. Who would have dared to say one word against his choice? I don't mind telling you, I had my eye on the tailor's son but my father cared as much about my dreams as he did about last year's snowfall.' And she gave the rug an extra thump.

Down in one corner of the yard, women with rolled-up sleeves carried buckets of water which splashed over their laced-up boots as they walked. Boys in baggy breeches and peaked caps chased each other and teased the girls in long pinafores who tucked up their skirts in their bloomers to play hopscotch. The language that echoed around these walls was Yiddish. Today housewives still hang eiderdowns on the railings and children still play hopscotch in the yard, but the Jewish voices have been silenced.

The sound of children shrieking in the yard floated up while Daniel's prospective tenant was looking around the apartment. When my grandfather noticed the Chassid's solemn little boy standing beside his father, his eyes lit up. This child would be an ideal companion for Avner.

The father bent down to his son whose pale red hair hung in straight strands in front of his ears. 'Nu, so what do you think of this place?' he asked in Yiddish. While the little boy looked around the apartment, Daniel asked him whether he knew any Hebrew. When the boy nodded, Daniel nudged Avner to come forward. 'My son knows some Hebrew words too,' he said.

'What's the Hebrew word for wall, then?' the Chassid's unsmiling child asked Avner in Yiddish. Avner stood planted on his sturdy legs, his pointed chin thrust out with a confident tilt. But when he tried to guess the answer, the boy shook his head. 'That's not the right word!' he said disdainfully.

'It is so!' Avner retorted.

The little boy turned to his father. 'Tateh, let's go,' he said. 'This place is not for us!'

The man shrugged his hunched shoulders and spread his white hands as if to say, 'What can I do?' and left.

With every passing year, Avner resented his upbringing more and more. A mischievous child with an exuberant sense of fun, he felt suffocated by religious rules and strangled by the restrictions which his father imposed on every aspect of his existence. He especially loathed the Chassidic costume he had to wear, the long coat with the fringed prayer tassels hanging outside his trousers. He began to feel like Isaac being sacrificed to God by Abraham in a Biblical pact.

But no matter how distressed he was about these restrictions, it was impossible to tell his father how he really felt, unthinkable to upset or disappoint him. It wasn't fear of his power, but awe of his authority. When his children thought of the Almighty, they saw Daniel as God's role model: omniscient, omnipotent and awesome, and yet compassionate.

Daniel was a strict disciplinarian who never made idle threats. He would give one quiet warning but never shouted or lost his temper. After a belting with the leather shaving strap had been administered, he took his son's little hand in his. '*Git?*' he would to ask, meaning 'Friends?', and curved his little finger to denote that the episode was over. Instead of replying with the same gesture, Avner usually turned away his angry face and raised his index finger, which meant that he was '*broiges*', or offended.

Half a century later, whenever I was upset with my father, he would curve his little finger and ask in a jocular tone, 'Git or *broiges?*' This overture only added to my sense of grievance, and irritated me just as it must have irritated Daniel's children.

Avner felt that he was choking on this religious diet, but at a time when most of the people of Galicia were illiterate, there wasn't a Jewish boy over five who couldn't read Hebrew. Apart from studying ancient commentaries which analysed, dissected, and interpreted the meaning of the Torah in minute detail, the Talmud also examined issues of justice, law and morality, and taught boys to think. They sharpened their wits by looking at problems in different ways and considering various options. 'Two men find a coin,' the *melamed* would say. 'Whose is it?' Or 'A farmer's bull gores a cow. Who is responsible? Should he pay compensation? How much?'

Avner didn't have a cow and couldn't care less whether it got gored or if anyone received compensation, but his active mind loved the mental acrobatics involved in exploring all the possibilities, and he soon became the star pupil. Whenever visitors came to check on the boys' progress, the teachers knew that he could always be relied on to give the smartest answers.

By then he was no longer the only child, although he always remained Daniel's best-loved son. From the moment they were born, the other children knew that their eldest brother was the smartest child in the family, a paragon they could never match. It's no wonder that with such adulation Avner developed an overinflated ego. The others admired him excessively in their youth but turned against him unmercifully in their old age.

Over eighty years later, the telephone rings in my Sydney home and I hear a quavery voice speaking in a Jewish-American accent with a European intonation. 'This is Avner.'

It's the first time in my life that I've spoken to this legendary uncle about whom I've heard so much. 'I got your letter about your father,' he told me. 'How come no-one else told me that my brother died? Someone should have told me.'

All my life I'd heard about his chequered career, his ups and downs, the grandiose schemes and their subsequent failure in Vienna, Antwerp, Rio and New York. Of all the family, Avner arouses the strongest emotions, good and bad. Their father's favourite, the showpiece of the family, I've heard him described as extraordinarily bright, extraordinarily selfish, self-assured, self-absorbed, a storyteller, a user, a charmer, a fraud.

And now this fabled old uncle in New York is speaking to me. 'What can one say?' he muses in his indeterminate accent. It's a rhetorical question. He has nothing to say about his brother's death, except to complain that he wasn't notified earlier. As we speak, I recall being told about his prodigious memory and inexhaustible fund of anecdotes, and ask whether he plans to write his memoirs. 'No,' he replies. 'There is nothing in my childhood that I remember with any pleasure. Nothing. I did *not* have a happy childhood.' He emphasises the word 'not' with a New York drawl.

'My father was a strict disciplinarian,' he continues. 'He sent me to a religious school where I didn't fit in. I always felt like a white raven in a black flock. To this day I don't know why my father did that to me. Perhaps he was counting on me to become a rabbi and intercede for him in the other world. And one day, when he was dead, I was to say Kaddish for him. I don't want to go into all that at this stage of my life.'

'My father was very fond of you,' I tell him.

'And I of him!' he cries. 'Sometimes I tried to get him out of going to *cheder*. I don't know why they didn't tell me. It's not right,' he repeats querulously. Then he asks, 'Are you planning to visit the States?'

'Not at the moment. Maybe later on.'

'I hope I'll still be here when you come,' he sighs.

He wasn't.

It was Avner's death in 1985 that spurred me on to collect information about the family. Whenever I asked my relatives about their childhood, their response was invariably: 'Ah, if only Avner were still here, the stories he'd be able to tell you! Avner knew everything. If only you'd spoken to him!' It's devastating for a researcher to hear that the best source has just died, but although I'd missed Avner, I was determined not to miss the rest. Five of my father's brothers and sisters were still alive, scattered around the globe. I would create a mosaic out of their memories.

In 1897, when Avner was eighteen months old, Daniel and Lieba's first daughter, Serla, was born. Lunia, as she came to be called, lacked Avner's mercurial mind and self-assurance but this little girl with light brown hair and level grey eyes was shrewd and observant.

Because she was a girl and not allowed to learn Hebrew or study the Torah, she was sent to the state school instead of *cheder*. Lessons bored her but she read voraciously. Reading was a passion she shared with Avner and they often fought over books. Hiding a torch under the bedclothes for fear her mother would catch her reading late into the night, Lunia lost herself in aristocratic worlds of princely suitors and refined heroines.

From an early age Lunia felt that her life fell far short of her ideal world. Avner teased her and grabbed her books when she wasn't looking; her teachers criticised her for inattention, while her mother never had time to play with her. Her father's reserved though forceful presence also didn't measure up to the courtly behaviour of princes in storybooks. Instead of rescuing damsels in distress, all he did was fix gas pipes.

On Tuesdays and Sundays, when weddings were held in the temple across the road, Lunia used to stand in the doorway of their house, breathless with excitement as the brides arrived in their horse-drawn *doroskys*. They resembled the princesses in her storybooks and she dreamed of a Prince Charming who would take her away from Miodowa Street and gallop with her to a castle where the walls would be covered with tapestries and the platters would be made of gold.

In 1901, when she was four, Lunia smiled at her reflection in the looking glass. In her new muslin dress and laced-up white boots which squeaked, she finally looked like a princess. It was the wedding day of her mother's sister Karola, and she couldn't wait to go. Suddenly she gave an outraged howl: Avner, restless in his sailor suit of navy velvet with gold buttons and matching beret, tugged at the big white bow perched on top of Lunia's well-brushed hair and the bow collapsed like a dead bird dangling over her eyes. When the bow was retied and peace was restored once again, Lunia looked into her parents' bedroom and stood riveted by what she saw. Time stopped, and the image she saw remained engraved in her mind forever.

Ninety years later, in a nursing home in Petach Tikvah in Israel, a grey-haired woman with a stylish hairdo, level grey eyes and the aristocratic air of an old dowager, recalls how her mother, whom she always called Mamuncia, had dressed for her younger sister's wedding so long ago. Speaking slowly with a beatific smile, Aunty Lunia recalls the scene she'd witnessed as an enthralled four-year-old. 'Mamuncia sat in front of her mahogany dressing table with the cheval mirror where she kept her tasselled perfume phial. Her head was bent forward, and Tatunciu, my father, stood behind her, fastening the clasp of a magnificent diamond choker he had given her,' she said. For one brief moment, life and fable had merged in one perfect image. Aunty Lunia reminisces with a fond smile, 'Mamuncia loved dressing up, she was very vain. She used to say to me in German, "A woman is vain from the moment she is born until the day she dies."'

The bride was the prettiest of the three Spira sisters, in spite of the mole on the end of her nose. In her wasp-waisted gown with a bustle and long lace veil, Karola was a vision from a fairy tale. There was a big wedding breakfast, with guests Lunia had never seen before who made a fuss of the wide-eyed little girl with the big bow in her hair.

Then the band struck up. The adults formed themselves into rows and began to dance the stately quadrille. Later they twirled around the hotel ballroom to the strains of the Polonaise, while little Lunia watched intently, determined not to forget a single waft of perfume or secret glance. She tapped her little laced-up boots as the newlyweds waltzed around the parquet floor. Suddenly Uncle Ozjasz, the dashing bridegroom, bowed in front of the child and bent down to invite her to dance the waltz. Straining on tiptoe to reach her new uncle's hand, Lunia closed her eyes and wished the music would never stop.

Aunty Lunia is wallowing in the romance of the past, but suddenly her eyes narrow and she fixes me with a look stern enough to wither the roses that I've brought her. 'Nobody needs this history of yours,' she says. 'Nobody. There is nothing there that brings honour to the family, no-one you can be proud of.' She shakes an arthritic forefinger at me like an ancient sibyl. 'Don't do it,' she warns. 'Your children won't thank you for it.'

By 1901, Daniel and Lieba had two more children, Jerzy and Rozia. Lieba, who only five years earlier had been distraught wondering whether she'd ever have any children, was now distracted trying to take care of four youngsters. Adam and Eve, who had been commanded to go forth and multiply, had stopped at two, but Daniel intended to have as many as the Almighty blessed him with.

Daniel loved looking after the babies as soon as he came home. Throughout their lives his children recalled fondly how he used to cradle them in the crook of his firm, comforting arm and put them on the potty at night. 'I want to do wee-wee with Tatunciu,' was a plaintive cry often heard at 19 Miodowa Street in the middle of the night.

Both Jerzy and Rozia had problems with their ears. Jerzy was born with one misshapen ear which was stuck to the side of his head like an unfurled flower. Physical irregularities were regarded with suspicion at the time, and women wondered whether some misshapen dwarf had stepped in Lieba's path while she was pregnant. Perhaps, may God protect us, some malevolent crone had cast a spell on her. Lunia hated going out with her little brother because everyone stared at him. She never noticed that he was a good-looking, friendly child who looked people straight in the eye. Even now after all these years, the only thing she mentions about him is his deformed ear.

Rozia, who was born in 1899, was hard of hearing as a result of scarlet fever. The frustration of never being able to hear properly affected her all her life. She had a narrow face and would have been attractive if not for her anxious expression and highly-strung personality. Lieba, who got on well with Lunia, had very little patience with her deaf daughter. But despite her difficult nature, Rozia had a loyal and loving heart, as her mother was to discover in the terrifying years to come.

Privileged because he was the favourite son, Avner felt superior to his younger siblings but he waged a continual power struggle with his father. Apart from resenting the fact that he was imprisoned in *cheder* every day at the mercy of the strict *melamed*, he felt alien among boys who looked down on him because his father was neither a Talmudic scholar nor a professional man. 'How come Baldinger's son is so smart?' visitors used to mutter whenever Avner shone with his quick answers. He knew that they were asking 'How come the son of a mere tradesman is brighter than the sons of lawyers and scholars?' and hated their condescension.

Avner felt as alien at home as he did at *cheder* because he was the only one of the children whom Daniel dressed like a Chassid, with the Chassidic peaked cap and long side-locks. The neighbouring boys and his cousins made fun of him. 'Avner the Chassid! Avner the Chassid!' they chanted in sing-song voices. He wished he could make them all disappear.

The Chassidic sect had started during the eighteenth century when mainstream Judaism had grown stagnant. By the time Daniel was born, most of the Jews in *shtetls* all over Poland had been swept along by this religious revival which initially prized joy and fervour above scholarly learning. My grandfather, like his father before him, was ambivalent about the Chassids. Reserved by nature, he disliked their exuberant dancing and singing and the way they paraded the accoutrements of their faith outside their clothes. In spite of that, he consulted a Chassidic rebbe and sent his children to be educated in their *cheder*.

Since it was unthinkable to oppose his father openly, Avner tried one ruse after another to induce Daniel into allowing him to discard his Chassidic clothes. One day he returned home from the barber's without his hated side curls. Looking very pleased with himself, he told his mother with an innocent expression, 'The barber accidentally cut one *peyis* off, so naturally he had to cut off the other one too, to make them even.'

One afternoon Avner came home from *cheder* with the peak on his cap missing. 'Avner, what have you done to your cap?' Lieba cried, her hands flying to her face while she looked accusingly at her eldest son. 'Always up to some mischief!' she grumbled. Lieba hated waste and unnecessary expense. Now they'd have to buy him a new cap.

As the battle of wills continued, Daniel became increasingly disappointed at Avner's defiance. Lieba could only watch the power struggle and shake her head. Secretly she sympathised with her son's desire to look like his friends, but she never argued with Daniel in front of the children.

Lunia looked up from the sampler she was embroidering for her mother with rose-coloured Filoflos thread. 'Don't fight with Tatunciu about this,' she would advise her oldest brother. 'You can't win.'

Avner usually listened to Lunia, but he knew that these skirmishes were part of a larger battle and refused to surrender. 'I don't care what Tateh does. I'm not going to wear those horrible clothes and be laughed at,' he said.

So when his mother bought him a new cap, he did exactly the same, fully aware of the consequences. 'I hear you've ruined your new cap,' Daniel said quietly when he returned home. 'You know what I told you last time. Go into the bedroom, pull down your trousers, lie across the chair and wait for me.' While Avner lay across the chair, trying not to tremble, his father, who understood the punitive value of anticipation, took his time.

Slowly he walked into the room, closed the door and reached for the shaving strap. For the next few moments the others listened to the dreaded swish of the strap with the mixed feelings children have when the favourite is being punished. With each blow, Daniel repeated in the same quiet voice, 'Are you still going to ruin your clothes?' But after the punishment had been administered, he hung up his strap and took his son's hand. '*Git*? No hard feelings,' he said cordially. The cordiality was one-sided.

Lieba let out a sigh of relief when Avner emerged from the room, white-faced but nonchalant. Rozia ran up to comfort him but he shook her off. 'Didn't hurt,' he told Jerzy, but he sat on the edge of his chair for the rest of the evening.

But that wasn't the end of the affair. Next Avner used all his ingenuity to get rid of the long caftan he loathed. Eventually Daniel realised that Avner had no interest in the religious life and that his dream of turning his eldest son into a rabbi was not going to be realised. Graceful in defeat, Daniel accepted his son's decision, but he never stopped hoping that his firstborn would one day discover the solace of religion. And he was comforted by the knowledge that no matter what path Avner would follow in life, one day he would say Kaddish for him.

CHAPTER 3

Hesiu hopped over the lozenge-shaped tiles on the entrance floor and skipped out into the street. Suddenly the smile froze on his lips and his boots seemed nailed to the ground. It was dark and gas lamps cast eerie shadows on the street over which hung a crescent of new moon no wider than a sliver of lemon peel. In front of him, men in long coats, big black hats and tangled black beards formed a circle on the pavement. As the men moved, their grotesquely elongated shadows looked like phantoms. In the centre of their circle sat a small boy.

Hesiu's eyes were fixed on the child who reminded him of stories that his older sister Lunia sometimes read aloud, about helpless children captured by witches and *dybbuks*. And now he was seeing that happen right here in Miodowa Street. Somewhere inside the sinister folds of those black caftans lurked cruel knives, and as soon as they'd finished their magic rituals, he knew that these demons would sacrifice the child.

Heart pounding, Hesiu dropped the letter that his father had asked him to slip into the postbox and raced indoors as fast as his chubby legs would carry him, too terrified to tell anyone what he had witnessed in case the sorcerers came after him too. Wriggling to avoid his brother Jerzy's bony knees in the bed they shared, he pulled his eiderdown high over his head and waited, too frightened to close his eyes.

My father Hesiu, who was born in 1901, was delivered by

Ewa Silbermann the midwife, given the name Hirsch, and circumcised eight days later by Szymon Fischer the *mohel*. It seems that once Daniel and Lieba had finally found the recipe for having children, they didn't know how to stop, because Hesiu was their fifth child within six years. With three sons to study the Torah and say Kaddish for him, it looked as though Daniel's prayers had been generously answered but, as my grandfather was to discover, you can't cheat fate.

Many years later my father told me that what his overactive imagination had turned into a satanic sacrifice was in fact a prayer of thanksgiving which Chassidic Jews offer for the new moon. The little boy must have been the son of one of the worshippers waiting for the prayers to finish so that he could go home. But the damage had been done. For years to come, Hesiu had only to glimpse a Chassid to quake with terror. Perhaps it was this experience that turned my father against religion for the rest of his life.

There was no point telling his mother about his terror. By this time Lieba already had two more children, Izio and Andzia. With a new baby in her arms and a brood of youngsters to look after, she was rushed off her feet from morning till night and had no time to listen to her children's nightmares or their dreams.

One evening Hesiu noticed a strange woman in their house, bossing everyone around and taking charge. A big slow-moving woman whose body reminded him of billowing pillows, she walked into his parents' bedroom with a large enamel basin steaming with water and a pile of clean white towels, and closed the door quickly behind her. It was the midwife. She rarely hurried, knowing that anxious husbands always called her too soon, but she'd already delivered seven of Mrs Baldinger's babies and figured that this one wouldn't take long to join their crowded household. Throughout the night, Hesiu heard strange muffled noises. Next morning, his father announced with a happy smile that they now had a new baby brother, Jakub, who was later called Janek.

In between her babies, Lieba had several miscarriages as well, so the woman who in 1895 was worried about being barren had remained in a state of almost continual pregnancy ever since. She had ample opportunity to ponder the wisdom of the proverb that when the gods wish to punish someone, they make their dreams come true.

Lieba appreciated her husband who was hard-working, kind and generous. He bought her jewellery, treated her with respect and provided well for the family. She had everything that a woman could wish for, except the one thing she wanted most of all: the right to limit the number of children she bore.

None of the Baldinger children shared Daniel's joy about the new baby whom they saw as yet another rival for their adored father's attention. Hesiu, a sensitive child, always craved more of his parents' affection than they were able to give him. At the age of seventy, my silver-haired father could still recall the longing he'd felt when he watched his father cradling the new baby in his arms. Daniel sat in his wooden rocking chair, tenderly smiling at the baby and stroking his cheek. But when Hesiu tried to clamber onto his father's lap, Daniel turned a surprised gaze on his four-year-old son. 'You want to sit on my lap? But, Hesiu, you're already a big boy, and he's only a baby,' he said with a hint of reproach. Hesiu's face burned with humiliation at his father's rebuff. He remembered that rejection for the rest of his life.

Hesiu's feeling of deprivation became even more acute shortly afterwards when he was sent to *cheder*. Daniel had intended to start his Jewish education at three, like that of his older brothers Avner and Jerzy, but when Lieba's family criticised him for sending babies to Talmud-Torah classes, he agreed to wait one more year. To Hesiu, going to *cheder* meant being banished from home, but to Daniel it meant being given the keys to heaven. 'You're very lucky, Hesiu, you're going to learn our holy language, read the sacred books of the Torah, and study the commentaries of the sages,' Daniel explained. Perhaps this son would become the rabbi he longed for.

But while his father regaled him with the wonders of learning, his older brothers warned him about its tortures. 'You'd better listen to every word, because if you don't, the *melamed* will give you such a wallop that you'll feel that birch cane on your *toches* for a month,' Jerzy smirked.

On his first day, Hesiu dragged the heels of his new boots along the narrow streets of Kazimierz as Daniel led him by the hand towards Chevre Tilem. Inside the cold, bare classroom, a group of little boys surveyed him with the superiority of the initiated. Looking at Hesiu out of the corner of his eyes, one boy spat saliva through a gap in his front teeth as he shrilled, 'Remember when they had to run for the doctor because the *melamed* cracked Shmuel's skull and all his brains dripped out on the floor?'

Hesiu began to tremble. Encouraged by his reaction, his classmates soared to greater heights. 'That's nothing! What about the kid he bashed to death last week for not knowing his *aleph bet*?' a skinny boy sniggered. Hesiu looked longingly at the door. He wanted to run away but didn't know the way home.

From my father's description of *cheder*, I know that it was sheer torture for a lively little boy who could hardly sit still for a minute to have to spend six hours each day in this confined classroom. As he was the smallest in the class, the teacher had to place two wooden blocks under his feet so that his head would be visible above the table. This made the others titter, which always brought tears to his eyes, and then they giggled and pointed, which made it worse.

The *melamed* had a scruffy beard the colour of winter carrots, and watery red-rimmed eyes, probably from studying over flickering candlelight long into the night. Whenever the boys couldn't answer a question, he slid his hand into their trouser pocket and pinched their thighs with pincer-hard fingers. These teachers of religion saw no anomaly in using violent methods to inculcate love of God. Nor did most parents. But one parent did object. At the end of one day's lessons, when the *melamed* emerged from *cheder*, Srulek's father was waiting for him. Planting himself in front of the teacher, the burly butcher slapped his face so hard that he left the imprint of his huge hand on his cheek. 'That will teach you to hit my Srulek!' he shouted.

Perhaps it was as a peace offering that soon afterwards the *melamed* announced a walk in the park. Excursions were a rare treat and the boys ran to pull on the patched, fraying jackets that had been passed down from brother to brother. The prospect of being outdoors in the warm sunshine made them jump around in a frenzy of excitement, like prisoners unexpectedly set free. Skipping and chattering, they set off for the Planty Gardens.

This straggly line of little boys in stiff peaked caps and sidelocks hanging in front of their ears, shepherded by the stooped *melamed* in his long caftan and untrimmed beard, aroused the immediate notice of some Polish youths playing in the park. While kicking an acorn along the path, Hesiu suddenly felt a sharp stinging sensation on his arm. Then another on the back of his neck. Recoiling with shock, he thought he must have been struck by lightning, until he heard jeering laughter and scuffles behind the trees.

As they pelted the *cheder* boys with lumps of dirt and handfuls of acorns, the larrikins yelled, 'Take that, you lousy

Jewboys! Get out of our park, you filthy Christ-killers!' Hesiu had heard Polish children jeering at Jews but he'd never been physically attacked before. As the teacher shepherded them quickly away from the park, he felt humiliated for them all, as though they'd been belittled by the attack.

After several months a new teacher arrived. This one had a dreamy expression and a flustered manner. He had no idea how to keep little boys in order. At the end of the first week, when the old rabbi who ran the *cheder* unexpectedly stood in the doorway, an uneasy silence descended over the classroom. The rabbi was an ancient man with a flowing beard who reminded Hesiu of Methuseleh. The classroom smelt of fear. 'Translate the first word of the chapter you've been learning this week from Hebrew into Yiddish,' the rabbi commanded.

From his seat at the far end of the row, Hesiu watched as the rabbi stepped up to the first boy. Chaim rose, scraping his wooden stool against the bare wooden floorboards. 'What does the word *"bechaloschu"* mean?' the principal snapped. Chaim cleared his throat and surveyed his inky fingers. 'I don't know,' he mumbled. Without a word, the rabbi raised his veined hand and, with the elegance of a samurai wielding a sword, struck the boy across the face.

While the shocked child rubbed his red cheek, the rabbi moved on to the next pupil, who also didn't know the answer. Again a sharp retort resounded in the silent room. By the time he reached Hesiu, the rabbi had slapped every single boy in the class. As it happened, my father did know the answer, but he was terrified in case the old man struck him from sheer reflex. Damp with perspiration, Hesiu blurted out the answer even before the rabbi had finished asking the question, and sank to his chair in relief.

But the episode wasn't over. The bridge of his bony nose pinched with anger, the rabbi strode towards the white-faced *melamed.* Before anyone had time to realise what was happening, he whacked the startled teacher so hard across the face that the young man staggered, fell backwards, and only came to a stop when he landed with a thump against a cupboard. The force with which he fell made his legs fly up in the air, and in that instant Hesiu saw that his trousers, which were usually concealed by his long coat, were threadbare and torn, and that his frayed shirt showed through the hole. This wasn't unusual for the boys, but it was shocking to see a teacher's clothes in that wretched state. The boys tittered and pointed, but Hesiu couldn't join in their derision. He felt sorry for the *melamed* whose poverty had been exposed in such a humiliating way.

To add to his misery at *cheder*, Hesiu was lonely. He didn't fit in with Chassidic boys who sneered at him because his father wore western clothes and trimmed his beard. They called him a '*dajsche*'. As the progressive Jewish movement had originated in Germany, the word 'German' became a derogatory term for assimilated Jews.

When finally one boy accepted his invitation to come home to play, Hesiu was overjoyed. At last he had a friend. During the visit, while his brothers and sisters came in and out of the house, he noticed his new friend frowning as he strained to hear what they were saying. In Chassidic homes, Yiddish was the only language spoken. But in the Baldinger household, Daniel spoke to Lieba and Avner in Yiddish, to Jerzy in German, and to the others in Polish, which the children used amongst themselves. As the realisation hit him that he was hearing the language of nonbelievers, Hesiu's playmate stared at him accusingly, jumped to his feet and ran out of the house as though pursued by the devil with a pitchfork. He'd never been inside a home where Polish was spoken and was frightened of staying in such an ungodly environment. Resigned to his loneliness, Hesiu gave up trying to make friends.

Although there were no lessons on Saturdays, the Baldinger boys had to go to *cheder* even on the Sabbath, probably to keep them out of mischief at home and to give their parents a few hours of peace and privacy. The boys hated having to spend even the day of rest in the hated schoolroom while most of their friends were running around the Blonia playing fields and having fun.

Sitting in the classroom one Saturday afternoon, almost jumping out of his skin with boredom, Hesiu began fiddling with the enamel inkwell which fitted into a hole in his desk. As Jews are forbidden to touch any work implements on the Sabbath, the boy next to him immediately called out, '*Muktzeh!* Forbidden!'

Hesiu had an inquiring, argumentative mind. 'Why is it forbidden?' he asked.

'Because that's what it says,' the other boy replied.

'Who says so?'

'Moses.'

'And who told him?'

'Hashem did.'

The devil was goading Hesiu's tongue. 'Prove it!' he shouted.

For a moment the boy fell silent, and then he spat out one word which ended all discussion. '*Apikojres!*' Calling someone Epicurus, or heretic, was the worst insult, because no self-respecting Jew would stoop to speak to such a despicable person. Hesiu abandoned the argument but seethed even more at the stifling restrictions of his father's religion.

No matter how much work he had, Daniel always came home early on Fridays to observe the Sabbath. On Saturday mornings he donned his top hat and walked with his measured gait to the Alte Shule Synagogue at the top of Szeroka Street, not far from the smaller Remu Synagogue in whose cemetery

Lieba's famous ancestors, Rabbi Moses Isserles and the scholar Nathan Spira lie buried. 'Gut shabbes, Reb Danil,' the other worshippers would greet him as he made his way towards his seat near the wrought-iron bimah, where generous donors like him used to sit.

Wrapping his fringed prayer shawl around him, Daniel began to doven in that swaying motion whose rhythm helps worshippers focus on the Almighty and tap into five thousand years of prayer, dialogue and supplication. During the service, the buzz of conversation formed a low hum in the synagogue whose walls had heard news, gossip and rumours for over three hundred years. Looking up from their well-thumbed siddurs, the men whispered into their neighbour's ear the latest gossip and scandal about embezzlement, fraud, law suits and adultery. Daniel took no part in these conversations. He disapproved of gossiping and despised the hypocrisy of those who came to synagogue to pray to the Almighty but spent their time judging their fellow man.

Back home after the service, Daniel sat contentedly in the wooden rocking chair with the rush back which was always known as 'Tatunciu's chair'. No-one ever presumed to sit in his chair, or to take his place at the head of the table. In my own home, too, my father's chair and place at table were sacrosanct, so although as a child Hesiu rebelled against his father's restrictions, in adult life he imposed some of them on me. While relaxing in his wooden rocking chair, Daniel sipped a small glass of brandy while Lieba brought him a plate of the crescent-shaped kichelech which she baked for him every Friday and placed on top of the glass-fronted sideboard out of the children's reach. Although the children eyed the plate longingly, they knew that this treat was for Tatunciu, but if they hovered around when he returned from shule, he always offered them one of the coveted cookies.

Although the law of the Sabbath forbids any physical labour, its spirit requires Jews to abstain from even thinking about work. My father always marvelled that no matter what pressing personal or professional problems Daniel had, he would spend the Sabbath contemplating the gifts and pleasures of life with a tranquil mind.

Lieba, on the other hand, found it difficult to sit still and do nothing, as her anxious thoughts jumped from Lunia's poor marks at school to Rozia's poor hearing, Izio's bad report card, Andzia's scarlet fever and Hesiu's latest escapade. Would the washerwoman manage to wash and dry all the family's laundry, would she have time to scour every single cupboard in time for Passover? Where would the money come from to pay for all the extra Hebrew, French, maths and piano lessons the children had?

Smiling indulgently at his preoccupied wife while he crunched the cinnamon-spiced cookies, Daniel urged her not to worry. 'You'll see, everything will work out,' he used to say. 'You must trust the Almighty.'

Lieba gave him her uncertain sidelong glance. 'I try not to worry,' she sighed. 'But somehow my mind seems to worry all by itself.'

Financially Lieba didn't need to worry. By 1906 Daniel's business was thriving. Gas had replaced coal and kerosine, and his team of labourers was busy installing gas and water pipes throughout Krakow. As Avner later put it, Daniel became a plumbing contractor before plumbing was invented. A masterbuilder had alerted him to the fact that water was going to be installed in people's homes. 'Soon everyone will want a bathroom of their own and if you can install those pipes, you'll have the field almost to yourself,' he pointed out. Daniel followed his advice and prospered.

Even though at this stage they had no money problems,

Lieba was always anxious in case there wouldn't be enough. As a result she ran a frugal household in which nothing was wasted. Early each morning the baker's boy delivered a fragrant basket of freshly baked rolls whose yeasty scent curled into every corner of their home. He brought snail-shaped rolls, round rolls sprinkled with poppy seed, horseshoe rolls encrusted with salt, and crusty kaiser rolls.

Each child was allowed to take three buttered rolls to school or *cheder*, but if they wanted more, they had to do without butter. Lieba didn't believe that any child could eat four rolls, so she saw no point in wasting butter. But if they were really hungry, then they wouldn't mind an unbuttered roll. Daniel backed her up. He prized moderation in all things it seems, except procreation, and disapproved of gluttony. 'You should always leave the table feeling as if you could eat more,' he used to say. It was a healthy concept but not one that his growing sons appreciated.

Hesiu, who was always hungry, used to take three rolls every day but one morning he asked for four. Lieba looked at him suspiciously. 'Are you giving them away?' she asked. He shook his head, hurt that she mistrusted him. When his lunch was ready, he saw that she'd left one roll unbuttered. 'I'm not taking any of them then!' he cried, and stomped off without his lunch. Mid-morning there was a loud knock on the classroom door. 'Baldinger, someone has brought this for you,' the *melamed* said, handing him a small package. Inside were four rolls. They were all buttered.

There was always some commotion over food in the Baldinger house because keeping a strictly kosher home required constant vigilance. If there was the slightest risk that the food may have been contaminated, Lieba sent one of the children to the rabbi's house to check if it was fit for consumption. If the cook accidentally spilled one drop of milk into the chicken soup, the rabbi had to pronounce whether it was still kosher. Often Lieba gave a chicken to the caretaker's wife because she didn't like the look of its innards or had found a suspicious spot on its liver.

By 1911, when Hesiu was ten years old, there were ten Baldinger children. Karola, born in 1908, was followed by Matus in 1910. Although she had a cook and a servant, Lieba never stopped working. Every day Hesiu watched his mother darning socks, bathing babies and braiding the girls' hair. Every four weeks, when the washerwoman arrived, Lieba worked side by side with her, sweat pouring down her face as she bent over to rub clothes and linen with yellow Ridler soap, drubbing it rhythmically on the washboard. Every evening she sat down beside her servant Anielcia, plucking feathers for down pillows, polishing the silver or mending the boys' torn trousers.

Reflecting on his mother's life much later, my father used to wonder what she got out of her life of unremitting toil. My grandmother Lieba has always been a shadowy figure in a family so dominated by Daniel. Whenever his children reminisced about their childhood in later years, it was invariably their godlike father they discussed. Where their mother was concerned, however, they only recalled how overworked and harassed she was, how well she looked after their physical needs and how efficiently she ran the household. Of her as an individual, they had only a hazy notion. As in so many families, the centre of everyone's attention was the powerful, charismatic father, while the mother who spent her time looking after everybody's needs and organising the household seemed far less interesting.

Hesiu loved Friday nights. From the moment his father came home singing traditional songs to welcome the Sabbath, a festive atmosphere pervaded the household. Lieba made sure that the children scrubbed their hands and faces, brushed their hair and changed into their best clothes. The table was always set with a snowy damask cloth which was smooth to the touch. Like a priestess presiding over an ancient rite, Lieba held her white shawl over her head and covered her face as she lit the candles in the heavy silver candlesticks. Then she broke up the fluffy braided *challahs* which she had baked herself, a plain one for the men and a braided one for the women.

Each one lay beneath a royal blue velvet cover with a lion and the tablet with the ten commandments embroidered in thick gold thread. Lifting the chased silver *kiddush* cup to his lips, Daniel made the blessing over the fragrant raisin wine which he used to make himself, and thanked the Almighty for the gift of the Sabbath. Then looking fondly at Lieba, he said the special thanksgiving prayer for the mother of the family. 'She looks after her household and eats not the bread of idleness,' the prayer says. It might have been written with Lieba in mind.

Finally the meal began. While he savoured his mother's satin-smooth goose broth thickened with fine semolina, Hesiu's attention was drawn to the candles which sputtered more than usual. He knew that it was forbidden to blow out Sabbath candles because his father had impressed on them that no matter what happened, Jews must never touch fire on the Sabbath.

Hesiu saw the burning wick break off onto the tablecloth. It sparked and almost at once a tiny tongue of flame licked the air. Lunia grabbed her mother's arm. 'Mamuncia! Look!' she gasped. Unperturbed, Daniel held up his hands to make sure that no-one tried to blow it out. The children stole petrified glances at each other as the flame grew higher, but Hesiu saw that his father's expression was as calm as ever. Even if the whole house was going up in flames, his father would never break God's law.

Rising to her feet, Lieba cried: 'Oy gewalt! Quickly, Luniu, call Anielcia, and the rest of you, come away from the table, run!' Soon the plump maid came running, her ruddy face flushed. 'Oyey, Jesus Maria, Mrs Baldinger, the whole house could end up a pile of ashes!' She clucked her tongue as she smothered the flames. Anielcia was a good-hearted country woman with a husband who begrudged a piece of lard for her black bread. No-one had ever fed her as generously or treated her as well as Mrs Baldinger, but there were times when she could only shake her head at the strange ways of these Jews.

After Anielcia had extinguished the flames and opened all the windows, and the last wisp of smoke had vanished, they settled down to continue their interrupted dinner. Lieba served the carp. She always gave Daniel the head. Hesiu used to watch as his father sucked, picked and teased out every fragment of moist, sweet fish. Daniel always sliced off part of the head to share with Lieba, saying with an affectionate smile, 'One sweet little mouth deserves another!' It was one of the rare expressions of affection that the Baldinger children ever witnessed between their parents.

While Lieba carved the chicken with deft movements, Hesiu watched her place the largest piece on his father's plate as usual. Sometimes Daniel brought home a stranger from synagogue to share their Sabbath meal, but no matter how many sat at the table, Lieba always managed to make the food go around, and each child always received their favourite part of the chicken. Hesiu sighed when she placed a piece of the leg on his plate and wondered whether God knew how often he wished that there were fewer children so he could have the leg all to himself. Chewing the crisply roasted chicken rubbed with garlic, he studied the tiny stitches on his slice of stuffed neck and tried to take small bites to make it last longer.

He glanced up at his father at the head of the table. His

face usually so stern and serious, now looked relaxed, and his deep-set eyes glowed with a softer light. Only a few moments earlier their home could have been reduced to ashes, but his father's trust in the Almighty hadn't wavered. What if God hadn't noticed the flame, or had decided to let their house burn down? His father's absolute faith reminded him of the story of Abraham being ready to sacrifice his son just because God told him to do so. Hesiu already knew that he didn't share his father's faith in the Almighty: he preferred to trust in himself.

Every year my father rebelled more against Daniel's regime. When *cheder* was over for the day, he ran wild. He played in the street, ran around barefoot with a gang of neighbourhood boys, and joined in their scrapes. He learned to grab shiny red apples from the market stalls and bolt while Salcia the blousy fruitseller waddled after him, fist raised. 'Wait till I catch you, you little *ganev*!' she panted at his retreating back, 'You'll be sorry you were born!'

Once he amused himself by standing still on the tram lines on Dietla Street while the pug-nosed red tram clanged towards him. He didn't budge even though he could see the choleric face of the driver shaking his fist at him. Only when the tram was so close that he could feel its metallic breath brush his face did he leap aside. On one occasion he felt a stinging blow on his ear. 'Have you gone crazy? Are you trying to get yourself killed? Just wait till I tell your father!' Unfortunately for him, one of his older cousins had caught him playing chicken with the tram.

Daniel didn't seem to understand that children needed toys or that boys had to let off steam, and it seemed to Hesiu that whenever he was enjoying himself, his father always punished him. In winter, when frost etched leaf patterns on their windows, the ponds froze and hillsides billowed with soft snow, the children of Kazimierz skated and slid down the slopes on toboggans. The Baldinger boys had no skates or toboggans. Hesiu would watch enviously while his brother Jerzy glided lopsidedly on a single skate he'd found somewhere, as if on a scooter. 'Let me have one turn,' he pleaded. 'Just one!' but Jerzy ignored him. Hesiu went inside, head down, hands in his pockets. When he spotted a goose breast bone in the kitchen, he tied it onto his boot. Now he had a skate too. But as soon as he put his weight on it, the bone broke.

The water that collected in the gutters froze solid, creating a miniature skating rink just wide enough for one boot. He ran outside to join the boys who were sliding around. His cheeks smarted from the cold, and he stamped his feet on the icy ground while waiting his turn, but finally Hesiu was sliding and laughing with the others. Within a few minutes, however, his father was striding towards him. Daniel took him inside, pulled down his trousers, laid him across his knee and picked up the strap as if to strike him. Arm raised, he asked quietly, 'Are you going to slide in the street again and ruin your boots?' Miserably, Hesiu shook his head but he had no idea why having fun was a crime.

It's one of the ironies of parenthood that parents so often inflict on their children the same restrictions that made their own lives miserable. When I was small, my father forbade me to play outside with the neighbouring children. I seethed with the injustice of it. 'It's not fair. This is Australia, not Krakow, all the kids are allowed to play outside except me. Who can I play with?' A glacial expression would harden my father's bright blue eyes and in a voice that made argument impossible he would reply, 'Find more suitable friends. Only common children play in the street.'

Added to all his other grievances as a child, my father didn't have a single place to call his own. Not even his bed, which he had to share with his older brother Jerzy. There wasn't a corner, a shelf, or even part of a drawer where he could keep his little treasures. He had to keep them in his pockets away from the prying eyes of his brothers who pulled apart whatever came into their curious fingers.

When Hesiu came home from *cheder* one afternoon and saw a handsome roll-top desk in the living room next to the piano, he slid his hand appreciatively over the highly polished surface of swirled walnut. It was the most beautiful thing he'd ever seen. There were three big drawers down each side and four smaller ones across the top which only became visible when they rolled back the concertina-like top. Each little keyhole was beautifully edged in brass. Hesiu opened each drawer in turn, looking for a concealed recess like the ones in the storybooks which always contained secret talismans. 'Tatunciu already has his big American desk, so he must have bought this one for us,' Avner said.

Hesiu's heart pounded with excitement. If Avner said so, it must be true. A desk just for them! There was no time to waste: this time he wasn't going to miss out. Appropriating the bottom drawer, he placed his treasured possessions inside it: two chipped marbles, a Chanukkah *dreidl* which spun in a lopsided way, and a battered cloth ball. He locked the drawer and dropped the small brass key safely in his pocket. Next morning, he set off for *cheder* with a secret smile. Now he had a place of his very own.

That day the lessons dragged even more than usual. He couldn't stop stroking the key, longing to unlock his drawer. As he burst into the living room that afternoon, he stopped and blinked as he looked around, hardly able to believe his eyes. The desk was gone. His father had returned it, along with all his prize possessions. All he had left was a useless key.

CHAPTER 4

Dragging his feet towards *cheder*, Hesiu crossed a works yard stacked with timber, sheet metal and wooden crates. Outside the soda water bottling shed, the delivery man was whistling one of Souza's marches while he adjusted his horse's bridle. He winked when he caught sight of Hesiu's eager face.

The sky was blue, the air felt warm on his face, catkins were hanging off the chestnut trees, and a yearning for something beyond his daily life squeezed Hesiu's heart. '*Prosze pana*, please sir, would you take me with you on your deliveries today?' he asked.

'Oho! So the young master wants to have a ride!' the carter chuckled and hauled him onto the coachbox.

Hesiu jigged on the narrow seat. Instead of going to his lessons, he was setting off on an adventure. The horse clip-clopped along Miodowa Street, past the familiar shop signs advertising Luxus Shoe Polish, Grynberg's hats and Fyszer's down feathers, past the market square, and then through the crumbling stone archway which led out of Kazimierz towards Wawel Castle. He craned his head to see the fortress perched high on its bluff above the torpid Vistula River, delighted at his own daring. But when he next looked around, he didn't recognise a single building. Panic swept over him. He was a long way from home. What if his father found out that he hadn't gone to *cheder*?

Involuntarily, he rubbed his bottom. The last time his father had found out that he'd not only played truant but also forged his signature, he'd marched him to *cheder* and, in front of the other boys, made him pull down his trousers and whipped him with a piece of rubber hose. Angry tears still came to his eyes at the memory of that public humiliation which had wounded him far more than the hose.

When I think about my father's childhood, it amazes me that even in later life he never held Daniel's strictness against him. On the contrary, my father felt an unwavering admiration for his father's character and consistency and regretted causing him so much trouble as a boy. Perhaps that strict upbringing had helped forge the strong character which later helped him to survive.

Riding beside the ice carter, Hesiu twisted around, vainly hoping to see a familiar landmark. '*Prosze pana*, when will we be back in Miodowa Street?' he stammered.

Tugging on the well-worn reins, the carter hooted with laughter, showing teeth like brown tombstones. 'Back in Miodowa Street? And who said I was going back to Miodowa Street?' Hesiu was wondering whether he should jump off and try and find his own way home when he saw something that nearly made him topple off the waggon.

Surely his guilty conscience was playing cruel tricks on him. Striding purposefully along the road was the neat, immaculately dressed figure he knew so well. And his father was coming straight towards him. Hesiu closed his eyes and wished that he could vanish off the face of the earth. 'That's my father there, oh please, quick, can you hide me?' he whispered in a strange, hoarse voice. The coachman rose and lifted the top of his seat. 'Get in there,' he said. Hesiu's legs shook as he crawled into the recess, but there was so little room that when the carter sat down again, the seat pressed on Hesiu's head.

Immediately he was swathed in a fog of freezing air. He was inside a tin-lined icebox, and his teeth chattered so violently that he was sure his father would hear him.

He could hear muffled voices. Was his father demanding that the carter let him out of the ice chest so that he could deal with him? The voices grew faint and he heard nothing more. Was his father waiting out there for him?

The cold of the cabin seeped into his marrow. Even a belting would be better than this numbing ache. When the carter finally opened the trapdoor, Hesiu's brows and eyelashes were rimed with frost, and his face and hands had the bruised tinge of a fowl left in the icebox too long.

Looking down at him, the man held his ample sides and laughed so much that he could hardly speak. 'Your gentleman father only stopped for a moment to ask directions,' he chuckled, ruffling the boy's ice-spiked head. 'He's been gone a while now, but I thought you might enjoy hiding in there!' As the waggon rumbled back towards Miodowa Street, Hesiu shivered. How was he going to explain his wet boots and soaking jacket to his mother?

When Daniel came home that evening, Lieba's set face and her arms folded across her round body warned him of trouble. 'It's Hesiu again,' she said. 'That child gives me nothing but *tzures*. On a sunny day he comes home wet through and won't say what he's been doing. You have to do something about him.'

After the birth of Matus the preceding year, Lieba was finding life more hectic than ever. Hardly a day went by that she wasn't complaining to Daniel about Hesiu's ripped trousers, lost caps, skinned knees and scraped elbows. He came home late from *cheder*, didn't do his homework, and caused upsets every single day. How was she supposed to run this household and look after ten children when this one took up so much energy and gave her no peace?

Daniel looked grave. The problem of what to do with his wayward son had been weighing heavily on his mind for some time. Although he had hoped that Hesiu would settle down as he grew older, he was now more unruly than ever and had even started playing truant and writing his own absence notes.

It wasn't just that Hesiu rebelled against *cheder*, as Avner and Jerzy had done. He was becoming a delinquent. Daniel looked at Lieba who was mending yet another pair of trousers the child had ripped. 'You're right,' he said. 'If we don't do something about it, who knows how he'll end up. But I think I have the solution.'

Looking up from her mending, Lieba glanced at her husband. Daniel's jutting brow had grown wider as his hair receded, and his neat beard had gone completely grey, but his gaze was more intense than ever. 'My brother Samuel wrote to say that he can arrange for Hesiu to go to boarding school at Igru and spend the holidays with him at Shepesvaria. I'm going to send him there,' he said. Daniel's two brothers lived in what was then Hungary but later became part of Czechoslovakia. One was a vet, while the other, Samuel, had a big brewery, hotel and restaurant.

Apart from hoping that their wayward son would become more controllable in a different environment, they must both have looked forward to a welcome break from the constant aggravation. Hungary seemed the perfect solution. Since Galicia was part of the Austro-Hungarian Empire, its citizens could travel freely from one part of the realm to another. Daniel and Lieba, who had property and relatives in Vienna, often travelled to the capital by train as if they were going to another suburb.

As soon as Daniel began arranging Hesiu's departure, Lieba started having qualms. Her loving nature, so often swamped by the demands of everyday life, now asserted itself. 'How will the child manage among strangers? He can't speak a single word of Hungarian. Who will look after him?' she fretted. But Daniel's thinking wasn't clouded by emotion. 'You'll see, in a new school, among different boys, he'll change for the better.'

Apprehensive about her son's reaction, Lieba let Daniel break the news. When his father called him, Hesiu hastily tried to rearrange his crumpled trousers so that the latest tear wouldn't show. Without hurrying, his father dipped his nib into the brass-edged porcelain ink pot, scraped the excess ink against the side and signed his name at the bottom of his letterhead which said '*Instalateur für Wasserleitung und Gasbeleuchtung, Krakau*'. Water and Gas Installer, Krakow.

After placing the account on top of a neat stack of papers on his big American desk, Daniel closed the lid and turned to face his son with a concerned expression. While Lieba looked on, Daniel told him that in the new school year, he'd be going to boarding school in Hungary. Hesiu could hardly contain his excitement. At last he'd get away from his strict father and his mother who never had enough time for him.

He'd lately begun to wonder whether his mother cared deeply about any of her children. One evening, when it was already dark and the courtyard had grown quiet, his little brother Janek still hadn't come home. Suddenly there was a loud knock on the door. It was the mother of Janek's playmate Moishe. Her face was white and her words tumbled over one another as she pulled at her grey shawl. 'My Moishe hasn't come home yet and I know he's with your Janek. Let's hire the town crier together so he can go all over the neighbourhood shouting our children's names. God willing, perhaps someone has seen them,' she wailed. Lieba, however, didn't do as her neighbour suggested. Although she was anxious for her son to come home, her shrewd, frugal mind saw no point in wasting money. Since the two boys had been playing together, presumably they were still together. 'If her Moishe turns up, our Janek is sure to be with him, so there's no need for me to pay as well,' she said.

As Lieba had predicted, the crier her neighbour engaged soon located both boys who were playing in another yard, so she didn't have to spend a single *groschen*, but her cool thinking upset Hesiu deeply. He wished that she'd been as distressed as Moishe's mother. Being an only child, Moishe was probably more precious to his family, he reasoned to himself. After all, the Baldingers already had ten.

Hesiu couldn't wait to get away from his brothers and sisters. As the number of children increased, so did the friction between them. The boys belted each other with savage fury, the girls pulled each other's hair and told tales, and the babies howled. Even at night Hesiu couldn't get away from them because he had to share a bed with his younger brother. He often woke up in the middle of the night feeling something hot and wet spreading underneath him. To his affronted nose, it seemed that no amount of washing ever got the cloying ammonia smell of his brother's urine out of the bedclothes. His older sister Rozia made his life a misery. Because of her poor hearing, Rozia was angry at the whole world, but he always felt he bore the brunt of her frustrations. From the moment he was born, she tormented, teased and picked on him incessantly. Without a kindred soul at home, Hesiu felt lonely and misunderstood.

To make matters worse, there was always some commotion in the family. If it wasn't the birth of a new baby, it was the death of some old relatives that constantly required his parents' attention. Daniel's mother Ryfka Baldinger had died the previous year. Reminiscing eighty years later in Tel-Aviv, Aunty Andzia recalls that her parents Daniel and Lieba had been playing cards at home with friends when the telephone shrilled. It was a call from Nowy Sacz to tell Daniel that his mother had died. After replacing the trumpet-like receiver, he tamped out his cigarette and, according to Aunty Andzia, never smoked or played cards again, because he felt so guilty that, while his mother lay dying, he'd been enjoying himself.

Shortly afterwards, Daniel brought his father to live with them in Sebastiana Street, so that he could keep an eye on him. It seemed to Hesiu that his grandfather was older than the universe. My great-grandfather Matus Baldinger was ninety-three years old, a stout old man with a bald head and a long grey beard, like a distinguished looking rabbi. Aristocratic looking, according to Aunty Lunia. He wore a black satin coat and a shirt as white as snow which his devoted granddaughter Berta, who had moved to Krakow to look after her grandfather, used to launder.

After one year in Krakow, Matus Baldinger decided to return to Nowy Sacz where he died soon afterwards. He was buried in the cemetery there, like the Sanzer Rebbe, and each year, on the anniversary of his death, Daniel went on foot over the mountains to pray at his grave. At the same time, he always left a *kvitl*, a note of supplication, at the tomb of the Sanzer Rebbe.

With all the commotion about his grandfather, Hesiu felt even more neglected. It seemed as though there was nobody in that huge family who was interested in him. Not even his oldest sister Lunia, whom he admired from a distance. Lunia had no time for her brother. She had taken her younger sisters Andzia and Karola under her wing. Like my father, Andzia was lost in the middle of this large family. A sharp-eyed little girl with straight dark hair worn in a heavy fringe across her forehead, she was discontented and envious.

The greatest object of Andzia's envy was her younger sister Karola who was their mother's favourite. At the age of four, little Karola resembled a porcelain doll, with her blonde curls, rosebud mouth and eyes the colour of delphiniums. Lunia loved taking her little sister for walks in the Planty Gardens because no-one passed them without stopping to admire her.

Dressed in the fetching outfits that her mother ordered from Mrs Koralowa, the best children's dressmaker in Krakow, Karola turned heads in her velvet pelisse with its matching beret. Andzia used to go with them too, but nobody ever stopped to admire her, not even when she wore the same outfit as Karola. Worried in case someone should cast a spell on her beautiful daughter, Lieba always said, 'Khanaynahora,' or spat, 'Pfui, pfui, may the evil spirits not hear you,' whenever anyone praised the child. Just in case, she tied a red silk thread around her wrist to ward off the evil spirits and covered her little face with a veil.

Lunia, who always aspired to a life of refinement, almost died of embarrassment every time her mother gave birth to yet another baby. Controlling one's reproductive ability was one of the hallmarks of educated, modern couples, and it offended Lunia's sense of decorum that an intelligent woman of middle age, in comfortable circumstances, should continue having babies year after year like an ignorant peasant.

Lunia never forgot the day she came home from the state school she attended to find her mother soaking her feet in a basin of scalding water. Lieba's head was in her hands and she was weeping. Although private matters were not discussed in those times, Lunia was perceptive enough to realise that Mamuncia was pregnant once again and was following some folk remedy in the hope of bringing about a miscarriage. It didn't work, and six months later another child, the tenth, was born. He was called Matus after his grandfather.

Influenced by her older sister, Andzia also became critical of their father for inflicting so many pregnancies on his wife.

Thinking back over her childhood in her sunny flat near Diezengoff Street in Tel-Aviv, Aunty Andzia looks pensive. 'Father must have had a high sex drive. Otherwise he wouldn't have had so many children.'

She immediately regrets voicing that opinion. Now she's jabbing the air between us with her crimson spear-shaped nail and I can hear Lunia's voice as Andzia echoes her older sister's warning. 'In my opinion, no-one needs this book. Why do people need to know that your grandfather was a plumber? Or that we had to sleep two to a bed?'

By 1912 the Baldingers had moved to 20 Sebastiana Street. Daniel and Lieba had bought a three-storey block at the better end of the street, near the Planty Gardens, where the professional people lived. According to Aunty Lunia, they moved because Lieba wanted her daughters to live in a more socially desirable area. But soon even that apartment was so overcrowded that they ran out of beds.

While Matus was a toddler, they put two chairs together to make his bed. Recalling his sleeping arrangements over eighty years later in Paris, Marcel, as he came to be called, puts a large fleshy hand on his large bald forehead and makes his beer coloured eyes bulge in mock alarm. '*Mon Dieu!* You'd better not mention that I slept on two chairs!' he laughs. 'Lunia wouldn't like it!'

It was at the end of the summer of 1912 that eleven-year-old Hesiu sat on the train bound for Hungary, thrilled to be leaving Krakow behind. He pressed his nose against the window so as not to miss a single detail of the landscape. The countryside resembled a large quilt scattered with clusters of farmhouses. Rich brown potato fields with small white flowers, meadows of rapeseed as yellow as melted butter, and stubbled wheatfields stretched out under a domed sky. How beautiful it was!

Peasants with brawny arms pitched hay and rolled it into stacks just as their ancestors had done for centuries. Hesiu smiled at the sight of the conical stooks which seemed to stand on the field like legless people. Peasant women with sun-browned faces worked barefoot in the fields with an easy rhythm.

Sitting beside him was his grandfather, old Abraham Spira, who was accompanying his grandson to Hungary. The stern old man, whom the little boy feared, hardly spoke during the entire journey. The only thing my father could remember his grandfather saying to him in all that time was a rebuke. 'Turn the peak of your cap down, Hesiu,' he barked. 'Only common boys wear their hats like that.'

When they reached the school, Abraham filled in the enrolment forms, turned on the heel of his well-polished shoe, and left without saying goodbye. Perhaps he was afraid that his grandson would burst into tears. Little did he know that Hesiu was relieved to see his taciturn grandfather stride away. Although he didn't know anyone and didn't speak any Hungarian, he felt as though he'd just laid down a heavy burden.

His new school had a good reputation among Jewish parents in neighbouring countries because the pupils received a good secular as well as spiritual education. Although the headmaster was a rabbi, the school was subsidised by the government and employed non-Jewish teachers as well. The children received kosher food and excellent religious instruction from Rabbi Koppelreich who later became the Chief Rabbi of Hungary.

Twice every day the Jewish boys attended synagogue, but the rest of the time they studied secular subjects, like children at state schools. To Haydn's melody, which later became the tune of 'Deutschland Uber Alles', Hesiu and the other boys sang the anthem to Kaiser Franz Jozef: 'May God defend, may

God protect, our emperor and our land.' No-one could yet suspect that God's support for this obsolete empire was drawing to an end.

Boys living away from home were billeted with private families, and my father was sent to live with his Hebrew teacher Mr Goldsztain. He was thrilled when he saw the dormitory. A bed all to himself!

He was even more delighted with the meals. Mrs Goldsztain was a warm-hearted woman who understood that growing boys had voracious appetites. On his first Saturday Hesiu sat expectantly at the long table with the other boys while she served each of them a big slice of cake, overflowing with minced poppy seed, sweetened with plump raisins and spiced with cinnamon. More than sixty years later, the memory of this poppy slice still made my father's mouth water. The following Saturday he tasted another ambrosial cake, this time filled with chopped walnuts. The cakes were delicious and cut in generous portions but, even more wonderful, you could get a second helping just by asking for it.

Life in Hungary was full of new pleasures. For the first time Hesiu had his own bookshelf where he could keep his treasures without worrying that someone would grab them. He could play with boys his own age, run outside and play games without getting into trouble. In summer they played soccer on the playing field with a real ball pumped up with air, not a cloth one like in Krakow. There were excursions to nearby villages and hikes into the woods. Nobody thought he was a larrikin.

During the holidays he stayed with his Uncle Samuel and played with his cousins. Sometimes they sneaked into the cellar and tasted the wine fermenting in the bulging oak casks. The biggest thrill was being allowed to climb aboard the truck in which his uncle delivered his spirits. In 1912 this vehicle was the sensation of the little town, and riding in it with his cousins, Hesiu felt like a celebrity.

At the end of the first school year, Lieba came to fetch him home for the summer holidays. After not seeing her son for a whole year, her first words were, 'So, has your maths improved?' When Hesiu nodded, she started peppering questions to test him. 'Nine nines? Eight sevens? Six elevens?' The moment his mother started setting him sums, Hesiu's confidence melted away and he got them all wrong.

Lieba looked annoyed. 'So you've been wasting your time here too?' she said.

'Well, it just comes out differently in Hungarian,' he mumbled. The moment his parents appeared, things started going wrong.

Maths had always been my father's weak point, and I can remember him at seventy, poring over 'Teach Yourself Maths' books, determined to master in old age what had eluded him in childhood. When he was five, Lunia had tried to teach him elementary sums without success. If she wrote down 1 + 1 = 2, he could understand it, but when she wrote 1 + 1 = ? or 1 + 2 = ?, he thought that a question mark was a number and couldn't understand how it could equal two as well as three.

Mathematical ineptitude must be hereditary because I also had trouble with mathematics, the only subject I've ever failed in my entire scholastic career. For a conscientious student like me, failing a subject was distressing enough, but my father's reaction upset me even more. His eyes, bluer than ever against his smoothly combed silver hair, glinted with disapproval. 'You failed!' he said, and turned away without another word.

In spite of Hesiu's poor maths, Daniel and Lieba obviously felt that the school was having a good effect on him, or perhaps his absence was having a good effect on them, because to his delight they let him stay another year. This time his younger brother Izio joined him.

At the age of eighty-seven in Los Angeles, Uncle Izio takes a few tottering steps down the bare corridor of his boxlike apartment in Woodland Hills and stands there just looking at me. Tears splash down his jowly cheeks. As he wraps his thin arms around me, his frail body trembles with emotion at seeing me after so many years. Later, in a tremulous voice, he explains how he came to join his older brother at boarding school. 'When I was travelling with my father, taking Hesiu back to Hungary after the summer holidays, I misbehaved, and father said curtly, "I'll deal with you when we get home."'

That was all he said but it was enough. For the rest of the journey Izio squirmed on the hard seat, trembling at the thought of what awaited him when they returned to Krakow. Nothing more was said, but Daniel must have pondered over his fourth son while the lush Slovak countryside flashed past. Izio, who was one year younger than my father, didn't resemble him in appearance or temperament. He had dark hair, dark eyes which sparkled in his oval face, was sports mad and had an outgoing personality.

Izio had never done well at school, and as the train clacked over the railway tracks, it occurred to Daniel that a change of environment might benefit him too. As they approached the school in strained silence, Daniel suddenly asked, 'How would you like to stay here with your brother?'

Uncle Izio chuckles at the recollection. 'Naturally I jumped at the opportunity. It saved me from getting a belting at home!' He stares into the distance and sighs. 'Father didn't show us any affection,' he recalls. 'Mother was warmer but she was rushed off her feet. Only once in my entire life I can remember Father patting my hand for a moment. We were in *shule* and he leaned forward and patted my hand. That was the only time.' He looks at me with his intense gaze. 'Do you have any idea what that means?'

As I feel his pain and think about his words, it strikes me that my father wasn't demonstrative either. He revealed his love in caring, considerate actions, but apart from a peck on the cheek for greetings, goodbyes and special occasions, I can't recall any show of affection. I wonder whether that was because he inherited Daniel's reserved nature, or because he had never received affection from his parents.

The new school didn't turn Izio into a better scholar. According to him, it only confused him and made things worse. 'I learnt nothing that year,' he recalls in his sardonic way. 'I didn't understand Hungarian, I forgot my Polish, didn't improve my German and learnt no French. Your father managed much better, but he was much brighter and had a much stronger character than me.'

But going to Hungary had one unexpected benefit: it created a close bond between the two brothers which lasted throughout their lives, probably the only close bond my father ever had with any of his siblings. At the end of his second year in Hungary, when Daniel arrived to take both boys home, my father was sorry to return to the repressive, grey world of Krakow.

His oldest brother Avner, who was working for his father on the railways in Oderberg at the time, joined them on the train and, as usual, had a store of entertaining anecdotes. His father smiled and nodded, while Izio listened enthralled, but Hesiu kept wriggling. He couldn't get his left leg comfortable. Perhaps he'd hurt his knee while playing soccer. The clackety-clack of the locomotive and the peaceful landscape of wheat-fields and pine forests speeding past the windows finally lulled him to sleep.

When he awoke, the train was pulling into Krakow's central

station and his left knee felt as though it had been speared with a long shard of glass. The pain transfixed him so that he could neither speak nor stand, and it took the three of them to help him off the train and bundle him into *a dorosky* to go home.

Excitement at his homecoming turned to gloom. His father looked worried, and his mother put the new baby in her crib to place a compress on his swollen knee and feel his burning forehead. While he'd been away at school, Lieba had given birth to another baby, Freide, who became known as Fridzia. Her name means joy, but Lieba didn't feel elated after her eleventh confinement and she took a long time to recover.

Hesiu winced with pain when the baby screamed in her cradle. Whenever somebody shouted or slammed a door, he felt as though his leg was going to explode. His brothers and sisters often came to peer at his distended knee, but being the centre of his family's attention for once in his life didn't comfort him. His knee had swollen like a balloon and the mercury on the thermometer rose to forty degrees. The doctor was called. After placing the ends of his wooden stethoscope into his ears and listening to Hesiu's chest, he examined the knee and slowly placed his instruments back in his pouchy leather bag. The knee was severely infected. This was a case for the surgeon.

Professor Rutkowski was a tall thin man with a long dour face and an English overcoat with a sable collar. He peered at my father's knee through his shiny pince-nez. 'Your son has acute inflammation of the bone marrow,' he pronounced. 'It's dangerous because the infection could spread. He must be operated on as soon as possible.' Before leaving the house, the professor informed them that they owed him thirty crowns for the visit and another five for his transport. Daniel's courteous manner did not betray his shock. The usual fee was two or three crowns. Apart from this exorbitant sum, he was shocked at being charged for transport as well, especially when he looked out of the front window and watched the professor climb into his own carriage and drive away.

As Hesiu lay in bed, writhing from side to side feeling as though red-hot pincers were squeezing his knee joint, he heard his parents discussing his illness. The words operation and hospital were often mentioned, and his father paced around the house. The following day Daniel set off to Nowy Sacz to consult his rebbe. The rebbes were regarded as miracle workers, blessed with extraordinary insight and wisdom, and whenever their followers got together, they boasted about their miraculous deeds. After a word from the rebbe, barren women became pregnant, dying men recovered, and disastrous businesses prospered. The Sanzer Rebbe had predicted the birth of Avner. He'd know what should be done about Hesiu's knee.

On the way to Nowy Sacz, my grandfather turned his dilemma over in his mind. Firstly there was the vexing issue of an operation. When he was young, hospitals were places where people died. This was in pre-Lister times, before the introduction of antiseptics, and was no longer true in 1914 when hospitals were scrubbed, swabbed and disinfected, but fear of hospitals was still deeply ingrained in his mind.

On the other hand, he knew that Hesiu's condition was serious. In the days before antibiotics, people often died from blood poisoning. Then there was the problem of finance. If the professor charged thirty-five crowns for one house visit, he'd demand a fortune for an operation in a private clinic. And apart from medical and financial considerations, there was a religious problem as well. Food in hospitals was *treif*, not kosher. He'd have to ask the rebbe not only whether Hesiu should have the operation, but whether it would be a sin for him to eat nonkosher food during his stay.

At the rebbe's modest court his devout followers sat around a scrubbed oak table in an austere room with bare walls. Aron Halberstamm stroked the two points of his long grey beard as he considered Daniel's dilemma. Finally the rebbe pronounced that my father could go into hospital as long as he said the *viddui* before he was admitted. This was the prayer devout Jews said just before death which absolved them of all their sins. It wasn't a promising portent, but Hesiu was in too much pain to dwell on the sinister significance of the prayer which he mumbled through fever-scabbed lips.

When he opened his eyes after the operation, the chloroform hadn't yet worn off and its penetrating odour made him feel queasy. He was lying in a large ward of the public hospital where ten iron beds stood on each side of a long room with a well-polished grey linoleum floor. The sharp smell of disinfectant bit his throat. A sister in a long veil and stern expression walked up and down the aisle shaking thermometers and carrying bedpans.

Suddenly a searing pain almost hurled Hesiu into the air. He wanted to scream to the sister that someone was tearing his leg out of his hip socket. When he could unclench his eyes again, he saw that his left leg was suspended from a peculiar contraption with weights slung over the end. His leg was in traction to stop the tissues in his knee from knitting together but he didn't care if his knee knitted together or not. He would have gladly chopped it off to stop the torture.

Although the pain was excruciating, he was given nothing to relieve it. The only painkiller was morphine, and they were reluctant to administer it in case patients became addicted. Hesiu gripped the iron frame of the bed, tossed his head from side to side, and sobbed until he was exhausted. He begged the other patients in the ward to take some of the weights off the pulley when the sister was out of the ward.

Upset by the boy's anguish, a patient on the other side of the ward crept over to him. Looking over his shoulder to make sure the sister's laced-up shoes weren't striding down the linoleum corridor, he unfastened some of the weights and placed them at the bottom of a tin bucket in the corridor. A long sigh escaped from Hesiu's chest and he almost wept with relief.

While he lay in hospital, he heard people discussing strange names and distant places. The words Sarajevo and Archduke Ferdinand kept cropping up. It was August 1914. World War I had begun. As hospital beds were now needed for wounded soldiers, they sent him home before his leg had healed.

Back in Sebastiana Street, Hesiu waited impatiently for his knee to bend again, checking it anxiously every morning. Months passed and his leg remained as stiff as a block of granite. The knee joint had knitted together and would never bend again. The boy who had just discovered the joy of sport and the fun of living had become a cripple who hobbled like an old man, dragging a stiff leg behind him. Life had tricked him.

When he was able to walk without pain, he returned to the boarding school in Hungary. This time he travelled alone. It was winter, and the bare brown fields looked desolate under leaden skies. Because he arrived in Hungary in the middle of the school year, he didn't get a certificate. Daniel was upset with the rabbi for not letting him know beforehand that this year wouldn't be counted. He'd paid the train fare, tuition and boarding fees for nothing.

Hesiu became moody and withdrawn. Throughout his angry adolescence he blamed his lameness on the war and his own stupidity. He thought that if they hadn't sent him home too soon, if he hadn't taken the weights off the pulley, his knee joint wouldn't have knitted together.

For the rest of his life, my father was self-conscious about his disability. 'You know he has a complex because of his leg,' my mother sometimes said to defuse an argument. It was awkward for him to travel by plane, and even a visit to the movies was fraught with tension. As people were about to squeeze past him, he'd point to his outstretched limb and say to each one in turn, 'Please step over my leg.'

During a family reunion in 1966, my father was amazed to hear that Avner, Izio, Lunia and Andzia all blamed Daniel for his misfortune. They maintained that Daniel was an affluent man who owned several houses in Krakow and Vienna and could have afforded the best treatment for his son. If the operation had been performed at a private clinic, they said, the outcome would have been different. But their opinion didn't affect my father who steadfastly refused to blame his father who, he said, had done his best.

Not being able to play sport, run or kick a ball was a huge loss, but as he got older, he discovered a more agonising aspect of his handicap. From early adolescence my father had an eye for a pretty face and shapely figure, but now whenever his friends talked about meeting girls, he looked away so that they wouldn't see how distressed he was. Girls liked good-looking active boys, not cripples.

Just once, he summoned up the courage to approach a girl who lived across the road. She had a blotchy complexion and greasy hair so he figured that she wouldn't turn him down. When he saw her outside her gate, he brushed his thick brown hair back from his forehead feverishly, grabbed a few sprigs of lily-of-the-valley out of his mother's vase and hobbled over to her house.

Holding out the fragrant little bells towards her, he

stammered, 'These are for you,' and flushed to the roots of his hair. The girl just stood there staring at him, not saying a word or taking the flowers. Bright red with embarrassment, he let the flowers drop to the ground and limped home.

CHAPTER 5

While my father was an unhappy teenager battling with his disability, a battle on a much greater scale was being waged in Europe. World War I had begun, and on 13 September 1914, Avner was called up to fight in Kaiser Franz Jozef's Imperial Austrian Army.

On a warm Sunday in August when dark roses perfumed the Planty Gardens and spiky green pods swung from the boughs of the chestnut trees, Daniel took Avner by the arm and tried to persuade him not to be in a hurry to report for duty.

Krakow was a garrison city, and the park swarmed with soldiers in their gold-embroidered Austrian uniforms and stiff shakos adorned with plumes. Everyone was buzzing with the exploits of a heroic young Pole, Jozef Pilsudski, whose band of riflemen had advanced against Russia even before hostilities had officially commenced. Although the assault had ended in a fiasco, reports of his audacity inspired the patriotic youths who swaggered around boasting that they'd soon show the Tsar who was boss.

Along the dappled paths of the park, housemaids on their day off wore their best white collars and adoring glances as they clung onto the arms of their soldier sweethearts. In the bandstand, regimental bands struck up stirring Souza marches. Drums beat, cymbals clashed, trumpets blared, and young couples looked yearningly into each other's eyes. Sombre in his well-cut overcoat and homburg, Daniel argued about army life with his eldest son who rarely agreed with him about anything. Daniel's heart sank at the thought that his favourite son was going to risk his life to further the ambitions of two old kaisers whose war-mongering threatened to engulf the whole of Europe.

Daniel, who had been a soldier back in the days of compulsory conscription, wanted to give Avner the benefit of his experience, but while his father talked, Avner's eyes kept darting to look at the delicious young women who returned his openly admiring gaze with flirtatious smiles under their large gauzy hats. Unlike his lame brother Hesiu, Avner didn't doubt his ability to charm women. Despite Daniel's efforts to delay his departure, he refused to wait. At nineteen he was carried away by the stirring talk about patriotism, gallantry and heroic deeds. Somewhere outside Krakow, life was waiting for him and like everyone else, he couldn't wait to be part of this carnival called war.

After the Austrian Archduke Ferdinand was assassinated in Sarajevo, things happened so fast that people hardly had time to digest one shocking event before another one followed. In rapid succession Austria–Hungary declared war on Serbia, Serbia asked for Russian help, the Russians mobilised, the Imperial War Council of Germany declared war on Russia and its ally France, and England came in on the side of the western allies. Global war had begun. The Central Powers—Germany, Austria–Hungary and Turkey—were aligned against Russia, France and England. The strongest nation among the Central Powers was Germany with its modern, well-disciplined troops armed with heavy howitzers, flaming patriotism, and a sense of national destiny which twenty years later was to lead to another, deadlier conflict. Meanwhile, the ally of Kaiser

Wilhelm of Germany, Kaiser Franz Jozef, ruled an anachronistic, declining empire peopled by a mishmash of ethnic groups seething to throw off the Austro-Hungarian yoke.

Ever since the first partition of Poland in 1772, the country had been divided up between Russia, Prussia and Austria and had ceased to exist as a sovereign state. Although the imperial aspirations and rivalries of the great powers had nothing to do with Poland, Polish soldiers in the three partitioned regions ended up fighting on different sides. As Krakow was part of the Austro-Hungarian Empire, Avner was conscripted into the Austrian army.

By now Daniel Baldinger was a prosperous plumbing contractor with eleven children, several apartment houses in Krakow and Vienna, and a lucrative government contract. Krakow was linked with Vienna by the Kaiserferdnandnord-bahn, one of the first railways ever built in the Austro-Hungarian Empire, to transport salt from the mines in Wieliczka. Before the war Daniel had won a highly profitable contract with the Imperial Austrian Railways. He kept meticulous records and accounts in his neat, firm handwriting, and listed the cost of every nail and the name of every labourer he employed, including the plumber's mate who carried the tools. Every Monday morning the mate brought a list of materials that were needed, and the railway master had to authorise their issue. Daniel was responsible for maintenance work on the station buildings and for water and gas on the trains. He also won the concession to supply teams of labourers for government jobs. In keeping with his religious beliefs, Daniel did not allow any of his employees to work on the Sabbath, even though he paid their wages for that day's work.

Aunty Lunia told me several years ago that by 1914 the name Baldinger, inscribed in powder blue letters on cream porcelain sinks, had become familiar to tens of thousands who washed their hands on trains and in private homes. Daniel's sinks displayed the prestigious sign 'Contrahend'. By Royal Appointment. Being connected with the Kaiser in this tenuous way was the only thing that ever impressed Aunty Lunia about her father's business. Even at the age of ninety-three, her eyes gleam with pride as she repeats, 'Tatunciu's sinks had "Contrahend" written on them. "Contrahend"!'

Before the outbreak of war Avner, who had refused to become a rabbi, had become apprenticed to his father as a gasfitter instead. The son who had been destined to minister to men's souls began to install gas and water pipes for their homes, and soon discovered that he had more aptitude for business than religion. Daniel recorded Avner's four-year apprenticeship in an employment book which Avner kept all his life. Writing in German, in his fine, assertive hand, Daniel certified that Avner had begun his apprenticeship in 1909 and completed it to his satisfaction in 1912. Then he sent his son to Oderberg in Austria to supervise his business there.

War, which brings so much misery, initially brought my grandfather good fortune. As the Austrian army needed copper to boost its armaments, the Imperial Metal Authority gave him the contract for confiscating every fragment of brass and copper in Galicia. This involved tearing out copper pipes as well as the copper tanks and cylinder heaters which heated water for people's baths. All the copper was sent back to Austria and melted down for arms, and Daniel began installing steel pipes instead. Carrying out this order didn't make him popular but it was extremely lucrative.

Avner had only been in the army for a short time when he heard his name called out. He couldn't believe his ears. 'You have permission to go home,' the sergeant barked. It was Rosh Hashana, Jewish New Year, and Daniel had arranged for his favourite son to come home for lunch.

Avner's eyes lit up at the thought of getting away from the austere army fare and of sitting at the festive table covered with the white cloth, drinking his father's fruity raisin wine and eating his mother's goose broth, carrot *tzimmes* and brisket braised with onions.

They were all sitting around the table waiting for Avner to arrive when the shrill ring of the doorbell shocked everyone into sudden silence. No-one in the Baldinger household would have dared to use the telephone or ring the doorbell on the Sabbath or on holy days. By ringing the small key-shaped bell, which is still attached to the front door of 20 Sebastiana Street to this day, Avner was flouting a religious rule he'd known all his life.

The family exchanged glances and everyone looked at their father to see what he would say. 'Why did you ring the doorbell on Shabbes?' he asked in his quiet, deliberate way.

Full of bravado in his high-necked grey military uniform with the peaked military cap, Avner thought he was too grown-up and too important to be rebuked. With a sarcastic laugh, he quipped, 'I must have forgotten that a bell was a bell.'

Without raising his voice, Daniel looked at him with his even gaze. 'But surely you haven't forgotten that a Jew is a Jew?' he retorted.

Daniel was realistic enough to know that Avner wouldn't be able to observe many religious laws while in the army, but he did expect him to obey them at home. 'Being unable to observe the laws is one thing,' he pointed out, 'but choosing not to is a different matter.'

Lieba changed the subject, but Avner's chair suddenly felt hard, and his collar chafed his neck. Daniel's dignity made it difficult to get the better of him, and anyone who tried usually regretted it.

Although Avner had been keen to join the army, he soon found that it didn't live up to his expectations so he was very pleased when a misunderstanding enabled him to stay at home for the next eighteen months. This protracted furlough came about because of a mix-up which resembles the plot of a Viennese farce. His name had been mistakenly entered in military records as Waldinger, and it took the Austrian army eighteen months to realise that Waldinger and Baldinger were the same person.

Meanwhile war was being waged with increased fury. While English, French and German soldiers died hideous deaths in the trenches and Australian troops were sacrificed on the cruel beaches of Gallipoli, Russian and Austrian armies advanced across Poland, turning the country into a battlefield. In the process, the villages of Galicia were torched and trampled, and at one point the Tsar's Cossacks came perilously close to Krakow.

When the Austrian army finally discovered its spelling error, Avner was sent to Vienna in the army reserve. The army recruited tradesmen of all kinds and on the day when Avner arrived, they happened to call for plumbers, so he stepped forward along with several others. They were taken to an enormous Garbanz pump where the officer in charge explained that when it rained in the Alps, water poured over the Italian and Austrian armies in the ditches below, so they needed pumps had to siphon out the water and dispose of it. Avner's group was ordered to build a platform high enough for this powerful pump to push the water up and empty it over the other side of the mountain.

Perplexed by the intricacies of this Garbanz pump, Avner's superior officer kept making mistakes and miscalculations, but having already installed these pumps with his father, Avner knew how they worked. As he was the only one in the entire outfit who did, the captain summoned him. Sitting in a makeshift office which was cluttered like a newspaper kiosk, Captain Austerlitzer looked up with bleary eyes when Avner entered, and made a weary gesture with his hand. 'What do I know about pumps?' he shrugged. 'I'm a paper merchant not a plumber! Go ahead and do whatever needs doing.' And he put Avner in charge of the entire operation.

Recounting Avner's adventures eighty years later, his son Adam can't get over his lucky breaks. 'My father never saw the front line,' he says in his stroke-slurred speech. 'He became a pump consultant, stayed in a hotel and wore fancy uniforms. He was a *dreikopf*. A smartarse,' he chuckles. 'Just listen to how he got out of the army!'

What happened next was typical of Avner's life, where nothing ever went in a straight line. When Daniel received a huge contract, he was entitled to employ tradesmen from the military reserves, so he applied for Avner to be detached from the army to work for him. Daniel's contract was to construct railway tracks in those parts of Poland which were then occupied by the Austrian army, so as the army advanced, his business expanded with it. When Daniel requested that Avner, his employee, be permitted to join his railway team, the application went astray, so it wasn't approved. Determined to go home anyway, Avner forged a pass, attached his own photograph to it, and travelled home with his falsified document.

Several months later an official letter bearing the imperial eagle was delivered to his home. The military police were looking for Avner Baldinger. He was ordered to report immediately to his superior officer. While clearing up the files, someone had come across Daniel's letter and realised that the subject of this application had left the army long before approval had been granted.

This time Avner was worried. Forging documents, deceiving

the army and being absent without leave were serious charges. His stomach churned as he travelled to the appointed place for the interview with the officer who had uncovered his absence, trying to figure out how to extricate himself from this tricky situation. At the officer's instigation, they met inside an opulent hotel furnished with crimson plush armchairs and crystal chandeliers. Avner noted that the officer arrived with a fawning entourage. He studied the man's neck, which bulged over his army collar, the features flushed and coarsened by too much food and wine, and the well-buffed fingernails on his smooth white hands.

Sizing the officer up, Avner took a deep breath. He was about to take an enormous risk. 'How much will it cost me to go home for good, so that no-one will ever know I was missing?' he asked. A knowing look crossed the officer's bloated face. 'Three hundred crowns,' he replied, not taking his heavy lidded eyes off Avner's face. Avner's audacity paid off. The officer signed his approval into the order of the day, and the army entered it into their records. 'By order of the Dept of War, private Avner Baldinger has been detached and sent home.' That was the end of Avner's army career.

Seventy-five years later on a damp Manhattan afternoon, Avner is telling his story to his grandson Barry. Avner's face is now cadaverous, his cheeks are sunken, and the huge blue eyes have a despairing look, but he still marvels at his past. 'It's a whole chain,' he says in wonderment. 'A whole chain of happenings.' Barry asks about his childhood but Avner mumbles that he can't remember. 'I'll tell you about it tomorrow,' he promises. That tomorrow never came.

While Avner was playing hide and seek with the Austrian army, Daniel and Lieba were far more worried about their second son Jerzy who was interned as an enemy alien in France. Like Avner, Jerzy had refused to become a rabbi. Since he hadn't matriculated, his options had been limited, and Daniel had decided to apprentice him to a furrier. Jerzy, who had a quiet sense of humour, was amused at the way his father introduced him to his employer. 'My son doesn't want to be a *mensch*, so let him be a furrier!' he said. *Mensch* means man, but its Yiddish connotation is that of an honourable, ethical person. Daniel hadn't intended to insult the furrier but couldn't hide his disappointment that Jerzy was going to become a furrier when he could have been a rabbi.

The fur trade had indirectly caused Jerzy's internment. As Paris was the heart of the fur trade in Europe, he'd travelled there to complete his apprenticeship, but being a citizen of the Austro-Hungarian Empire in 1914 automatically made him an enemy of the French and he was interned as an enemy alien. He was so badly treated that for many years he couldn't bring himself to talk about his experiences. Twenty years later, he was to be interned again, but from that internment there was to be no release.

For the Baldinger girls, however, war made little impact on their lives. Lunia had become a coquettish young woman, handsome rather than pretty, with her fleshy face, long upper lip and thick ankles which she tried to hide by wearing high heels and long skirts. Lunia resembled her mother, but she had a more commanding presence. She was tall, dressed well, and carried herself with such an air of self-importance that everyone noticed her. 'If you act as though you are a nobody, people will treat you like a nobody,' she used to say.

When Kaiser Franz Josef expired in November 1916, shortly before his empire did, Lunia leapt at the opportunity of travelling to Vienna for his funeral. She was to collect rent from her parents' apartment block in Herminenstrasse, give some of the rent money to Tatunciu's impoverished cousins, and stay for the funeral which promised to be the spectacle of a lifetime. The prospect of visiting Vienna was exhilarating. Although Krakow was the cultural and intellectual centre of Galicia, it didn't compare with Vienna, an effervescent city where life was lived with style, verve and charm. Everyone tapped their feet to Johann Strauss waltzes, hummed melodies from Franz Lehar's frothy operettas and copied Viennese fashions.

In normal times Vienna was an easy train journey from Krakow on the Kaiserferdnandnordbahn railway but because of the war, Lunia needed a special permit from the police. At nineteen she was a self-possessed young woman, not easily intimidated. While waiting at the police station for the permit, Lunia noticed a strange wooden contraption about one metre high in the next room. 'I'd like to know what that is,' she said.

The policeman reddened to the roots of his hair and twirled his bushy moustache in embarrassment as he looked at this elegant young woman with her coil of tawny hair, houndstooth travelling suit, and fancy blouse tied at the throat. 'Now, my dear young lady, it's ... ahem ... it's a chair ... a special chair ... it's for examining certain women that we bring here ... you wouldn't know about that, a fine young *panienka* like you,' he stuttered, while Lunia, wide-eyed and enjoying his discomfiture, hung on every word. Too embarrassed to continue, the policeman cleared his throat. 'Here's your permit for Vienna, Miss Baldinger.'

Determined to make a good impression in Vienna, Lunia sewed feverishly for weeks before her departure and arrived in her new travelling outfit, a flared navy skirt nipped in at the waist and a jacket with fake chinchilla cuffs. Vienna was a revelation. Like a child let loose in a toy shop, Lunia stared at the fashions in the shop windows and the exquisitely turned-out Viennese women who made the women of Krakow seem like country bumpkins.

Unable to resist the stylish fashions, she tried on shoes, suits and hunting hats and convinced herself that spending some of Mamuncia's rent money on clothes was a much better investment than giving the money away to poor relatives. She couldn't wait to see the faces of her friends turn green with envy as she made a grand entrance in her new finery.

In 1990, when she can no longer walk without a frame, let alone wear stylish shoes, Aunty Lunia can still recall the pumps she bought in Vienna in 1916. 'The shoes I bought were high-heeled to make my legs look more shapely, with little straps across the instep, in suede with contrasting toe pieces in patent leather. No-one in Krakow had shoes like that. Only young ladies who'd been to a funeral in Vienna!'

On the day of the funeral, she stood with the crowds near St Stephen's Cathedral as the cortege went past. Staring intently to absorb every enthralling detail, she watched the never-ending procession of dignitaries in feathered cockades and flowing capes, the high-trotting Lippizaners caparisoned in white plumes, the gilded carriages and liveried coachmen. She was plunged into the world she'd always dreamed of, a realm of chivalry, beauty and style, and she never wanted to go home.

When Lunia unpacked her new outfits, Andzia, who always hung on her eldest sister's words, widened her dark eyes. 'What will Mamuncia say when she sees that you bought six pairs of shoes?' she asked, awed and horrified by her sister's daring. 'I'll have to face the music,' Lunia shrugged. 'But it's worth it. After all, she can't kill me. And I'll never see suits and shoes like that again!' Then she proceeded to explain the finer points of haute couture to her younger sister.

In the midst of these recollections, Aunty Lunia's eyes harden. 'I was always very good to Andzia but unfortunately she hasn't been good to me,' she sighs. 'She doesn't even come to visit me any more.'

Throughout their lives, these two sisters have been locked in a symbiotic relationship. Living in the same city and knowing each other's weak points, they always knew how to draw blood. Fierce rivals and intimate friends, they loved and loathed each other, yet could not live without each other.

Lieba did not share Lunia's excitement about her new wardrobe. 'Luniu, how could you be so irresponsible? That money was supposed to go to my cousin. I can't trust you. That's the last time I'll ever send you anywhere on business again!'

Not long after Lunia's return, Leo, the son of Daniel's cousin from Vienna, came to visit them on leave from the army. Lunia thought that this tall young man in his Austrian shako, snappy uniform and sword in its tasselled scabbard was very dashing, but Lieba was more interested in what he had to say. Concern creased her kind face as she heard that his mother, the one to whom Lunia had been instructed to take some of the rent money, was struggling to make ends meet. After Leo had left, Lieba, remembering her eldest daughter's selfishness, said to Andzia, 'Let's go to Vienna and take Aunty some food.'

For some reason she decided to take eggs to Vienna. After buying two hundred of the biggest eggs she could find, she carefully arranged them in a big flat basket in layers, with tissue paper in between. At the station she handed the basket to the railway porter who placed it on the rack above their seats. While recounting this story, Aunty Andzia shakes with laughter which transforms her discontented expression. 'He must have put the basket down too roughly because for the whole journey those wretched scrambled eggs kept dripping down onto our heads. We kept wiping the slimy stuff off our foreheads, hoping that no-one noticed! By the time the train pulled into Vienna, we were too embarrassed to own up that the basket was ours, and left the whole sorry mess, basket and all, on the train. On the way to our cousin's place we didn't know whether to laugh or cry. After all that, poor Mama arrived at her cousin's empty-handed!'

Like Lunia, Lieba also had a weakness for clothes, but unlike Lunia, who looked at herself with a kind eye, Lieba rarely liked the way she looked in the clothes she ordered. Often she sent outfits back to the dressmaker, and hats back to the milliner, because she felt that they made her look too fat, too dowdy or too old.

According to Aunty Andzia, Lieba got her love of dressing up from her own mother, Ryfka Spira. The photograph I have of my great-grandmother bears this out. Taken several years before World War I, it shows her in a long patterned skirt, shiny blouse puffed out at the shoulders, and an exuberantly wide-brimmed hat trimmed with feathers. At the age of eighty-seven, Aunty Andzia herself is a fashion plate. She's slim and attractive, her hair is fashionably blow-waved, and she wears smartly tailored slacks with an Italian silk shirt.

When I comment on her clothes, she runs into the bedroom and brings out a new outfit which she has recently bought in Switzerland. Talking about clothes has obviously put her in a good mood, because an hour earlier she refused point-blank to talk about the past, but now she can't wait to tell me about the time her grandmother Ryfka Spira turned up in Krakow.

During the first year of the war, Ryfka apparently became restless in Szczakowa. 'Am I going to sit at the cash register in this department store for the rest of my life?' she said, and talked her husband into going to Krakow. Lieba was very attached to her mother and immediately gave notice to some tenants so that her parents could live in her house in Sebastiana Street.

When my great-grandmother Ryfka saw how lively life was in Krakow, she didn't want to go back to Szczakowa. At first my great-grandfather Abraham enjoyed the novelty of strolling in the Planty Gardens beneath the ancient towers and gates of the city. He liked browsing around Krakow's Glowny Rynek, the vast cobbled square which resembled an Italian piazza. At the stroke of twelve, he stood beneath the lacy tower of the Mariacki Church and listened to the bugler playing his haunting fanfare, which always stopped mid-note. This had been a tradition ever since the Middle Ages, in memory of the ancient bugler who was pierced by a Tartar arrow while warning the people of imminent invasion, and it seemed particularly apt now that the Great War was raging.

Aunty Lunia also remembers her grandparents' visit. Sometimes Abraham took his wife shopping. 'Come, Ryfka,' he'd say to her affectionately in German, 'I saw some nice taffeta with flowers printed all over it in a shop on Florianska Street, it will make a nice blouse for you.' As she recalls this, Aunty Lunia's wrinkled face creases into a beatific smile. For a moment she forgets that she's in an old people's home surrounded by people who are not refined enough for her, abandoned by her sister, feuding with her niece, and trapped in a place with religious fanatics she despises. The years roll away. 'I can remember it like yesterday,' she whispers.

On Saturdays Abraham walked to the Old Synagogue with Daniel, two well-dressed men with neatly trimmed grey beards in their silk top hats strolling through the quiet streets of Kazimierz. Later, he visited his sons and daughters, many of whom had already settled in Krakow. Like Ignacy, who imported Sarotti chocolates and lived in a mansion facing the Planty Gardens on Straszewskiego Street with his wife Pepcia. Ignacy was a distinguished looking man with a stern glance and the bearing of an Austrian officer, and my mother used to tell me that, of all his uncles, my father most resembled this one.

During World War I, Daniel and Lieba's house must have been bursting at the seams because in addition to Daniel's sisters and their children, whom he had brought to Krakow, there were also Lieba's parents. Then, when Lieba found out that her sister Berta was struggling in Chrzanow because her husband didn't support his family, she hired a horse and carriage and brought them with their five children to Sebastiana Street as well.

Little Andzia used to run upstairs to Grandmother Ryfka's, her heavy fringe bobbing over dark eyes which missed nothing. Seeing the candy box on the sideboard, she used to ask her for a sweet but she rarely got one. 'But you gave some to Aunty Berta's children!' Andzia would complain.

'That's because Aunty Berta is poor and her children never see sweets. Your mother is well off, so you don't need them,' her grandmother told her. Berta was badly off because her husband preferred drinking mead to working. 'Uncle was ... Uncle was ... he wasn't rich,' Aunty Andzia falters. She doesn't want to say that he drank.

For my great-grandfather Abraham, Krakow was a wonderful place for a holiday, but he didn't want to live there. He missed Szczakowa, especially his business, although he'd left the running of the store to his son Herman. Although his wife didn't want to leave Krakow, he insisted on going home and so Ryfka packed her bags regretfully and went back with him.

But before long she was back. Unable to settle down in the small provincial town, she braved her husband's displeasure, packed her bags once more, and returned to Krakow. This time, however, there was no room in Sebastiana Street, so Lieba found her mother a room in a widow's house in Agnieszka Street. From the moment Ryfka laid her deep-set dark eyes on her landlady, she had it in for her. 'May God forgive me, but my fingers tingle when I look at that woman. She's as ugly as sin,' she shuddered.

Before long she was saying, 'When she brings my coffee in the morning, she stares at me with those malevolent eyes of hers. I'm sure she's going to give me the evil eye.'

Although Lieba considered this to be *'bube meise'* or old wives' tales, she tried to reason with her. 'But Mama, why would she do that? She has nothing against you, she's a respectable woman. Perhaps you're imagining it.'

But no amount of reassurance could shake Ryfka's conviction that the woman would bring her bad luck. 'She'll be the death of me, you'll see,' she insisted. 'I'm sure I'm going to die in this room.'

Not long afterwards, my great-grandmother started getting headaches. Looking at her daughter meaningfully, she nodded with some satisfaction despite her pain: 'You didn't believe me, Lieba, but that's what I've been telling you. That woman has cast the evil eye on me.'

When Ryfka's headache persisted, Lieba became so concerned that she called Professor Eckstein, who recommended hot compresses. 'So much for your evil eye, mama,' Lieba teased her as she applied a compress to her mother's frowning brow. 'You'll see, *bilineder*, in a few days your head will be like new, God willing.'

Ryfka gave her daughter a sceptical look. 'From your mouth to God's ear,' she sighed.

But instead of improving, the headaches grew worse. Within a short time, Ryfka died in that room on Agnieszka Street, just as she had predicted. It was November 1917, just after the Bolshevik Revolution which shook the world, but this event went almost unnoticed in the Baldinger household which was mourning for Ryfka Spira.

Lieba had a black outfit made for her mother's funeral at

an expensive salon in Krakow. Andzia, who was thirteen years old at the time, watched her mother getting ready for the funeral. Usually energetic and matter-of-fact, Lieba sobbed so much that she could hardly fasten her blouse. 'Why are you crying so much, Mama?' Andzia asked. 'After all, Grandmother was so old!'

Wiping the large tears that rolled down her cheeks, Lieba said, 'You're too young to understand. Old or young, a mother is a mother and can never be replaced.'

Aunty Andzia can still remember the horror she felt when Lieba put her outfit on the floor, rumpled it and tore the lapel before putting it on. 'Mama, your new suit!' she cried.

'That's the custom, to show humility when we're in mourning,' Lieba explained. To Andzia, even then, spoiling a smart outfit was sacrilege.

By the time the war ended in 1918, instead of elation, there was chaos and uncertainty in Krakow. The Austro-Hungarian Empire had collapsed and suddenly there was a dangerous power void. But politics abhors a vacuum. The nation of Poland, which had not existed since 1772, now arose like Phoenix out of the ashes of the burnt-out empire. The creation of the independent Polish state resulted in popular euphoria, but the proud Polish eagle had claws as well as wings.

The new atmosphere of aggressive patriotism increasingly defined itself by marginalising and scapegoating the Jews. Already during World War I, there had been pogroms against Jews who were blamed for food shortages and escalating prices. In 1918 a wave of demonstrations hit Krakow and a mob comprised of students, General Haller's legionnaires and various rabble-rousers rampaged down Grodzka Street where Lieba's sisters Berta and Karola had their shops. They looted market stalls, tore the beards of old Jews, set houses on fire and bludgeoned people, while policemen looked the other way.

Anti-Semitic slogans and ditties echoed all over the city: 'Father Leo drowned in the lake because he sold the Jews some cake!' 'The Jews have millions but we've got Legions, let's show them what our Legions can do!' The rabble-rousers jeered and brandished sticks as they shattered shop fronts and kicked the shopkeepers.

The Baldingers had been Jewish citizens of the Austro-Hungarian Empire but they were about to become Jews in a Polish state. All over Europe, the swords of war had been replaced by ploughshares, but those with sensitive hearing could already detect the sound of cymbals clashing in the distance.

CHAPTER 6

Soon after Poland gained its independence, Avner lost his. One week after the Armistice was signed in November 1918, he married his sweetheart, Hela Majerczyk.

Abraham Majerczyk's kosher sausages were famous throughout Krakow, but for many of his customers, the girl who served behind the counter was far more delectable than the salamis she sold. Hela resembled the early Hollywood movie stars, a plump, strikingly pretty girl with large blue eyes, masses of wavy hair the colour of shiny new chestnuts, and a smile that cheered up the most miserable customers. There was a lushness in Hela's beauty, a promise of sensuality in her soft mouth, and a gaiety that attracted everyone she met.

Avner, who had an eye for a pretty face until the day he died, fell madly in love. His postcards from Austria palpitated with longing, and during his long leave from the army he bought enough salami to feed an entire army. Before long Hela's heart was racing whenever he came in. Dashing in his high-collared army jacket and peaked cap, Avner had a cheeky way of looking deep into her eyes in a way that made her blush right down to her little toes. She was entranced by his easy flow of conversation, effortless compliments and inexhaustible fund of stories which made her peal with laughter.

Hela was not just a pretty face. From the age of sixteen she had been running her father's busy shop on her own. When in 1914 her father had moved to Holland to escape conscription, he took the five younger children with him and left his eldest daughter to look after the business. Hela, who was an excellent pupil, never forgave her mother for not letting her finish high school. 'Why didn't Mother look after the shop herself instead of taking me out of school?' she used to say.

On the other side of the globe in Connecticut, Hela's daughter Wanda, who has been telling me about her mother and their stormy relationship, is suddenly struck by an interesting thought. 'Mother always blamed her mother for taking her out of school. Why wasn't she angry with her father? After all, he was equally responsible.' Suddenly another insight takes her by surprise. 'You know, I'm just like her!' my cousin exclaims. 'She blamed her mother all her life, and I've been doing exactly the same thing!'

Avner and Hela's wedding festivities lasted for one week. Avner was resplendent in tails, a stiff wing-collar shirt with four black buttons, and silk top hat; and Hela, with her delicate face, plump little figure and masses of curls, looked enchanting in her lace gown and long filmy veil. It was a large wedding—the relatives alone on both sides must have added up to over a hundred guests, with all the cousins on the Spira and Baldinger side, as well as Hela's large family.

Fridzia, the youngest of the eleven Baldinger children, remembers attending her big brother's wedding. She was a five-year-old with a round face and a winning smile, and everyone made a fuss of her because of her sore knee. Two months before, she'd come home from kindergarten in her black shoes, ribbed stockings and red overcoat trimmed with fur. When she had tried to clamber up onto a bench to see what was cooking on the big tiled stove, the bench had overbalanced and she'd fallen into the basin of boiling water which Anielcia had left on the floor.

For weeks her father Daniel was the only one she would allow near her scalded knee. A faraway look comes into my aunt's dark eyes while she talks. 'I remember sitting in the little bath while Daddy tried to get me to straighten my leg bit by bit, because it hurt. As I straightened it, and the knee started to disappear underwater, he'd say, "Big fishy, little fishy," and then, "Look! Fishy all gone!"' Her eyes tremble with tears. 'He was so patient with us children.'

She is the only one of the Baldinger children who recalls Daniel as an affectionate father. 'My first memory is sitting on Father's lap at the age of two or three and peeing on him! I can still remember the gentle touch of his hand on my head when he stroked me.' Thirteen years earlier, when my father, at the age of three, had wanted to sit on Daniel's lap, he was rebuked because this privilege was reserved for babies, but being the last, Fridzia was allowed to be a baby as long as she liked.

By the time her brother Avner got married, Fridzia's knee had almost healed and everyone smiled indulgently when this chubby little girl clambered up onto a chair in her black taffeta dress with flounces edged with pink, her fat little legs in black patent pumps and white stockings, beamed at the upturned faces of her relatives and recited a poem which she remembers to this day.

As we talk in her flat in Krakow, which is still furnished with her sister Karola's sideboard, Lunia's divan and her brother Jerzy's white-painted kitchen cupboard, this short plump woman with straight grey hair and a beaming smile recites the ditty she sang for her family almost eighty years ago, probably in the same sing-song way. 'All gather round on this special date, for a wedding we shall celebrate. Let us show how much we care, and congratulate the happy pair!'

It was Fridzia's older sister Rozia who taught her this, and all the other poems she knew. 'Rozia kept me in such a stern grip that you can't imagine! She was like a mother, only more strict. I used to howl like a banshee because I didn't want to learn all these verses but she wouldn't relent. She was always angry and upset and I copped it because I was the youngest. It was because she was deaf. But underneath it all, she was very good-hearted.' My aunt gives a deep sigh, recalling Rozia's tragic fate.

Unlike Fridzia, Matus, the youngest Baldinger son, did not attend his big brother's wedding. Distressing experiences linger longer and more vividly in the memory than happy ones, and even at the age of eighty, Matus, who has been called Marcel ever since he arrived in Paris in 1928, could still remember how he felt when the whole family went to Avner's wedding and he was the only one left behind. Even now, decades later, that memory clouds his amber-coloured eyes. 'Perhaps I'd ripped my trousers and didn't have anything suitable to wear,' he muses. 'Or maybe it was after I'd thrown a glass which cut Fridzia's chin. I was always in trouble. One day Father tied me to a chair so I couldn't run away.' Marcel is a big, generous-hearted man with enough warmth to thaw an iceberg, but anger simmers just beneath the surface waiting to explode, like a dormant volcano. 'I wanted to go to Avner's wedding so badly that to make sure I stayed home, my father tied me to the door handle with a rope and left me there,' he recalls.

One year later, however, Matus was allowed to attend his sister Lunia's wedding. The reception was held at the elegant Hotel Londres. As Szymon Spira, one of Lieba's brothers, had married the daughter of the hotel owners, the family probably got special rates. A beatific smile crosses Aunty Lunia's wrinkled face, and her papery hands flutter with emotion when she recalls her wedding day. 'Oh, my wedding!' she exclaims, and immediately she's swept away on a flood of euphoria.

For a moment the hated convalescent home disappears and Lunia is twenty-two again, radiant in her bridal gown, like the brides she used to watch as a child. Her faded grey eyes gleam inside their crumpled pouches as she declaims in an awed whisper, 'What a wedding that was! You see, I was the first Baldinger daughter to get married.'

Almost thirty years after the china merchant had told Daniel about a marriageable young woman in Szczakowa, another *shadchen* stepped up to him in the Chevre Tilem Synagogue after morning prayers. 'Reb Danil, you have a marriageable daughter, and I know a respectable young man from a good family who would make her a good husband,' he told him.

Lunia was already at an age when most girls were already married, so she listened with interest when her father reported the *shadchen*'s offer. She still read love stories and yearned for romance, but her mother never stopped trying to bring her down to earth. 'Luniu, you'll find out that life isn't like novels,' Lieba used to sigh. 'Especially when you're married. You'll have to learn to accept what comes your way and adjust to your husband's wishes.' Lunia looked sharply at her mother. There was no way she was going to marry a man whose wishes included having a baby every year and running her life.

Lunia's first meeting with Berus took place at her parents' home in Sebastiana Street. He was a serious-looking young man of twenty-nine with shiny glasses, but she liked his quiet manner, dimpled chin and nicely shaped mouth. 'I'm a lucky woman because I married the man I loved, while my sister Andzia, on the other hand ...' my aunt says, and looks at Andzia's daughter who has accompanied me to the nursing home. Krysia is pointedly staring into the distance, her jaw set in an angry line. She is furious with her aunt because she feels betrayed and can hardly bear to look at her. 'Everyone loved Berus,' Aunty Lunia is saying. 'You loved him too, Krysienka,' she says in a honeyed voice, trying to woo her angry niece.

Krysia nods. 'That's true. I did. And if he hadn't asked me to take care of you before he died, I wouldn't have put up with you all these years.'

Lunia gives her niece a long pained look, and raises her pencilled eyebrows. 'That's news to me,' she sighs.

The first time they met, Berus Selinger's sister impressed Lunia almost as much as her suitor did. While they sat in the Baldingers' sitting room, near the piano with the flowered shawl thrown over it, trying to make polite conversation, Lunia's eyes kept straying to the sister's diamond ring and diamond earrings. To this day she can't forget them. 'Her diamonds were this big,' she says, making a circle of her crooked thumb and index finger.

After Berus left, Lunia's heart was thumping. 'Mamunciu,' she said with a blush, 'if Mr Selinger wants me, I'd be very happy to have him, because he really appealed to me.'

Lieba was shocked at this unmaidenly expression of desire. 'Luniu!' she rebuked her daughter. 'One doesn't say such things!'

Lunia didn't take rebukes lightly. 'Mamunciu,' she replied tartly, 'I'm not telling strangers, I'm only telling you so that you'll know how I feel.'

Lieba looked doubtful. 'But you know, your suitor doesn't have any profession,' she pointed out. Berus had done a year or two of economics but had interrupted his course and become a railway clerk so that he wouldn't be conscripted into the army.

Lunia wasn't put off. 'It doesn't matter, I like him and I'll be happy to eat dry bread with him!' Now she giggles girlishly at herself. 'See, I told you I was brought up on romantic novels!'

When the betrothal was announced and Berus was invited to meet the rest of the family, Lunia noticed that he was looking at the necks of the older female relatives and his expression made it clear that he didn't like what he saw. Lieba, her sisters Berta and Karola, and Auntie Pepcia, Uncle Ignacy's wife, all had thick necks that billowed beneath their chins. Lunia could tell that he was wondering whether his fiancée would end up looking like her mother and her aunts.

The following day Lunia took more care than usual dressing for her date with Berus, selecting a three-quarter jacket in forest green and a matching skirt with an inverted pleat. To complete the outfit, she wore a dashing little hunting hat that she'd made from one of her father's hats and wore at a rakish angle over her forehead. She didn't forget to drape one of those new tricot scarfs to hide her neck, but as they walked along the dappled avenues in the Planty Gardens, she could feel Berus's eyes boring into her neck through the scarf.

Laughing, she points to a faint scar on her neck. 'From that day on, I was always self-conscious about my neck. I had it operated on here in Tel-Aviv in 1942, but the surgeon messed it up and severed a nerve and for a time I couldn't even talk.'

Convinced that appearance was everything, Lunia spent much of her time looking into dress shops, poring over fashion magazines and studying how the couturiers achieved their effect. She knew exactly how her wedding dress of French silk should be cut to make her look slimmer and more willowy, how the train should make a shell-like circle on the floor behind her, and how her veil should drift around her face and flow down her back, accentuating the elegant fall of the skirt. She was very explicit that the train be wide enough to twirl as she danced, but not long enough to trip over it.

The dressmaker was accustomed to Miss Lunia's detailed instructions and her gimlet glance which picked up the slightest imperfection. But the veil was made by a high-class couturière who disliked this self-important young woman with the bossy manner.

When Lunia saw the veil for the first time on her wedding day, she couldn't believe her eyes. Surely this flimsy scrap of gauze wasn't her bridal veil. White faced with anger, she shouted at the dressmaker, 'I told you exactly what I wanted. What is this supposed to be? I don't know whether to put it on my head or blow my nose on it. That's not a veil, it's a handkerchief with four corners flapping over my face! You did this to spite me!' she stormed. No amount of explaining that long veils were old-fashioned while shorter ones were more chic could placate the furious bride. Shaking with fury she put the ridiculous little gauzy scarf on her carefully coiled hair, dried her eyes, put her chin up, and stepped outside.

The fracas about the veil made her so late that by the time she emerged from her house, everyone in Sebastiana Street was standing on the pavement to gawk at the bride. Lunia tried to put the hideous veil out of her mind and gave the onlookers a wan smile and regal wave as she stepped into a landau lined with white satin and drawn by four white horses. Just like the brides of her dreams, except for the veil which irritated her throughout the reception because whenever someone came to kiss her cheek or invite her to dance, it kept sliding off her head.

Lieba also spent a great deal of time planning her outfit for her daughter's wedding, but whereas Lunia always knew exactly what she wanted and thought that she looked magnificent in her clothes, her mother rarely felt right in hers. Lunia was horrified when her mother returned the diamond bracelet which Daniel had bought for her. Even though they owned several buildings in Krakow and Vienna and had a big income, Lieba thought it was too extravagant. She had always been modest, and didn't feel comfortable accepting expensive gifts, almost as though she didn't feel she deserved them.

There was an element of self-interest in Lunia's dismay. She felt that her dowry of 50 000 zlotys had been inadequate, and figured that if Mamuncia had kept the bracelet, she would have been able to provide a better dowry. Lunia had no qualms about letting her parents know that she was disappointed because 50 000 zlotys wasn't enough to buy an apartment.

Seventy years later, in the nursing home in Tel-Aviv, she still resents the fact that her parents didn't buy her a house when she got married. She thinks it's because she wasn't selfish enough, because she didn't push hard enough for what she wanted. 'I can see now that I was a fool all my life. I wasn't down to earth,' she sighs. She glances at Krysia. 'Not like her mother Andzia ...' The rivalry that's lasted almost as long as this century rises to the surface like scum on bathwater. 'Andzia was always smart. She demanded things regardless of whether our parents could afford them or not. She had to have a three-room flat on an elegant street, she had to have furniture, she had to have everything.'

Krysia, who rarely defends her mother, is now caught between the tough old aunt who has exploited her, and the mother who has flagellated her with words all her life. On this occasion, bitterness towards her aunt prevails. 'But she didn't get a dowry like you of 50 000 zlotys, which gave you half a house and an income for life!' she snaps.

Lunia doesn't budge. 'All I know is that at the time your mother got married, nine years after me, our parents were badly off, but she still insisted that they buy her a home. For me, they just rented an upstairs room at the Gonskis.'

Krysia is shaking her head with disbelief. 'But you ended up with a half share in your house!'

Lunia passes a weary hand over her face. 'I can't remember

every detail, and some things I don't want to say. But Andzia was very clever and very envious, and remains so to this day.' The look which my cousin Krysia gives her could dissolve steel.

The most popular holiday resort for the Jews of Krakow was the little spa town of Krynica, and that's where Lunia and Berus spent their honeymoon. Each day Lunia promenaded in a different outfit, her fashionably long tight skirts worn with matching shoes and head-hugging hats. Her favourite outfit was a slinky black crepe dress worn with a white fox fur and a delicious little hat shaped like a miniature Austrian officer's shako. As she didn't want her feet to look big, she always wore shoes that were a size too small, which made her walk as though she were treading on eggshells. Taking her husband by the arm, she checked that his new overcoat was neatly belted at the back and that his brown homburg was tilted at just the right angle. As they strolled arm in arm through the rose gardens of Krynica, everyone turned to look at this elegant couple. At least that's what Lunia thought.

After four passionate weeks which exceeded all of Lunia's romantic fantasies, they returned to Krakow and the hated second-floor room which her parents rented for them. Lunia hated living on the second floor. Clinging to her new husband's arm with one hand and to the balcony railing with the other, she acted as though she was living on top of the Eiffel Tower. Whenever she ventured out on the balcony, she shivered and clutched the door as if her legs were about to give way. 'My parents have always lived on the ground floor, so I'm not used to being so high up,' she used to complain.

Living in someone else's house was also embarrassing. Demurely attired for bed, Lunia wore a frilled mob cap, silken nightdress and satin dressing gown with contrasting piping on the lapels, but at night a less demure aspect of her nature emerged. Her wedded bliss was inhibited by the fact that the landlady could hear the creaking of the bed, the rhythmic banging against the bedhead, the murmuring, giggling and ecstatic moaning. In the nursing home at Petah Tikva, Aunty Lunia leans towards me and lowers her voice. 'It's not nice to talk about these things, but sex is one of the greatest pleasures in life.'

Daniel and Lieba adored Berus, a sincere, considerate young man who wasn't demanding like their daughter who took every opportunity to make some dig about her flat. 'Really, Mamunciu, the flat is fine, it's just that those people are not my type. They're not cultured. And that balcony terrifies me, I always feel as if I'm going to fall over the edge. You don't know how it feels, you've never had to live in an upstairs flat,' she would add pointedly. Finally Daniel and Lieba agreed to put in another 50 000 zlotys and bought a house jointly with Lunia on Panska Street. This kept her happy, but it was to cause her parents a great deal of heartache later when their situation deteriorated and their daughter's selfishness became more blatant.

Berus didn't have a job, so when Lunia found out that Avner had become a partner in Hela's family company which imported sausage casings, she seized the opportunity. 'Why don't you take Berus into the business? That way you'll have a bookkeeper you can trust,' she suggested. It was a brilliant move for both parties and, later, when the business grew, they expanded to Vienna and Berus became a partner. Lunia was finally able to start turning her apartment into the palatial home she'd always dreamed about.

Two years after their marriage, in 1921, Tusiek was born after a long and difficult labour which lasted for three days. When Lunia was completely exhausted and no longer cared whether she gave birth or not, it became obvious that there was a serious problem, so the midwife called a doctor. When the baby was finally delivered, Lunia's first reaction on seeing her son was utter dismay. He was bright yellow. Such an embarrassment. She cringed whenever relatives came to see the baby, mortified about his appearance. Later, whenever she was wheeling the pram in the park and saw someone she knew, she would duck behind a tree until they'd passed.

While Lunia was still recovering from childbirth, the Russo-Polish war broke out, and Berus fled to Vienna to avoid conscription. Aunty Lunia can recall the day he left as clearly as if it were yesterday. 'I remember when I got up from my childbed my mother-in-law was with me—I'm embarrassed to tell you this—Uncle Berus knelt beside my bed and kissed my breasts. My mother-in-law looked at me in horror, she was scandalised. I sprang out of bed when Berus went to leave the room, I clung to his legs, I kissed his knees, I can't tell you how miserable I was that he was going away. And my mother-in-law could only say, with pity in her eyes, "Luniu, what are you doing, what are you thinking of? Get back into bed, don't, you mustn't . . ."'

As soon as she could manage it, Lunia followed Berus to Vienna. Lieba came to say goodbye to her daughter before she left. 'Lunia, take care that you don't have another child straightaway,' she cautioned. She was speaking, as Lunia well knew, from bitter experience.

Aunty Lunia is reminiscing about her son. 'When Tusiek got over the jaundice, he was so gorgeous, so beautiful, he had such a lovely round face, such bright blue eyes,' she says. 'When he started walking, whenever we tried to stop him falling, he'd go "Na na na na!"' Meaning no. Then she frowns. 'Later he wasn't so lovely,' she says coolly. 'Later his nose grew too big.'

While Lunia was discovering the pangs and pleasures of

motherhood, and Poland was rediscovering the joys of nation-
hood, Daniel's fortunes began to decline. When the Austro-
Hungarian Empire was dismembered and Galicia became part
of the newly independent nation of Poland, his lucrative
railway contracts came to an end. Daniel and Lieba still had
apartment houses in Krakow and Vienna, but misfortunes
rarely come singly.

In the postwar inflation, money lost value rapidly and the
income from their houses was worth less day by day. They'd
bought the houses on Kopernika and Zielona Streets in Krakow
on a mortgage, aiming to sell them for a capital gain, but in
the deteriorating economy it was impossible to keep up the
payments and equally impossible to sell for a profit.

Daniel's inner serenity and absolute trust in God prevented
him from worrying about their financial situation, but Lieba,
who had been apprehensive even in the good times, always
worried about the future, even though by now the household
was smaller and the children were less dependent financially.
Avner and Lunia were married, Jerzy and Janek were apprenticed
to furriers, Izio had begun manufacturing prams with his father,
and my father Hesiu had left school without matriculating and
was working as a dental technician.

Rozia was still living at home, as was Karola who was doing
well at high school. From an exceptionally beautiful child, she
had grown into a willowy, attractive teenager and was the
only one of the eleven children who finished high school and
matriculated. Andzia, who was very shrewd and resourceful,
had never done well at school, but she had inherited Lieba's
efficiency and flair for cooking, and helped her mother run
the household. Matus was, in his own words, growing up
neglected as a weed, while little Fridzia kept smiling and
wound everyone around her podgy little finger.

From an early age Fridzia had learned how to manipulate

her parents. With an innocent expression, she used to say to Daniel, 'Mummy said to give me ten cents.' After he'd placed the coin into her plump litle hand, she would sidle over to her mother. 'Daddy said to give me ten cents.' She didn't get away with it for very long. Daniel would look up from the exercise book where he and Lieba kept detailed accounts of every cent they spent, and say, 'You asked me to give Fridzia ten cents, but I can see that you gave her ten cents yourself.' Lieba was astonished. 'But she told me that you said to give her ten cents!'

Fridzia must have quaked in her little shoes when her father called her over to explain, but she had nothing to fear. 'My father never smacked me,' she says in that hushed, reverent tone she uses whenever she speaks about him. 'He was always very gentle.' In his firm, quiet way, Daniel admonished his daughter. 'Fridziu, it's wrong to tell lies. If you need ten cents, don't make up stories, just come and ask.' The trouble was, she didn't usually get the money when she asked for it.

So little Fridzia kept scheming. In spite of her delinquencies, she was often sent on errands, like fetching two litres of creamy milk from the dairy in a big metal container with a long spout. On Thursdays she was sent to Korn's grocery shop around the corner, in Ditla Street, to buy flour, sugar, salt, whatever was needed for the Sabbath. Up three broken steps and she was inside the dark shop that smelled of wax, cloves and herrings. Jars, bottles, boxes and sacks were heaped on the wooden floor and shelves, but on the counter Mrs Korn displayed something Fridzia couldn't resist—coconut candies called Kokoski. Although she wasn't allowed to buy anything for herself, she had a terribly sweet tooth, and it killed her not to have five cents to buy one. Since everything was bought on credit, she just added the Delta chocolate biscuits or the coconut Kokoski sticks to the list and ate them, but when at the end of the month Lieba checked the bill, she would ask with a frown, 'What are these Kokoski doing here?' Rather than own up, Fridzia invented stories. 'There was a family called Baumger in there, so Mrs Korn must have mixed us up.'

By now Daniel had started a new business. Whenever Lunia arrived with the baby, she complained that it was impossible to buy a nice pram. The best prams were made by Opel in Vienna, but the falling value of the zloty had made the Austrian prams prohibitively expensive, while the Polish factory in Czestochowa couldn't keep up with the demand.

Lieba, who had inherited her parents' business instincts, was quick to see the opportunity. 'Why don't we make prams?' she suggested to Daniel one evening after Lunia had gone. 'You're a good organiser, and you still have all your workmen,' she pointed out. 'They could make prams and then I could sell them.' She'd always wanted a shop of her own and this seemed the perfect opportunity. Daniel was in his late sixties, but his energy hadn't flagged and he enjoyed working with his hands. He set up his pram workshop in a shed at the back of their yard in Sebastiana Street.

At the beginning the pram factory went well, and the dolls' pram which little Fridzia pushed up the stairs to show off to her friends upstairs came from Daniel's workshop. My cousin Wanda still remembers the big, fancy English-style prams our grandfather used to produce. But Avner, who always had big ideas, talked his father into expanding the business to premises in Przegozala Street.

A bad move according to Uncle Izio who helped Daniel make the prams. 'My father used to say that everything you do has its cost, and that in the learning process you have to pay your dues, but he didn't pay his dues when he started making prams. That factory was a disaster because he knew nothing about making prams, and he was competing with the automotive firm Opel which also manufactured baby carriages. Father should have employed an expert, but he insisted on us doing everything ourselves. And then times changed, and more modern styles were needed, and he couldn't compete with the prams they made in Czestochowa.'

The retail outlet for Daniel's prams was a shop called Syrena which Lieba opened on Szpitalna Street. Shops were in her blood, and after Daniel closed down the pram business, she and Izio kept the shop going.

According to Lieba's niece Rozia Johannes, Izio was Lieba's favourite son. I had no idea that my father had a cousin called Rozia Johannes or that she was living in Tel-Aviv until Aunty Andzia mentioned her in passing. The following morning a proud old lady of eighty-seven with wiry grey hair twisted into a French roll walked slowly up the path to Krysia's place, leaning on a cane. The daughter of Lieba's brother Judah, Rozia had lived in the same apartment block as my grandparents in Miodowa Street. Luckily for me, Rozia had a mind as sharp as a laserbeam and, addressing me formally in the third person in the old-world Polish manner, she proceeded to regale me with fascinating stories about her Aunty Lieba, Uncle Daniel and the eleven cousins.

'Izio and his mother were a mutual admiration society,' Rozia recalls. 'Whenever he came home, she delighted in making delicacies for him, and whatever she placed in front of him, he praised to the skies. "Mama, that's the best soup I ever tasted, no-one makes apple slice like you," he'd say, and ask for another helping.' But when I ask Uncle Izio about his mother, he sounds upset and doesn't want to talk. Much later I understand why talking about her is so painful for him.

After finishing elementary school, Fridzia longed to go to the academic high school like Karola where the girls wore pleated navy skirts, but her parents couldn't afford to send her there. It was Lunia who paid for Fridzia's secondary education at the commercial school where she learned bookkeeping and stenography.

But Aunty Fridzia has no warm feelings for her eldest sister. 'If I wanted to visit her in her home on Szlak Street, I had to take the number three tram. But when I asked her for twenty cents for the tram, she'd shoo me away, saying "Off you go, you little beggar!" She wouldn't give me twenty cents!'

The only one of her siblings whom she remembers with love is her older brother Jerzy who was caring and affectionate. Fridzia's eyes grow misty when she thinks about him. 'Jerzy had one ear curled over like a flower,' she says with great affection. 'He had a pet name for me—Fioradelko. My little Fioradelko he used to call me. I loved Jerzy. Even though times were tough, he always managed to find a few cents for me. Always. Poor Jerzy.'

During the mid-1920s, while his youngest sister was still at school, my father stopped working as a dental technician. He wanted to study medicine but because of the small quota of Jewish students admitted to Polish universities at the time, he wasn't admitted, and enrolled in dentistry instead. But as he hadn't matriculated, he had to pass his school leaving certificate first, which was very rare for an adult at the time.

Poland was in the grip of devaluation so severe that people had to lug wheelbarrows full of banknotes just to make the simplest purchases. To make my father's life more difficult, he had to move away from home because Warsaw University was the only one which offered a dentistry degree. Although Daniel helped him financially, it wasn't enough to cover basic expenses but knowing his father's straitened circumstances, he refused to ask for more money. Throughout his studies my father lived in the cheapest lodgings he could find in Warsaw's Jewish quarter, where frost encrusted patterns on cracked windowpanes, and ill-fitting doors rattled and banged. He blew on his reddened fingers and shivered in the damp room he shared with two equally impoverished students.

Hesiu wore shoes with gaping holes, walked to save tram fares, bought the discarded books of older students, and ate meagre meals. He used to tell me that on the rare occasions when he could afford a piece of herring, he used to slide it towards the back of his black bread to make it last longer. With fingers so stiff with cold that they could hardly hold a needle, he mended his threadbare clothes. But bad experiences often produce good stories. In later years my father's mime depicting the painstaking efforts of a man trying to sew a button onto his shirt and sewing it onto his finger instead, became his popular party piece.

My father never forgot an incident he witnessed from his window one day. 'A boy of about five was standing in front of the gate holding a willow switch in his hand. Whenever a Jew walked past, the boy hit him with his stick. People crossed the road to avoid him, but no-one dared to punish him, scared of provoking a pogrom.

'They feared it wouldn't take much for the father, who was watching from the other side of the gate, to shout that the Jews were killing a Catholic child to use his blood for *matzoh*. When one passer-by found the courage to scold the child, his father ran outside and made excuses. "After all, *prosze pana*, he's only a child!"'

If at the end of the week my father had a few zloty left, he spent them on a ticket at the very back of the opera house. In the foyer he was dazzled by unattainable young women with bobbed hair and dropped waistlines who glided around on the arms of supercilious men in stiff white collars and well-polished shoes. But when the lights went out and the conductor struck up the overture, the passion and pathos of the music would help him forget his crippled leg and abject poverty. For the rest of his life my father used to whistle tunes from his favourite operas, and to this day I never hear a well-known aria without recalling how his eyes would close with pleasure while his hand moved in time to the music.

My father was too proud to complain to his parents about his plight, and my grandparents would never have known how bad things were if not for a friend of my father's who happened to be visiting Krakow and dropped in to see Lieba. 'Hesiu would kill me if he knew I told you this, Pani Baldinger, but I'm sure you'd want to know how hard it is for him to study. He can't afford to buy books, and there are days when he only eats dry bread,' he said.

Shocked, Lieba took the train to Warsaw and astonished her son by turning up on his grimy doorstep. It was even worse than she'd imagined. Hesiu was living in a freezing, slummy room, wearing threadbare clothes and, although he wouldn't admit it, she was sure he hadn't eaten all day. Taking a wad of zlotys out of her well-worn wallet, she insisted he rent a better room and send all his laundry home. Many years later in Tel-Aviv, Aunty Andzia recalled mending his shirts and trousers and folding them into a parcel ready to send back to Warsaw.

After obtaining his dental degree in 1926, my father decided to have another operation on his stiff knee. According to Aunty Lunia, he had the operation in Berlin where he was doing a postgraduate course. His mother wept and pleaded with him not to have more surgery. 'I'll never speak to you again if you insist on going ahead with this,' she said. 'You said yourself that the surgeon warned you there was no guarantee of success. You'll go through all that pain and expense for nothing.' But Hesiu wouldn't listen. Once my father decided to do something, there was no stopping him.

He had the operation, lay with his leg in traction for four long weeks, refusing to be discouraged by what anyone said. But at the end of it all, his leg remained as stiff as ever. And that disability, according to Lunia, was why he refused to marry. He was a handsome young man, with thick brown hair brushed back from his forehead, eyes that shone with intelligence, and regular features. Looking at her handsome, educated, and kind-hearted son whose strong character she admired, Lieba's heart ached for him. She kept suggesting eligible girls until he became furious with her. 'Mama, if you don't stop driving me crazy with these girls, I'll stop coming to see you,' he fumed. 'I don't intend to get married, and that's that.'

CHAPTER 7

The noises from the street had died down, the last of the worshippers in their fur *streimls* and long coats had vanished from the street, and peace had descended on Kazimierz as families gathered around the table to observe the annual festival of Passover. Inside the Baldingers' flat in Sebastiana Street, ten-year-old Matus was clean and uncomfortable in his new corduroy suit. 'This one he won't tear in a hurry, this is the thickest material I have!' the wizened tailor had cackled, wagging a thimbled finger at him.

Sitting at the festive table beside his brothers and sisters, Matus watched his father, impressive as a Roman emperor in his snowy white *kitl*, its high neck embroidered with a broad band of silver, reclining on his side while he went through the Passover prayers. It was like a fancy dress party where Father was *Melech*, or King, and at the other end of the table, Mother was *Malka*, the Queen.

As Daniel intoned a prayer thanking God who led our forefathers out of the land of bondage, Matus remembered that this festival had something to do with Egypt. Why people in Krakow should go to all this trouble on account of something that happened so long ago and far away he couldn't fathom, but he loved the rituals of Seder night, the evening that ushered in the Passover festival. It was like a party, with special food and singing at the end. Matus liked the part of the service when his father dipped his finger repeatedly in the silver *kiddush* goblet, and named each of the plagues that Moses brought onto the wicked Pharaoh who made slaves of the Jews. He didn't know whether to believe that story or not, but there was no point asking anyone about it. They would just tell him not to be stupid.

Now Daniel was putting salt onto his soup spoon and submerging the spoon in the golden broth because it was forbidden to do work of any kind on holy days, and Matus knew that even shaking salt into the soup could be considered work. It was unthinkable to question his father about any religious matters, while his brothers would only wallop him for being ignorant, so it was better to keep quiet and stay out of trouble. Any minute now his father would look his way and ask him to recite the Manishtana, and his mind tried feverishly to recall the four questions he always had to ask during the Passover meal. He didn't want to get them wrong and make a fool of himself as usual.

The best thing about Seder night was the food and wine. As his older brother Izio poured their father's homemade wine into the silver goblet from which they all were permitted to sip, Matus glanced around the table, his amber-coloured eyes shining in his eager face. Father made the wine out of raisins which he soaked in water, brought to the boil very slowly, and kept in long-necked bottles on top of the mahogany cupboard in the living room.

As his brother Izio poured the wine out for all the children, Matus was careful not to spill any for fear of getting a clip on the ear. After the bitter herbs had been dipped in the salt water in memory of bitter years of slavery, his mother served the golden-coloured goose broth she always served with *matzoh* dumplings. Avner used to joke that their mother's dumplings were like cannonballs, and everyone agreed that Andzia's were the lightest. Andzia was whispering behind her hand with Lunia, and Karola was joking with Janek. Matus envied the conspiratorial relationship of his older sisters and the bantering of his older brothers and wished that he wasn't the youngest son.

After the broth came a succulent turkey stuffed with minced meat. Biting into the piece of *matzoh* that his father broke off for each of them, Matus tried to remember why they ate this dry flat bread on Passover. 'The Israelites had to flee for their lives before their bread was baked, so it was flat, and that's why we eat *matzohs* on Pesach,' Lunia said. He looked at his eldest sister admiringly. She knew everything. That's what it was, the Israelites hadn't had time to let their bread rise, and that's why they didn't have anything with yeast in it for the eight days of Passover. At least he'd know the answer to that one.

The previous night he'd watched the baker making their *matzohs*. Staying up late the night before the Seder was a treat. They'd set off to the baker's at ten o'clock and stayed there until three or four in the morning when all the *matzohs* were ready. 'You can't be certain that a speck of *chometz* won't get into the mixture,' Daniel always cautioned, and to make sure that the *matzohs* weren't contaminated by a speck of leavened flour, they used to watch the baker at work. Matus liked to see the way he rolled and shaped the mixture into rounds by hand and ran his little roller along the dough to puncture the small holes that made it easy to break strips off. He would have liked to trace that roller along the dough. The oven door was like a furnace, making the baker's red face stream with sweat, and Matus sometimes wondered whether some of the sweat ever ran into the dough. When at three or four in the morning all the *matzohs* they needed for the next eight days were ready, they piled up a laundry basket as big as a room and lugged it all home. For the next eight days of Pesach, the basket was kept underneath the piano, and day by day the pile became smaller.

The week before Pesach was Lieba's busiest time and the household was in a frenzy of cleaning, scouring and washing. It wasn't just that all the everyday vessels, dishes and utensils had to be put away, but the stove had to be scraped, every drawer, shelf and cupboard had to be scoured, and the dishes, cutlery, pots and pans used only for Pesach were brought out.

The night before Pesach, when every corner of every room had been swept and scrubbed, there was one more ritual. Just before sunset, Daniel and Lieba hunted for any traces of *chometz* that might have escaped Lieba's sharp eyes. Daniel went around with a candle, peering into every nook and cranny, accompanied by Lieba with her feather duster. When they came to the small pile of dust which she had deliberately left for him to find, they swept it up ceremoniously, and with it the last vestiges of yeast and leaven had officially been removed. The house was now clean for Pesach.

For the rest of his life Uncle Marcel felt a pang of nostalgia whenever he thought of the Seder night celebration at his parents' home. Pesach would have been perfect if he hadn't had to recite the Manishtana, the traditional four questions asked by the youngest child in the family on Seder night. Matus's only reprieve would have been if his mama had another son, but his youngest sister Fridzia was already seven, so it didn't look as if any more children were coming.

When he was little, everyone laughed indulgently when the round-faced toddler lisped and stuttered his way through the questions, but by now he was expected to be able to read Hebrew and remember the prayers. He felt ashamed that he couldn't. He hated *cheder*, especially the bad-tempered *melamed* who lashed out at his pupils with a stick whenever they didn't know the answer. The strange squiggles that ran back to front on the page made no sense to him, and even if he managed to read a word correctly, he had no idea what it meant, so he didn't remember it next time. One day he ran home crying because the teacher had hit him harder than usual. To his delight, for once Daniel took his side and denounced the *melamed*'s behaviour at the next synagogue meeting. My grandfather must have mellowed with time.

Munching on a crisp piece of *matzoh* piled with his mother's delicious haroset, a mixture of grated apple, ground walnuts, raisin wine and cinnamon that represented the mortar the Hebrew slaves used for building the pyramids, he tried not to think about the coming ordeal because it made his tummy feel as if it was being squeezed tight with ropes. He knew he'd never remember all the questions. His father would be disappointed, his mother would complain, and his brothers would make fun of him. He'd learned the words at *cheder*, but when it came to saying them out loud in front of everyone, he panicked and his mind went blank.

He could feel Daniel's quiet gaze rest on him. Not yet, he thought, not yet. 'Now it's time for Matus to say the Manishtana,' his father said with a smile. Matus put down his fork, which clattered to the floor, and shuffled his feet, but he couldn't move his chair back and his hands felt clammy. Nervously, he glanced at his father. 'Manish—' he whispered. 'Manishta . . .'

'I can't hear him,' his older brother Jerzy was saying. 'What's wrong with him? Speak up, Matus.'

The boy cleared his throat and began again in a strange piping voice. '*Manishtana, halilah . . . halilah . . .*' He stopped, looked down at the table.

'*Hazeh*,' Karola prompted. She winked at him and he looked gratefully at his lovely sister. By now everyone was staring, thinking what a dunce he was, as usual. Matus went bright red and stammered, 'I can't remember the rest.'

'What's the matter with that boy? Hasn't he learned anything at *cheder*? I'll have to take him in hand,' Jerzy threatened. Matus winced. He knew what Jerzy had in mind.

Then Izio chimed in, 'How come after all this time you don't know the Manishtana? A three-year-old would know it.' He turned to his mother and said in a grim tone, 'Mama, leave him to me, I'll make a *mensch* out of him if it's the last thing I do!' In Paris, seventy-five years later, Uncle Marcel could still remember the exact words his older brother had used.

Tears splashed down Matus's plump cheeks. His brothers were always taking him in hand, as if they were his parents, bashing him whenever they pleased. His brother Jerzy once broke a stick on his back, and no-one said anything.

Maybe Izio was right and he was a dunce. A few days earlier, he'd gone outside to see Daniel in his overalls, doing something in the workshop at the back of the yard. Happy to have a few moments alone with his father, he stood and watched for a time before asking what he was doing.

'I'm making a copper pot for the washing,' Daniel said. 'The one we have is made of iron and when they fill it up with water, it's too heavy for the women to lift. Copper is much lighter,' he explained. Happy to be inducted into the mysteries of the workshop, Matus watched his father's dexterous fingers weld the metal. Daniel bent down to pick up a small piece of metal off the floor. 'Can you guess what this bit is for?' he asked his son.

Perplexed, Matus studied the flat piece of metal his father had begun to shape. He longed to give the right answer so that his father would think he was smart, but the more he stared at the object, the more blank his mind became. Just then, his little sister skipped into the workshop. 'Fridziu, can you guess what this is for?' Daniel asked.

115

Fridzia looked at the scrap of metal in his hand for a moment. 'A handle for the pot,' she said.

'Good girl!' Daniel nodded.

Matus slunk away mortified. To think that his little sister knew the answer and he didn't. Ten is an unlucky number, he thought to himself, because he was the tenth of a family of eleven and that's why he didn't get much attention. All the others had some special talent, but he had nothing at all, not one single quality to be proud of. He wasn't clever, hard-working, bright or witty, wasn't as important as the oldest or as lovable as the youngest, and the only attention he got was for running wild. His only toy was a diabolo, a reel which he threw up in the air and then tried to catch on a piece of string attached to two sticks. The trick was to throw the reel up high enough to give you time to twist the string behind your knee or over your shoulder and still catch the reel in it.

'I never had a real ball,' he reminisces. The walls of his high-ceilinged apartment in a narrow Paris street are lined with beautiful paintings, and there are Persian rugs on the polished floor. Across the road there's a synagogue, but although my uncle has lived here for over thirty years, he has never been inside. He has found his niche among the Masons in whose rituals, activities and camaraderie he has found acceptance, warmth and personal satisfaction.

'Of course I would have liked a proper ball, what do you think?' he roars suddenly in answer to my question and I remember how his outbursts of temper used to frighten me when I was a child. 'You keep asking me if I wanted this or that. I'm telling you, there was no point wanting anything in those days, no point asking. It never occurred to me to ask.' Uncle Marcel has a short fuse. A Baldinger trait, my mother used to say indulgently.

'I grew up like a wild plant,' Uncle Marcel tells me in his

wistful way. 'I never washed my hands properly, I didn't pay attention at school, I was noisy and tore my clothes. No-one taught me anything, no-one saw to it that I learned anything. I was so stupid that I never even learned to read or write properly, and to this day my hand shakes when I have to write something down and that's why I never write letters. I was scared of Izio and Jerzy because they bashed me. Your father was the only one who never bashed me.'

Like all his brothers, Matus loathed *cheder* and hated going to the Chevre Tilem Synagogue with his father on Saturday mornings, especially as it meant going without breakfast because one always prayed on an empty stomach. Matus longed to run around with his mates, kicking the cloth football in the playing fields of Blonia, but to tell Daniel that was unthinkable. 'To this day, it's still unthinkable,' he muses, his large topaz eyes full of wonder in his fleshy face. 'Everyone respected him. He didn't impose his ideas and he wasn't demanding. He never reproached us. It was a question of respect. That's how we were brought up. No-one was forced to do anything.' He inclines his head towards his wife Jako and says, 'She can't understand that.'

Jako is bursting to argue, even her short cropped hair seems to bristle. 'Oof,' she says, blowing air out of her pursed lips in that typically Parisian sound of disparagement and flapping her hands so hard it's a wonder they don't fly off her wrists. 'His father dominated the family and his sons couldn't live up to his expectations. Neither Jean nor Marcel ever did, and from what I've heard the others say, I don't think Avner or the others did either.'

While his wife airs her views, Marcel shakes his head impatiently. 'She can't understand that we respected Father so much that we couldn't think of disappointing him,' he says, irritated at her criticism of his father. 'Some of my brothers had a grievance towards him, but I never did. I loved him. Father didn't say much, but when he spoke, we listened and never forgot his words.'

When Matus turned thirteen, his Bar Mitzvah was held at Chevre Tilem, but like everything else in his life, this was another painful reminder of his incompetence. Unlike his older brothers' Bar Mitzvahs which were big celebrations held on Saturdays, his father arranged his for a week day. Matus had so much trouble learning his portion of the Torah that, to avoid embarrassment, they chose a day when fewer worshippers were present to witness his ineptitude.

Like a man going to the gallows, his legs trembled as he mounted the four steps that led to the *Bimah*, and stood in front of the Ark where the Torah was usually kept, behind an embroidered velvet curtain with gold tassels. There was no rabbi in this prayer house and members of the congregation conducted the service. 'God hears our prayers so there's no need to have anyone to pray on our behalf,' Daniel used to explain. There was a cantor but some worshippers complained that he sounded as if he had last year's *matzoh* ball caught in his throat, while others were shocked that he sang ancient prayers to modern tunes.

When it was Matus's turn to chant his *parsha*, his hand shook as he tried to move the pointer along the line, the new *tallith*, the prayer shawl that he now wore for the first time, kept slipping off his shoulders, and his voice rose to a squeak. As he stumbled and hesitated over his words, Daniel had to prompt and correct him. Although the whole episode couldn't have lasted more than half an hour, Matus was bathed in perspiration and thought that his ordeal would never end.

Although Matus was a poor student, he was alert and curious, and wondered about some of the traditions his father followed. Before Yom Kippur, when Daniel used to bless all the children, he gathered them all around the sacrificial rooster and raised his finger. 'Now all of our sins have entered the rooster,' he explained. Unaware of the symbolic nature of this ritual, Matus was puzzled. If their sins really were inside the fowl, wouldn't they swallow them all back again when they ate it?

At the age of eighty-five, Uncle Marcel could still see his mother take a big white shawl embroidered with little eyelet petals, fold it diagonally and hold it over her head while she lit the candles on Friday nights. Then she would sit down and wait for Daniel to come in, singing melodious Shabbes songs which created such a festive atmosphere in their home.

When Sabbath ended, at sunset on Saturday, Lieba lit thin, finely plaited Havdalah candles, yellow, green and red ones, and again Daniel made *kiddush* with wine. Matus knew that the small silver spice box with aromatic cloves that stung the inside of his nose was intended to make the whole week smell good.

Melancholy lurks behind Uncle Marcel's jollity, I can see it in the depths of his amber eyes. Suddenly the years roll away, and a stout man with a large bald head sits forward, looks into my face with his candid gaze and says in a confidential way, 'You know, in all my childhood I can't remember anyone ever saying a loving word to me. I don't know if you can understand what this means, that no-one ever stroked me. No-one,' he says, plunged in sadness for what he missed.

My heart aches for this warm, affectionate man who has yearned so much to be loved. It's ironic that those who long most desperately for close family relationships so often end up having the most turbulent ones. 'Your mother must have cuddled you when you were small,' I say.

'Where would she have found the time?' he scoffs. 'I can't recall ever seeing her showing affection to the others either.

In our home there was no cuddling. But I've never held that against my parents,' he says. 'Not like Avner and Izio.'

I feel sad for Daniel too. This man who had longed so much for children didn't know how to show the love that he undoubtedly felt for them. He must have been too reserved, too self-conscious. Perhaps he thought that they would feel his love without him showing it. Or perhaps he just didn't know how. As far as Uncle Marcel can remember, the only member of the family from whom he received any affection was Jerzy's dog, Lord, a labrador who regarded Matus as his master. One day Matus walked out of the living room and whistled, forgetting that he'd closed the double glass door behind him, Lord hurled himself through the two glass doors to get to Matus!

My uncle's face glows as he tells me about his dog. 'Lord knew he wasn't allowed to stay in the room while Father was praying, so as soon as Father went to wash his hands before praying, he'd creep into the kitchen, and didn't come back until the prayers were over!'

When Matus left school, his father had a brief talk with him about his future. 'With what you have learned, you can make shoes or furs,' he said. Matus decided to follow his brother Janek's example and become a furrier's apprentice in Krakow. The furrier's workshop had the stuffy, sweetish odour of Persian lamb whose fibres tickled Matus's nose. He didn't like the work and didn't show much aptitude for it, but he had no idea what else to do. For the next two years, his employer taught him to use a sewing machine but didn't teach him how to cut the skins, which was about as useful as training a surgeon without showing him how to use a scalpel. Jealous of his craft, the boss shut himself up in his cutting room so that his apprentices couldn't watch.

In 1928 Matus Baldinger, a round-faced youth with a shy

smile and an insatiable curiosity about the world, climbed aboard the train at Krakow's Central Station bound for Paris. For an eighteen-year-old making his first train journey, this was an exciting adventure. The feel of his wallet packed with the money which he had saved, the sharp smell of the leather seats, the clackety-clack sound of the pug-nosed locomotive as it chugged along its shiny tracks, whistling and spewing black smoke. The thought that in a few days he'd be arriving in Paris made his head whir in time with the rolling wheels. Going to Paris, going to Paris, sang the locomotive as the bare branches and frost-coated fields of Poland rushed past. No bird released from a cage ever felt freedom more deliciously than Matus that day. He was leaving the grey world of Poland behind, to meet his brother Janek who'd lived in Paris since 1925. The world was waiting.

One of the most liberating aspects of his departure was that he had left his phylacteries behind. Incredibly, this had been Daniel's suggestion. Every single day Daniel would wake his sons at dawn for morning prayer and insist that they wind the symbols of their faith around their arms and across their foreheads to remember their commitment to God, even though he knew that they only did it to please him. Matus was the sixth and last of the sons he had longed for but, like the others, he had no interest in religion or the orthodox way of life. The God of his father had no appeal for him. His love was too conditional, his power too overwhelming. The relationship was too unequal, it made too many demands.

By the time Matus left for Paris, Daniel must have realised that although the Almighty had granted his wish to have sons, the spirit of his wish had not been fulfilled. Devout though he was, my grandfather was obviously a realist who could face unpalatable facts. He realised that once Matus left home, he wouldn't continue laying phylacteries, and he didn't want the sacred objects of his faith being treated with disrespect. 'There's no point taking them with you, because you won't wear them when you're away from home,' he told his astonished son.

When Matus arrived in Paris, he felt like a blind man whose sight has suddenly been restored. Even the people here seemed a different breed. They were bursting with life and seemed connected to each other in a way that made him feel joyously connected too. In Krakow there was such stifling formality, such a distance between people, but here everyone talked to strangers and welcomed them. No-one cared about religious rules or what the neighbours thought. Matus loved the generosity and free spirit of the Parisians and blossomed in this climate of friendly sensuality, acceptance and fun. This was what he had always yearned for without even knowing that it existed. He had finally found his home.

As soon as he arrived he handed over all his money to his brother Janek who now called himself Jean. 'I never saw that 10 000 francs again,' he chuckles wryly. 'That money was to cause a lot of misunderstandings between Jean and me.' He arrived in Paris on a Tuesday, and on Thursday he was already working. At first he lived with Jean at Rue Grande Jobelle not far from the Place de la Republique. All week he worked in the same workshop with his brother until late at night when his skin was saturated with the smell of tanned hides, but on Saturday afternoons and Sundays his time was his own. Jean introduced him to his friends. Soon one of the great delights of his new life was meeting friends at a table in a pavement cafe on the Left Bank and talking for hours about life, love and politics. He learned to drink aperitifs in bistros, munch baguettes for lunch and drink bowls of café au lait with croissants for breakfast. On Sundays they took a train out of Paris to the Marne. They rowed pretty girls in boats and later lay under the willows on the riverbank, talking, laughing and flirting.

Matus, who changed his name to Marcel, was dazed by la vie Parisienne, and especially by the Parisiennes. Charming, vivacious and full of fun, they seemed as free as men. They didn't play the games that women played in Krakow. No-one needed formal introductions. If girls enjoyed your company, they showed it without requiring a betrothal contract. Marcel noticed that his older brother's dark good looks and sharp wit made him very popular. But although Marcel was shyer, more self-conscious and less handsome than his brother, people liked his company as well. He was friendly and ingenuous, had an insatiable curiosity and interest in people, and an infectious lust for life.

Everything he saw fascinated him. One afternoon soon after his arrival he was sipping pernod at his favourite bistro while an old woman in a battered fedora was sitting on a folding chair on the street corner outside, selling papers and cigars. It was winter and she drew the woollen shawl tighter around her thin shoulders and blew on her fingers. He watched amazed as she left all her merchandise unattended in the street and walked into the bistro to warm herself up. While she took her time sipping her pernod, passers-by stopped to pick up newspapers or cigars wrapped in cellophane and dropped their money in the box she'd placed on the chair, often leaving more than the item cost. A delighted smile split Matus's face. Pointing outside, he turned to the man sitting at the next table. 'In Krakow she wouldn't have dared turn her back or all her merchandise would have disappeared, and the chair as well!' he laughed, and his neighbour laughed with him. He thought he was going to burst out of his overcoat with sheer happiness. 'Mind you, she wouldn't risk doing that in Paris these days!' he chuckles. Outside in the large garden of his country house, the cherry trees are bathed in early morning light and he springs to his feet with a speed which belies his years. 'Let's pick cherries!' he says, slaps a straw hat on his head, clambers up a ladder, and soon we're laughing as we pop more fruit into our eager red-stained mouths than into the bowl. Glancing at my uncle I suddenly feel a twinge of sadness. Relaxed and glowing with this simple pleasure, he reminds me so much of my father.

Back inside the house, Uncle Marcel continues reminiscing. For the first few years in Paris, he was in a state of perpetual infatuation, with the city and with a succession of delicious girls. He'd never imagined that life could be so carefree, so enjoyable. Then he met a young milliner who personified the spirit of Paris more than any girl he'd ever met. Rolande Guyot, who worked in Christian Dior's fashion house, was effervescent, spontaneous and utterly irresistible. It seemed as though she hadn't a care in the world, and her funny remarks and bubbly laughter always made him laugh. She was also very pretty, with delicate features, soft fair curls and shining eyes. Marcel was swept away.

Even now a dreamy look comes over his face when he recalls those enchanted far-off days. 'Ah, Rolande was a fantastic girl. Fantastic. She had a light-heartedness about her, a gaiety that made you feel dizzy. I can't explain it.' Suddenly he grows restless. 'Speaking Polish is exhausting me,' he says curtly. 'Don't forget it's sixty years since I left Poland.' But when I suggest speaking French he shakes his big head. 'I'm so muddled now, I can't speak one or the other.'

I wonder whether recollections of his early years in Paris have made him irritable. His life would have been perfect except for one thing. Rolande fell passionately in love with his brother.

CHAPTER 8

Bent over his notebook, Daniel was absorbed in balancing his expenses. For the first time in his life he had no change to drop into the alms box in the synagogue, no spare coins for the beggars and no money to spend. Looking up, he caught Lieba's tired glance. She'd regained some of her old energy after having a goitre removed in Berlin several years ago, but these days she walked more heavily and there were pouches under her eyes.

He thought about his brother's invitation. Samuel, whose brewery in Hungary had continued to prosper, had invited them for a holiday to the spa town of Krynica. The crisp mountain air would be invigorating and the mineral baths would soothe their old bones, but pride made it hard to accept his brother's generosity.

Izio, who was still living with his parents, occasionally tried to slip his father a few zlotys, but Daniel didn't want to take them. In the end, Izio persuaded his father to accept forty zlotys and go on holiday. When he describes the incident many years later, Uncle Izio's face crumples with regret. 'I'm ashamed that I didn't do more to make Father's life easier, knowing how hard up he was. I should have organised a regular allowance for him.' At eighty-nine Uncle Izio is thin and frail and his eyes resemble gumdrops when the flavour has been sucked out of them, but he's as dapper as ever. The crease in his trousers is impeccable, his shirt is crisply ironed, and he wears his peaked cap at a jaunty angle.

Errors of omission jab us like needles concealed in the lining of our conscience. But when I remind him that he'd given his father money for a holiday, my uncle's moist lips tremble. 'I only did it once. And anyway Father gave it all back to me when he returned from Krynica. He hadn't spent a single groszy.'

As I sit in my sun-drenched study in Sydney and listen to the honeyeaters twittering on the branches of the pepper tree outside, I look at a photograph of Daniel and Lieba during that holiday in Krynica. A fine-looking old man with a grey beard and a gold watch chain draped across his well-cut waistcoat is leaning on a blackwood cane with a silver handle, alongside a stout woman with thick ankles, softly waving grey hair and a motherly face. Standing beside her ageing parents is Karola, a typical twenties flapper in a dress with a dropped waistline and a head-hugging hat which accentuates her well-defined Grace Kelly jawline and the lovely mouth shaped like Cupid's bow.

The late 1920s were hard for Karola too. Although she'd graduated as a gym teacher, she couldn't find a teaching job in Krakow and was becoming increasingly despondent. During a recent visit to Paris, among the family letters and documents my cousin Aline keeps in a big trunk, I came across a letter Karola wrote to her brother Janek in 1927. Aline, who has retained the surname Baldinger along with her married name Achour, has become the custodian of these precious papers her father kept all his life.

Sitting on the floor of Aline's rustic house on the banks of the Marne, my hands tremble with excitement as I unfold the thick cream writing paper with the initials KB in the corner. This letter is like meeting my young aunt in the flesh; it's so infused with her high spirits that reading it feels as immediate as physical contact. I feel as though I'm watching the words tumble out of her impatient pen as she writes.

> *Dear Janek,*
>
> *Again I'm sitting down to write even though I haven't received any news whatever from you. Well it can't be helped. What am I to do with such a wayward fellow? I'd like to box your ears, but what's the use when you are there and I am here. So I'll set you a good example and write myself.*
>
> *I'm very disappointed that you're not coming to visit us because I was so excited about your visit and told all my friends that my handsome brother (I don't even know if that's true!) was coming to Krakow, and now you've spoiled my wonderful plans and reduced them to ashes. Instead of you, all we get is a letter saying that 'most probably I'll go to Australia!' Don't you dare go there, I forbid you to even think about it, and I don't want to hear about it anymore. I've thought it over and I'll let you go but on one condition—a great big heavy condition—I mean me. Big because I'm 165 cm tall, and heavy because I weigh around 60 kilos. So if you're set on going, and nothing I say will stop you, you'll just have to take me with you. That's fair, isn't it?*
>
> *So I suppose now you'll give up the idea of that journey because I found the right remedy to knock it out of your silly little head. I'm not going to write about this anymore and I don't ever want to hear about it again! Last week Avner was here, he'd just got back from Vienna. He was barely here for a day but we hope to see him again soon. You're the only one who doesn't come, and not only don't you come, but you don't even*

write. I wonder why? Is it to save money . . . or is it just laziness?

Aha, I guessed, didn't I? Right? You probably find it hard to get round to writing. I can understand that because it's a Baldinger defect. But difficulties have to be overcome so just write whatever is on your mind. The hard part is sitting down, but once you're sitting down at the table, or at the desk with a letter in front of you, your hand just moves by itself and the thoughts will somehow arrange themselves in your curly little head.

Now that I've given you such a telling off, I'm sure that you'll write straightaway, out of fear, in case you get another one of these letters.

What's new with you? Do you have any work? I don't have a job at the moment and feel like a lost soul. Well, there's nothing I can do about it. Somehow it will work out. Surely God won't forget about his children and let us perish for nothing.

The poignant prophecy of her last sentence sends a shiver down my spine.

Within two years, however, Karola's life improved dramatically. She was finally appointed gym teacher in a high school in Sosnowiec north of Krakow and met the man she later married. While Karola was teaching schoolgirls who were infatuated with their beautiful young teacher, her brother Izio was running the shop with his mother on Szpitalna Street where they still sold prams, even though Daniel had stopped producing them.

Izio was still living with his parents and every day when he came home for lunch Lieba greeted him as if she hadn't seen him for weeks, and he in turn complimented her cooking as if he hadn't eaten for weeks. 'Mama, that's the best chicken soup I've ever tasted!' he would say, licking his lips appreciatively while Lieba basked in his praise.

Halfway through a plate of crisply fried potato *latkes* and cucumbers pickled just the way he liked them—with plenty of dill and garlic—Izio suddenly dropped a bombshell. 'I want to marry Lola Haubenstock,' he told his parents. Daniel was shaken. Although Lola's father was Jewish, her mother wasn't, so according to Jewish law, Lola herself wasn't Jewish.

Intermarriage had become more common in Poland during the 1930s, but it was still regarded as a tragedy by most orthodox parents. Some disowned their children, while others even sat *shivah* for them as though they had died, observing seven days of mourning with slippers on their feet and ashes on their head.

Until now, each of the married Baldinger children had chosen Jewish partners. The latest was Andzia who'd married Zygmunt Rosenbaum in 1928. Lieba was bitterly disappointed at Izio's decision. Why couldn't a handsome, charming young man like her son find himself a nice Jewish girl from the thousands of eligible girls in Krakow?

I understand how my grandmother must have felt. Even though Michael and I hadn't led an observant Jewish life or sent our children to Jewish schools, I still felt a sharp sense of loss when our son Jonathan fell in love with a girl who wasn't Jewish. I was upset that five thousand years of history were about to come to a dead end in our family. It wasn't a matter of one religion being better than another; it was a question of continuity being broken, of the end of our traditions, of grandchildren who wouldn't follow in our footsteps or those of their grandparents. After the Holocaust, it seemed like a betrayal of the millions who'd been slaughtered because of their religion.

For a devout Jew like Daniel, this was a terrible blow.

During the turmoil over Izio's proposed marriage, my father tried to persuade his parents not to oppose the match. 'I don't think that Lola is the right person for Izio but he's very stubborn,' he said. 'The more you try to talk him out of it, the more he'll dig his heels in, but if you leave him alone, he might see for himself that they're not compatible,' he advised.

But the conflict continued until one of Daniel's friends, a restaurateur called Szwartz, persuaded him to search for a compromise. 'If your son won't listen, talk to a rabbi. If he can't come up with a solution, ask another and another.' Eventually Daniel decided that the only way of averting a rift between himself and his son was for Lola to convert.

Izio knew his strong-minded fiancée well enough to know that this option would be coldly received. 'It's not as if she's really Christian,' he argued. 'Her father is Jewish!'

Daniel remained calm. 'You know very well that if her mother isn't Jewish, then she isn't Jewish either, so you can't be married in a synagogue.'

Izio, who was becoming increasingly angry, tried to keep his voice under control. 'This is utter hypocrisy. I'm not even religious!'

Daniel fixed his penetrating gaze on his angry son. 'But you are a Jew,' he pointed out quietly, 'and you're a grown man. You have to think about the future. Unless your wife converts, your children won't be Jewish either.'

Izio leapt to his feet as if catapulted out of his chair. 'So I won't have any children! I don't even want to have any children,' he stormed.

Izio had met his fiancée in Zakopane, high in the Tatra Mountains. While gliding down the thick powdery snow, Lola had caught sight of a handsome young man with a sensual mouth, and eyes like glowing coals which seemed to devour her face. Soon they were racing each other down the slopes, and sometimes their races ended with them tumbling on the soft snow, exploding with laughter.

Before long they spent every minute together, taking rides in little horse-drawn *doroskys* driven by mountain men in their pudding-basin hats and short embroidered jackets. Arm in arm, they strolled around the snow-covered village whose chalets and churches were built without a single nail. Past beech trees and clusters of hornbeams with fluted trunks, they climbed to the stone chapel on the hilltop. While they gazed down at the vista of spruce-covered hills, Izio told Lola how the chapel came to be built. 'The priest told his parishioners to bring one stone for every sin they'd committed, so it didn't take long to collect enough building material!' he chuckled. Both sports mad, they hiked along the steep track to the summit of Mount Gubalowka, and rafted down the foaming Dunajec River.

Izio loved women, but in all his thirty-one years he hadn't met one he wanted to marry. But Lola excited and intrigued him. He loved her directness, coolness and independence. Lola was German and lived in Berlin but had come to visit Poland because it was her father's birthplace. Unlike any woman he'd ever met, Lola said whatever she thought and didn't play games. As they sat close together by the blazing fire in the ski lodge, sipping spiced wine, he looked into her brilliant dark eyes whose slightly mocking expression he found so exciting, and knew that he'd fallen hopelessly in love.

More down to earth than her lover, Lola had some reservations about their future. The idea of living in Krakow appalled her. Compared with the vitality and modernity of Berlin, Krakow was small, grey and provincial. Then there were the cultural and religious differences. She had been brought up in a big city, in a liberal German household, unfettered by religion, but even though Izio himself wasn't religious, she could see that he was attached to his orthodox parents.

And to make matters worse, there was this outrageous demand that she should convert. She was angry that their marriage depended on her conversion. 'What does conversion involve?' she asked in the awkward, German-accented Polish Izio found so delightful.

'You'd have to study a few things about the Jewish religion.' After a pause, he added with embarrassment. 'And you'd have to go to a *mikveh*.'

Lola opened her large dark eyes even wider. 'What's that?' Izio cleared his throat and tried to explain about the ritual purification of women which took place in a communal bathhouse before their wedding, and each month after menstruation. Lola's horrified expression left no room for doubt as to her opinion of this tradition. Anyway, why should she convert just to keep an old man happy? She was inclined to return to Berlin and forget the whole thing.

Caught between the two most powerful people in his life, Izio consulted everyone he knew in the hope of finding an acceptable solution. When he came to see Lola one afternoon, his eyes were dancing with optimism. 'If you can find some Jewish women on your mother's side of the family, maybe you won't have to convert,' he said.

Lola's arched eyebrows shot up towards her widow's peak hairline. 'Are you suggesting that in Germany in 1934 I should ask my mother to look for Jewish blood?'

It wasn't a great time to be searching for Jewish relatives. One year after Hitler had become Chancellor, anti-Semitism had already started to poison the German air. Although he pretended to dissociate himself from the brown-shirted thugs organised by his evil propaganda minister, those who'd read the Nazi party policy formulated in 1920 knew that Hitler planned to strip Jews of German citizenship and civil rights.

Hitler had already told Major Josef Hell: 'The annihilation of the Jews will be my first and foremost task.' With chilling political opportunism he went on to tell the major that all revolutions needed a focus of hostility and predicted that the battle against the Jews would be popular and successful. 'The Jews will be hanged, one after another, and they will stay hanging until they stink. As soon as one is untied, the next will take his place, and that will go on until the last Jew in Munich is obliterated. Exactly the same thing will happen in the other cities until Germany is cleansed of its last Jew.' In 1934, however, Hitler still wasn't ready to reveal his plans publicly, although his vicious speeches increasingly vilified Jews.

Despite all the obstacles, Izio and Lola were so passionate about each other that they resolved to get married and Lola agreed to convert. When Lieba and Daniel finally asked Izio to introduce his fiancée, he was anxious for her to make a good impression on his parents.

'They'll serve either a *milschich* meal or a *fleischich* meal,' he alerted her beforehand, explaining that milk and meat were never served at the same meal in kosher homes. 'So if they serve meat, don't ask for milk in your coffee.' When she asked how many brothers and sisters he had, all he said was, 'Enough.' He was too embarrassed to tell her that he had ten.

Lola's first meeting with the Baldingers did little to allay her misgivings. As if having to convert wasn't enough, she was annoyed that Izio's mother expected a dowry. She thought his parents looked old and sounded old, more like grandparents, and she had nothing in common with them. During one of the many awkward pauses, she looked around the living room at the grand piano with its old-fashioned embroidered shawl flung across the top, the heavy mahogany sideboard with the *kiddush* cup, menorah and candelabra on the shelves, the big glass-fronted china cabinet in the dining room, and the wooden rocking chair that no-one except Daniel ever sat in, and couldn't help comparing them with her progressive parents and their modern, spacious apartment with its elegant carved furniture and Persian rugs.

Daniel always let his wife do the talking, but Lieba, with her soft short grey hair and kind, homely face, was ill at ease and darted sidelong glances at Lola, trying to figure out why her son had chosen this young woman who spoke such poor Polish and made so little effort to be friendly. Tension crackled all around them and Lola couldn't wait to leave.

Sensing Lola's growing resentment and homesickness, Izio realised that if he didn't speed things up, she'd lose patience and return to Berlin for good. Eventually they both travelled to Berlin where Lola converted. 'That's the kind of thing you do when you're young and in love,' she tells me when we meet many years later, and her dark eyes gleam with that bemused expression that captivated my uncle sixty years ago. She's still sharp-witted and fiercely independent, and hasn't lost her sardonic sense of humour and candid manner, although the sleek black hair has turned iron-grey. To this day she speaks with a strong German accent and still lives in Krakow, the city she once hated so much.

Their wedding in Berlin was a very quiet affair. Daniel and Lieba didn't want to travel so far, while Lola's mother opposed the marriage and didn't attend. While they stood under the *chuppah* during the wedding ceremony, just as the rabbi said 'Mazeltov!' and Izio was about to place the wedding band on her index finger, he dropped the ring. Lola was a modern young woman who scoffed at superstitions and laughed at Izio's nervousness, but perhaps it was an omen.

Back in Krakow to begin their married life, Lola was homesick but she and Izio were so much in love that she soon forgot her unhappiness. He bought her an aristocratic looking Doberman for company and every day Lola put on her sensible shoes, belted tweed suit and cloche hat and took the dog for long walks. Izio was playful and passionate, and they used to chase each other around the flat like children. Aunty Lunia recalls that her brother was so besotted with his bride that he couldn't leave her alone, and loved playing with her glossy black hair which he sometimes plaited and tied with scarlet ribbons.

Lola's directness, which Izio found so refreshing, shocked his family. People in Poland weren't used to plain speaking, but Lola said exactly what she thought and even talked openly about sex, which scandalised Lunia and Andzia.

Lola found Lunia unbearable, a terrible snob, full of her own self-importance, always finding a way to put her down. 'How wonderful that you're not tired of wearing the same hat, Lolschen,' Lunia would say sweetly, exchanging a meaningful glance with her sister Andzia. 'Here in Krakow, we don't wear the same outfit until it falls apart.' One day she leaned forward and asked, a propos of nothing, 'Lola, how do you say Theory of Relativity in German?' Lola gave her a long, hard stare. 'Are you checking me out to see if I'm sufficiently educated for your brother?' she retorted.

Aunty Lunia hasn't changed. When I visit her in Tel-Aviv, I mention that I've recently seen Lola. Even at the age of ninety-four, her eyes gleam as she recalls the treasures that her sister-in-law brought with her to Krakow back in 1935. 'Her father was a Jewish aristocrat, you know. She brought fifteen Persian rugs with her from Berlin and her parents sent furniture as a dowry because they couldn't get money out. It took her all day to unpack. Of course we received her very well, but she always looked at us with critical eyes.' Then she adds, 'Their Doberman had a pedigree, you know.'

135

The only one of the Baldinger sisters Lola liked was Fridzia who was out with her boyfriend most of the time. At twenty-two, Fridzia was passionately in love with a law student called Wienio. Sixty years later, with a dreamy voice and rapt expression, she recalls their romantic meeting at the skating rink back in 1933. As she describes the scene, I can see the short young woman with the winning smile gliding on the ice to Strauss waltzes which crackled over the gramophone. In her chocolate-brown velvet skating dress trimmed with fur, matching velvet panties and fur-trimmed cap and muff, Fridzia was convinced that she was the most fetching girl on the icerink.

She was making her way towards the buffet table laden with canapes when she almost collided with a young man who blocked her way. 'Could you please let me pass?' she asked and with a lopsided smile, he replied, 'For a princess like you, I'll do anything!' and bowed with a flourish, like a medieval knight. When they started going out, he drank in every word and said that her speech was like poetry. When they went skating, he insisted on removing her boots and skates to save her the effort. Fridzia had met the man of her dreams.

Lola dreaded Friday evenings when the whole family got together, but Izio often managed to talk her into going. She had to sit through dreary evenings of trivial conversations, endless quarrels and snide remarks. If Lunia said something was white, her sister Andzia immediately said it was black. If Andzia bought something, then Lunia pointed out why it was extravagant, overpriced or unfashionable. Later they would both turn on their mother and accuse her of playing favourites, of giving more to one than the other. Then Rozia would complain about one of them in her loud voice and that would start a whole new row. Lola felt sorry for poor deaf Rozia for whom no-one had any time, not even her mother whom she clearly adored.

Lola noticed that her mother-in-law was often irritated by Rozia's fussing and upset by Andzia and Lunia's quarrels. 'They're at it again,' she'd shake her grey head sadly. Sometimes she turned to Lola with an embarrassed smile and a wry proverb. 'Small children, small worries, bigger children, bigger worries,' she would say, or 'Small children in your arms, older ones on your mind. Small children don't let you sleep and big ones don't let you live!'

Lola especially hated visiting her in-laws in winter, when they had to take a horse-drawn sleigh through the frosty streets. 'Krakow is like a country town,' she used to scoff. 'In Berlin we haven't used horse-drawn sleighs in the city for years.' She much preferred to go dancing at Cyganeria on Szpitalna Street where the Rosner orchestra played seductive tangos, or to dine at smoky taverns, like Jutrzenka on Sienna Street, where *dorosky* drivers used to drop in for rich *bigos* stew which simmered on the stove all day.

There was another reason for Lola's reluctance to visit her in-laws. Riding through the streets of Krakow late at night in 1935 was a harrowing experience if you looked Jewish as Izio did. Like Spain, Germany and Hungary, Poland during the thirties had moved sharply towards the right, and from marches and demonstrations it was obvious that ultra right-wing groups like Endecja were gathering support. Members of this party roamed the streets armed with sticks and clubs looking for Jews. By day, Endecja members stood guard outside Jewish shops to stop gentiles from doing business with them; by night, roaming bands beat up any Jews who ventured out into the streets, while the police usually turned a blind eye.

They tried to avoid going home past the Glowny Rynek because the fascist-dominated student association had its headquarters there. Although they always put up the hood of the *dorosky*, angry-faced hooligans looked inside every carriage and scanned every face. Lola pressed herself against the back seat so that they wouldn't see her while Izio, his face tense with anger, clenched his fists and muttered, 'Those bastards! If I could get my hands on them!'

Lola was shocked by what was happening in Krakow. Poland seemed to be a nation of two distinct groups, Poles and Jews. She found it strange that only Catholics were regarded as Poles, as if being Jewish precluded citizens from being Polish. The street assaults horrified her because they indicated that anti-Semitism was a grass-roots movement. Distressed, she said to Izio: 'In Berlin, the anti-Jewish propaganda comes from the top, from Hitler and his Nazis, but here the hatred seems to come from the people.'

It was at about this time that Hitler escalated his persecution of the Jews. On 15 September 1935, the Nuremberg Decrees put into action Nazi policies formulated in 1920. The first lethal step towards turning the Jews into outcasts in their own country had begun. But in 1935 no-one could have guessed what Hitler had in mind when he warned that if the Nuremberg Laws didn't succeed, 'it might become necessary to hand over the problem to the National Socialist party for a final solution.'

CHAPTER 9

The band was playing Fibich's 'Poeme' the night my parents met, and as he twirled Bronia around the dance floor, my father knew that this was the woman he was going to marry. For the rest of their lives, whenever that tender melody came on the radio, they would stop in mid-sentence, get that sentimental look in their eyes, and my mother would say, 'Remember?' and my father would take off his glasses, smile, and hum a few bars.

It's hard to imagine your parents being young, impetuous and in love, but judging by the way he swelled with pride whenever he looked at her even when she was well past middle-age, I can imagine how dazzled he was in the days when she resembled Carole Lombard, the blonde American film star. 'Mummy was far the prettiest woman at the party,' he would often tell me, while she would wave a disparaging hand and tell him not to be silly.

From the moment they met, my father was bewitched by this small blonde with skin which glowed like ivory and a smile which lit up the room. But Bronia wasn't just another pretty face: there was something strong and spirited about her, and her high cheekbones and slanting cat-green eyes hinted at Slav horsemen galloping across the steppes.

My mother was flattered by the attentiveness of this older man whose dignified bearing, slight limp and greying hair reminded her of an Austrian officer. He was witty, cultured and so much more interesting than her younger admirers. 'He was transparently straightforward,' she would reminisce later, moving her small hand in front of her in a slicing motion. 'I liked his honesty from the moment we met.' As they became acquainted, she was touched by the vulnerability behind his reserved manner. 'He's always had a complex because of his stiff leg,' she used to tell me.

When they met in the late summer of 1935, my father was thirty-four years old, unmarried and already set in his ways. An old fuddy-duddy, my mother used to mutter whenever she was angry with him. Once, when I was a teenager trying to figure out how you knew when you'd met the right person, I asked him whether it had been love at first sight. By then my father was more distinguished-looking than ever. His white hair made his blue eyes even bluer and the grey moustache emphasised his nicely shaped lips. My mother said that he resembled Sir Anthony Eden, the English Prime Minister at the time.

My father was sitting in his armchair by the window, above a curve in the wide tree-lined street that swept down towards Bondi Beach. Looking up from the Golden Delicious apple he was peeling in one long unbroken spiral, he mused, 'Love at first sight? I'm not sure if that ever happens. I think there comes a time when you're ready to meet someone and settle down, and when you meet someone suitable, that's it.'

My romantic soul was affronted by this version of events. Perhaps at that moment he'd forgotten the rapture of their courtship in Poland, or maybe he was just being prosaic so that I wouldn't get too carried away by unrealistic notions. Certainly the intensity with which he pursued my mother is inconsistent with his explanation. But maybe you really can fall in love with almost anyone if you make up your mind to do so, so perhaps there was some truth in what he said.

I repeated my father's remarks to my mother during an argument we were having one day. Twenty-two years after their first meeting, she had grown rounder, but she was still blonde and pretty, with a flawless, unlined complexion that all my friends remarked on, and quick, firm footsteps which reflected her quick, firm mind. Leaning against the red laminex bench top in the kitchen of our Sydney flat where she was rolling out pastry for her mushroom pie, I lashed out at her with all the spite of a wounded seventeen-year-old: 'Daddy said he was never really in love with you!'

She fixed her sharp green gaze on me and to my amazement burst out laughing. 'That's a good one! He was so smitten, he wouldn't let me out of his sight from the moment we met!'

I know that it was my mother's sister Mania who met my father first. They were all staying at a guesthouse in the fishing port of Hel. For city dwellers from land-locked places like Krakow and Lwow, the Hel Peninsula, a triangular sandbar jutting out into the Baltic Sea, was a magical place of vast skies and endless seas. Above the beaches, among pine trees twisted into strange shapes by the wind, guesthouses catered for holiday-makers who descended on the small fishing port each summer. They smeared perfumed Nivea cream onto their pallid limbs and lay on the white sand in their demure knitted swimsuits, soaking up the sunshine while children played with buckets and spades beside them.

While they were dressing for dinner, Mania was thinking about the interesting man she'd met that afternoon. Flipping open her silver cigarette case with a flourish, she lit up and narrowed her khaki-coloured eyes with pleasure as the smoke hit her lungs. Glancing over at her sister whose complexion was smooth and white as alabaster, she sighed. 'You're so lucky, Bronia, to have such good skin.' My mother flashed her a disapproving glance. 'Your skin would probably look better if you didn't smoke,' she retorted.

Mania shrugged. She was used to her sister's remarks. Straightening her flowered silk dress over her slim hips, she looked approvingly at the long-legged silhouette in the mirror. From that angle, her rounded shoulders were hardly noticeable. 'I met a dentist from Krakow this afternoon,' she said. 'Henek Baldinger. He's a fair bit older than us, but he's good-looking and there's something very nice about him. I think he'd be fantastic for you. Let's go to the dance tonight and I'll introduce you.' My mother waved a dismissive hand. Mania was always enthusing about some man or other, and anyway she'd had enough of men for the time being. She'd travelled across Poland to the Hel Peninsula to get away from involvements, not to look for new ones.

But later that evening, floating in his arms to the languorous strains of the tango, she had to admit that she was drawn to this man whose cornflower blue eyes rested on her face while his hand felt pleasantly firm on her rose-coloured crepe dress. Looking into Bronia's slanting emerald eyes during the foxtrot, my father Hesiu, who had Aryanised his Jewish name to Henryk, or Henek for short, marvelled how well this little woman followed his steps, not missing a beat in spite of his stiff leg. He started saying: 'I met your older sister before—' when my mother blurted out, 'Everyone thinks that Mania's older, but she's actually younger than me.' Her honesty made him smile. Most women would have jumped at the chance of appearing younger.

Over the next few days the dentist from Krakow monopolised Bronia day and night. Just once, when another man asked her to dance, his eyes resembled icepicks. Later I came to know and dread that glacial look that came into his eyes whenever he was angry or upset. From that moment he made sure that no-one got near my mother again. 'I can see that Henek is getting serious,' Mania chuckled. 'You won't get rid of him so easily!' But my mother shook her head impatiently. 'You're always dramatising things,' she scoffed. 'We're going home soon and he'll go back to Krakow so we'll never see each other again.'

Krakow and Lwow were at opposite ends of Galicia, almost seven hundred kilometres apart, a vast distance in the days before mass air travel. But as far as my father was concerned, distance was an inconvenience but not an impediment. He made it clear that for him this wasn't just a holiday romance, and although she blushed whenever he spoke of love, my mother had to admit that each morning the thought of seeing him again made her heart beat in a peculiar but delicious way. After all the turmoil of the past year, it felt wonderful to enjoy herself again.

My father too had recently broken off a serious relationship. His girlfriend had been a beautiful woman with one major defect: she was very religious. The thought of reverting to the lifestyle that had been drummed into him at home, of keeping a kosher home, attending synagogue and observing religious rituals he didn't believe in, obviously outweighed his love for her and he'd ended the relationship shortly before coming to Hel.

But this girl from Lwow had a down-to-earth attitude about everything and, to my father's delight, she shared his views about religion. Bronia's father, who was a socialist, ate ham, didn't fast on Yom Kippur and had no time for rabbis, synagogues or organised religion. 'If God really is everywhere, then people don't need synagogues to talk to him,' he used to say.

My mother agreed. 'I hate the way hypocrites go to synagogue on Yom Kippur and then sneak around the corner to smoke cigarettes. They pray on Saturdays and break the command-ments on Mondays,' she told my father. She had a definite way of stating her views that he found enchanting, especially when she raised her straight black eyebrows and furrowed her ivory forehead.

Apart from Mania, one other guest had noticed that my father had fallen in love. This was Henek's favourite nephew Tusiek, Lunia's son, whom he'd brought with him on holiday. Tusiek noticed that his uncle's step had become much lighter ever since he'd met the new blonde, and that his eyes never stopped following her around the room. Although Tusiek was only fifteen, he was unusually perceptive. He had an impish wit and adored spending time with his uncle who shared his sense of humour. When Tusiek noticed how impatient my father was to get down to dinner each night, he gave his uncle a shrewd glance. 'Uncle Henek, run for your life, 'cos if you stay here one more day you've had it! You'll chase her till she catches you!' he teased.

My mother revealed her unusual situation to my father soon after they met, though it wasn't on their first date in Hel, which was a disaster. Thinking that sailing would be romantic, my father invited her for a boat trip around the peninsula, but while he was enthusing about the pretty coastline and the turquoise water, my mother's face was turning the same colour as her eyes. She couldn't wait to get off the boat and could feel the ground swaying under her feet for hours afterwards. All her life she was a terrible sailor. 'Don't talk to me about boats!' she would shudder.

She told him later, while they were strolling past the old fishermen's huts on the seashore. He liked the sound of her small, energetic footsteps resounding on the long wooden pier that jutted into the Baltic Sea. While the late summer sun warmed her bare arms and the sea breeze ruffled her fine hair, she turned towards him. 'There's something I have to tell you,' she said. 'I'm married.'

He stopped walking and they both stood looking at the iridescent sea that shimmered like taffeta all around them. 'So where is your husband?' he asked, a strained look around his eyes.

'We're separated,' she said quickly. 'I'm trying to get a divorce,' she added and blushed, looking away from his intense blue gaze. He breathed out again. 'I don't know how long it will take,' she was saying. Henek wasn't perturbed. He'd waited a long time to find the woman he wanted to share his life with, and now that he'd found her, he could wait a little longer.

Throughout her life, my mother kept her first marriage secret from me and I only found out about it by accident after my father's death. While we were going through his papers, I found a yellowing Polish document at the back of a drawer. It recorded the marriage of Hirsch Baldinger and Berta Wechslerowa. I knew that Hirsch Baldinger was my father's name before he changed it to Henryk Boguslawski, and that my mother had also changed her given name from Berta to Bronia, to sound less Jewish. But her maiden name was Bratter. So who was this Mrs Wechsler?

My mother snatched the document out of my hand and tried to stuff it back into the drawer. Aunty Mania, who was there at the time, lit one of the low-tar cigarettes she now smoked, put her head back and blew a funnel of smoke towards the plaster rosettes on the bedroom ceiling. Happy to have a distraction, my mother grumbled, 'Always with the cigarettes!'

Mania rolled her eyes in my direction, and pointed to the document half sticking out of the drawer. 'For heaven's sake, Bronia, Diane isn't a baby any more,' she said.

Speaking rapidly and avoiding my eyes as she spoke, my

mother said, 'Well, I was once married to someone else before I met Daddy. It was just a marriage on paper and that's all.' Then her face snapped shut, and I knew her well enough to realise that she wouldn't say another word.

My mind was reeling. Parents expect bombshells from their children, but no matter how old or sophisticated you are, the revelation of a parent's secret life comes as a shock. Several years passed before she talked about this enigmatic marriage again, but I was never sure whether she'd told me the whole story. It seems she'd had a boyfriend in Lwow—Izko Liebermann—whom her parents liked. He was dynamic and extroverted but had an aggressive streak and was pathologically jealous.

When my mother finally broke off with Izko, he stalked her and wouldn't leave her alone. Lwow, the capital of Galicia, was a bustling university town of about 100 000 people, but it wasn't big enough for the two of them. If she was strolling with her girlfriends along the leafy avenue leading to the opera house, he turned up with a bunch of roses. If she went for iced coffee to the Cafe de la Paix on Legionow Street with her younger sister Hania, there he was at the next table, blowing kisses. Even his parents badgered her to take him back.

Finally my mother hit on the solution. She'd get married, but to someone else so that Izko would have to leave her alone. 'I had another admirer, Samek Wechsler, and married him just to get rid of Izko, but it wasn't a real marriage,' she says. 'He knew I didn't love him and that I wouldn't have anything to do with him.' She gives me an embarrassed look. 'You know what I mean.' Shaking her head in wonder, she says, 'Fancy agreeing to such a proposition!' Fancy making it, I think.

I know that the past is a different country, but this story

mystifies me. I'm speechless at the idea of my sensible, straightforward mother being a femme fatale at the centre of all this turmoil, and concocting such a devious scheme. 'What did your parents think about these weird goings on?' I ask.

She shrugs. 'They thought that marrying Samek was a smart thing to do, otherwise Izko and his parents would never have left me alone. It worked. Izko was angry but there was nothing he could do. Samek and I were only together for three months.'

Back in 1935 divorce was rare, so it took courage to take such a major step. There's nothing shameful about it, and I don't understand why she feels so embarrassed, but every life has a corner that never sees the light. Secrets contribute to our individuality and uniqueness, they define and distance us at the same time. I never asked her about this episode again. In my search for the past, am I betraying her by writing about this? But would omitting it not betray the quest? As I struggle with this problem, it strikes me that my mother, who was one of the most honest, fearless people I've ever known, feared only one thing: that I would think less of her if I knew that she'd been married before she met my father.

'So what happened to Izko after you married Samek?' I ask my mother the last time we talk about her mysterious marriage. By now she has a tremor which she tries to conceal by clasping her hands together under the table. She shrugs. 'It was a big blow to him when I married Samek. Izko was too sure of himself, he wasn't used to being turned down.' I ask what became of them all. She raises her straight eyebrows. 'Don't you know what happened to the Jews in Poland?'

When Bronia returned home from Hel, her parents met her at the door with astonished faces. 'Who is this Henek Baldinger you met in Hel? He's certainly a fast worker!' her mother said, looking searchingly into her eldest daughter's face while holding out a letter. With growing astonishment, my mother read my father's handwriting which swept along the page revealing his determined, impetuous personality in every energetic stroke. As soon as he'd returned to Krakow, he'd written to the Bratters, asking for their daughter's hand in marriage. 'I can tell you, I was dumbfounded,' my mother told me. 'He hadn't talked to me about getting married. I had no idea that he was going to propose so soon. The trouble was that my husband Samek didn't want to give me a *gett*.'

Now that it's too late to ask, I wonder why Samek was reluctant to divorce her since he'd agreed to this marriage of convenience. Research always starts too late and ends too soon and my questions are destined to remain unanswered.

During their courtship, my father used to visit her every weekend. He spent most of Friday night trundling the seven hundred kilometres on the train, arrived in Lwow on Saturday, and left on Sunday. And this was the man who'd said he hadn't fallen in love!

My maternal grandparents were Berisch and Taube Bratter, who had Aryanised their given names to Bernard and Toni, as many Jews used to. I don't know whether they did it because it was a disadvantage to have Jewish names, or because many progressive city Jews associated such typically Yiddish names with backward *stetls*. My mother's given name was Berta but she changed it to Bronia. Berisch was born in 1883 in the little town of Zolkwa fifty kilometres outside Lwow. When he was born, his mother Ester was fifty-two and his father had just died, so his married brother Samuel became his father figure.

My grandmother Taube came from Budy Lancutskie where her father, Chaim Goldman, was a landowner. My grandmother must have been an unusually independent girl because at the turn of the century she left home and went to live with an uncle in Lwow. Apparently she didn't get on with her despotic father. Chaim was an imposing figure of a man with a white beard. My mother remembered seeing him riding around his wheatfields, and the farm workers greeting him: 'Good morning, Chaim Hil.' It's rare to hear of Jews in Poland being farmers, so I was fascinated to hear that my great-grandfather owned land, grew wheat, and rode around his property on horseback.

My mother didn't like her grandfather, a harsh despotic man who made his wife Breindl's life miserable, and treated his children with no consideration. 'When my mother inherited a piece of land from a relative, her father just gave it away to one of her sisters, without even telling her,' my mother told me. 'He didn't care about anyone's feelings.' Daughters often choose husbands who resemble their fathers, but in choosing the gentle, easy-going Bernard, whom she married in 1910, my grandmother Toni had chosen a man very different from her father.

According to my mother, her parents were opposites in character and temperament. 'My father was very laid-back,' she recalls. 'When they first met, he only worked two days a week and played billiards the rest of the time. Money wasn't important to him.'

Toni, on the other hand, was shrewd, quick-tempered and energetic. She was the driving force behind their marriage as well as the steel business, which was located two doors away from their home in Sloneczna Street.

Bernard and Toni liked my father from the moment they met him. Bernard could tell that he could entrust his favourite daughter to this man. They were impressed by the fact that Henek had just moved out of his own apartment so that his brother Izio and his bride Lola could live there while their own flat was being renovated. 'Not many brothers would do that,' my mother used to tell me. They were also impressed by the fact that my father helped his parents financially and refused to accept a dowry from his in-laws because it was against his principles.

The affection was mutual. Henek liked Bernard's gentle, noninterfering nature, and Toni's direct, commonsense way of looking at life. He knew that girls often ended up resembling their mothers, and when he looked at this youthful well-groomed woman, with her clear complexion, high cheekbones and fine features, he knew he'd chosen well. Curiously, that was exactly what my husband Michael thought the first time he met my mother.

When my grandparents made discreet inquiries about this ardent suitor who seemed to have fallen out of the sky, they heard that he had an excellent reputation professionally as well as personally and came from a respected family. The father, Reb Danil as he was called, was a wise and devout man, who was a member of the Chevra Kadisha, the Jewish burial society, a voluntary position which commanded great respect in the community. When the time came to meet their future in-laws in person and discuss the wedding plans, Toni Bratter, who was the mover and shaker of the family, travelled to Krakow. Sitting in an armchair in the sitting room at the Baldingers' home in Sebastiana Street, she glanced at the heavy mahogany sideboard with the silver candelabra inside, and the piano with the flowered shawl thrown across it, so much darker and more old-fashioned than her sunny flat in Lwow which she'd recently renovated and in which she had installed a modern kitchen and bathroom.

Although Henek's father said little, there was an aura of dignity about the old gentleman who looked at her with kind, deep-set eyes. Toni noticed that Mr Baldinger's jacket had modern lapels, and that his trousers, of fashionable houndstooth check, were superbly cut. It was Mrs Baldinger, his plump, grey-haired wife with very round shoulders, who did most of the talking. The two women discussed their respective families, checked for mutual acquaintances and compared life in their cities. It turned out that in both cities life had become more menacing with right-wing nationalist groups smashing shops and threatening those who did business with Jews.

My grandmother Toni told the Baldingers about the day when her daughter Mania arrived at the Lwow Polytechnic to be ordered to sit on the left side which was now reserved for Jewish students. 'And you know what hurt the most?' she sighed. 'Her friends, girls with whom she'd been friends for years, turned their backs on her, as if they didn't know her.'

While Lieba served tea and her legendary apple slice, they moved on to the impending marriage. 'Your Henek is an intelligent, good-hearted man, and he and Bronia seem very much in love,' Toni remarked.

Lieba gave a heartfelt sigh. 'I never had any romance in my life myself,' she said. Personal revelations were unusual, especially to a stranger, so perhaps this remark escaped from her lips before she realised what she'd said.

Toni was taken aback. 'You've had eleven children, and yet you say you've had no love?' she repeated incredulously.

They discussed plans for the wedding and the reception, but it was Lieba's remark about romance that stayed in Toni Bratter's mind. She repeated it to her family, shaking her head in wonder. Knowing Lieba's life story, I think I understand what she meant. She had grown to respect and love her husband, who respected and loved her in return, but that had nothing to do with the romantic love she had dreamed about as a girl.

When Bronia arrived in Krakow before the wedding, Daniel refused to meet her. As she hadn't yet been granted a *gett*, according to Jewish law she was still a married woman. As we talk about this fifty years later, something strikes my mother for the first time. 'I wonder why it bothered him so much that I was getting a divorce. After all, he'd been divorced himself!'

One of the first members of the Baldinger family whom my mother met was Lunia. Many years later, in the arid little garden of her nursing home, Aunty Lunia recalls the occasion with a malicious cackle. 'Your father told me: "Luniu, I've met the most gorgeous girl I've ever seen. She's got blonde hair, but it's natural, it isn't bleached, her eyebrows are black, they're not pencilled, and she has a fantastic figure."'

Now Aunty Lunia leans forward and from the expression on her ravaged face it's obvious that she's relishing every moment of this story. 'Naturally I couldn't wait to see this paragon. Well! She did have blonde hair, but it was bleached; she had black eyelashes and eyebrows but they were painted; and as for her figure, well she was very short. I must have made it obvious that I was disappointed, because your father was offended, but that's how I am, I can't pretend. I loved your mother and still do, and if they were happy, that was enough for me. But I must say, I was taken aback.' She laughs heartily, and now I understand why my mother could never stand her sister-in-law.

On 22 May 1936 my parents married in the synagogue in Rzeszow. They chose this city because it was halfway between Lwow and Krakow. At eighty-one, Daniel felt that he was too old to travel all the way to Lwow, while my mother's parents couldn't see why they should travel seven hundred kilometres to their own daughter's wedding. Near the end of her life, all my mother could remember about her wedding was that she wore a cream suit and matching hat, and that her family had attended, as well as Henek's parents, and his brother and sister-in-law, Izio and Lola. They danced till the small hours of the morning at an elegant restaurant, and the lilac trees were in full frothy bloom.

The only aspect of Bronia's marriage which distressed her parents was that she had to live so far away. Of their four children, she was the one they loved best. For all his charm, their only son, who was also called Izio, spent most of his time chasing girls instead of studying. Like many Jewish students, he couldn't get into university in Lwow so they sent him to study medicine in Pisa, but he spent his time chasing the Italian signorinas with their flashing black eyes and flirtatious glances instead of studying. Hania was soft-hearted but she was hypersensitive, always upset about something. Mania was always gallivanting. Bronia was the one they relied on.

On the eve of my mother's wedding day, her father took her aside. 'I don't know what life will bring you but I wish you one thing,' he told her. 'When you have a daughter, I hope that she'll be as good to you as you've been to us.'

We are crossing a busy Sydney street when my mother tells me this, and I'm holding her hand. 'Your hand feels exactly like my mother's did,' she says suddenly, full of wonder. By now, she's starting to fade away, we've changed roles and, in a way, I have become her mother. It's not a role I relish.

'My father's wish came true,' she says, squeezing my hand gratefully. But I don't think it did. I feel that when she most needed me, I let her down.

CHAPTER 10

In Antwerp in the late summer of 1937, while my parents were settling down to married life in Krakow, Avner announced to his family that they were going for a trip to Poland. Wanda and Adam looked at their father in astonishment. They'd just returned from a holiday at the Belgian seaside, and the new school year was about to begin. 'If we don't go now, I have a feeling that I'll never see my parents again,' he said.

During the worldwide depression of 1929, Avner had travelled to Antwerp on business for one of Hela's relatives and had ended up staying in this dynamic but damp Belgian city with his family. Not long after they had arrived, when Daniel and Lieba came to visit, Lieba was shocked to see him and Hela sitting by candlelight because they couldn't afford electricity. They were broke. It must have upset them deeply to see their eldest son living in such conditions, but Daniel kept his thoughts to himself. It wasn't his nature to criticise or give gratuitous advice but he volunteered one suggestion. 'Perhaps you should pray and lay *tefillin*,' he told his son. Avner wasn't interested. He didn't keep a kosher home, observe any Jewish traditions or even fast on Yom Kippur. 'We don't serve food on Yom Kippur,' he used to joke. 'Everyone just helps themselves.'

By the time they settled in Antwerp, Avner had made and lost several fortunes in various countries. The boy whom his father had consecrated to the service of God had turned into an entrepreneur, but perhaps God had meant him to be a rabbi after all, because his schemes never came to fruition.

After World War I, when Daniel's business had collapsed, Avner had got the idea of importing leather into Poland with one of Hela's uncles. Their firm, Opus Vienna, brought in sought-after leather from Italy by the carload, but when the bank called in their loan, they were wiped out overnight. They were selling in one currency in Poland and buying in another in Italy, and when the Polish zloty plummeted, they couldn't cover the shortfall.

As part of his dowry when he married Hela, Avner had received a share in the Majerczyk sausage factory, but when he saw the possibilities of importing sausage casings from China and Australia, he went into business with Hela's uncle. With his flair for publicity, Avner bundled up the merchandise with the shape of a pig cut out of brown cardboard, labelled *Hog ze Swinki*. Hog and piglets. I presume that these casings weren't intended for the kosher market! This lucrative enterprise had come to an end when the partners had quarrelled. The end of their partnership turned out to be Lunia's good fortune, however, because she persuaded Avner to sell the business to her husband Berus, who had been the accountant.

By then Avner was already planning to leave for Vienna, but before he left he discovered that there was fast money to be made in paraffin. Paraffin, which was controlled by a Polish cartel, was very expensive in Poland, but was exported much more cheaply to other countries. Avner crossed the border and, while in Czechoslovakia, placed an order for two carloads of paraffin from the Polish cartel to be delivered to himself in that country. As soon as it arrived, he sent it straight back to Poland where he had trucks waiting to buy it from him at a cheaper price than the cartel charged. He made several trips before packing his family up and moving to Vienna.

The indulgent lifestyle of Vienna suited Avner's expansive personality. He relished the intimate charm of its cafes where people sat for hours over the best coffee and richest pastries in the world. While the deferential waiter served him *sacher torte* smothered in whipped cream one afternoon, Avner looked around at the other relaxed patrons tucking into their chocolate cake and had a vision.

He foresaw that every table of every cafe and restaurant in Vienna would have a small vending machine which dispensed chocolates at the drop of a coin. As they gossiped with their friends over coffee, diners wouldn't be able to resist inserting money and nibbling the chocolates. In 1927 vending machines were a novelty, and Avner couldn't see how this concept could possibly fail.

As the venture needed capital, Avner turned all his persuasive powers on his parents. When he needed to, Avner could charm a mountain into flying, and he made chocolate vending machines sound like the best invention since the motorcar. Daniel and Lieba were in financial straits themselves but, after considerable discussion, they agreed to mortgage their apartment house in Vienna to lend him the money.

Unfortunately, Avner's enterprise didn't succeed. Avner had gone into partnership with a businessman who had less vision than he did and wasn't prepared to outlay enough money to get the best designer. Their prototype was badly designed, badly made, and dispensed only one type of chocolate. It was a flop. Later, after he'd lost his money, someone else designed a better machine and made the millions that Avner had dreamed of.

When his venture failed, Daniel and Lieba lost more than money. According to Avner's brother Izio, who told me this several years ago in his small flat in Woodland Hills in Los

Angeles, his parents lost the block of flats they'd mortgaged. By the time he told me this, Uncle Izio was ninety years old, depressed and embittered. 'I idolised Avner all my life, but ten years ago I suddenly woke up and realised that he'd always been completely selfish. From that moment, I couldn't bear to see him again.' Nothing is smashed as violently as an idol that is discovered to have feet of clay.

After two years in Vienna, Avner arrived in Antwerp. Life was difficult at first but before long his fertile mind had hatched another scheme. Women were always complaining about the time they spent going from shop to shop looking for fabrics. He would make their life easier by sending the shop to them. His offer was inexpensive and attractive. He advertised three metres of printed silk enticingly packaged in a miniature suitcase. Although this offer proved popular, he was undercapitalised and the enterprise went bust, but he didn't lose heart. 'Making the first million is the problem,' he used to chuckle. 'After that, making money gets much easier!'

Ever in search of the golden goose, Avner turned his attention to lotteries. During a visit to his brothers Janek and Marcel in Paris in 1934, he noticed that everyone was feverishly buying lottery tickets. Lottery fever was at such a pitch that apart from trying their luck in the Lotterie Nationale, people were even buying tickets in the Irish Sweepstakes. By the time Avner returned to Antwerp, he had it all figured out. He would sell French lottery tickets in Belgium. Initially the exchange rate worked in his favour, but before long the French government made it illegal for people in foreign countries to make money on French lottery tickets. Avner had to quit.

As long as business flourished, Avner bought expensive clothes for Hela, kept a maid, frequented the best restaurants and sent Adam and Wanda to private schools. But even when things were bad, he believed it was important to keep up appearances. 'A clerk who applies for a position in a torn jacket won't get the job,' he used to say. One day when Wanda asked the headmistress for Greek and Latin lessons, she retorted, 'Tell your father that when he pays his bills, we'll arrange a tutor for you!'

Whether their ups and downs were due to extravagance, bad management or just a sign of the times, Avner always remained philosophical. Musing about her father's personality, Wanda says, 'It's true that my father was a bit of a fraud, but he was a likeable fraud. He believed in himself, was generous to others and lived life to the hilt.'

According to my cousin Adam, who loves talking about his father's seesawing business career, Avner decided to resuscitate the mail order business, but instead of silk he sold watches and jewellery. Proudly opening up one of his father's old brochures, Adam points to advertisements in the form of testimonials from satisfied customers. 'I am a dentist and know nothing about diamonds, but when I examined yours under the microscope, I was amazed by their purity,' one of them said. Adam reckons that some of his father's slogans in the 1935 prospectus were the forerunners of epigrams later used by DeBeers. 'A woman without a diamond is like spring without roses.' 'Fortune in the palm of your hand.' 'A carat that you buy today for forty francs will in ten years be worth 16 000.' Some of his claims were so extravagant that he upset the Antwerp jewellers who made him publish a disclaimer saying that he meant to cast no aspersions on any other retailer!

By the summer of 1937 Avner's mail order diamond business was doing well, and it was at this stage that he decided to visit Poland. As they left the suburbs of Antwerp behind, Avner accelerated, revelling in the power of his big beige Pontiac which could devour nine hundred kilometres in a single day with no effort. Driving across Germany, they stopped several times for spicy bratwurst, sauerkraut and cherry *kuchen* in the towns they passed. The pristine prettiness of German towns resembled lavish operetta sets with every window adorned with boxes of geraniums, every front path lined with neat rows of phlox and asters, every house scrubbed until it shone.

Wherever they looked, people were weeding, hoeing, scrubbing and sweeping as if their lives depended on it. There was energy in this land and vigour in its people. Even the stooks in the fields and the grass in the meadows bristled with vitality. It was hard not to admire these people in whom industriousness and duty were as deeply ingrained as their fingerprints, but Avner knew that a dark shadow was spreading across this perfect landscape. He'd read *Mein Kampf* and had no illusions about Hitler's grandiose plans.

Past Hanover, Avner sped along the autobahn until Hela complained that he was about to take off and fly. 'Leave the driving to me, Dzidzia, just sing us a song,' he laughed, using his pet name for her. While Hela's melodious voice filled the car with Franz Lehar's waltzes, seventeen-year-old Adam egged his father on to see how fast the Pontiac could go. Wanda, who was three years younger, was lost in a reverie about their last visit to Krakow. Her cousin Tusiek would be sixteen now. Years ago, she remembered him as a sallow, sickly child who used to vomit all over the place, but four years ago he'd changed into a good-looking teenager and she was looking forward to seeing him again. She giggled to herself when she remembered her little cousin Krysia, an angelic toddler who called everyone an arsehole, which made all the adults roar with laughter, except her mother, Aunty Andzia, who was mortified.

Wanda's mouth watered at the memory of the round blue-black blueberries and the bittersweet wild strawberries which peasant women used to bring every morning in their straw baskets, along with jugs full of thick cream which they poured over their berries and sprinkled thickly with sugar. Wanda sighed and pulled her sweater down self-consciously. She'd put on pounds and pounds during that holiday, and ever since then Adam had called her Fatty, and her mother had warned that no-one would ever marry such a fat girl.

One relative Wanda didn't want to see was Aunty Rozia who was quite different from the other aunties, so abrupt and impatient, always bossing her around. Rozia was often held up to Wanda as an example of what she might become if she didn't learn to control her moods. Whenever Wanda lost her temper or shouted, her mother would say, 'Just listen to you! You're a *hystericzka* like Rozia. You'll end up an old maid just like her!' As an adult looking back on her aunt's life, Wanda muses, 'I didn't realise that Rozia was difficult because she was unhappy and frustrated. She couldn't hear what people were saying, no-one really needed her, and the man she'd wanted to marry hadn't wanted her.'

Adam, too, was day-dreaming. He was looking forward to seeing their Aunt Karola whose sexy figure and flirtatious nature he'd found so exciting when she'd visited them in Antwerp the previous year. Avner had enjoyed showing off his attractive sister around town and had taken her on a shopping spree which had made Wanda intensely jealous. 'He's like a lover taking his young mistress around,' she thought resentfully, wishing that her father would lavish the same kind of attention on her.

To this day Adam can't forget the way Karola kept pulling at a silk blouse which she'd recently had made. 'I can't understand it,' she said. 'It fitted perfectly a few weeks ago.' Next morning, she burst out laughing. 'I've figured out why it didn't fit. I forgot to wear a brassiere!' After fifty years, Adam's eyes light up with devilry. 'I sneaked up behind her and flicked the back of her brassiere so that it came undone! Imagine what a superb figure she had, that she didn't know she wasn't wearing a bra!'

Adam tells me this when we meet for the first time at his sister Wanda's house in Connecticut in 1990. My cousin is seventy years old, and his smooth white hair and royal blue eyes remind me of my father whose nephew he was. A stroke has left Adam's speech slightly slurred but hasn't affected his astonishing memory. Waving his hand deprecatingly whenever he can't pronounce a word, he mimics himself good-naturedly. 'You see how I talk, burrrr . . .' he shrugs.

As the Pontiac sped through Germany, Wanda looked at her father, so confident behind the wheel in his fashionable, well-cut suit. Before leaving the house, he always brushed his homburg with his special hat brush and made sure that his black and white shoes were immaculate. He was proud of Hela's appearance too, loved to choose clothes for her busty, overweight figure, and discouraged her from dieting. 'Losing weight will spoil your lovely face,' he used to say. It was a prophetic statement. Many years later, Hela's severe dieting did more than spoil her face: it cost her her life.

The accident happened out of the blue at a township called Neumark. As Avner sped around the bend, happily tooting his horn, a cyclist suddenly swerved in front of him. Avner rammed his foot on the brake, but at one hundred and twenty kilometres an hour the big Pontiac skidded across the road as if on skates, turned over a few times and landed on its side. For a long moment there was silence. Then a voice screamed, 'My leg! My leg!'

Adam had seen the accident coming and had tensed up so much that when the car careered out of control, his leg stuck out of the open window and became pinned under the car when it overturned. 'You're all standing on my leg! I can't move it!' he yelled. Hela's face was white. Something hurt just below her throat and, holding her hand against her broken collarbone, she screamed, 'Where is Adam's leg?' She couldn't see it because it was trapped beneath the car.

From his awkward position, Adam looked at the road. No sign of the cyclist. 'The sonofabitch caused the accident and then ran away!' he swore, partly from anger but also from pain, because all the skin had been flayed off his leg which resembled a lump of raw meat. Soon a big black Porsche pulled up, and its well-dressed occupants craned their necks to see through the broken glass. Using a crowbar, their liveried chauffeur lifted the car, helped to pull them out and offered to go for the police.

By the time the policeman arrived, Hela and Avner had found the cyclist. He was lying in the ditch, unconscious. The local gendarme was an elderly man who was about to retire in a week's time and grumbled that he didn't need the hassle of wrecked cars, injured cyclists and foreigners who didn't know how to drive.

The ambulance took Adam, Hela and the cyclist to hospital, while the policeman escorted Avner to the courthouse. Shortly afterwards, the cyclist died of a broken skull. The situation looked bad for Avner, a foreign Jew involved in a fatal car accident. In the magistrate's court the policeman asked his nationality and religion and as he wrote down *Polnische Jude*, Avner's heart raced with anxiety. The magistrate was courteous. 'You have nothing to worry about, *mein Herr*,' he said. 'Those stories about Germans being anti-Semitic are lies, but we have to keep you here until the hearing tomorrow morning.'

The magistrate confiscated their passports and put them up at a hotel for the night, but they couldn't rest because all evening people stomped up and down outside their room.

When Avner became exasperated enough to put his head out of the door to see what was going on, he quickly closed it again, ashen-faced. Men in well-polished leather boots and peaked caps, with Nazi swastikas on their left arms, were striding along the corridor, greeting each other with snappy salutes and enthusiastic 'Heil Hitlers!' The room next door was the headquarters of the local Nazi party.

The doctor who came back to check on Hela's collarbone and change Adam's dressing was a chatty fellow and Avner began to relax. 'Are there any Jews in Neumark?' he wanted to know.

'*Jawohl*,' the doctor replied. 'One has a liquor store, the other is a grocer.'

'And are they making a living?' Avner asked. 'I suppose that the grocer buys liquor from the wine merchant and the wine merchant buys groceries from the grocer?' he said facetiously.

The doctor looked at him in astonishment. '*Bitte*? What do you mean?' he asked. 'We all shop there!' He too was anxious to dispel the idea of German anti-Semitism.

Next morning, standing in the dock, Avner's chest tightened with apprehension. Who knew what would happen to a Jew charged with killing a German citizen? Suddenly there was a flurry as the court officer announced that a witness had come forward to give evidence. It was the liveried chauffeur from the Porsche. Avner swallowed. His fate depended on this man.

'I witnessed the whole accident,' the chauffeur was saying. 'It wasn't the driver's fault. The cyclist was weaving back and forth as if he was drunk and when the Pontiac tried to pass, he suddenly swerved in front of it. Herr Baldinger tried to avoid him but caught the rear wheel of the bicycle on his licence plate.'

Avner breathed out again, hardly able to believe his luck,

especially when the old policeman testified that the cyclist was the village drunkard. In spite of their testimonies, however, the magistrate decided that the case would have to be heard in court at a later date, and asked for 10 000 marks bail to allow them to continue their journey.

Having regained his equanimity, Avner spoke up. 'That's out of the question. I don't have that kind of money with me, I'm travelling with my family to visit my parents in Poland,' he explained. To his relief, the judge accepted 3000 Belgian francs instead, which he placed neatly into a large white envelope. As they continued their interrupted journey, Avner mused that no matter how bad things seemed, it usually worked out well for him in the end.

Before long, the Pontiac swung into Krakow's labyrinth of narrow cobbled streets, and as usual when he visited his home town with his family, Avner pointed to the sombre fortress on Wawel Hill and the slow river that flowed beneath its ramparts. As the car slowed down along one of the narrow cobbled streets leading to his parents' house, Wanda was upset to see barefoot urchins in tattered shirts running beside them, hands outstretched. She hadn't seen beggars before, and as she looked around at the haggard women crouching along the pavements trying to sell their withered posies, and at the tired horses pulling old-fashioned black *doroskys* along the thoroughfares, she was glad she lived in Antwerp and not in this sad impoverished city.

Avner's visits always created great excitement in the family. He was jovial and generous and impressed everyone with his big car, lavish spending and entertaining stories. Life in the 1930s was hard for Daniel and Lieba but years seemed to fall off them when he was around.

Their daughter Lunia couldn't wait to show the visitors her luxurious apartment with its oak panelling, expensive Persian rugs, and bathroom with a separate little sink just for brushing your teeth. To this day my cousin Wanda can't forget her aunt's morning ritual. After Gizia the maid had served her breakfast in bed, she laced Lunia into her corset and then dropped to the floor on her knees to pick up her mistress's high-heeled shoes and ease her large feet into them.

Lunia had prospered when her husband Berus had taken over the sausage casing business from Avner. With her shrewd direction and assistance, Berus used the basement of their home to package the merchandise and had gradually built up the business. 'They did well because they were prepared to start small and wait until they'd built the business up, unlike my father who always had big ideas and wanted to get rich quick,' says Adam.

While Avner kept his family enthralled with stories about his enterprises and escapades, Wanda was falling in love with her cousin Tusiek, a skinny seventeen-year-old whose sense of humour kept her giggling helplessly. Like the rest of the family Tusiek was smitten with this vivacious girl whose raven tresses fell across her expressive face when she talked. Wanda revelled in the admiration of the whole family, especially her uncles who loved taking her out. Her Uncle Izio took her kayaking on the Vistula in Krakow; my father showed her around Wawel Castle; and Uncle Jerzy, who had a car agency at the time, took her and Tusiek for a drive in the countryside. While she and her cousin were kissing in the back seat, she glanced up and flushed scarlet when she saw Jerzy watching them in the rear-view mirror with an indulgent smile.

To Adam's relief, he was staying with Uncle Izio and Aunty Lola and not with his religious grandparents. Yom Kippur was approaching, and he was glad that, like his parents, Izio and Lola didn't fast. Adam liked talking to his uncle about sport, while his new aunty Lola was excitingly frank about matters that he'd never heard adults mention before. When he remarked that Uncle Izio wasn't wearing a wedding band, Lola, ever the realist, just shrugged. 'Wearing a ring doesn't mean anything,' she said in her strong German accent. 'If a man wants to pretend he isn't married, all he has to do is just flick his ring off, like this, and that's it!'

One morning he noticed that she wore a nightgown, not pyjamas like his mother and sister, and he asked her about it. 'Aunty Lola, you look so old-fashioned in that nightgown, why do you wear it?'

She fixed her large dark eyes on him and shrugged. 'It's too much of a nuisance having to remove pyjamas in the middle of the night. Nightgowns are much easier, you just pull them up!'

Soon after Yom Kippur, Avner and his family headed back to Antwerp but this time he chose a different route. After the car accident, he wanted to avoid Germany. Berlin was at a fever pitch of excitement because Benito Mussolini had just arrived, and Hitler was pulling out all stops to impress his guest with the might of the Third Reich. Like thousands of poisonous black spiders about to be released on an unsuspecting world, swastikas fluttered on scarlet banners all over the city. Tens of thousands of helmeted troops goosestepped with spine-tingling precision, and an endless convoy of tanks and armoured trucks roared past while bands blared and ecstatic spectators roared approval for their Teutonic Messiah.

Avner was enjoying the beautiful drive home past the jagged peaks of the Swiss Alps, but when he arrived home, bad news was awaiting him. The court in Neumark had issued a warrant for his arrest. Bail had been revoked and he was to stand trial for manslaughter. Several months later, however, he received an unexpected letter from Germany. Out of the large white envelope fluttered three banknotes, the same three 1000

Belgian franc bills that he'd lodged as bail! His trial had been cancelled because of an amnesty and they were returning his bail money.

This incident, so typical of the reverses and reprieves that marked Avner's life, added to his repertoire of anecdotes. He couldn't get over the fact that although Nazis were confiscating Jewish property and stripping Jews of all their rights, in this isolated case they were keeping to the letter of the law and restoring to one Jew the small sum they'd taken from him legally. 'They even returned my bail money in the original envelope!' he used to say. 'In Poland, they'd never find the envelope. In Belgium, the money would have disappeared. Such meticulous attention to detail could only happen in Germany!'

CHAPTER 11

Daniel was slowing up. At the table he often raised his trumpet to his ear to catch the conversation, and when strolling in the Planty Gardens he leaned more heavily on the shiny blackwood cane with its chased silver handle. But his gaze hadn't lost its piercing clarity, he still had an air of distinction, and his houndstooth trousers still had their razor-sharp creases. When he wore the homburg elegantly tilted on his bald head, it was hard to believe that he was eighty-three years old.

Unlike most of us who try to hide from God, Daniel had never ceased seeking Him out. He still rose at dawn, laid *teffilin*, and thanked the Almighty for the world which seemed more marvellous to him every day. Although on the rebbe's advice he'd sold the house on Sebastiana Street to ease his financial situation, he and Lieba continued to live there and pay rent.

Daniel had never sought power or position. Several years earlier, when his colleagues had offered to make him president or *gabai* of the Chevra Kadisha Burial Society, he'd declined the honour. 'Being elected "*gabai*" is a fine thing,' he told my father one day. 'But to be voted out and become the "*aus-gabai*", that's not so pleasant. I'd rather not become president than to become ex-president.'

By 1938 my grandfather realised that the longer you live,

the less life turns out as you expect. Over the years most of his dreams for his children had turned to dust. He'd longed to have children so that he could pass on the religious faith which had sustained him all his life, but in this he hadn't succeeded.

He had known who he was, while his sons knew what they didn't want to be. Instead of becoming a rabbi and consecrating his mind to the service of God, his beloved Avner had devoted his talents to Mammon. None of the other sons found solace in the sacred Torah whose vision of perfection had inspired him throughout his life. None of them laid *teffilin* or kept kosher homes, but he accepted their right as adults to choose their own paths and never interfered in their lives.

Apart from Rozia, none of his daughters were religious either. As a young girl, Lunia had once asked him, 'Tatunciu, why do you believe in God?' It was a daring question which verged on blasphemy but he gave her his considered answer. 'Luniu, religion is not a matter for discussion,' he said. 'Either you believe or you don't. But I would strongly urge you to believe.' He knew that the believer was blessed in many ways, but to believe in God you had to transcend the limits of the physical world. Faith was beyond reason.

With schooling too, the children had disappointed him. In spite of all the money he'd spent on private tutors over the years, most of them hadn't finished high school. Apart from Hesiu, who'd educated himself as an adult, only Karola had matriculated and gone on to university. At the thought of his favourite daughter, Daniel checked the time on the fob watch hanging off the gold chain draped across his waistcoat. Although the newlyweds lived in Sosnowiec where Karola was still teaching, they visited every Sunday and lit up the house on Sebastiana Street with their light-heartedness. Lunia and Andzia had already arrived and Lieba was grumbling that

Karola was an hour late for lunch and the roast chicken would be ruined.

Karola was married to Stasiek Neufeld, an attorney she'd met while teaching in Sosnowiec. Stasiek was tall, dark, handsome and full of charm, and soon became a favourite with the whole family. According to Uncle Izio, who had a nostalgic smile on his face while he talked about his genial brother-in-law, Stasiek had been a prominent attorney in Sosnowiec who would have gone to the top of his profession if he hadn't been Jewish. 'He was offered a high position on condition that he converted to Catholicism, but my sister Karola told him that if he did that, she would no longer be his wife.'

Finally the bell shrilled, and there she was, tall, slender and more radiant than ever, in peals of laughter at something that Stasiek had said. 'The chicken has dried out,' Lieba sighed but her son-in-law soon disarmed her. 'I really can't understand why we're so late, Mother,' he said with an innocent expression. 'We woke up on the dot of one, jumped out of bed and drove to Krakow as fast as we could!'

Turning to Lunia, he pointed to a small pimple on his wife's face. Putting his arm affectionately around her shoulder, he said, 'Don't you agree I'm entitled to compensation? Even with the cheapest watch, you get a twelve-month guarantee, but I've only been married six months and this face is already marked!'

While everyone laughed, including Lieba, Lunia was looking approvingly at the understated dress Karola wore with such an air of casual elegance, while Andzia thought how happy she and Stasiek looked together. Everyone loved this golden couple. Perhaps this adulation made them too trusting of others and too sure of themselves so that they weren't prepared for the inhumanity that was soon to engulf the world.

Sitting at the table with her in-laws, my mother liked to listen to her father-in-law whom she adored. 'Daniel was a perfect gentleman, he had innate courtesy,' she used to reminisce. 'He always made me and the other daughters-in-law feel very welcome. That's more than I could say for some of his daughters,' she would add darkly. Whenever Lunia and Andzia made malicious comments about their 'out-laws' or whispered behind their hands, a pained look would cross Daniel's face. 'Please remember that we have guests and be polite,' he would admonish his daughters, who blushed at their father's mild rebuke. Daniel's gentleness was his strength.

Although Andzia's tongue was lacerating, and her eyes as unforgiving as needles, my mother adored hearing stories about her little son Fredzio who was like a sunbeam with his fair curls, blue eyes, and precocious mind. 'Come on, sing your song, Fredzio,' urged his older sister Krysia, and soon they were all laughing until tears rolled down their faces as the toddler lisped the words of a popular love song: 'We had a date last night at nine but then she said she won't be mine!'

Daniel watched admiringly while Lieba served apricot cake. Loyal, dependable and as efficient as ever, she still ran the household like clockwork and remembered what each one of them liked. He glanced at Karola, holding the floor with one of her lively anecdotes. 'Before they let me train as a gym teacher, I had to pass a fitness test, but the course was so tough, it's a wonder I didn't have a heart attack!' Although Daniel listened far more than he spoke, his attentive manner made him part of the conversation. He enjoyed having the family around him and regretted that his two youngest sons lived so far away in Paris.

The year before, Janek had made one of his rare visits, but it was fraught with tension and had prompted Lieba to comment that small children tug at your apron strings but big children tug at your heart strings. Janek had come to ask his father's consent to marry a young Frenchwoman. Although Rolande Guyot had been a devout Catholic, she had converted to Judaism. For one thing, she regarded religions as different paths leading to the same creator, and for another, she was so much in love with this handsome, debonair and witty man that she would have walked through fire if he was on the other side. Rolande's father was the famous sculptor Georges Lucien Guyot, whose massive bronze lions still embellish the Trocadero in Paris. Monsieur Guyot wrote to Daniel, saying that he'd consented to his daughter's conversion and her marriage, and he hoped that Monsieur Baldinger would do the same.

Enclosed inside his letter was a certificate from a French rabbi who confirmed Rolande's conversion and recommended that the marriage should proceed. But according to my cousin Adam, who heard this story from his father Avner, Daniel wrote back to say that he didn't consider it appropriate for a rabbi to recommend that his son marry a woman who wasn't Jewish by birth.

Displeased with his reply, the Paris Rabbinate wrote to the Chief Rabbi of Krakow saying that once someone has converted, they cannot be refused. Daniel was then summoned by the Chief Rabbi who made it clear that the Krakow Rabbinate expected him to consent to the marriage. As always, Daniel was graceful in defeat. In a telegram she sent off to her brother in Paris, Lunia wired: 'Parents give their consent to the Rabbi's request.' In a moving letter Daniel wrote to Avner, he asked his eldest son to represent him at the wedding in August 1938, as he was too old to make such a long journey. Quoting the story of Ruth the Moabite from the Torah, Daniel requested that Rolande be received warmly and whole-heartedly into the Baldinger family.

After lunch, when all the young people had left, Daniel looked fondly at Lieba having one of her brief catnaps in the chair. Any moment now she'd open her eyes, fully awake, and say, 'I feel as if I've slept for hours!' They'd share a few more happy years together, God willing.

Several weeks later, when Czechoslovakia was about to be sacrificed on the altar of allied appeasement, and the death knell for Europe had begun, Daniel and Lieba travelled to the little Polish spa town of Iwonicz for a holiday, eager to breathe country air again and soak their tired limbs in mineral baths. Even though the guesthouse was kosher, Daniel had brought his own salt shaker in case the owner forgot to keep condiments for *milschich* and *fleischich* dishes separate.

They spent several pleasant days taking the cure and strolling in the gardens which bloomed with late summer roses. In spite of the warm weather, Daniel complained of feeling cold, and when his warm dressing gown didn't stop the shivering, Lieba borrowed a hot-water bottle from one of the guests. The following day, when she wanted to return it, however, she was told that the woman had left suddenly because she felt ill.

When they returned to Krakow, Daniel felt worse. His muscles ached and he felt exhausted, but when Rosh Hashana dawned, he insisted on attending the synagogue service. Looking at his pale face and lacklustre eyes, Lieba followed him around, grumbling and nagging that he should stay home. She had to help him knot the striped tie over the stiff white collar and pull on his cutaway jacket, and when he was ready, she noticed that the silk top hat had become too big and accentuated the pallor of his face and the shadows under his eyes. 'You shouldn't go out,' she insisted, but to no avail. At Rosh Hashana, it was decided who would live and who would die. It was unthinkable not to attend that solemn service, not to watch the cantor's cheeks puff out with the effort of blowing the ram's horn, and then hear the thrilling fanfare which signified the hope of redemption and the start of a new year.

But when he returned home, he went straight to bed. As usual, Lunia took charge. 'We must send for the best doctor,' she pronounced.

After placing his wooden stethoscope against the patient's chest and examining his coated tongue, the professor closed the bedroom door quietly and stepped into the living room where tense faces awaited his diagnosis. 'Your husband has typhoid fever,' he told Lieba. 'Make sure that he rests and drinks plenty of water. I'll return tomorrow with an injection.'

Lieba clucked her tongue in distress. 'He must have caught it in Iwonicz when he borrowed that woman's hot-water bottle.'

When injections of saline and glucose didn't help, the doctor tried camphor and caffeine to stimulate Daniel's heartbeat. On Yom Kippur, the Day of Atonement on which he had always fasted, for once Daniel allowed a little fluid to go down his parched throat.

During the Yom Kippur service, Fridzia prayed fervently as never before, tears flowing down her plump cheeks. 'I'll never ever do anything mean again, just let Father get well,' she promised.

Sukkoth, the harvest festival, had begun but Daniel was deteriorating and his weakened body was now racked by hiccups which gave him no peace. 'Is it Hoshana Raba yet?' he asked Fridzia through fever-scabbed lips when he felt her soft gaze resting on his face. Hoshana Raba, the seventh day of Sukkoth, has a mystical religious significance because it offers universal salvation.

'Not yet,' she replied.

'The souls of those who die on Hoshana Raba go straight to heaven without being judged,' he told her in a hoarse whisper. Tears welled in her brown eyes. In the bedroom on Sebastiana

Street where she herself had been born, the forces of life and death were locked in a struggle which only one could win.

The following day, as the family sat around him, the bed suddenly made a loud crack, as if it had snapped in two. Lieba's head swivelled towards her daughter, terror in her eyes. 'Did you hear that sound?' she asked. Fridzia nodded, her mouth too dry to speak. 'It's a premonition of death, it means that the end is near,' her mother said.

While Daniel was clinging to life by sheer effort of will, Neville Chamberlain was signing the Munich agreement. On the day when the fate of Czechoslovakia and the western world had been sealed, my grandfather recited the Shema, the Jew's affirmation of faith in one God. 'Hear O Israel, the Lord our God, the Lord is one.' With these words, the last breath left his body.

It was Hoshana Raba.

Karola crumpled and slid onto the floor in a faint while Lunia tore her hair and shook with loud, despairing sobs. 'Tatunciu,' she sobbed. 'Tatunciu.' For the first time in Fridzia's life, her brother Izio put his arms around her. When she glanced up at Jerzy, she saw that tears as big as peas were rolling down his face although he wept without making a sound. 'There are moments in life that are carved into your memory and this was one of them,' she tells me, wiping her own tears with a big handkerchief.

After fifty years Uncle Izio's voice quavers when he recalls his father's body laid out on the floor. The scene which he witnessed remains indelibly etched in his memory, and even at the age of ninety he can't talk about it without breaking down. Inside his modest flat in Los Angeles, my uncle stares into the distance and I can tell that he has the scene in front of his eyes as he speaks.

'When my father died, the Chassids in their long black

coats and big hats came in, lit candles and placed them around his body. Then they said prayers to honour him because he was a member of the Chevra Kadisha. I was too upset to stay and watch, but I heard them chanting and praying for a long time.' Suddenly a wily smile brightens my uncle's morose face. 'But the most interesting story of all, I can't tell you,' he says.

'What story? Why can't you tell me?' I ask.

He wags a bony forefinger at me. 'Don't be so curious!' he says, delighted with his secret. I hate it when he plays these perverse games, but at least this time he's talking about the past, because a year ago he was so agitated that he refused to tell me anything at all.

Finally he relents and tells me his secret. Several years after his father's death the undertaker told him that Daniel had asked to be buried in the same grave as Lieba's grandfather who had died back in 1872. By the time Daniel died in 1938, a new Jewish cemetery had been consecrated and the old one in Miodowa Street was no longer being used, but they gave special permission to open the family grave in the cemetery where the Spira family have been buried for three hundred years.

Fascinated by the conversation, Uncle Izio's daughter widens her eyes in astonishment. My cousin Lee, an attractive woman in her forties, has finely chiselled features and a crisp, no-nonsense manner. Her days are divided between chauffering her two teenage children and taking care of her frail parents. Eyes blazing with indignation, she turns to her father. 'I was in Krakow two years ago, but you didn't tell me anything about a family grave. If I'd known, I would have gone to see it!' I'm amazed to learn that she knows nothing about her father's past or about her grandparents either.

Uncle Izio's lips quiver with emotion. 'You'll never be able to understand,' he says. 'Never. My father weighed me down with hundreds of religious rules. You can't possibly understand what a strain that was. What does she need it for? I don't even want her to hear any of this.'

Lee flushes and her topaz-coloured eyes spark with anger. 'All my life he's kept the past a secret from me. Okay, I'll leave the room so I won't hear anything about it,' she retorts and stalks out, banging the door behind her.

Her father's pained eyes follow her. 'Why did she go so suddenly?' he wants to know, but before I can explain, he shakes his head. 'To this day I wash my hands hundreds of times because that's what my father taught me. After I touch my hair I must wash my hands, when I sneeze I must say a prayer, when I see a rainbow I'm supposed to recite a benediction. To this day the rules buzz around in my head and drive me mad. I didn't want her to be burdened with all this superstition.' He's looking forlornly at the closed door. 'And now she's angry with me.'

At the graveside, one by one, Daniel's sons, brothers and sons-in-law threw earth onto the coffin and winced as it struck the simple wooden casket. Swaying back and forth, the Chassids intoned the ancient prayers for the dead. 'The time is short, the labour is great, and the Master of the House is waiting. It is not your duty to finish the task but neither are you free to desist from it.'

There remained one final prayer to be said. Uncle Izio looks pensive. 'Life is so ironic. My father divorced his first wife because he wanted a son to say Kaddish for him when he died. Finally he had six sons but only three of us came to the funeral. Avner was in Antwerp, and Jean and Marcel were in Paris. And those of us who did come didn't say Kaddish for him the way he wanted it said, every day for a year. We recited it once at the funeral and that was all. There's an ironic half smile on Uncle Izio's face. 'It seems to me that my father wasn't meant to have children. You can't cheat destiny.'

Half a century after my grandfather's funeral, I stand on the withered leaves of the cemetery whose tombstones are sinking into the decaying loam. The canopy of chestnut trees allows so little light to filter through that leaves rot on the overgrown paths and a musty smell, the smell of death, rises from the ground. An air of reproach emanates from these sagging stones. This cemetery was desecrated by the Germans who smashed most of the gravestones and carted them away to pave roads. Big raindrops patter on the splayed leaves and slide down the family memorial as I read the inscription.

Here lies a man who walked a straight path.
Beloved by all and kind to his fellow creatures
He arrived early and stayed late at the house of study
A lifelong student of the Torah
He worked diligently and faithfully
And his hand was always open to the poor.

Daniel Baldinger of blessed memory.
Passed away with a good name on Hoshana Raba 21
   Tishri 1938
May he rest in peace.

A few weeks after Daniel died, the sound of glass shattering in Berlin resounded all over Europe and heralded the beginning of a reign of terror unequalled in the history of mankind. It's true that the Almighty hadn't granted Daniel's fervent wish for devout sons who would say Kaddish for him, but God must have loved my grandfather after all, because he gathered him up before Poland became a charnel house and the way of life he loved so much had vanished forever.

PART TWO

CHAPTER 12

Not a single breeze cooled the sultry September heat and my father's shirt clung damply to his body as he limped along a road jammed with people fleeing from Krakow. He was already regretting his decision to leave. It would be impossible to reach Lwow at a time when the country was being mobilised and trains had been commandeered by the army. Desperate civilians had paid exorbitant sums to hire cars, carts and horse waggons, and there wasn't a single wheel left for sale or hire.

Swept along by the throng, my father felt like a single cell in a huge organism pushed by forces outside its control. The sun beat down on exhausted parents dragging whimpering children, on unshaven men pushing barrows and perspiring women clutching unwieldy bundles. Babies wailed, dogs barked, carts clattered, waggons rumbled, and wherever Henek looked, a mass of humanity surged along the road. What had made him think that he could walk seven hundred kilometres to Lwow with his stiff leg? As his well-worn leather suitcase with the ridged handle dragged on his right arm, he changed hands yet again and wished that he hadn't succumbed to the general panic when Colonel Umiastowski had ordered men of military age to leave Krakow and head east.

In the turmoil over his decision, only one thought consoled him: that Bronia had refused to leave with him. This was no journey for a woman with a new baby. As he hobbled along, his thoughts drifted to his tiny daughter who was only six weeks old. I was born under the astrological sign of Cancer, but it should have been during the transit of Mars because shortly after my birth German tanks rolled into Poland and World War II began. The miracle was that I was born at all, because my father had decided not to have any children. He felt that he hadn't received enough love and attention from his own parents and had no desire to inflict unhappiness on his own offspring.

There was another reason too. From the moment he and my mother had married in 1936, the spectre of war had haunted eastern Europe. It wasn't right to bring children into the world at a time like this, he argued. My mother Bronia, on the other hand, couldn't wait to have children and peered longingly into every pram she passed. 'One child isn't going to change the course of history,' she used to tell him in her matter-of-fact way. As it turned out, she was mistaken, because having me did affect their history. Many years later she told me that if it hadn't been for me, they may not have found the strength to cling to life during the years when every day of their existence was as precarious as treading a tightrope.

When they were first married, my mother went along with my father's ideas about children in that resolute nonconfronting way of hers, but when the biological urge grew too strong, she just did what nature intended. The deciding factor was my cousin Fredzio, without whom, she later told me, I would never have been born. When my father's sister Andzia went away for a holiday and left Fredzio in my mother's care, she became besotted with his melting eyes of celestial blue, his fair curls, affectionate nature, and astonishing memory. At the age of two he knew every make of car and could identify them at a glance. Perhaps I absorbed my mother's love for him while I was still in the womb because throughout our lives there has been a powerful bond between my cousin Fredzio and me which even forty years of separation did not weaken.

When Andzia returned from her holiday and took her little son home, my mother's apartment felt as lifeless as a tomb and she knew she couldn't live without a child of her own. She was then in her late twenties and her biological clock was hammering. By this time she'd already been pregnant and had an abortion. This fact slipped out accidentally, many decades later, amid great embarrassment because she was very reticent about revealing anything in her life that deviated from the perfect picture she presented of herself.

So when this story spilled out, and it was too late to kick it back into the dark closet of life's secrets, her cat-green eyes darted sideways and an embarrassed expression pulled her mouth into a straight line. 'I didn't want to have a baby so soon after I got married, that's all,' she said curtly. Whether she had an abortion because she thought tongues might wag if she had a baby so soon after getting married, or because my father didn't want to have a child at that time, I never found out.

It's ironic that my father, the son of a man who'd been desperate to have children, was equally determined not to have any. Ironic, too, that he married a woman whose need for a baby echoed his own father's yearning. I don't know whether my father gave in, or whether my mother simply took matters into her own hands and faced him with a foetus accompli, but in the darkening autumn of 1938, while Daniel lay dying, my own life began to form.

My father's reaction would have upset a less determined woman. 'It's crazy to bring a new life into the world at this point,' he said. Hitler had already annexed Austria, marched into the Sudetenland, occupied Czechoslovakia and grabbed Memel, and from his vituperative attacks on Poland it was obvious that country would be next.

This failed to disturb my mother who glowed with happiness, her eyes more lustrous than ever under straight black brows slanting above her Tartar cheekbones. Some faces consist of curves; my mother's were straight lines sketched with a fine pen. 'You're worried about the future, but there's no future without children,' she told him. They were living in a spacious apartment on Potockiego Street, a tree-lined boulevard whose handsome stone-faced buildings had graceful balconies over-looking the park. Autumn lingered that year, and fallen leaves crackled under her small, quick footsteps as she strolled under the linden trees. Let politicians worry about politics: she was going to have a baby.

I was born during a sweltering July night which my mother thought would be her last. As if I had some foreboding about the world awaiting me, I refused to emerge from the warm security of the womb, until finally the obstetrician clamped his forceps round my stubborn skull and yanked me out with so much force that I had the outline of the forceps imprinted on my head for weeks. 'You looked like a war casualty, but from the moment you were born you were the image of your father,' my mother used to tell me. I think she emphasised this resemblance to create a bond between my father and the child he hadn't really wanted.

My father was thrilled to have a girl—boys had caused too much uproar in his own family, whereas girls at least were more controllable. He wanted to call me after his father, but as his brother Jean in Paris had just named his baby Danielle, my father chose Diana, the Roman goddess of the moon and of the hunt. It was an original choice. Too original for Poland where children were usually named after Catholic saints and martyrs like Teresa, Zofia and Cecilia, and whose namedays were marked on the calendar and celebrated on that day for the rest of their lives. When my father applied to register the birth, the thin-lipped registrar wiped the surplus ink off his nib, placed it neatly on the ink stand and looked up from his ledger with a frown. 'Diana? Isn't that a pagan name?' So in deference to the prevailing culture which made things hard enough for Jews without having heathen names, I became Danusia. It took another nine years, and a journey to the other end of the earth, before I was to reclaim the name my father had chosen for me.

I have a photo of my mother holding me when she came home from the clinic. She's wearing a percale dress with zigzag patterns and a triumphant expression. But when a month later I was still waking them every night with my howling, my father decided to take action. One night, without telling her, he moved my cradle into the furthest room and closed all the doors so that she couldn't hear my indignant screams. I slept through the night after that.

This was probably just as well because soon there was enough tumult in the world without me adding to it. In that hot Indian summer of 1939, when wheat fields and pasture lands shimmered in the sun and the orchards hung heavy with fruit, Poland itself resembled an overripe plum ready to be plucked. The whole nation awaited the inevitable attack with such tension that the announcement of war came almost as a relief from the uncertainty.

For months newspapers had carried increasingly grave reports about the gathering storm, but nobody understood the significance of the nonaggression pact signed by the German Foreign Minister von Ribbentrop and his Russian counterpart, Molotov. By securing Russia's neutrality during the impending conflict, Hitler had paved the way for his invasion of Poland.

As Hitler's tirades became more hysterical, in cafes and taverns all over Poland, fists crashed on counters and glasses shook as people argued about what was going to happen. On

Polish Radio the stirring voice of Commander-in-Chief Marshal Smigly-Rydz reaffirmed that Poland would never surrender Gdansk or the Corridor. Buoying up national morale, the Marshal kept praising the brave, invincible Polish army and harking back to the victorious battle of Grunwald five hundred years ago. 'We defeated the Teutonic menace once and we'll do it again, we'll show them another Grunwald!' the optimists cried, shaking their fists.

In Krakow's main square at midday, the bugler's haunting fanfare floated down from the gothic towers of the Mariacki Church, as it had done for centuries. As always, the trumpeter stopped abruptly mid-note in memory of his heroic predecessor. On that stifling August day, no-one could suspect that the interrupted fanfare of this bugler would usher a period of barbarism and carnage unequalled in the annals of the western world.

Now, on the eve of another barbarian invasion, a tremulous soprano voice brimming with emotion began singing Poland's national anthem. *'Jeszcze Polska nie zginela i nie zginac bedzie.'* 'Poland has never been annihilated and will never perish.' Others took up the song and the square resounded with the stirring words. It's not surprising that Poland's anthem related to war and conquest. For the past 1000 years, Poland had not enjoyed twenty-one consecutive years of peace.

In the lemony light of dawn on 1 September, a droning sound of engines from above drew my mother to the window. She looked at the dainty Tissot watch my father had given her for their third wedding anniversary. It was five o'clock. The roar grew louder, and she stood frozen while big black aeroplanes of the Luftwaffe flew low over Krakow, grotesque black stains blotting out the light. Then they vanished like a disturbing dream.

Along with the rest of Poland, my parents heard the

announcement which was to change their lives forever. German radio relayed Hitler's hysterical screaming. Poland had supposedly attacked the Third Reich and the two nations were now at war. Heydrich's scheme to disguise a band of German criminals as Polish soldiers and stage a phony attack on a German radio station at Gleiwitz had provided Hitler with a pretext for starting World War II. Tuned in to their radios, disbelieving Poles heard the Führer's cynical words: '*Heute morgen haben wir zurückgeschlagen!*' 'This morning we've hit back!' Several hours later, a million and a half German soldiers were pouring across the Polish frontier to avenge this trumped-up attack.

Throughout the day, shortwave radio stuttered warnings in code. Warsaw: air alert. Krakow: air alert. Lwow: air alert. With the droning sound which made people tremble, German warplanes roared towards their targets and dropped bombs on major Polish cities, railways and columns of soldiers trying to reach the front.

Glass shattered, buildings crumbled, and teams of first-aid workers pushed their way through fallen bricks, burrowed through mountains of debris to free those who were trapped underneath. Newspaper headlines shrieked WAR!, the ground shook, and all over Poland grave faces gathered around the radio, trying to figure out what would happen next.

While the fighter planes and dive bombers of the Luftwaffe poured death and destruction from the skies, German Panzer divisions were flooding over Polish plains. Driving eastwards from Pomerania and westward from East Prussia, thousands of tanks with heavy armaments thrust deeper and deeper into Poland. Helmeted soldiers in motorised vehicles laughed and joked as they rolled inexorably over rutted country roads, meadows and barley fields, pushing onward to entrap Warsaw in a giant pincer movement from which there would be no escape. They couldn't wait to show these Slavs and Jews who was the master race.

On the third day of the war there were terrifying rumours that the entire Polish airforce had been wiped out, even before most of its planes had time to get off the ground. Day after day, people gathered around their radios hungry for news. Most of the time they only heard the defiant strains of Chopin's Military Polonaise which raised their spirits while it broke their hearts.

There was still no news about the ground battles. How could an army whose cavalry still used lances hold out against howitzers, tanks and cannons? Whenever she thought about the soldiers, my mother's anxious thoughts flew to their nephew Tusiek, who'd enlisted just before the war. She saw his tousled fair hair and heard his bantering voice, and tried to ignore a growing sense of foreboding.

While they sat beside their wireless sets anxious for news my parents heard Colonel Umiastowski's broadcast: 'All men of military age must withdraw immediately to the east.' Perhaps the High Command planned to assemble an extra group of fighting men to hold off the German offensive some time in the future. Acording to rumours, Polish defeat was imminent, the remnants of the dazed Polish army was in retreat, and the government had packed its archives and gold reserves and fled eastwards.

At first the idea of fleeing from Krakow seemed nonsensical to Henek, who tried to dissuade his friends and relatives from leaving. Andzia and Zygmunt had already left for Lwow, as had my father's cousin Kuba Spira with his wife Niusia and their children Alinka and Bronek. 'There's no point in running away,' my father argued. 'Where will you go? How will you live?' But as more and more people fled, he got sucked into that spinning vortex of panic which gripped the city. He would to go to Lwow to Bronia's family.

'I'm certainly not going to trundle across Poland with a tiny baby,' my mother had said when he told her of his decision to leave. She didn't believe that he'd really go until she watched him folding two white shirts and placing them together with some underpants and undershirts into the worn brown suitcase. After wrapping several thick slices of rye bread and butter in rustling pergamom paper, Henek unlocked a small drawer at the back of his mahogany desk, took out some money, and divided it equally between them. There wasn't much.

'When you're ready to travel, I'll arrange for you to come and join me in Lwow,' he told her. It never crossed anyone's mind in September 1939 that a woman with a baby wouldn't be safe in a city occupied by a civilised nation like the Germans. My mother's face was white and her heart bumped crazily in her chest but she remained resolute. Before leaving, my father asked her to move in with his mother. 'You'll be safer there than on your own,' he said.

As Henek limped along the road heading east, he noticed that everybody was overtaking him. If it wasn't for his gammy leg, he wouldn't be falling behind, but he couldn't allow himself to dwell on that old grievance. All around him vehicles were bursting with passengers and bulging with parcels and packages. Pigskin suitcases and billowing bundles of pillows and eiderdowns, candlesticks, birdcages and heirlooms swayed from the roofs of cars or tottered from rickety horse waggons whose carters had to keep whipping their bony nags to keep them pulling the loads. Wayfarers dropping with exhaustion sometimes hung onto the sides of the carts which swayed and tilted until the cursing drivers shook them off.

From time to time Henek managed to get a ride on a cart and rest his blistered feet, but the rides were all too brief, and when they ended, Lwow seemed as far away as ever. And at the end of each exhausting day, he faced the problem of finding a safe place for the night. As he hobbled towards Staszow along the dusty road, trying to avoid the potholes which tripped him up, he mopped his perspiring neck with a handkerchief and moved to the edge, where tall poplars gave grudging shade. As the last shafts of sunlight slanted through the trees, he wondered where to spend the night. Nearby, a group of travellers were discussing an offer of lodging. Apparently a local farmer had invited them to spend the night in his barn. Glad to have some company, Henek went with them, because he'd heard that solitary travellers were sometimes lured into farmhouses, robbed and murdered.

But just as he was stretching out on the prickly straw in the barn, pulling his shoes off his swollen, blistered feet, he overheard one of his companions murmuring to his neighbour. 'My cousin Maciej knows the village blacksmith here, and he reckons that some of the peasants around here wouldn't think twice about doing someone in to get their money,' he said, and drew the edge of his large hand across his throat in an explicit gesture.

Henek's heart was thumping. Any moment they might appear and slit their throats. He pushed his sore feet back into his dust-encrusted shoes, picked up his case and crept out onto the moonlit road. Better to die standing on your blistered feet than be slaughtered in your sleep.

In his memoirs my father describes the stress of having to be on his guard day and night. Not far from Przemysl he stopped near a wayside shrine of the Virgin Mary garlanded with poppies and cornflowers. When Henek looked up, he saw a barefoot peasant in a loose shirt who walked out of the forest and planted himself in front of him, scythe over his shoulder. His eyes slid quickly down my father's herringbone suit and leather shoes. '*Szczesc boze!*' he said in the traditional

Polish greeting which means 'God bless you'. 'You look tired, honoured sir. Come to my hut and rest. I've already got thirty souls there, all nice and comfortable, like. They're going to stay with me until the Germans are gone. You'll be as snug as a mouse behind the stove. Why wear yourself out on the road?' he said with an ingratiating smile. Feeling uneasy, my father thanked him but scrambled to his feet and continued on his way.

He still had over four hundred kilometres to go.

The countryside had never looked so seductive. The sun felt warm on Henek's arms and he breathed in the juicy scent of summer grass. High in the branches a lark was warbling above the tree tops. Along a winding stretch of road which skirted barley fields, he watched women in headscarves tied low over their foreheads threshing the grain and tying the sun-scented bundles into pointed stooks. Further along, the harvesters lifted the cut wheat high into the air with their rakes and tossed it onto a waggon, pausing occasionally to wipe the sweat off their foreheads. Engrossed by this timeless scene, Henek was startled by a voice. '*Ej, prosze pana*, why did you leave your home?' drawled a toothless peasant with grizzled hair. 'There's no need to worry, good sir. The Germans are civilised people.'

My father was incredulous. 'But don't you care that Poland is being overrun by foreigners?'

The man shrugged. 'Us peasants are always exploited by one landowner or another,' he said in his slow, drawn-out way. 'No matter who rules Poland, it's all the same to us, our lot never improves. But mark you now, the Germans, at least they'll get rid of the lousy Jews at last!' And he spat a gob of phlegm onto the dust.

Henek looked away. With his incisive glance, bright blue eyes and reserved manner, he didn't fit the stereotype of a

Jew, so people didn't curb their anti-Semitic comments in front of him. He couldn't get the peasant's words out of his mind. 'We're going to have two enemies against us in this war, not just one,' he thought bitterly as he trudged on.

By the time my father reached the outskirts of Przemysl, his legs felt like blocks of granite, and such a weariness fell over him that he sank under a plane tree by the roadside, staring at its spiky green pods. He knew that the Germans were catching up but he didn't have the strength to go any further. Resigned, he abandoned himself to his fate.

But on this occasion fate was good to him. Suddenly, as if in a dream, a carriage appeared with two magnificent horses, the kind of lacquered landau that wealthy landowners rode. To see an elegant chariot like that, with only the driver inside, travelling along this road, with the Germans so close behind, made Henek wonder whether exhaustion had made him delirious.

Forgetting his weariness, he leapt to his feet and hailed the driver, even though he didn't expect him to stop. To his boundless astonishment, the man pulled on the reins, whistled softly to the horses and motioned for my father to climb in. 'I'm delivering this landau to a man in Krakowiec, but I can take you there if you like,' he said. The driver was a good-natured, chatty fellow, and for the next twenty-seven kilometres Henek couldn't get over his good fortune.

The almost magical quality of that episode lifted his spirits and gave him the strength to walk on to Jaworow, which was only fifty kilometres from his destination. But here his spirits sank again. Jaworow buzzed with the rumour that soldiers weren't letting any more refugees into Lwow because the city was full of homeless people. This looked like the end of the road. He couldn't go forward and he couldn't turn back. Henek wandered around the town square trying to figure out what to do. While prowling around he noticed a Polish army officer pushing a wounded soldier into a taxi. 'Take this man immediately to the main hospital in Lwow,' the officer ordered. He slammed the car door and strode away.

In one of those instinctive actions which were to save his life several times in years to come, Henek poked his head into the driver's window. 'Excuse me, I'm a doctor,' he heard himself saying. Glancing at the injured soldier's greenish face and the red-stained bandage around his chest, he improvised, 'Your passenger looks very bad. Perhaps I should come and keep an eye on him. If he bleeds to death while in your care, you'll be in trouble.' The driver was an impassive man with sleepy eyes and a droopy moustache. He didn't look overly impressed by my father's argument but he shrugged and nodded. '*Dobrze, co mi zalezy*. Okay, what do I care, get in,' he said.

As the car lurched towards Lwow, Henek realised that this wouldn't be an easy ride. He couldn't stand up because the roof was too low, and he couldn't sit down because the injured soldier took up the whole back seat. He glanced longingly at the empty seat beside the driver, but since he was supposed to be taking care of the wounded man, he couldn't very well sit in the front. Somehow he managed to extend his stiff leg, hold onto the edge of the seat with one hand and to the roof with the other, all the while pretending to be ministering to the patient along the way.

Finally in Lwow he rang the doorbell of his in-laws' home, swayed on the doorstep and collapsed.

CHAPTER 13

While Henek was recovering from his ordeal, his sister Lunia with her husband Berus were stumbling around the town square in Radom with glazed eyes that saw nothing. People turned to look at the stately woman with her upswept hair, stylishly tailored suit and distracted manner. Like sleepwalkers, the couple pushed open the door of the first cafe they came to and slumped at the nearest table. While Berus stared into the distance, his face white and taut, Lunia covered her face with her hands and repeated one word over and over. 'Tusiek! Tusiek!'

This is the name that Aunty Lunia is repeating now in her cramped bedroom at the Beth Hadekel Nursing Home near Tel-Aviv when I show her a family photograph taken in Krakow in 1934. 'Tusiek! There's my Tusiek in the flesh!' she exclaims. She kisses the photograph and fondles it with her arthritic hands. 'Look! Look! They are all there!' she cries, tracing outlines with her crooked forefinger. 'Tatunciu and Mamuncia, and there's Avner.' In a calmer voice she says, 'We took that photo because Avner had come to visit us. And look, there's Rozia and Jerzy, there's your father and Izio and, oh, here's Karola, see how beautiful she was? And look, here's my dear Tusiek. They're as real as if they were here in this room with me now!'

She's in that photograph too, self-possessed as ever with

her upswept hair. Standing in front of Berus, Tusiek has that self-conscious look of teenagers being photographed, uncertain what expression to assume. Avner looks portly and successful. I hardly recognise my father without a moustache; his brown hair brushed back and a half smile that reminds me of my son Jonathan. He stands shyly at the back, as he does in so many prewar family photographs. There's Fridzia, with her sweet smile and full-moon face, and Andzia, attractive and sharp-eyed. Sitting in the front holding their little granddaughter Krysia, Daniel and Lieba have that complacent look of parents who have successfully navigated the vicissitudes of family life.

Past and present vanish, decades roll away, and half a century is concentrated in that moment frozen by the click of a camera at a time when life was still predictable and neighbours could be relied on. Tears stream down Aunty Lunia's wrinkled face as she stares at the ghosts of her past. Holding the photograph towards the light, she peers closely into the beloved faces, as if willpower and close scrutiny might breathe life into those so long dead, captured at a moment when they were so intensely alive and oblivious of what was to befall them.

Four years after that photograph was taken, Lunia had her first intimation of impending war. Hundreds of destitute Jews who had been expelled from Germany arrived in Krakow bewildered at being thrown out of the country they regarded as home. Although Lieba was still stunned by Daniel's death, the plight of these refugees touched her. As she and Rozia now lived alone in the large apartment in Sebastiana Street, she decided to take in one of these homeless families. Winter had begun, and as she rode in a *dorosky* to Krakow's central station where trains disgorged these homeless people, she pulled her fur collar over her ears and watched large white flakes dissolve in front of the horse's hooves. How terrible to be thrown out of your comfortable home, forced to leave everything you own behind, and be thrown on the mercy of strangers. She brought home a couple with three adult children.

As they described the pogrom euphemistically referred to as Kristallnacht, Lunia could visualise the thud of staves smashing down Jewish doors, the sound of shattering glass, the screams of old men being bashed in the streets, the smell of fire, the sight of flames rising up from 192 synagogues torched by hate. She held her hand against her mouth as they described the mass hysteria of the Third Reich, the rallies that evoked primitive Teutonic legends and medieval witch-hunts, the cold-eyed schoolboys marching under crimson banners with crooked black crosses, the high-stepping jackboots, the inflamed crowds screaming for Jewish blood.

But that was Germany. In Krakow life went on as usual. Several months later Lunia was strolling through the Planty Gardens, breathing in the fragrance of a bunch of lilies-of-the-valley she'd just bought, when she bumped into Izio's wife Lola. Sweeping her eyes up and down her sister-in-law's tailored suit and sturdy shoes, she said sweetly, 'I've just been to my dressmaker's for a fitting. She's making me such an elegant suit, a Paris model . . .'

Lola cut her short. She'd just returned from her father's funeral in Berlin and was still shaken by what she'd witnessed during Hitler's birthday celebrations. 'You should see the war preparations in Germany—they staged a military parade with thousands and thousands of the most terrifying soldiers, all marching like machines. And their armaments! The tanks just kept coming. The people even have coupons ready for coffee and imported goods. Lunia, you can smell war in the air of Berlin.' Lola was usually cool and unemotional, but for once there was anxiety in her voice. In her German-accented Polish and incorrect grammar, she fumbled for words to convey the gravity of the situation.

Lunia forced a smile. 'Don't get carried away by all that Germanic posturing, Lolschen,' she said. 'Whatever Hitler does, we'll be ready for him.' When Lola persisted, Lunia sounded annoyed. 'I don't think it's wise, carrying on like this. You'll create a panic. I can assure you, we're not so backward here that we don't understand what's happening in the world,' she snapped. 'I read all the best papers, and I can assure you that our army will protect us.'

Half an hour later, over iced coffee at the Pavilon Cafe, Lunia was saying to her sister Andzia, 'Lola's such a *yecker*,' using the insulting term that denoted the meticulous Germanic personality. 'So heavy-going. She gave me a headache with all her prophesies of doom. And you won't believe it, she's still wearing that brown suit!'

But several weeks later she recalled Lola's words when two visitors came to see her. One of them was Leo, their father's relative from Nowy Targ who used to visit the family during World War I. She remembered how her teenage heart used to flutter whenever she saw him in his officer's shako and braided jacket, a long sabre hanging in his tasselled scabbard. Now, twenty-five years later, he was no longer a dashing officer in the Austro-Hungarian army but a middle-aged engineer with a worried face. 'I'm leaving for England and you should leave too,' he told her. 'Hitler is a madman but he's a dangerous madman and it's only a matter of time before he invades. And you know what will happen to the Jews when he does.' Until that moment his companion hadn't spoken a word, but now he spoke in a slow, prophetic way that was chilling. 'In three weeks Hitler will be in Poland. And then there will be hell on earth.'

Haunted by his words, Lunia began to consider the situation. In 1939 she was living in the style to which she'd always wished to be accustomed. When Avner had left Poland, Berus had taken over the sausage casings business, and with her shrewd help they'd built it up so well that she'd been able to buy a beautiful apartment on Szlak Street, some diamonds, and a block of flats for investment.

My aunt's apartment was palatial. The floors wouldn't have looked out of place in Wawel Castle. Lunia had engaged the finest parquetry specialist in Krakow, but when he ran out of the timber she'd selected and had to finish off the entrance with an inferior wood, she was distraught and bought a richly patterned Turkish kilim to cover the hated floor. Her drapes, of the finest French silk, were ordered from the most exclusive curtain-maker in Krakow. There was oak panelling in the lounge room, with a rail for exquisite little knick-knacks. As a wide-eyed little girl, Lunia had stared covetously at her grandmother Ryfka Spira's carved Biedemeier sideboard with its Sevres porcelain. Now she had a house that was the envy of everyone she knew.

The only thing that hadn't gone according to Lunia's plans was her son Tusiek who'd fallen madly in love with a sixteen-year-old called Lula. The intensity of his feelings worried her. Although he was only eighteen, he was impetuous and romantic. The jaundiced baby she'd covered up in his pram so that no-one would see how ugly he was had grown into a good-looking young man with fair hair, a twinkle in his blue eyes and an irrepressible sense of fun.

His uncles adored him. My father had invited him to Hel on holiday and two years later, when he matriculated, Uncle Izio gave him a magnificent watch, a snappy style with a mesh cover to protect the glass. Tusiek couldn't stop looking at it on his suntanned wrist and checked the time every few minutes. 'I'll never take it off as long as I live,' he said. Everyone laughed at his boyish enthusiasm, little suspecting that he would keep his word.

Determined to break up Tusiek's love affair, Lunia convinced Berus that they must get him away from Lula and out of the country as fast as possible. They would send him to study at a textile college in Manchester. With new friends in another country, in no time he'd forget this girl. Berus, who always did whatever Lunia wanted, wrote to Avner in Antwerp asking him to arrange the enrolment. But before Avner received a reply from England, a second letter arrived from Berus, asking him to cancel the arrangements. 'As Tusiek has enlisted in the Polish army, he won't be attending the college in Manchester after all,' he wrote.

My mother always maintained that if Lunia hadn't meddled to break up the relationship, Tusiek wouldn't have joined the army because he only enlisted so that he could stay in Poland. So in that fateful summer of 1939, Tusiek entered cadet school with his best friend. As in the universities, there was also a *numerus clausus* in the army, limiting the number of Jews, but thanks to his friend's father, Professor Taubenschlag, Tusiek was accepted into the officers' school.

I have a photo of Tusiek taken in the winter of 1939, just before he enlisted. He's slightly built, not very tall, and wears a striped suit with wide lapels and a jaunty polka-dot tie. His fair hair is smoothly brushed to the side, and he has a nicely shaped mouth with a full lower lip. He has his arm around Lula, a pleasant looking girl with a placid face who is taller than him and looks much older than sixteen.

While in the army Tusiek fretted in case Lula found another boyfriend. Aunty Lunia heaves a sigh. 'He was so infatuated with that girl that when he heard that she was going to a ball with someone else, he was beside himself. I tried to make him see reason. "Tusiu," I said, "don't get so upset. The girl can't go to the ball on her own, but it doesn't mean anything." But he wouldn't listen and sneaked out without permission because he couldn't stand the thought of her dancing with someone else. And who knows, maybe because of his disobedience, they sent him straight to the front soon afterwards,' she laments.

Avner's son Adam, who loves to gossip, supplies an ironic postscript to Tusiek's love story. 'Decades later, in New York, at a New Year's party, I meet this Polish guy, a stamp dealer from Krakow. We get talking about old times, and it turns out that he knew our cousin Tusiek.' Adam's bright blue eyes are gleaming as he leans forward with another revelation. 'Then he starts reminiscing about a girl he was madly in love with, called Lula! No wonder Tusiek refused to go to Manchester. He knew he had a rival!'

Aunty Lunia and I sit in silence as she broods about her son. Then her trembling hands fly to her mouth and her eyes widen with distress. 'Several weeks later, that must have been in late August, we received a card from Tusiek from cadet school. He asked us to send him one hundred zlotys, because he didn't know what would happen and thought he might need some cash. He wrote, "Please take care of my Lula because she and you are my dearest ones in the whole world." Of course he wasn't allowed to reveal where he was being sent, but I saw that the postmark was Radom, close to Warsaw.'

Tusiek's letter galvanised Lunia into action. It was time to pack up, leave Krakow and travel east, as far away from the German border as possible. But first they'd go to Radom to say goodbye to Tusiek. Feverishly they packed their clothes, silver and eiderdowns, took banknotes, gold and diamonds out of the safe, hired a car, and set off.

They arrived too late. Tusiek's regiment had just left for the field. When she realised what this meant, Lunia began to tremble. 'Berus and I stumbled into a cafe, sank onto the nearest chairs, covered our heads in our hands and wept,' she tells me.

War broke out while Lunia and Berus were fleeing eastwards, without any news of Tusiek. 'I remember being in some small Polish town when suddenly I stopped walking and the blood seemed to freeze in my veins,' she tells me. 'At that moment I knew in my heart that my son was dead. I just knew it. Tusiek was dead. I sank to my knees on the street and started screaming and tearing clumps of hair out of my head. "Tusiek! My only son! I've lost him forever."' Tears roll down her furrowed cheeks.

'Did you know that Tusiek died at Ozarow?' asks Uncle Izio when we talk about his nephew several weeks later. 'He died in one of the first battles between the Polish army and the Wehrmacht. His entire regiment was wiped out, every single one of them.' There was a mass grave at Ozarow, and in 1945, along with the relatives of other soldiers, Izio was granted permission to have the grave opened up so that he could have his nephew buried in Krakow's Jewish cemetery beside his grandfather Daniel.

Standing on the edge of that mass grave where so many young men lay, Izio wondered how he'd be able to identify Tusiek. Suddenly he spotted something which sent a tremor of recognition through his body. A watch with an unusual mesh cover. Tusiek had kept his promise.

When I was looking through my father's papers after he had passed away, a small card, discoloured with age, fluttered out of an envelope. The kind of card that might have accompanied a bouquet of flowers. On one side someone had written in an impatient boyish scrawl: 'Dear Uncle Henek and Aunty Bronia, Congratulations on your marriage. Sorry I haven't written sooner.' The date was May 1936. The name on the other side was Tusiek Selinger. All through the war years, all through his life, my father had kept this memento of the nephew he loved.

Lunia's thin shoulders are shaking and she sobs with noisy gulps. 'My poor Tusiek! I only hit him once when he was little. Only once. Because he'd broken my best pink vase.' Now she's weeping softly. 'I wanted him to have the best of everything. But whenever I think about him I console myself that life never gives you any peace. And life with all its problems and all its pain has passed him by.' Looking at me beseechingly, she says, 'Every night I pray for eternal sleep but God refuses to answer my prayers. I just vegetate and suffer in this horrible nursing home.'

Then she glances around and drops her voice to a whisper. 'I don't talk about my son here because I don't want them to know how old I am. I tell them that he died in Europe, that he was with relatives at the time.' I don't know whether to laugh or cry at this ninety-three-year-old woman who is too vain to admit that in 1939 she had an eighteen-year-old son who died fighting for his country.

CHAPTER 14

Looking out of the window of their black Skoda convertible, Krysia could feel the car being pressed and pushed by the throngs moving along the road like one monstrous body with thousands of legs. They reminded her of the marionettes she'd seen at the Planty Gardens, stiff and unreal, as if someone in the sky was pulling the strings that kept their legs moving. The hum of voices rose above the dusty road, became dense and solid, and suddenly she tasted something sour in her throat.

'Mummy, quick, I'm going to vomit!'

Andzia turned around and saw her daughter's hand across her mouth, her face the colour of pea soup. 'Zygmunt! Stop the car!' she shouted, and as Krysia tumbled out, her head bent forward in successive spasms, spewing bits of undigested bread and sausage, Andzia stood over her impatiently. 'This is a fine time to get sick, when we have to get away from Krakow as fast as possible. I told you not to eat so much. Look at all these people, how are we ever going to get past them?'

Zygmunt patted his daughter's heaving shoulders. 'Feel better now?' he asked smiling into her face. 'That was a good idea, getting rid of all that food. Now we'll have more room in the car!'

In spite of the bitter taste in her mouth, Krysia managed a smile. Her father always knew how to cheer her up. Every evening at home when he started playing jolly tunes on his small mouth organ, the tip of his duck's-bill nose moving in time to the music, she forgot all about her mother's biting comments.

Right now, however, home seemed very far away. Like her older sister Lunia, Andzia was also fleeing eastwards. The last few days had been very confusing for Krysia. She'd been on holidays with her mother and little brother Fredzio at the seaside at Zawoja, when suddenly her mother started packing up their buckets, spades and swimming costumes and they rushed back to Krakow. All the adults looked nervous and sounded worried but she couldn't see that anything had changed.

Back in their flat she'd watched her mother rushing around, opening drawers, pulling out clothes, stacking pillows. With decisive movements, she piled up two eiderdowns and four pillows, wrapped all the silver cutlery and laid out the children's best outfits, many of which she'd knitted herself. Her fingers flew as she placed everything on tarpaulins and roped them into neat bundles. The following day Krysia's father, handsome in his Polish army uniform, had picked them up in the Skoda and soon they were speeding away from Krakow with their valuables tied on the roof.

Krysia looked out of the car window at the throngs choking the road, coats caked with dust and faces streaked with sweat. Some people swayed on carts piled to the sky with bedding and bundles, while others pushed rickety barrows, dragged children and lugged suitcases or carried cages with their pet canaries. Krysia clutched her doll. If only she was still at home among the people and places she knew.

She always looked forward to the mornings when she trotted beside her mother to visit Aunty Lunia who was usually still sipping coffee in bed when they arrived. Aunty Lunia was tall and important, and when she spoke everybody listened, even her mother who didn't think much of anyone. Without hurrying, Lunia would finish the last drop of her coffee, put down the fluted gold-edged cup delicately on her bedside table, and hold out her arms while Gizia the maid laced up her corset.

'Lunia lives like a duchess, she's done well for herself marrying Berus,' she sometimes overheard her mother saying. Her mother didn't consider herself nearly as lucky, but to Krysia, her father was the most wonderful person in the whole world.

She loved visiting Uncle Henek and playing with his dog, Charush. 'What kind of dog is it?' she used to ask, and her uncle would say with a serious face, 'A very special breed. A muttsbury.' Charush was funny. Whenever he did anything naughty, Uncle Henek would say, 'Charush, go to the corner!' And the small brown dog would stand on his hind legs in the corner, like a child who has misbehaved.

Now, fidgeting on the back seat of the black Skoda whose low-slung bouncing motion and acrid leather upholstery was making her feel queasy again, Krysia thought about her shiny red scooter which she was sometimes allowed to ride to her grandmother's house in Sebastiana Street. The only time she didn't like going there was on Saturday mornings, when the Chassids walked past on their way to synagogue. They terrified her and even now the memory of the black-coated men with their big black fur hats and long beards made her shiver.

For her ninth birthday Uncle Izio and Aunty Lola had given her doll's furniture painted cream and pink, and her mother had crocheted a satin blanket for the doll's pram. Her best friend Tamara Fruchtlender would have done anything to have doll's furniture like that. At her birthday party Krysia had stood on a chair to be pelted with sweets and raisins by

Tamara, Ignac and the other children who lived in their building on Gancarska Street.

Lost in happy memories, Krysia had almost forgotten her nausea when she felt the car vibrate. First came the relentless grinding noise of warplanes, closer and closer, until they seemed to drill right into the raw nerve of the world. A high-pitched whine made her clamp her hands over her ears. 'They're German Stukas, probably bombing Krakow,' her father said.

As she looked up she saw a pilot above them, his head encased in a tight brown leather helmet. He was grinning as if this was a carnival. Suddenly the earth began to explode all around them. German warplanes were shelling thousands of defenceless refugees, bearded old men, haggard women and exhausted children trudging along the country road.

'Quick! Out of the car!' her father shouted, and before she knew it, she'd leapt outside, raced to the edge of the road and flung herself into the ditch. Zygmunt covered Krysia's trembling body, his soothing voice trying to calm her down while she pressed her hands even tighter over her ears. Lying on the ground, smelling the dry sweet odour of the barley sheaves standing on the stubbled field, she felt as if the shuddering earth was splitting open and would soon swallow her up.

Krysia tried to block out the shrieks of pain and the cries of lost children. She tried not to look at the mangled bodies lying on the road, or at the woman sitting motionless on the ground, staring with glazed eyes at the limp body of her baby. A man took off his dusty hat as he came up to the mother and asked in a soft voice, 'Would you like me to say Kaddish for your baby?' but the woman just stared at him and shook her head rhythmically from side to side like the pendulum of a clock.

When the bombardment was over and the black Stukas

had become specks in the sky, they piled back into the car and drove on, too shaken to speak. As they passed through peaceful villages, smoke curled up from the chimneys and wheat stooks squatted on the fields, it was as if the bombardment had never happened. The sun was setting and the last swallows flitted against the darkening sky when they decided to stop for the night and Krysia sobbed with relief that their ordeal was over. But just as her mother started hauling the baggage off the car, the inexorable high-pitched whine started all over again.

As she lay trembling with terror in a ditch, eyes clenched, Krysia wondered how long they could keep dropping bombs on the world before it crumbled into fragments. It seemed as though the Luftwaffe was on a mission to destroy her, for no matter how far they travelled, the Stukas always caught up.

They were sitting in the car next morning, ready to drive on, when a warplane swooped so low that its wings lopped off the boughs overhead and showered them with russet maple leaves. A peasant standing in the doorway of his hut crossed himself. 'Jesus Maria, that pilot didn't need any bombs: he was so close, he could have lopped your heads off with a scythe!'

For the next fifteen days the road that stretched eastwards towards the Russian border was a river of refugees who looked more haggard and more haunted every day. They didn't know where they would end up or whether they could survive the bombing. By now most of them had jettisoned their heavy cases and trudged on, clutching a few essentials and their exhausted children.

At Zamosc a wall of flames blocked their path. The whole city was on fire. The smoke choked Krysia's throat and stung her eyes. Andzia's voice sounded shaky. 'How in heaven's name are we going to get through?' All around them poplars and birches blazed and foliage crackled. Only the ground was not burning.

'We have to get through, we can't go back,' Zygmunt said and jammed his foot down on the accelerator until it almost went through the floor, while they bent down and covered their heads with a blanket. As the car tore through the blistering heat and pungent smoke, Krysia whispered into her doll's porcelain ear, 'Don't worry, you'll see, everything will be all right.' They emerged on the other side of the inferno, all blackened with soot, her mother holding Fredzio tightly against her and Krysia clutching her doll.

Ten days later in a village close to the Russian border, Krysia awoke to see her father, now dressed in a peasant's loose shirt and baggy trousers, digging a hole in the yard where hens scrabbled in the dirt. Standing beside him, the farmhouse owner kept looking around. 'Quick! Be quick!' he urged. 'When the Russians see a Polish army uniform, they'll shoot.' During the night the Bolshevik army had occupied their town and other Polish towns to the east.

When they were ready to drive on, they went out to the car, and looked around bewildered. It had vanished. They were stranded. Strolling up to Andzia, a villager said, '*Prosze pani*, those thieving commies took your car last night.' Not wasting a moment, Andzia grabbed Krysia's hand, dragged her along the dusty road and marched into the Russian headquarters. She barged into a room where a thick-set soldier with lumpy features was smoking an aromatic cigarette, his legs sprawled out.

'Who's in charge here?' she stormed, the air around her crackling with anger. 'One of your people stole our car last night. That's not the way for a civilised army to behave, it's disgraceful. Communists should set people a good example, not rob them. How do you expect anyone to trust you if you

Baldinger family portrait. This photo was taken in 1934 when Uncle Avner
visited Krakow. Back row, left to right, standing: Fridzia (Slawa), Izio, Rutka,
Jerzy, Rozia, Tusiek, Lunia, Berus, Hesiu (Henek, my father), Andzia, Zygmunt.
Front row, sitting: Avner, Lieba, Krysia, Daniel, Karola.

My great-grandparents Abraham and Ryfka Spira, with their daughter-in-law Salomea (the wife of their son Julek), and her sons Janek (left) and Albert (right), around 1906.

Above: My mother Bronia's family. This was taken in Lwow in February 1938, at the wedding of Hania and Dolek Korner, who are not in the photograph. Fifth from left is Bronia, and sitting on her right are her parents Toni and Bernard Bratter. Standing behind my mother is my father Henek. Standing next to him is Aunty Mania and her husband Misko Schwartz.

Left: My grandparents Daniel and Lieba on their last holiday in Krynica, August 1938.

Above: Uncle Avner and Aunty Hela in New York, around 1970.

Left: Hela and Avner on their wedding day, Krakow, 1918.

Avner with his regiment, Vienna, July 1916. Avner is in the back row, third from left. The tools of their trade are displayed in front. Avner had this photograph made into a postcard which he sent to Hela. On the back he wrote: 'My dearest darling Helunia, I think I'll be able to organise everything so that we can be together this week. I can't wait to see you!'

Fred Ross with grandson Coby in California, 1997.

Adam, me and Wanda during our reunion in Connecticut, 1990.

Hela and Avner's son Adam in Madrid, en route to Brazil in 1940.

Their daughter Wanda in Rio de Janeiro, 1942.

Aunty Rozia with her niece Krysia in the Planty Gardens in Krakow in 1936.

Aunty Lunia's passport photograph, 1940.

Aunty Karola with her brothers: left, Janek (Jean) and right, Izio, taken in Zakopane in Poland, 1937.

Aunty Lunia's son Tusiek and his girlfriend Lula, 1939.

Aunty Lunia at Beth Hadekel nursing home, Petach Tikvah, Israel, 1990.

Aunty Andzia with Krysia's daughter Ronit, Tel-Aviv, 1957.

Above: The last family photograph of Aunty Andzia, Uncle Zygmunt and their children Krysia and Fredzio. Lwow, 1940.

Right: Wedding photo of Krysia and Marcel Ginzig, Krakow, 1949.

Above: Uncle Izio with Aunty Zosia and their daughter Lee, Montreal, 1959.

Right: Izio in Los Angeles, 1990.

The three brothers. From left, Uncle Izio, my father Henek with Phyllis Ross, my cousin Fred's wife behind him, and Uncle Avner. Taken in New York in 1967, during the only trip my parents made from Australia to see the family.

steal their belongings? I demand that you find our car and
return it to us at once.'

Through narrowed eyes the officer surveyed the fiery brunette
with the angelic-looking daughter and continued puffing on
his cigarette without saying a word. Krysia quailed at her
mother's audacity. There was nothing to stop the captain from
arresting them both.

'*Krasnaja dziewiczka*,' he said, smiling at Krysia. 'Pretty little
girl.' Then he stubbed out his cigarette, tossed the butt on the
floor, clapped his hands together, called, 'Sasha! *Dawaj!*' and
gave some instructions in Russian to a young soldier whose
cap was nonchalantly perched on the back of his thick brown
hair. A few minutes later he drove the Skoda up to the front
of the building and handed Andzia the key.

They drove on until they reached Chrzemieniec where
Zygmunt knew someone who offered him a job operating
machinery in the local peat mine. In the narrow potholed
streets of the Jewish quarter in whose rickety wooden huts
impoverished Jews had lived for centuries, they found accommodation with one of the Russian families who had moved
here in the wake of the Bolshevik occupation. Their fat,
voluble landlady poured tchai all day from a samovar and
sweetened it with thick raspberry jam which she spooned onto
her saucer.

The Russians who had settled in Chrzemieniec had become
the laughing stock of the town. Never having seen modern
clothes before, they had no idea how to dress, and Krysia
laughed to see the women wearing men's longjohns instead of
stockings, and nightdresses instead of ballgowns. Polish buildings
puzzled the Russians as well. When the commissar built a
grand house for his family, his wife was shocked at the sight
of an indoor toilet. 'No way will I have such a filthy thing in
my home! I've worked in mansions in Russia where tasselled

209

tapestries hung on the walls, but they didn't crap inside their homes!' she raged. Andzia was appalled at the ignorance of these primitive people and wished she was back in the cultured world of Krakow, but Krysia liked the childlike spontaneity of the Russians.

Krysia went to school, made new friends, and played with her black Scotch terrier. But hardly had she started to enjoy life in Chrzemieniec when she watched dismayed as her mother started packing up their belongings once again. 'Can't I even take my toboggan or my dog?' she pleaded, her large sea-green eyes swimming in tears. But Andzia was adamant. 'At a time like this, she's worrying about a dog, as if I haven't got enough to think about!' she scolded. 'We're going to Lwow to join up with Uncle Henek and Aunty Bronia.'

It's 1990, and my cousin Krysia and I are sitting in an Arabic cafe in Jaffa, drinking rich black coffee and gazing out at the cobalt water of the Mediterranean, while we talk about life in a sad and distant land. Krysia, now a grandmother, still has the same luminous eyes, warm personality, and placid disposition, and in her slow, musical voice she reminisces about the time we spent together in Lwow so long ago.

'I loved playing with you,' she says with a nostalgic smile. 'You were my favourite doll. By the time you were two years old you knew the names of all the animals in Polish and Latin and your father loved showing off how clever you were. But you had a temper. Once when you were crying, your grandmother Toni and I tried to calm you down. 'It's all right, Danusia, nothing happened,' your grandmother said, but you stamped your little foot and shouted: 'It did happen! It did happen!' Sometimes I took you tobogganing. You were my favourite doll.' She looks at me with a loving expression and my eyes fill with tears as I recover a fragment of my truncated childhood.

*

My mother and I had joined my father in Lwow at the end of 1939. We had remained in Krakow for the first few months of the war because my mother didn't feel ready to undertake the long journey to her home town until I was five months old. In those first days of September 1939, living with her husband's family in Krakow bothered my mother far more than the war itself, which still seemed far away. As Bronia bent over to bathe me, she sensed that her mother-in-law was watching her. 'Always make sure that you test the water with your elbow first,' Lieba said. 'You don't want to scald the baby.' Bronia sighed. As soon as Henek had left Krakow, she'd moved to Sebastiana Street as she had promised, but she felt like a creature in a cage, under constant scrutiny.

An uneasy lull hung over Krakow as people waited to see what would happen. The broadcast of Walter von Brauchitsch, the commander of the German armed forces, comforted those who chose to believe his words. 'We don't regard the people of Poland as our enemies,' he said in an ingratiating tone. 'We will observe all international laws, and Jews have nothing to fear.' Although disturbing reports of the massacre of Polish troops on battlefields around the country had already begun filtering in from neighbouring townships, in Krakow itself nothing was happening.

But within a few days the residents of Krakow were shaken out of their illusions. In the suburb of Podgorze, where my grandfather had once had his pram factory, long columns of trucks carrying triumphant soldiers armed with rifles began roaring along the streets, followed by heavy artillery which struck terror into the hearts of the silent onlookers. Soon fourteen divisions of the Wehrmacht had spread their tentacles over Krakow. The city was now ruled by cold-eyed men with harsh voices, gleaming boots, peaked hats with death's-head insignia, and ominously immaculate uniforms which seemed to have been stitched onto their flesh.

It was no longer possible to ignore the shocking truth. It had taken Germany forty-eight hours to knock out the Polish air force, and seven days to annihilate its army. No-one yet knew the full extent of the carnage that had taken place in Polish fields and forests. There was still no news of Tusiek. The President of Krakow had left, taking most of his staff and secret documents with him. Warsaw was encircled, and President Moscicki's government had fled to Lublin. The people of Krakow were left to the mercy of the invaders.

Sparks flew from the cobblestones as helmeted soldiers swaggered around the city as though they owned it. Army trucks rattled along Krakow's cobbled medieval streets, then pulled up suddenly as soldiers jumped out and yelled orders in guttural voices. They took a special delight in humiliating defenceless old Jews whom they knocked down and kicked before pulling and cutting off their beards. Witnesses told terrifying stories of brutish soldiers who rounded up people in the street and pushed them into trucks, grabbed women's rings and bracelets, smashed shops and looted merchandise. Those who tried to resist had their faces smashed with shiny rifle butts. Shots retorted in narrow streets and blood flowed over cobblestones.

Each day new decrees limiting people's freedom were posted up around the city. The penalty for breaking each one was death. 'You'll never believe what I've just seen, you won't believe what the Germans are doing,' gasped Rozia who rushed home with the news two days after the Wehrmacht's arrival. 'Every Jewish shop, restaurant and cafe, even the market stalls, all have to display a Star of David! I saw the decrees posted all around the Glowny Rynek with my own eyes, signed by SS Brigadefuhrer Bruno Streckenbach!'

Bronia stopped rocking the baby for a moment and shook her head with disbelief. As she put the bottle into my mouth, Lieba shot her a warning look. 'Are you sure you tested the milk properly?' she asked.

Having brought up eleven children, Lieba dispensed child-rearing advice without being asked. The milk was too hot, it would burn poor little Danusia's mouth, or it was too cold and would give the child a sore throat. The bath water was too hot, it would scald her, or it was too cold and would give her a chill. She wasn't dressing the child warmly enough, surely she knew that autumn was treacherous. Why didn't she wind a red thread around her little wrist to ward off the evil spirits? My mother was already like a coiled spring because of my father's departure. As well as her mother-in-law's constant advice, there were Rozia's hysterical outbursts and her well-meant but wearying offers of help.

One day, irritated beyond endurance by this surfeit of well-meant assistance, my mother grabbed me and fled back to her own flat on Potockiego Street. It would be better to live alone than endure this interference. By then most of the family had left Krakow. Apart from Lunia and Berus, who'd fled before war had been declared, Andzia and Zygmunt had also fled east with the children, while Fridzia, who had recently married, was living in Vilno with her new husband Jerzyk Szapiro. Apart from Lieba, Rozia and my mother, the only ones still left in Krakow were Karola and Stasiek, Izio and Lola, and Jerzy and Rutka.

Every afternoon, after finishing work at the Skoda agency, Jerzy used to drop in to see whether my mother needed anything, and to play with me. Sometimes he brought a ring of Polish country sausage, smoky and spiced with garlic, a rare treat in those days. My mother loved Jerzy and his friendly, unpretentious wife Rutka. Some afternoons Izio's wife came over to help her bath the baby, but Lola's blunt manner had an unsettling effect on her. Whenever my mother talked about rejoining her family in Lwow, Lola's comments weren't comforting. 'I don't see how you're going to get to Lwow with Danusia now that the Germans are here,' she would say.

Life in Krakow became increasingly dangerous. The ancient capital of Poland had become the capital of Germany's General Government and, like a latter-day monarch, Dr Hans Frank installed himself in the royal apartments of the city's Wawel Castle and dispensed injustice under its medieval arcades and coffered ceilings. Decrees followed thick and fast, each one calculated to isolate, crush, ruin and demoralise the Jews.

By November, Jews were ordered to wear armbands in the street, for easy identification. 'The Germans are very exact,' Izio remarked. 'They've specified how wide the white band has to be, and the size of the blue Star of David!' No-one suspected that this meticulous attention to detail would shortly ensure the methodical murder of millions.

One day a new order was issued. 'Under a just system, every person must work for his daily bread,' the proclamation began. 'There will be no room for political dissidents, commercial hyenas or Jewish exploiters.' It went on to say that all Jewish males aged between twelve and sixty had to labour in street gangs along with Polish males aged between eighteen and sixty. German soldiers soon turned this into a sport. It amused them to see frail old scholars, rabbis and professional men sweeping dirt, shovelling snow, and hauling bricks, and they spat, kicked and tormented them whenever they wanted a diversion, sometimes encouraged by jeering Polish by-standers. 'Let them have it. Make the Jews work!' they'd call out.

My grandmother Lieba, who idolised her son Izio, was determined to save him from this degradation, and managed to bribe someone to get his name off the list. But according to her niece, Rozia Johannes, she didn't pay a bribe for her son-in-law Stasiek. Rozia tells me this when we meet in Tel-Aviv many years later. 'Poor Karola was very upset that her mother hadn't paid a bribe for Stasiek,' she recalls. 'By then no-one was allowed to employ Jews, and Jews weren't even allowed to withdraw money from the bank, so Karola had no income and hated being financially dependent on her mother. She learned to knit sweaters and earned a few zloty from that.'

The brutality of the conquerors continually caught people off balance. No-one was safe. The whole city was stunned when German trucks pulled up outside the Jagellonian University and helmeted soldiers marched across the arcaded medieval campus where Kopernicus had once studied astronomy, arrested one hundred and eighty-three professors, pushed them into a waiting truck and deported them to concentration camps in Germany where many of them were killed.

No-one knew where the next blow was coming from. Early in December several parts of Kazimierz were cordoned off and residents were forbidden to leave their homes. Soldiers trained their rifles at these houses and fired at anyone looking out of the window. The goal of this blockade was armed robbery on a grand scale. While the residents were under siege, soldiers carried out brutal and thorough searches of the premises. They held screaming women down at gun-point and probed their vaginas in search of valuables.

That same day German soldiers grabbed a Jew and ordered him to set a synagogue on fire. When he refused, they shot him. This was Ajzyk's Synagogue, where I heard voices on my first visit to Krakow.

By December my mother had become impatient to join my father and her parents in Lwow, but now she had a border to cross. Seventeen days after war was declared, the Bolsheviks had annexed the eastern part of Poland, so Lwow was now in

Russian hands and there was a frontier in Przemysl between the German and Russian areas.

But however bad things were under the Bolsheviks, at least they treated everyone equally badly and didn't single out Jews for persecution like the Nazis did. In mid-December, when snow settled in soft drifts in the woods, frost etched patterns on the windowpanes, and skies looked as sad and grey as people's faces, my father arranged for someone to guide us across the border.

Crossing from the German side was nerve-wracking because gimlet-eyed soldiers scrutinised every traveller, searching for Jews who might be travelling without armbands or carrying money or valuables. Any pretext was sufficient to beat, arrest or shoot. My mother's heart was pounding so loudly that she was sure they could hear it through her black karakul coat. A small group of Jews just ahead of her were taking a long time to go through. The guards were examining documents and shaking their heads, finally they motioned for them to step aside. Agitated, one of them started arguing but the soldiers shouted for silence and pushed them aside, yelling for them to stay where they were.

Just as my mother stepped resolutely towards the sentry post, a voice shouted 'Jude! Jude!' It was the man who'd been stopped from crossing; he must have realised that she was Jewish and was trying to stop her out of spite. Gripping me tightly in her arms, my mother kept her head high and hoped that the guard wouldn't realise that the man was shouting at her. With her ivory complexion, straight nose and direct green-eyed gaze, she didn't arouse any suspicion, and the guard waved her through.

Thank God. Now she only had to get past the Russian guards and they weren't likely to cause any difficulties. Only another step and she'd be on Russian soil, safe from the Nazi terror. But the thick-set Russian guard stepped in front of her, barring her way. 'Not so fast, *dziewiczka maya*, my dear girl,' he jeered. Grasping her arm, he started hustling her into a hut nearby that served as a border detention centre. All my mother's pent-up anxiety burst out and she started to berate the sentry guard. 'The German guards let us through, so why are you stopping us?' she argued. 'Look at me, with a baby and these bags, do I look like a criminal? Why are you keeping me here?'

The young guard wasn't used to being shouted at by a slip of a Polish girl who barely reached his shoulder. He spat out a torrent of abuse, words she'd never heard before. Leaning towards her he yelled into her face, '*Dziob twoja macie!*' She had no idea what that meant, and without stopping to think, she yelled back at him, '*Dziob TWOJA macie!*' He looked disbelievingly at the defiant little woman in front of him with the Tatar cheekbones and large green eyes. 'What did you say?' he roared. So she repeated it.

For the rest of her life, my mother couldn't get over her audacity. 'I must have been mad,' she'd say with a twinkle in her eye. 'Fancy swearing at a border guard. He could have bashed me up or had me deported. Do you think I had any idea what I was saying?' Here she'd lower her voice in embarrassment. 'I actually told him to go and fuck his mother!' Whenever she told this story, my children Justine and Jonathan would look fondly at their feisty little Nana who still hadn't lost her spirit at eighty.

Perhaps the guard had realised that she didn't know what it meant because someone trying to get across a border wouldn't abuse the guard. Or perhaps by flinging the insult back at him she'd taken him by surprise. He strode away from her and left her in the detention hut under the watchful eye of his colleague.

217

About thirty people were squashed into a tiny area. As there was no room to sit down, she had to stand, cradling me in her arms. Probably sensing the tension all around me, I began to bawl. The food my mother had brought for me was gone, and all she had left was an apple. Somewhere she found a little spoon and started scraping it for me. I swallowed the mushy bits but spat out the harder pieces, spraying them over those who stood nearby. As they watched me spitting out bits of apple, the tightly-furled faces around us relaxed and in spite of their anxiety, people began to smile as they recalled their own child-rearing experiences.

My mother managed to get to the window and looked outside. The branches of the slender birches were bare and stark and the frozen ground was scuffed by bootprints. Her stomach was churning. How long were they going to keep us in that hut? What would she give me to eat next time I was hungry? Outside the hut, she noticed a man in a cloth cap standing beside his wooden cart holding the reins of his solid mare. It would be wonderful to climb into that cart and ride all the way to Lwow.

The more she stared at the man, the more familiar he looked. No, she must be imagining it, it couldn't be. But it was. There was no mistaking those furrowed cheeks, the snub nose, that tuft of fair hair sticking up out of the cap. It was Antek, one of her father's customers in Lwow. She remembered him from the days when she used to keep the books for her father's business. Whenever a good customer needed more time to pay, she always extended credit for an extra few months, and she remembered giving Antek credit.

If only he'd turn around. Leaning eagerly out of the window, she tapped on the frosty pane and called his name softly so that the guards wouldn't hear. 'Antek! Antek! Over here!'

Finally he looked up and his face lit up with a grin when

he recognised her. 'Jesus Maria, Miss Bratter, what are you doing here?' he asked, his crinkled grey eyes wide with astonishment.

Glancing around to make sure that the guard didn't see her, my mother indicated that she wanted to get away. Antek nodded and motioned for her to throw her bundle of possessions out of the window. 'Go and stand near the door, I'll come and get you in a minute,' he whispered.

That night my mother and I slept on a mound of scratchy hay which tickled her nose and made her sneeze. Next morning Antek took us to the railway station and we arrived in Lwow that same day.

But it was no longer the Lwow my mother knew.

CHAPTER 15

While his family in Poland were living under foreign occupation, Avner was living a comfortable life in Antwerp as a diamond merchant. On 10 May 1940, however, the war caught up with Belgium. When bombs started falling on Antwerp, Avner's son Adam was drinking champagne with a married woman in their apartment building. At twenty, he was a bon vivant with a diffident personality and a bright mind which he'd never applied to anything for very long.

The bombardment resulted in a mass exodus from Antwerp and, like other refugees, Avner and his family packed hurriedly and left for France. They planned to change trains in Ghent but when the connecting train failed to arrive, they were stranded at the station. Since Belgian troops were using this railway line, the station became a target for German bombs and it shuddered all night with explosions. Later Adam heard that the stationmaster was a Nazi spy who used to signal to the Germans whenever trains were about to pull out.

While Adam was dozing on the platform, a bomb hit the stairs just above them. His mother Hela shook him. 'Quick, go and stand against the wall or under a doorway, it's too dangerous here!'

But Adam couldn't be bothered. 'I'm tired, leave me alone,' he grumbled. He is reminiscing about the first day of the war in Belgium at his sister Wanda's home in Connecticut where the three of us have gathered to talk about the past. 'In actual fact, I've never worried about anything,' Adam shrugs. '*Que sera, sera.*'

Wanda doesn't recall feeling frightened that day either. 'Of course my mother would have said that I wasn't scared because I had no heart. "You have a stone where a heart should be!" she always said.' Then she adds, 'Mother and I were always at cross purposes. I wanted her to love me, and she wanted me to love her.'

My heart aches as I think of all the missed opportunities, wasted time and tragic misunderstandings which undermine the closeness that all mothers and daughters long for.

This is the first time I've ever met these two cousins about whom I've heard so much. Wanda was my parents' favourite niece, and all my life I heard that she was vivacious and accomplished, that she spoke six languages and had been an interpreter at the United Nations. And so beautiful with her raven locks and bright blue eyes! When Wanda said that she would pick me up from JFK airport when I arrived, I expected to see a gorgeous young woman with masses of black hair. So I didn't notice the elderly woman with short-cropped grey hair standing next to me until she looked into my face with huge blue eyes and asked with a New England twang, 'Are you Diane?' I soon found out that my cousin was forthright, forceful and funny, with an irrepressible sense of humour which kept me in peals of laughter during my visit.

In 1939, however, Wanda was a striking but less assertive girl of seventeen who turned heads in the street because she looked like the actress Hedy Lamarr, but was more animated. Thinking back to their exodus from Antwerp, Wanda recalls one incident of panic. 'That was on the train heading for Cognac when I suddenly realised that our parents weren't on board.' She turns to her brother. 'But how did it happen that we got separated from our parents?'

Adam's smoothly combed white hair, deep lines on either side of his nose, and cornflower blue eyes remind me of my father. He gives Wanda a superior look and mutters, 'She never remembers anything,' as if she wasn't there. 'Mother felt so ill that she thought she was having a heart attack, and in the middle of the night she got off the train to look for a doctor and Father went to look for her. While they were still asking for a doctor, the train moved off with us on it. Our parents didn't have any money on them, no passports, nothing, and Father was in his slippers. When they realised that the train had gone with us on board, they sent a message for us to get off at the next station. Somehow they got hold of a caboose and caught up with us that way. I'll never forget the sight of them riding that contraption!' he chuckles.

Wanda leans forward. 'You know, a funny thing happened on the way to the gene bank. Adam got all the remembering genes and I got the forgetting genes! But I do remember that we were lucky to get off when we did, because all the refugees on that train were later interned in concentration camps.'

When it had become obvious that invasion was imminent, most of the diamond merchants of Antwerp decided to relocate in the Cognac region of France, and that's where Avner and his family were now headed. But it didn't take Avner long to figure out that Cognac wouldn't be suitable because it was an area of conservative vignerons who'd lived there for generations and wouldn't take kindly to Jewish merchants.

Avner's instinct proved right. Initially the wine producers seemed happy to have the added business in their area, but on Sunday, when they saw that not one of the newcomers attended Mass, they realised that they had Jews in their midst. Several days later the town authorities told the refugees that there was no room for them in Cognac but that they would find Royan more congenial.

No sooner had Avner rented an apartment in Royan than it became clear that France was about to fall to the Germans. They had to get away as soon as possible. 'Some of the Antwerp refugees asked my father to become their leader, as if he was Moses getting them out of Egypt. And really, if not for him, none of us would have got out of there,' Adam says.

Although private vehicles were almost unobtainable, Avner managed to buy a sixteen-seater bus. Strapping some of the luggage on the roof, he crammed the rest amongst the twenty-three passengers, some of whom had to sit in the aisle. On their way to Biarritz the bus guzzled gas at an alarming rate and at the top of a hill it suddenly conked out.

Adam's eyes gleam with nostalgic pleasure as he recalls how he saved the day. 'I lifted up the driver's seat, levered up the wooden planks, checked the battery and discovered what the problem was. One of the cables had worked loose!' He becomes so animated recalling his triumph that the stroke-induced slur in his speech almost disappears.

It was drizzling when they reached the southern town of Bayonne. The streets were jammed with the cars of refugees from all over Europe, including King Zog and his entourage who were also fleeing the Nazis because Albania had just been invaded. It was mid-June, Petain had already capitulated, and everyone was desperately trying to get visas for Spain.

There were no vacant rooms left in this postcard-pretty Basque town whose houses were painted in vibrant colours and shaded by orange trees whose scented blossoms made their heads swim. On the first night Adam slept under a bench at a bus stop, on the second inside a kiosk. Everyone was fleeing to Morocco, and after spending three days running to every travel office in town, Avner managed to obtain a boat passage for Morocco in exchange for their bus. But just as they arrived at the wharf, they watched their ship sailing away, leaving a flurry of foam in its wake. They ran along the jetty, shouting and gesticulating but to no avail. Their hopes of leaving Europe had been dashed. But Adam's face breaks into a smile. 'You never know when a disappointment can turn into a blessing: all the ships which got away from Bayonne that week were blown up by German submarines!'

Back in town they got their bus back and spent the next few days zigzagging along remote Pyrenean mountain roads to Perpignan. As soon as they arrived, Avner decided to try his luck at the Moroccan consulate. But when he went to pick up their passports the following day, the secretary told him that unfortunately they weren't eligible for Moroccan visas because they had Polish passports.

Avner spent a long time chatting up the secretary, turning on the full force of his charm and promising her a gift in return for the visas, but there was nothing to do but wait and hope. Drinking espresso coffee in one of the noisy smoke-filled bistros in town that afternoon, Avner noticed a young woman who suddenly lurched forward as the heel of her shoe snapped off. Recognising the secretary from the Moroccan office, he leapt to his feet, rushed outside, retrieved the heel, and announced with a flourish, 'Mademoiselle, today I'm returning your heel, but tomorrow, if you get us those visas, I'll bring you a bottle of perfume!' The next day he got the visas.

At the Spanish border they faced another problem. Refugees were forbidden to take any valuables out of France. 'The French were very crafty,' Adam recalls. 'When we arrived, they weren't interested in what we'd brought with us, but now that we were leaving, they weren't going to let us take our valuables out of their country. The diamonds were all we had, and we had to find some way of getting them out.'

As usual everyone turned to Avner for a solution. 'Leave it to me,' he assured them. 'I'll find a way.' Without telling the others where they planned to secrete the jewels, he and Adam dismantled part of the bus, put the diamonds in little packages, and pushed them into the hollow of one of the metal support poles. As Adam talks about this incident, he is no longer a slow-speaking seventy-year-old with a limp, but an eager young man again, sharing an adventure with his father.

Going through customs with their illicit cargo was nerve-wracking. 'Smile, Wanda!' Hela kept nudging her daughter, hoping that this pretty girl would distract the guards' attention from the contents of their bus. Finally they were driving across the border. As they sped into Spain, they whooped with joy. They'd made it safely out of France, their assets intact.

It was in Mataro, the first Spanish town they came to, that they discovered with a shock that while Avner and his family had Morocco stamped in their visas as they'd requested, all the others had received visas for Curaçao. After the initial dismay, Avner came to the conclusion that South America would be a much better option than North Africa, but when he asked about visas to Curaçao, he was told that this could only be arranged in Madrid.

Once in Madrid, Avner decided to try to migrate to the United States. As Wanda spoke English, he took her with him to the embassy as an interpreter. The secretary at the American Embassy sent them to the American Consulate. The consul took a fancy to Avner and Wanda and told them that he didn't have the authority to issue residents' visas, but if they could obtain a visa to any South American country, he could give them transit visas to the United States. Once they set foot in the States, they could apply for residency.

With that they began making the rounds of the South American consulates, and Avner hoped that his dazzling daughter would soften officials' hearts. It worked. At the Brazilian consulate the ambassador's Mexican secretary Enrique became so infatuated with her that he made it his mission to get them a visa. At the same time Avner kept sending gifts to persuade the ambassador: a little diamond here, a bonbonnière of Swiss chocolates there, and of course big bouquets for Madame l'Ambassadrice in between.

But while he was in the process of obtaining transit visas for New York, Avner heard that as soon as young men arrived in the United States they were drafted into the army and sent back to Europe. He wasn't going through all this so that his son would end up dead on some European battlefield. When the devoted Enrique produced visas for Brazil, Avner decided to start a new life there.

Before leaving Madrid Adam dismantled the bus support bars in the garage and brought them to their hotel where he sawed them in half to extricate their diamonds. 'That's how I started my career as a diamond cutter!' he quips, and adds, 'But if I'd been really smart, I'd have driven off with the whole van—it had about half a million dollars worth of diamonds in it. Unfortunately only a small share of that belonged to us!'

Later, when Wanda and I are alone on the sundeck sipping peppermint tea in the long New England twilight, she says, 'All his life Adash has been the boy who never grew up. He's extremely bright, with a photographic memory, but never wanted to study anything. My father sent him to a private school in Antwerp to refine him but he never learned to get on with people. He used to fly into terrible rages for no reason. He must have a lot of anger in him, but he's not prepared to deal with it.'

Finally, with visas in hand, they travelled to Lisbon where

they boarded a Brazilian vessel carrying mercury to South America for military purposes. It was a primitive ship with poor facilities, but they were thrilled to be on their way at last. The day after they sailed, however, the ship was apprehended by a British war vessel and kept in Gibraltar for a month.

In October they finally arrived in Brazil. Avner had never imagined a city as spectacular as Rio de Janeiro where volcanic peaks covered in tropical vegetation soared above dark blue bays, and palm-lined beaches created a permanent holiday atmosphere. With its sensual, fun-loving people, Rio was a hedonistic Garden of Eden, but Avner had a tough time making a living because he neither spoke the language nor understood the culture. Before long, however, his entrepreneurial instincts came to the fore once again. He bought a large villa on the Avenida Atlantica which skirts Copacabana Beach and persuaded a wealthy Belgian émigré to finance him to open a nightclub.

He decorated the nightclub in opulent Louis Quatorze style, with gilded trimmings and carved furniture. While waiters in tails carried flaming shashliks ceremoniously to the tables, a group of Russian gypsies wrung the diners' hearts with nostalgic Slavonic airs. Late at night jazz pianists made them tap their feet in time to the beat of George Gershwin and Glenn Miller. Avner congratulated himself on having created the kind of nightclub he himself loved to frequent.

It looked as if Avner's worries were over.

CHAPTER 16

The Russian occupation of Lwow which shocked my mother when she returned with me to her home town in December 1939, had taken the whole city by surprise three months before. On that sultry September day, her sister Mania Schwartz had been standing on her balcony when she witnessed a scene she would never forget. Turning to her husband, she called, 'Misko, quick, come and look at this!' Spilling along the entire width of Aleja Focha Avenue and down Grodecka Street came a ragged throng like debris floating on the current.

There were Russians, Kalmuks, Mongols and Turkomans, Uzbeks, Circassians, Georgians and Kirghiz, some with high cheekbones and flattened noses, others with slanting eyes. Some of this motley army wore conical fur hats with flaps and long dun-coloured coats that reached their ankles as if they'd just left their yurts in the steppes. In clothes powdered with dust, they straggled all over the road without any apparent formation. Their footwear was as oddly assorted as their outfits, and few wore boots. With her keen eye for detail Mania noted that many coats were fraying and unhemmed, with threads trailing from them. They looked as if they'd grabbed their clothes before the tailor had time to finish them, and rushed off to distant lands. And they just kept coming, a bobbing sea of men in ragged clothes streaming down the street.

These shabby soldiers were the advance guard of the million-strong Russian army coming to occupy Lwow. Mania gave a short laugh of derision. 'Just look at these conquerors! They look more like a horde of beggars!' She felt no terror, only contempt for their unkempt appearance. Terror she'd felt two weeks before when German bombs had exploded all over Lwow. She'd pressed her hands over her ears while her windows shattered and glass crashed into jagged splinters all over the room, and wished that she'd criss-crossed the panes with brown tape as she'd been instructed.

When Mania had heard the sirens' shrill whine that day, she didn't realise that war had started. It was a balmy September day of an unusually long, hot summer that smelled of red apples, ripe peaches and black cherries. They'd been alerted to expect a bomb drill, and she'd assumed that this was it. It was only when she heard explosions ripping buildings apart that she realised this was no rehearsal. German warplanes were dropping bombs on their city. War, whose possibility they'd all debated heatedly for so long, had actually begun.

From the yellowish pall of dust that had risen behind the railway tracks, she'd realised that the glass-domed central station and the streets around it had been hit. For hours Lwow had been torn apart by explosives and webbed by the sickening wail of sirens. Those who'd diligently attended first-aid courses grabbed their kits and rushed to bomb sites where they'd stared at the debris and devastation and wondered how to reattach severed limbs with rolls of bandage.

Mania couldn't believe that the good times could end. Lwow, which in Austro-Hungarian times had been the capital of Galicia, was a lively city of cafes, restaurants and nightclubs, and she frequented them all. By day she gossiped with her girlfriends over lemon gelato and iced coffee at the Cafe de la Paix on Legionow Street, and strolled along the promenade on Akademicka Street, choosing patterned silks for her new summer wardrobe. In the evenings she often persuaded Misko to go dancing.

She told me about her carefree prewar life many years later in Sydney when she was living in the same building as my mother. Like an enmeshed married couple who are miserable together but can't live apart, she and my mother were still fighting the same battles. In spite of all that she'd gone through, Aunty Mania hadn't lost her passion for clothes or her wry sense of humour. She was a good raconteur and a good listener, and I loved spending time with her, which provided my mother with yet another grievance against her sister.

As she places a big slice of her orange and almond torte on my plate, Aunty Mania recalls that while German bombs were falling over Lwow, she heard a strange message relayed over the airwaves. 'Because the Polish government has abandoned our brother Ukrainians, we are coming to your aid.' This enigmatic announcement from Russia was repeated several times each day. Everybody knew that the German and Russian foreign ministers Ribbentrop and Molotov had signed a pact, but no-one yet suspected the sinister significance of this statement.

On 17 September the world became silent. The bombing had stopped. When they switched on the radio they heard an excited Russian voice saying, 'Fellow Ukrainians, we are on our way to help you!' The Polish airforce had been demolished, the army had been decimated, and the Polish prime minister, along with his entire cabinet, had packed up the nation's gold reserves, state documents and historical archives, and fled to Romania. Now, to add to the shock of their devastating defeat, Poland had been carved up like a dead turkey between Germany and Russia, into east and west. The secret agenda of the Ribbentrop–Molotov Pact was now exposed in all its duplicity.

While the dark shadow of the Third Reich fell over western Poland, the areas to the east of the San River, including Lwow, were occupied by the Bolsheviks who had stabbed Poland in the back. There was no more Polish prime minister, no more Polish government, no more Poland.

And now, standing on her sunlit balcony that September morning, Mania watched the Russians streaming into Lwow ostensibly to rescue their Ukrainian colleagues. She sensed no menace in this ragtag army, not even in their big grey tanks decorated with scarlet hammer and sickles that followed like slow-moving monsters. But although she wasn't frightened, there was something inexorable about them that disturbed her. Perhaps in the oppressive air that hung around them she smelled the pillars of black smoke that they'd left behind, saw the funeral pyres of torched villages and heard the screams of a thousand women thrown down into wayside ditches and raped.

Lwow, the ancient city of lions, was part of Poland but its population was evenly divided between Poles, Ukrainians and Jews. The Ukrainians had chafed under Polish domination since 1659. Most of them hated the Polish Catholics who ruled over them, and detested the Jews they'd brought in their wake. In 1648 Boghdan Chmelnitsky's bloodthirsty hordes galloped across the rolling steppes and thundered through the narrow lanes of Polish towns. When their pogroms were over, Polish villages had been laid waste and over 100 000 Jews lay dead, some after being skinned alive.

Apart from religious anti-Semitism which had been inculcated by the church for centuries, many Ukrainians believed that all Jews were communists and blamed them for the country's economic problems, even for the famine caused by failure of the wheat crop. It was true that many Jews had become socialists as a reaction to the repressive, anti-Semitic policies of the government; after all, the socialists promised equality for everyone.

The most extreme right-wing party was Endecja, whose demonstrations struck fear into Jewish hearts. My mother saw Endecja members armed with lumps of wood standing outside Jewish stores to prevent shoppers from entering. As the boycotts continued, many Jews lost jobs and businesses and lived in abject poverty. Poor people sold off their belongings to survive, even their chairs and eiderdowns, covering themselves with newspapers on bitterly cold winter nights. In broad daylight students and hooligans roamed the streets brandishing sticks studded with razor blades, and slashed the faces and bodies of any Jews they encountered, confident that the police wouldn't intervene.

Now Mania watched the street below where young girls with apple cheeks and plaited coronets of fair hair and youths with snub noses and cloth caps lined the road to greet the Russians. Many waved blood-red flags decorated with hammer and sickle or threw garlands onto the tanks. 'Welcome to our Russian brothers!' they called. In fact, the arrival of the Bolsheviks didn't thrill either the Poles or the Ukrainians—both parties mistrusted the Russians—but for the time being the Ukrainians pretended to support their so-called liberators. Today they greeted the soldiers with flowers and offerings of bread and salt, the Slav symbols of hospitality. Later they would settle old scores.

My grandfather Bernard Bratter, who was a socialist, wasn't worried about the Russians. 'Things won't be so bad under the Bolsheviks,' he told Mania, sipping his tea in that painfully slow way of his, as if chewing each mouthful. 'You'll see, they'll treat everyone fairly, and there'll be plenty of food. Back in 1915 the Russians brought us buckets of caviar and slabs of halvah. They're not bad people.'

'My father was very laid back about most things,' my mother tells me. 'As a young man, he only worked for two days a week and played billiards the rest of the time. Money wasn't important to him. He was happiest when he could close the office and go to the pool hall. It used to make my mother mad!'

Even those who didn't share Bernard Bratter's optimism about the Russians agreed about one thing. At least Jews wouldn't be persecuted under the Bolsheviks as they were under the Nazis. From the moment they arrived, the Russians spread propaganda about the new workers' paradise in Russia. They stroked children's heads, gave them sweets, organised festive parades, and handed out photographs of Stalin, Lenin and Voroshilov like holy pictures. Communist Russia sounded like a utopia of liberty, equality and fraternity.

At first the workers of Lwow couldn't wait for this egalitarian wonderland. There is nothing as sweet as revenge, and the prospect of stripping their former bosses of their wealth, status and privileges warmed their hearts. At last the tide had turned. But it soon became obvious that the Soviet Union was a paradise without food or consumer goods, because instead of bringing buckets of caviar and slabs of halvah as my grandfather had predicted, the Russians bought up all the food they could lay their hands on and exported truckloads of Polish provisions back to Russia.

The sophisticated residents of Lwow watched with amusement as the Russians behaved like children let loose in a toyshop. Some of them had never seen watches or umbrellas, and it wasn't unusual to see grinning Russians rolling up their sleeves to reveal a dozen watches fastened all the way up to their elbows. They bought shoes by the dozen, handbags by the score. One day Mania's husband Misko came home with the latest Russian joke. 'I found out today why they're all so happy in the Soviet Union,' he said. 'When they can get bread, they're happy, when they can find butter they're very happy, and if they can find a pair of shoes to buy, they're absolutely ecstatic!'

But the backwardness of the Russians and their insatiable appetite for shopping soon ceased to be a laughing matter. Food became so scarce that long queues formed in front of every grocery and butcher shop, and people had to barter their belongings for butter, eggs, cheese or chickens when the peasants came to market. Their shrewd eyes were quick to spot the silken sheen of Mania's blouses and the trendy cut of her ankle-strap suede shoes, and they handed over slices of lightly smoked, pale pink ham or rings of garlic-spiced country sausage in exchange for clothes they would never have been able to afford in normal times.

Clothes were Mania's lifelong passion. She didn't have my mother's regular features or flawless complexion, but she had long shapely legs, slim hips, a devil-may-care smile and a foxy air of sophistication. People liked her because she always had an amusing anecdote to tell, often against herself. As a child she had contracted rheumatic fever which damaged her heart and made her prone to chest infections every winter, so her parents and her husband indulged her. According to my mother, Mania got good mileage out of her poor health.

When they were growing up my mother preferred working in her father's office to meeting friends in cafes, and had to be dragged to the dress-makers to have new clothes made. Mania, on the other hand, adored dressing up, flirting, shopping and gossiping, all of which was anathema to my mother. In today's psychological jargon, you could say that Mania was her sister's shadow self.

By the time my father arrived in Lwow, the city had swollen with refugees flooding in from the German-occupied zone.

While applying for his resident's permit, on a hunch he backdated his arrival in Lwow before the war. It occurred to him there might come a time when long-standing residents would be treated better than recent refugees.

Within a short time he found a job at the dental clinic in the Gas Company and also improvised a surgery in his small flat, so he earned enough to live on. For most of the refugees, however, life in Lwow was a struggle for survival. Haggard, destitute people roamed the streets and some became so desperate that thousands gathered each day in front of the German consulate, applying for visas to return to the German zone. Faced with starvation, they were unprepared to take their chances with the Nazis.

Among those who'd already returned to Krakow were my father's sister Karola and her husband Stasiek. Unlike most of the refugees in Lwow, Stasiek spoke Russian which meant that he could get a job, and when my grandfather Bernard heard that the municipal administration was looking for a Russian-speaking clerk, he'd recommended the attorney from Sosnowiec. To his amazement, Stasiek refused the offer. A clerical job was beneath him, and he didn't want to work for the Russians. He disapproved of their ideology and their methods and had no desire to be part of their machinery.

My grandmother shook her head in irritation. 'Your brother-in-law has his head in the clouds,' Toni muttered to my father. 'At a time like this you can't pick and choose where you work. Who else can can give him a job here except the Russians? The man's a fool.' Soon afterwards Stasiek decided to return to Krakow, despite the fact that Governor Frank's cruel grip was squeezing the Jews tighter every day. He argued that the Germans were cultured people, they loved art and music. They were hard but they were fair and law-abiding. Karola was a spirited woman with a mind of her own, but his persuasive manner convinced her to return with him. Life is made up of small decisions which, like brick upon brick, imperceptibly shape the structure of our existence. In wartime the smallest decision had enormous repercussions because once you veered off one path and followed another, there was no turning back.

As time went on, my grandfather Bernard grew more disillusioned with communism each passing day. No-one who had ever held a government position or had a business was safe from scrutiny, denunciation, confiscation and often deportation to Siberia as well. It was bad enough that the communists had deprived him of all his income by confiscating his steel business and his block of flats, but even the workers were badly treated, and people had to cheat and steal just to survive. One evening Misko came home with another Russian joke. 'Did you know that there are three categories of people in Russia? Those who've been to jail, those who are in jail, and all the others, who soon will be!' Like most jokes, this one was based on reality.

One day Bernard was shocked to receive a summons. He was ordered to appear before a tribunal on a charge of being a bourgeois, a major crime as far as the communists were concerned. Employers accused of exploiting or oppressing workers were hustled away, thrown in jail and brutally interrogated. After confessing to crimes they'd never committed, they were often sentenced to years of hard labour in the Siberian gulag from where many never returned.

Someone with a grudge must have denounced Bernard to the NKVD, the Soviet secret police, but at the hearing his former employees testified enthusiastically on his behalf. 'Comrade Bratter was not an exploiter, he was like a father to us,' they declared and gave numerous examples of his kindness over the years. Although the tribunal acquitted him, he was shaken by the experience. He'd coped with the blow of losing his business and having to work at some pointless job to justify his existence, but being hauled into court and charged with exploiting workers distressed him. He became depressed. Aunty Mania recalled that one morning an acquaintance stopped him in the street. 'Mr Bratter,' he said, 'do you realise that you're wearing pyjamas?' Bernard rubbed his bald head in embarrassment. He'd left home for work without getting dressed.

As accommodation in Lwow was scarce, the communists ordered people to share their apartments with strangers and that's how Misko's Russian boss at the railways came to move into their flat with his wife and teenage daughter. Although she was upset about the invasion, Mania was fascinated by her tenants. All that Nadia seemed to eat was herrings whose fishy smell permeated the flat. 'I'm telling you, from the minute Nadia opens her eyes in the morning, she drinks vodka and eats herrings. Even the curtains stink of herrings,' Mania confided to her parents in an attempt to cheer them up.

One day Nadia must have drunk more vodka than usual. 'I want to tell you something,' she hiccuped, bringing her bloated red face closer to Mania's. 'Did you know that we can't afford to buy any meat? Isn't that a joke?' she said bitterly in her sing-song voice. 'In Smolensk I was the director of a government sanatorium. All my life I've worked for the government, and now that I've retired, my pension isn't even enough for one lousy piece of meat!' She slid closer and was about to say something else when the front door opened and clicked shut. The words froze on her lips, a frightened look came into her eyes and she put a warning finger to her lips. Her daughter Olga was back from her Komsomol meeting.

The following day, when Olga had gone out, Nadia continued the conversation. 'It's dangerous to talk about these things in front of my daughter,' she sighed. 'Russian children are taught to report their parents' conversations. Then the NKVD come and take them away.' While Mania looked at her with horror, Nadia grabbed her sleeve and blurted, 'The Bolsheviks control every aspect of our lives, even our thoughts. Our only hope is the west. If you don't help us, how will we ever get to shake them off?'

So many people were leaving Lwow that the exodus was even reported in the foreign press. One day the city buzzed with news. The Russians had opened registration offices for those seeking to return to German-occupied territory. Those who wanted to return were jubilant, and soon the streets surrounding the German consulate became deserted. And that, my father reckoned, was exactly what the Russians intended, because the sight of vast numbers of people, especially Jews, who were clamoring to return to German rule wasn't good propaganda for the communist paradise.

All the refugees from the German zone were told to register but Henek had no intention of registering or returning to German rule. Knowing the political paranoia of the Bolsheviks, he didn't trust their promises. 'When you think about it,' he argued with his father-in-law, 'registration is unnecessary. If they intend to let people leave, why do they need lists of names and addresses? They could just issue permits on the spot.' But the Bratters kept insisting that he should register just in case he ever wanted to return. Worn down by their arguments, my father finally caved in, but when he signed his name, he gave a false address.

Several days later, around midnight, loud banging woke them with a start. Hastily wrapping her dressing-gown around her, Toni Bratter opened the door. Pushing past her, two thick-set men in heavy belted coats with collars turned up against the cold stared with hostile eyes at Bernard and Henek and demanded to see their papers. *'Dawaj! Dawaj!'* they barked

impatiently while my grandfather fumbled for his ID card and
resident's passport. Then it was my father's turn. They checked
his date of arrival, saw that he'd arrived in Lwow before the
war, thrust the papers back into his hands and stomped out,
banging the door behind them so that the crystal glasses
tinkled in the sideboard.

That night the NKVD scoured every home, shop, office
and warehouse in the city looking for those who'd registered
to return to the German zone. There was no escape because
the victims had supplied them with their names and addresses
themselves. Enemies of the Russian people who had applied
to return to the German zone were given a few minutes to
throw a few essentials into a small case before being pushed
into waiting trucks.

My father's instinct saved him from being deported to the
frozen wastes of Siberia, a fate which befell tens of thousands
of other refugees that very night. Among them was my mother's
second cousin, Srulek Kestecher, a gentle, slightly built boy of
thirteen who was something of a dreamer. Srulek was the
middle son of my grandmother Toni's favourite niece Balcia
who lived in the Polish village of Budy Lancutskie. When the
SS ordered all the Jews out of their homes, the family split
up. Srulek packed his rucksack and left for the Russian zone
with his father and two older brothers, while his mother stayed
behind with the two younger boys. Srulek was in Lwow the
night the Russian secret police banged on their door and
pushed them into a cattle truck.

As the train sped away from Poland, the people crammed
inside had no idea where they were going but Srulek was lost
in his own world as usual. He thought about his mother's tears
when they'd said goodbye, and about the last Yom Kippur
service which they'd held in a hut tucked deep in the woods
near his home. In his memoirs, written many years later, he

wrote: 'Yom Kippur night was glorious, there had never been such a night. The moon, which silhouetted every moving figure, had never shone so brightly but the silence and solemnity of the occasion were broken by exploding rockets and shellfire. Already leaves were falling in the orchards during that golden autumn. It was nature's way of bidding us goodbye.'

When the train finally came to a stop for the first time, Srulek saw dozens of similar trains which had converged there, each crammed with other unfortunates who had been captured that same night. Before it stopped again, one of Srulek's brothers jumped off the train and managed to escape. 'Many of the passengers envied his good fortune, but that was before we found out what happened to him,' he wrote.

In the crowded airless cattle truck, children were screaming, women were weeping and men were talking in low, depressed tones, but in spite of the gloom all around him, Srulek was captivated by the landscape unfurling before his eyes. 'It was early morning and the sun was rising above the horizon when the Volga came into sight,' he records. 'The sun reflected in the water, the wildflowers and birds singing made me temporarily forget my predicament. As we pushed deeper into Russia, fertile valleys were replaced by stark mountains and bare fields where no sun shone.'

As the train continued its interminable journey, further and further away from the world they knew, their destination was no longer in doubt. 'We are travelling to the end of the world, where polar bears roam and winter lasts for nine months of the year,' someone told him. Srulek knew that Siberia was the dreaded wasteland where political prisoners were exiled, and he wondered what political crimes he and the other children on the train had committed.

During their long journey into exile, the prophetic words of another passenger became seared into Srulek's memory. 'If and when this war will end, when the flames of burning towns and nations will subside, the survivors will return and trace the footsteps of their dearest ones and they will kiss those footsteps with such emotion as has never been known in the history of the world.'

CHAPTER 17

Eighteen months after the Russians had invaded Lwow, Mania was standing on her balcony once again, watching another conquering army march into her city. As my father had predicted, Hitler had broken the Ribbentrop–Molotov Pact and was invading eastern Poland. The German soldiers marched along the same road as the Russians, but the contrast between the two armies made Mania's throat tighten with dread. One behind the other, in strict military formation they marched, blond men with arrogant faces, spruce uniforms and shiny boots whose iron studs clattered on the cobblestones.

Down in the street the Ukrainians greeted the German soldiers with flowers, bread and salt, and rousing cheers. This time they weren't pretending. The Germans were their allies against the Poles, Russians and Jews. Now the old scores would be settled. Mania couldn't watch. With a sense of foreboding, she closed the door and went inside.

On the second day of the Nazi occupation of Lwow, my father Henek went to his dental clinic as usual, but as soon as he entered the courtyard he sensed that something was wrong. The other occupants of the building were standing around the large courtyard but when he approached they moved away as though he had a contagious disease. Another thing struck him as odd: although the Gas Company had many Jewish employees, he couldn't see a single one of them. Feeling uneasy, he turned to leave when two Ukrainians in German uniform barred his way.

One of them held his rifle so close to my father's face that its cold barrel brushed his cheek while the soldier said in a mocking voice, 'Maybe I'll shoot you right now.'

Henek's heart was drumming. 'Go ahead,' he said. 'Shoot.' The private's eyes were as cold as the barrel of his gun as he motioned my father to go inside.

In the makeshift interrogation room another Ukrainian guard glared at him. 'You're a Jew!' he hissed. When Henek denied it, the soldier snapped, 'Drop your trousers, we'll soon see who you are!' The ancient ritual which bound Jews to their God made them easily identifiable to their persecutors because only Jewish men were circumcised.

Realising that there'd come a time when being a Jew would be a death sentence, my father had organised a legal looking document which purported to explain how it came about that even though he wasn't Jewish, he'd been circumcised. Predated many years before the war, it stated that he was the illegitimate son of a Catholic woman who had been a servant in a Jewish family. When circumstances had made it necessary for her to leave him there, the Jews had brought him up and had him circumcised without her knowledge.

This affidavit was supposed to be a will written by his mother who had since married, inherited some money from her husband, and now wanted to bequeath it to her long-lost son. She offered a reward for finding him, along with payment for a newspaper advertisement searching for him. The story seemed watertight, and as my father handed it over to the Ukrainian guard he was convinced that it would ensure his immediate release.

But with a cursory glance at the document, the Ukrainian gave a sardonic laugh. 'Documents like this can be bought for three hundred zloty,' he scoffed.

Henek looked away quickly to conceal his dismay. That was exactly what he'd paid for it. So much for my foolproof plan, he thought. Nothing could save him now. But the German officer in charge was still mulling over the paper. Instead of handing Henek over to the Ukrainian militia, whose stony faces promised swift vengeance, he decided that the military police should investigate the story. A German corporal and Ukrainian guard were detailed to escort him to the town hall.

It was a radiant summer's day. Heat rose from the sun-warmed cobblestones and even the leafy lime trees beneath the copper domes of the Dominican church gave little shade. Past Lwow's solid ramparts, and the shingled roof of the medieval armory, Henek limped as fast as he could to keep up with the German corporal because the Ukrainian's hate-filled expression made him nervous.

As they crossed the avenue beside the opera house, Henek noticed that the open marketplace, which usually bustled with shoppers examining embroidered blouses, coral beads and wood carvings, was ominously quiet. He couldn't conceal his agitation. 'Why didn't they release me?' he asked the corporal in German. 'I haven't done anything.'

The corporal tried to calm him down. 'Don't worry, if you're innocent, you have nothing to fear,' he said. Henek wasn't convinced but he felt a little comforted by the soldier's kind manner.

Uneasy about the guard behind him, Henek glanced around and saw that in the far corner of the marketplace hooligans were knocking trestles over and smashing them to pieces. Suddenly, as if in response to some signal, they started rushing towards him, brandishing lengths of wood and yelling 'Ah, komisar!' as if he was a communist official. Bloodlust blazed out of their eyes, and their weapons promised no mercy. They were already bearing down on him, clubs poised to strike. Another second and their clubs would be raining down on his head and the corporal striding ahead of them wouldn't even know. With a strangled voice Henek called out to the soldier, who finally looked around and saw the gang rushing towards his captive. '*Weg ihr schweine!*' 'Get away, you scum!' he yelled, and to Henek's relief the louts slunk away like dogs whose bone has been taken away.

Past fountains whose statues of Jupiter and Diana spouted delicate jets of water in the four corners of the cobbled square, Henek limped up the steps of the town hall. Inside the weathered gate the corporal handed him over to the German security police, saying, '*Spionage verdächtig, aber so handweg kann man ihm nicht schiessen.*' 'Suspected of spying, but shouldn't be shot without further investigation.'

After he'd repeatedly denied being either a spy or a communist and insisted that he was just an ordinary dentist, they ordered him to join the other suspects. About twenty people stood in the courtyard, most of them Jews. The guards yelled that nobody was to move a muscle. A German private kept watch over them and whenever anyone made the slightest movement, he strode over and with a crisp motion struck their forehead with his truncheon so ferociously that they toppled over.

Standing in the searing heat as though nailed to the ground, Henek felt light-headed. Every cell in his body was shrieking for water, for the luxury of bending, stretching or just changing position. He could hear some sounds coming from the yard behind him. The Germans were setting up machine guns. 'They must be for us,' the man beside him murmured.

Henek nodded. The same thought had occurred to him. He was surprised how little emotion he felt. It would be better to be finished off right now, killed by a quick bullet than be hunted and live in terror and humiliation. While bracing himself for the inevitable he heard his name called out. Gritting his teeth, he walked towards the German officer. Any moment now he'd find out whether the Almighty, about whom his father had talked so often, really existed. But the officer was scrutinising his passport. 'Why were you brought here?' he asked.

'Because I'm a Jew and the Ukrainians hate Jews,' Henek explained. The officer handed back his passport and looked at his watch. 'It's now six-thirty,' he said. 'You will be released at seven, but not a moment earlier.'

On the dot of seven Henek walked out of the town hall as fast as his stiff leg would allow. The discomfort and anxiety of the past seven hours melted away. But when he looked around him, the blood froze in his veins and he slowed his pace. The streets of Lwow resembled a battlefield of ghostly, grotesque figures. Staggering along, clinging to the sides of buildings, were men bleeding from gashes on their heads, cradling broken arms or supporting those who could hardly walk. The sound of groaning was occasionally broken by racking spasms of sobbing. But the most terrifying sight was the haunted look in eyes which had witnessed cruelty they couldn't describe and would never forget. And these were the fortunate ones who had survived.

Henek had foreseen that Germany would eventually occupy Lwow, but neither he nor anybody else had envisaged that the city would soon resemble a slaughterhouse as Jews were hunted down and butchered more cruelly and relentlessly than in any other Polish city. In Lwow the Nazis had found enthusiastic accomplices. Like wolves licking their lips at the thought of the flock about to be placed in their care, some ultranationalistic Ukrainians had been eager to sink their fangs into Jewish flesh. They hadn't had long to wait.

On the day when he'd been detained, Germans had given the Ukrainians free rein to amuse themselves with the Jews any way they liked, but their fun had to end by seven p.m. That day, prison yards all over Lwow ran with blood, and their walls were spattered with fragments of human brains. By not releasing Henek until seven, the German officer had saved his life.

The next day Henek's cousin Janek Spira, an engineer who worked in the same building, was lined up with others against the courtyard wall to be shot. The rifle was already pointing at Janek's bald head when the German officer in charge of the execution squad suddenly threw his arms up in the air. 'Mein Gott!' he exclaimed. 'I'm a soldier, not an executioner. I can't take this any more!' and he strode away in disgust, letting his stunned prisoners go free.

Every day Jewish men were rounded up in the street. Some were lined up against the wall and peremptorily shot, many were press-ganged and later killed, while others were tortured to death in interrogation rooms. It was during those first days of the Nazi occupation that my young uncle Izio Bratter vanished.

From the descriptions of my mother and Aunty Mania who both adored their brother, I know that Izio was short but good-looking with fair hair and green eyes, good-hearted but lazy. A bit of a waster. The youngest of four children and the only son, he was probably spoilt. When he was little, whenever their mother put corn on the table, he used to say that he'd licked every single cob so that no-one would want theirs. Because of the small quota of Jewish students admitted to Polish universities during the thirties, his parents had sent him to Italy to study medicine, but according to my mother he'd studied girls instead of books and hadn't completed the course.

All that my mother ever said about the disappearance of her only brother was that he went out one day and never returned. There was no-one to ask, nowhere to go for help. In those tragic times gypsies did a thriving trade prophesying happy reunions. Like other desperate wives and mothers, my grandmother crossed a fortune-teller's palm with silver and was told that her son would return, but a neighbour told her that she had seen him being rounded up in the street by German soldiers. 'We kept hoping that one day he'd come back but he never did,' my mother said in the detached way she talked about these events. Much later I understood that she was keeping a tight lid over grief which, if released, might engulf her.

'Izio and Hania were crazy about you,' my mother used to tell me. 'You were our only sunbeam in those dark days.' As long as I can remember I've been the only child of an isolated nuclear family, so it's hard to imagine that I was once surrounded by adoring aunties, uncles and grandparents.

My mother's favourite sister Hania was a pretty strawberry blonde who cried whenever Mania called her 'Ginger' because of her hair. Another bad mark for Mania. Hania was so soft-hearted that she often brought home stray cats and dogs. As a teenager she thought she was too fat and drank vinegar to lose weight, but it gave her an ulcer and spoiled her complexion.

I listen avidly to my mother's recollections because I know so little about this young aunty. Suddenly she recalls something that makes me sit up. 'My parents sent Hania away to the country for a long time and when she came back to Lwow, she spoke with a country accent. Mania used to make fun of her and make her cry.' Perhaps now I'll discover something about Hania, but we've come to a dead end. My mother can't recall why her sister was sent away, or when she married Dolek Korner.

Aunty Mania once told me that both she and her sister Hania had become pregnant in 1941 but although she herself had an abortion, Hania had not and she had given birth to a little girl. But years later, when I was desperate to know more about this young aunty of whom not even one photograph has remained, my mother could no longer remember anything. Or perhaps she remembered too much. Our deepest feelings are often revealed in silences and my mother's silence screamed. By then Bronia looked as transparent as a Chinese porcelain saucer, the light had gone out of her cat-green eyes, and she clasped her small right hand in her left so that I wouldn't see how much it shook.

To each question I ask she stubbornly shakes her bouffant blonde head. She's eighty-one, still feisty and spirited, and as immaculately dressed and groomed as ever. What did Hania call the baby? She shrugs. No idea. Did Hania have the baby at a clinic? Sitting in my sunlit room in Sydney, one of the least introspective and most tolerant cities in the world, it's difficult to recreate a time when every doorknock meant death.

But my last question ignites a spark. My mother gives me a look that could have drilled through basalt. 'What clinic? How did Jews get to go to clinics?' She waves an irritated hand in my direction. 'Don't you know? Jews weren't people,' she says bitterly. 'Doctors and hospitals weren't allowed to treat them.'

Still I persist. 'So did Hania have the baby at home?' My mother stares out of the window but I know that she's not looking at the palms and frangipanis in the garden but at some indescribable scene inside her mind. Slowly she turns her eyes back on me and repeats in a hollow voice, 'At home. She had it at home. Don't ask. I don't want to think about it. I'll have nightmares.' I never asked about Hania again. On this occasion compassion triumphed over the tyranny of knowledge.

When the Germans decided that the annihilation of the Jews was proceeding too slowly because too many Jews were staying indoors, they put pressure on the Judenrat to supply Jews for their killing squads. The Judenrat, a Jewish organisation set up by the Germans to liaise between the Jewish community and themselves, had its own policemen who were now ordered to enter Jewish homes and take the women away. Two of these policemen once came into my grandparents' home for my mother and Mania. Fortunately Mania recognised one of them as a colleague of Misko's from the polytechnic. She started chatting with him about old times and mutual friends, until he felt too embarrassed to carry out his order and left them alone.

It wasn't long before two burly Volksdeutsch guards banged on the door, demanding wine that they'd heard was kept in the cellar. 'My father doesn't have any wine,' my mother said and offered to take them down there to see for themselves. One of them didn't like her tone of voice and threatened to hit her. 'Why don't you, then?' she taunted him, tilting her small chin. He stared at her, looked around the cellar and left. 'I don't know what got into me,' she says, shaking her fair hair in wonder. 'I must have been crazy. He could have killed me.'

It was around this time that Mania's husband Misko shot a German soldier. Everyone liked Misko, even his German employer who knew that he was Jewish. One morning the boss took Misko aside and told him that he kept a revolver in the top drawer of the desk and if he was ever in danger, he should use it.

Not long afterwards a menacing German soldier strode into the office, revolver in hand, and ordered Misko outside at once. With shaking fingers Misko slid the drawer open, put his hand around the pistol grip and pressed the trigger. He was shocked when the German staggered and crashed to the floor. He couldn't get over the fact that he'd killed someone. 'If you hadn't, he would have killed you and many others,' Mania tried to reason with him, but Misko was in a state of shock for a long time.

As it became increasingly difficult to evade the German soldiers, Ukrainian guards and Jewish police, my father and Hania's husband Dolek created a recess behind the stove by stacking firewood in a way that enabled them to crawl in through an opening at the top. After pushing their way inside, they covered the opening with a large enamel wash tub. They practised this manoeuvre over and over and slept on the kitchen floor fully clothed, ready to jump into their hiding place at a moment's notice.

According to my father, seeing so much suffering desensitised many people who became callous to protect themselves from feeling pain. He never forgot the shock of hearing a young married woman say, 'The Germans have taken Daddy away to make mincemeat out of him.' Reflecting about her comment many years later, he wrote: 'There was no time to cry over those who had perished because you had to think all the time of saving yourself. You had to become tough or you couldn't go on living.'

Shortly after Izio's disappearance, on a warm summer evening in 1941, there was a gentle knock on the door of the Bratters' home on Sloneczna Street. They lived in a handsome stone-faced block of flats decorated with ornamental balconies, pediments and plump cherubs carved above the entrance. But those angels didn't do their work, they didn't protect the owners of the building.

By then the Bratters, like most Jews in Lwow, didn't open the door to strangers any more because Ukrainian militia used to burst into Jewish homes and push the occupants into waiting trucks. On this particular day, 25 July, a rumour had spread that the Ukrainians were planning retaliation to avenge the murder of an anti-Semitic Ukrainian leader by a Jew. As the assassination had taken place in Paris in May 1926, this so-called anniversary was a thinly veiled pretext for a pogrom. But the gentle knock and the familiar voice on the other side of the door allayed the Bratters' suspicion. 'Panie Bratter, *prosze pana*, please open the door, I have something to tell you.' It was the caretaker. My grandfather opened the door.

In the doorway stood two Ukrainian guards with rifles, holding a list of names. 'Bernard Bratter? Come with us!' Glancing inside, they spotted my father. 'You too!' they snapped. Perhaps I watched them taking my father and grandfather away. I may have been looking at my animal picture book at the time, or chewing the precious Wedel chocolates Aunty Mania's husband Misko sometimes brought for me. I probably saw my grandmother's frozen face and heard her sobbing long after they had gone. It's hard for me to realise that I was actually there, a rosy two-year-old learning the names of animals on my father's knee while atrocities on a scale not seen in Europe since the days of Genghis Khan were being perpetrated all around me. For most of my life I've thought of the Holocaust as something that happened to my parents, not to me, so it's an effort to place myself on that terrifying stage and see myself as being inside the poisonous web that was ensnaring us. With a toddler's watchful gaze, I must have seen their frightened eyes darting towards the door and at each other, and sensed the terror in the words they couldn't articulate. My mother told me that for a long time afterwards, whenever someone knocked on the door, I would place a finger on the tip of my nose and whisper, 'Shh! Germs!', and in spite of their grief they would smile at my mispronunciation.

My father and grandfather were taken to the prison yard on Lackiego Street where about a hundred men were ordered to form two rows. A German officer with a thin mouth, hollow cheeks and a lantern jaw was surveying the prisoners while he caressed the truncheon he held in his right hand with long, loving strokes. He strode up to a man in the front row, raised his cudgel and with lightning speed struck his temple so hard that the man reeled and fell. While he lay on the ground, his head in his hands, the officer yelled at him to get up and kept beating the dazed man until he staggered to his feet.

Sauntering along the front row, the officer bored his colourless eyes into Henek's face. 'Who are you?' he demanded, and without waiting for a reply yelled with fury, 'You're a communist!' and struck him across the forehead with his bamboo pole. The sound of that blow reverberated in Henek's head like an echo chamber. 'At that instant,' my father writes in his memoirs, 'I experienced a strange olfactory sensation. Suddenly I smelt the sweet grassy fragrance of meadows in autumn. Like the man before me, I also fell backwards, but when the German yelled "Get up!", in spite of the pain and dizziness I leapt up like a marionette before he had time to beat me again.'

After a while the German officer lost interest in this game and handed them over to the Ukrainians who started battering their captives with sticks and clubs. Each time he saw one of the Ukrainians approaching him with a raised stick, Henek psyched himself up for the coming blow, which made the pain more bearable. It occurred to him that their tormentors puffed and panted just like the women who used to beat their rugs in the courtyard of his parents' home in Sebastiana Street. 'I suppose they'd been hard at work bludgeoning Jews for hours, so they were tired out,' he writes.

When the militia finally ordered the detainees to go inside

the prison building, my father heaved a sigh of relief, thinking that the beating was over. No way. Cracking whips, the guards started chasing the exhausted men up to the third floor like hounds lusting for blood. On each landing they had to run the gauntlet of Ukrainian guards who bashed them as they ran past. My father's hands swelled and became bruised because he used them as a shield to ward off blows to his head.

'When we finally got to the third floor,' my father writes, 'they crammed us into a long corridor, pushing us against those who were already up there. We could hear them moaning, begging us to move back because their bodies hurt so much. But this was impossible because a German was whipping us mercilessly to move forward. We were jammed together like sardines in a tin. They carried out one man, dead. The night was hot, we were thirsty, and we didn't have enough air to breathe, but that German kept lashing out with his whip, yelling "*Nasse säcke*", which meant "wet sacks". No-one was allowed to leave the room, and some men had wet themselves. Things improved whenever this soldier went outside for a break, because the young officer who replaced him let us go to the toilet, have a drink of water and even sit down on the floor. He hadn't had time to become corrupted by the bestiality of his colleagues. But as soon as the cruel one returned, we had to stand up again. And that's how we spent the whole night.'

In the morning their captors herded them out into the yard and beat them again. Sitting behind little tables in the yard, Gestapo officers called for any lawyers to come forward and made them load rocks into wheelbarrows and push them pointlessly backwards and forwards across the yard, just to torment and humiliate them.

Next they called for the doctors to come forward. Thinking that doctors were more likely to be spared, Henek stepped forward too, but when they announced that this didn't include dentists, he stepped back, though a hunch made him stand close to the doctors' group. When the soldier ordered everyone to throw all their possessions, including their passports, onto a pile, Henck's heart throbbed against his ears. 'They obviously intend to bury us all in a mass grave, because that's the only place where you don't need any documents,' he thought.

A moment later, however, the doctors were ordered to pick up their documents and, without hesitating for a second, Henek rushed forward, grabbed his passport and came back to the doctors' group. But the Ukrainians weren't taking any chances and started checking all the passports. Henek noticed that whenever they came across one which said Doctor of Dentistry, they sent its owner back to the group destined for death, but by a stroke of amazing luck my father's passport actually described him as a doctor. When applying for his passport during the Russian occupation, he'd said he was a doctor simply because he didn't like the Russian word for dentist. He didn't suspect that one day his life would hinge on his choice of words.

There were only about fifteen men in the doctors' group, and out of the hundreds of people gathered in the prison yard that day, they were the only ones whom the Germans released. All the others were loaded into trucks, driven to Piaskowa Gora and shot. On 25 July 1941, the Germans and their Ukrainian assistants killed over 5000 Jews. My grandfather Bernard Bratter was amongst them.

CHAPTER 18

In the village of Radlow north of Krakow, a stooped grey-haired woman tears opens a thick letter from Lwow with eager fingers. Lieba Baldinger's face lights up as she pulls out a sepia-toned photograph with serrated edges and gazes at a little girl with a solemn face who is digging with her spade. My father has sent my photo to his mother and writes that Danusia already knows the names of all the animals in Polish and Latin even though she's only two years old. But he doesn't tell her that he has been arrested and beaten, that his brother-in-law went out one day and never returned, or that his father-in-law has just been murdered by a death squad.

Lieba reads the letter over and over again, and then calls her daughter Rozia, who claps her hands with delight when she sees the photograph of her niece. 'Dear little Danusia is the image of Bronia's family, she doesn't take after our side, does she, Mamuncia?'

Tears spill out of Lieba's brown eyes because she longs to cuddle her little granddaughter and wonders whether she'll ever see her again. 'Such a lovely child,' she whispers while Rozia inserts the picture into the back of a double glass frame which already contains a photograph of Janek and Rolande's baby daughter, Danielle. Rozia places the frame on their dressing table so that one little granddaughter looks out from the frame while the other is reflected in the mirror.

I learned this from Rozia's letters which I found in Paris recently among a trunkful of family memorabilia kept by my cousin Aline. It's thrilling to hear this aunt's own voice in her well-spaced, rounded handwriting and a lump comes to my throat when I learn how much she and Lieba loved me. All I've ever heard about Rozia was that she was deaf, highly strung, and difficult, but in these letters to her brother Janek and sister-in-law Rolande, I encounter a devoted soul who is so involved with the family that she rarely mentions her own problems.

Even when she had been pistol-whipped by a German soldier in the streets of Krakow shortly before they'd moved to Radlow, Rozia had been more concerned about sparing her mother anxiety than about her own bruised face. That had happened just before Pesach, after they'd swept and scrubbed every nook and cranny in the house to make sure that not a crumb of bread or *chometz* remained. 'That soldier shook me up to make sure there wasn't any *chometz* left!' she joked, holding her hand across her cheek so Lieba wouldn't see the swelling.

Shortly afterwards Lieba had started to pack her menorah and candelabra, the bedroom suite and ice chest, and treasured family photographs of happier times. She moved slowly and sighed as she sorted possessions she'd accumulated over a lifetime in readiness to leave Krakow. In May 1940, in accordance with his plan to turn Krakow into a cleansed German city that was *Judenrein*, Governor Hans Frank ordered all Jews to leave. Those who left before 15 August could go wherever they chose, but after that date they'd be forcibly deported. Only Jews who were fit enough to work and be useful to the Germans were given permission to remain in the city, and Lieba's son Izio was amongst them.

At the age of sixty-eight, my grandmother, who had pitied

the Polish Jews in Germany when they were thrown out of their homes two years before, had become a refugee herself. For the first time in centuries the Jews of Krakow were forced to abandon their synagogues, *shtibls*, prayer houses, *mikvehs*, Talmud-Torah schools and the homes where the ghosts of their ancestors hovered above *mezuzah* scrolls on a thousand worn doorways.

Lieba and Rozia had moved to Radlowa because they had family there and thought that they'd be safe in this village which was little more than a huddle of poor huts. Lieba's brothers-in-law Ozjasz and Maks Kling came from here. From Rozia's letters, I learn that at this time my parents and Andzia and Zygmunt were in Lwow, Lunia and Berus were in Cyprus, Avner and Hela were waiting for a ship to Brazil, and Janek and Rolande were in Andorra.

Some of Rozia's letters are deceptively lively.

> *Our Dear Mamuncia—along with the rest of us—couldn't stop laughing at the story about Danielle doing weewee in bed. I'm not surprised that your in-laws are besotted with her, not because of the weewee, but because she sounds as though she has inherited Rolande's charm, although it sounds as if she gets her appetite from our tribe. I'm surprised she doesn't say: 'Mummy, mummy, me eat thwee swices of bwead but me still hungwy!' like Janek used to say! As for the olive oil, don't worry about it, it's not important, it was just a thought. On the whole, we have a lot to be thankful for. Let's hope that others won't forget us either. Henek and Andzia are with their families at the old address and Henek and Zygmunt are both working which makes us very happy.*

To each of Rozia's letters, Lieba adds a brief postscript sending her love in handwriting which trembles with agitation. Reading their letters fifty years after they were written, it's as though fictional characters have suddenly stepped out of their novels and begun speaking with their own voices.

One of the few highlights of Lieba's life in Radlowa was an unexpected visit from her daughter Fridzia who stayed with them in the room they rented in a villager's hut. Ever since she had married Jerzyk Shapiro in November 1938, Fridzia had been unsettled. He was a philologist from Vilno whom she'd met at a holiday resort at a time in her life when her bruised ego needed a boost. She was already twenty-five, the man she was in love with didn't want to make a commitment, and spinsterhood beckoned. There was no passion between her and Jerzyk but he said he loved her and she was impressed by his intellect. Many years later, looking back on her marriage, she comments, 'I married him to spite my boyfriend, but I ended up spiting myself.' It didn't take long to realise that marrying Jerzyk had been a terrible mistake. He was as dry and inaccessible as his textbooks, and to her warm, giving nature it felt like living in emotional permafrost. They had nothing in common.

Fridzia was so unhappy that as soon as war broke out she left him and went back to Krakow to live with her mother, but a few months later, when Jerzyk asked her to come back, she returned to Vilno hoping for a reconciliation. Vilno, which was part of Poland but inhabited mainly by Lithuanians, had by then been occupied by the Russians, and they both found work in the peat fields making bricks to sell for fuel. She still shudders when she thinks of that backbreaking work. She would to stand knee-deep in water for hours, her hands swollen and bleeding as she hacked the moist black peat out of the riverbed.

In 1941, when the Germans occupied that region, Fridzia

left Jerzyk once again. By then she'd obtained false papers and changed her name to Slawa which sounded more Aryan, and she has kept that name ever since. German soldiers caught her and locked her into a barn with other Jews they'd rounded up. The barn was bare except for some hay heaped in one corner. When her eyes had grown accustomed to the gloom, she noticed a pretty young girl with a mane of tawny, flowing locks, who had managed to climb onto the parapet of the only window and stood there wild-eyed and compelling. To this day my aunt has that scene carved into her mind. 'I couldn't stop looking at her and I couldn't believe what I was seeing,' she says in a hushed voice. 'The girl standing on the window ledge was tearing out her beautiful hair, pulling it out until whole strands of it were coming away in her distracted hands. I'll never forget the anguish in her voice when, oblivious of the clumps of hair in her hands, she screamed, "Let me out! Let me out! I'm young, I want to live!"'

'When I looked around, I saw that some people were saying the Shema, while others were feeding bread or apples to their children because none of us knew what was going to happen. But I felt optimistic. I couldn't believe that any harm would come to me because, in spite of everything, I've always believed that God does exist and knows what He is doing.

'When there were so many people crammed into the barn that there was no room to sit down, there was a commotion ouside and the Germans started shouting. "*Los! Los!*" "Hurry up!" They herded us outside, pushed us into a line, and we had to walk through the street while armed soldiers yelled at us and cracked whips. I heard people panicking that this was a death march, that they were taking us out of town to murder us all. My mind was whirring. I had to do something, there was no time to lose. My fingers were shaking as I unfastened my little gold brooch and sidled up to one of the young

Lithuanian guards. "Take this and look away for a moment so I can escape." He did. To this day I don't know what made me do that, or why he agreed. He could have taken the brooch and shot me anyway. Perhaps he wanted to have one good deed to his credit because half an hour later, at Ponary Woods, he helped to shoot down hundreds of women and children and to throw lime and earth over their still-warm bodies.'

Fridzia fled to the home of her Catholic friend Ziuta who hid her. While at Ziuta's place she used to play with her four-year-old daughter Basia, but one day she was puzzled to see the little girl take some pillows off the bed, tie their corners together with string, loop the cord around her waist, and pull them along the floor. 'I'm playing Jews,' the child explained. She had watched Jews being thrown out of their homes and escorted to the ghetto, pulling their belongings behind them along the ground.

When Jerzyk sent Slawa false papers, Ziuta's father helped her cross the border and she made her way back to her mother in Radlowa. By then German efforts to annihilate the Jews had intensified and life had become tenuous there too. During one ferocious raid, Slawa with her mother and sister ran to the woods where they hid until late at night, trembling when they heard salvos of gunfire. At night, when the shooting had stopped, they crept back to find that their home resembled a bomb site. Drawers had been emptied, plates lay smashed on the floor and everything of value had gone.

It was no longer safe to stay in Radlowa, but they had nowhere else to go. Izio was living in the Krakow ghetto, but apart from its residents no-one was allowed to enter. Izio and Lola had applied for a legal separation so that she wouldn't have to go into the ghetto with him. As far as the authorities were concerned, Lola was German and was permitted to keep working in their shop, Syrena, which had been taken over by a German. Although she and Izio were separated, she became a go-between for the family, minding furniture and valuables, passing on letters, and helping relatives who passed through Krakow.

Slawa decided to try her luck in Warsaw. She didn't look Jewish, and with her Aryan papers and excellent command of Polish, she might be able to pass as a Catholic in the capital where nobody knew her. When she heard that some of the villagers were going to Warsaw in a farmer's cart, she arranged to go with them. Before leaving, she promised her mother and Rozia that as soon as she'd found somewhere to live, she'd send for them. 'Don't take too long,' whispered Rozia, her brown eyes darting anxiously towards their mother. Lieba's spirits had plummeted since their home had been ransacked, and the threat of being caught was increasing day by day.

As the cart rumbled along the rough country road, Slawa wrapped her woollen scarf tightly around her neck and sank her chin into her overcoat to shut out the biting wind as she jolted up and down on the wooden seat. The bare branches of the poplars pointed towards the sky as if in supplication, and as they passed wayside shrines and the other occupants of the cart crossed themselves, Slawa wondered whether her God was watching what was happening to his people.

Her thoughts were interrupted when she heard someone say, 'Whatever they're doing to those stinking Jews, it isn't enough.' It was a wrinkled country woman with a threadbare shawl thrown around her thin shoulders.

Her neighbour leaned forward, eyes burning with almost religious zeal. 'I can smell a Jew a mile away,' she announced with a defiant glance around the cart.

Slawa stared straight ahead with a nonchalance she didn't feel. Suddenly she remembered the incriminating diary in her handbag. Pretending to search for something in her bag, she surreptitiously pulled out her notebook and clutched it under her coat, awaiting her opportunity. When the others were looking at a wayside shrine, she let her arm dangle over the side of the cart, opened her fingers, and dropped the diary into the muddy ditch.

By the end of 1942 Rozia's letters had become very brief, as if she had no more heart for trivia. Her last letter to her brother Janek breaks my heart. 'You shouldn't worry about us so much, as the good Lord has us in his care and we trust that He won't abandon us. Everyone does what they can. The main thing is, that God should let us survive.'

CHAPTER 19

All through the night the search for Jews continued. Skilled in the psychology of terror, the guards shone their torches on documents and then ran them up to people's faces, watching for their frightened expressions to give them away. Knowing this, my father's sister Andzia Rosenbaum boldly returned their gaze while they scanned her ID card. According to her *Kennkarte*, she was Janina Sulikowska, a Polish Catholic, travelling with her daughter Krysia and son Fredzio.

All through the night shouts and screams tore through the station. Documents were held up to the light and exposed as forgeries, rifle butts cracked on heads, whips lashed bare necks, and people were dragged away at gunpoint. For what seemed hours, the guard scrutinised Andzia's papers before he handed them back. After he'd walked on, she spotted a peasant's heavy overcoat lying on a bench. She looked around quickly, made sure that no-one was looking and pushed her small son underneath it out of sight.

Before dawn, when the waiting room was almost empty, an eerie stillness fell over those who remained. While Krysia dozed against her mother's shoulder, Andzia didn't take her eyes off the small shape bulging under the greatcoat. They mustn't find him.

Day and night German soldiers, armed Ukrainian militia and local extortionists prowled around Lwow's Central Station, hunting for Jews as eagerly as prospectors searching for gold. Andzia's thoughts throbbed with one refrain: Let the train come soon. Let the train come soon. She had to get the children away from Lwow and find some country town where they might have a chance to survive.

Suddenly the words froze in her head. A gaunt German soldier with a beak-like nose and a thin mouth turned down at the corners strode across the waiting room, stopped at the table and pulled the coat away, revealing a little boy who blinked sleepily into his face. Grabbing the child's arm, the soldier shouted, 'Whose kid is this?' and, without waiting for a reply, dragged him outside onto the platform.

Something exploded inside Andzia's head. Through the door, in the murky half-light, their lives were about to unravel while she watched. The shadowy figure was leaning over her child, fumbling with his trousers. Any second now the soldier would see that Fredzio was Jewish, take the revolver out of its polished leather holster and shoot him dead. Or pick him up by the legs, as she had once seen a German soldier do, and with a swift sharp motion let his soft skull swing into the brick wall, like an egg smashing onto a marble floor.

Like a tigress, propelled by a power beyond her conscious will, Andzia sprang forward, flew at the soldier and pummelled his uniformed arm just as it was tugging at the elastic waistband of Fredzio's knitted pants. Pretending to misunderstand what he was doing, she started scolding him like a fishmonger at the Friday market. 'How dare you? What do you think you're doing with my child? You should be ashamed of yourself! What are you, a pervert? Get away from my son this instant!' Taken aback by this tongue-lashing, the guard stepped away from the child and, taking advantage of his momentary hesitation, Andzia grasped her son's little hand and stalked back into the waiting room, pulling him behind her.

Instead of slumping down on the nearest seat as she longed to do, Andzia kept up a righteous tirade for the benefit of the other travellers, trying to appear like a simple Polish mother outraged at having her child molested. 'My God, imagine that! Grown men sticking their hands into a six-year-old's underpants. *Cholera psiakrew!*' she swore. 'To hell with them. They think they can do anything, the devil take them. What's the world coming to?'

The other travellers, mostly country women in kerchiefs with big wicker baskets, looked sympathetically at the feisty young woman with such beautiful children. They took in the angelic little boy with fair curls and long lashes, and the girl with the wistful expression of a Madonna.

Krysia looked at her brother, sighed, and looked away again. On their own, she and her mother would manage without any trouble, but Fredzio put all three of them in danger. All they had to do was look inside his trousers and they'd be finished. With her ash-blonde hair, creamy complexion and dreamy grey-green eyes, twelve-year-old Krysia had no trouble passing as a Polish child, especially with the little gold cross hanging around her neck.

It was the very shininess of that cross that caught the attention of a stout red-faced soldier a few minutes later when he came back to check the occupants of the waiting room yet again. It was that oppressive time just before dawn, when the sky resembled a crinkled sheet of pewter and the acrid smell of soot hung over the station. Peering into Krysia's frightened face, the soldier motioned her to go with him. '*Los! Los!*' he barked, and before Andzia could do anything to stop him, he'd gripped the girl's arm and propelled her out of the station.

Fifty years later, in her immaculate Tel-Aviv apartment decorated with Persian rugs and sparkling crystal, my Aunty Andzia, an erect, elegantly dressed woman of eighty-seven, leans forward and, jabbing her beautifully manicured fingernail in the air for emphasis, stares into my face and says in a slow, hypnotic way, 'The war lasted for five years. Each of those years lasted three hundred and sixty-five days, each day lasted twenty-four hours, and each hour lasted for sixty minutes. And every one of those minutes lasted an eternity.'

I've arrived to hear Aunty Andzia's life story, but at first she refuses to talk about her experiences. 'There are already too many stories about the Holocaust. The world is going to suffocate under them all. What good will it do me to talk about it? You'll have your story and I'll have nightmares.' From the hot street below, the noises of a Levantine city float up to her flat. Car tyres screech, a man shouts, someone is honking the horn. 'I don't need more unhappiness. As it is, sometimes I feel like jumping out of that window,' she sighs.

I know that I should respect her wishes, but I've travelled halfway around the globe to hear her story. There will never be another chance. I try once more. 'Your story is unique, it shouldn't be lost.' Finally she shrugs assent, bemused as well as annoyed by my persistence, and soon I'm sitting beside her in the waiting room of Lwow railway station, every muscle in her body taut with anxiety as she wonders what's happening to her daughter.

Although she longed to follow Krysia, Andzia knew she had to stay where she was. With the cross around her neck and her fair hair, Krysia could pass for a Polish girl, but it wouldn't take the soldiers long to find out that Fredzio was Jewish, and then they'd all be done for. For the tenth time that minute, Andzia unclenched her fists and tried to stop herself from glancing at her watch. Stay calm for God's sake, she told herself. Don't attract attention. How long could they question Krysia?

She sighed as she thought how her life had changed. Only

three years ago, in another lifetime, her biggest worry was which outfits to buy. Every morning, when Krysia was at school, Andzia used to visit Lunia and together they pored over the *Warsaw Illustrated Review* to study the Paris fashions. Then they'd go to their favourite cafe, Pavilon, in Krakow's Planty Gardens, and gossip about everyone they knew over tall glasses of iced coffee marbled with cream.

In those days, which now seemed a million years ago, she had a maid to do the housework and a husband who humoured her every whim. Zygmunt was a good-natured man, but no matter what he did, Andzia always found reason to carp and complain. She regretted it now. Some perverse spirit stopped her from enjoying what she had, envy poisoned all her relationships. The more placating Zygmunt was, the more shrewish she became. 'Aneczka,' he used to cajole her, 'be reasonable,' but she would only rage about her misfortune in marrying him, in not having the kind of apartment she longed for, in being saddled with two children. Everyone had better parents, kinder sisters, richer husbands and smarter children.

If only Zygmunt was with her now. Again she glanced at her watch. Would Krysia remember all the words of Our Father? Sometimes she stumbled over the words. That girl took after Zygmunt's family, she was so phlegmatic at times. Closing her eyes so that no-one would see the fear in them, Andzia thought, Dear God, let her remember that prayer.

An ironic smile fluttered across her mouth. If her father only knew that she was praying to God so that her daughter would remember a Christian prayer! Daniel Baldinger had prayed to his God every day of his life. She'd never seen the point of all that praying, but perhaps her father's God had taken care of him after all. Daniel had died before the war began, so he didn't have to run and hide like a hunted animal, wondering whether his children were going to be butchered in the street. Craning her neck to see out of the waiting room door, Andzia sighed again. If only Krysia would come back.

If only Mummy was here, Krysia was thinking as she stumbled on the chipped mosaic floor of the station, trying to keep up with the angry soldier. 'Hurry up, you Polish idiot, what's the matter with you? Do you want me to speed you up?' Her skin prickled with terror. Where was he taking her? What did he want? When would she be able to rejoin her mother? She looked back, hoping for some signal from Andzia, but she couldn't see the waiting room any more.

Her captor pushed her ahead of him across the street until she was standing in front of a building decorated with statues of lions. The soldier swung open the oak gate and pushed her inside. 'Wait here and don't budge! If I come back and find that you've moved one centimetre, I'll whip you till all your skin ends up on the floor in shreds!' he shouted and slammed the door behind him.

When the sharp clicking of the soldier's iron-studded boots on the cobbled street had faded away, Krysia looked around her. She was in a chilly cavernous room. At the far end three young soldiers flung a man across a wooden stool and began flogging his bare back. They beat him so hard that they grunted with each blow while he let out hollow moans that made her bite the inside of her cheek and stare fixedly at her shoes. She didn't want to see the blood trickling down his mushy back or hear the sound of their fists on his bones. 'Own up, Jewish scum! Tell the truth, *Schweinhund!*' they kept yelling.

Twisting her handkerchief around her numbed fingers, Krysia knew that they wanted him to admit that he was Jewish so that they could kill him. The prisoner didn't own up, and the beating continued. When he lay as limp as a rag doll, they tossed him into another room. She pressed her hand against her mouth. 'Now it's my turn,' she thought, longing for her mother to burst in and protect her. 'Now they're going to start on me.' She jumped when a door banged behind her, but it was only the guards going outside to get some air, puffing and panting from their exertion.

What would they do to her when they returned? Would she ever see her mother and little brother again, or the father she idolised? At the thought of her father, the handsomest, kindest person in the whole world, tears rolled down Krysia's pale cheeks. 'Be brave, I'll be with you as soon as my papers are ready,' Zygmunt had told her only hours ago, giving her one last hug.

She had believed him then, but now it seemed like a fairy tale. She thought of his kind face, so unlike her mother's critical glances which pierced her like hooks. Whenever she was upset, Father took his small mouth organ out of his pocket and played jolly tunes to cheer her up. If only he was here now.

The sound of guttural voices outside made Krysia glance nervously towards the door, but the door stayed shut. Her shoulders sagged. Thinking back over the past few years, it seemed as if someone was playing a deadly game with her, waiting just long enough till she felt safe, only to hunt her down again. Why did God allow that to happen? She hadn't done anything really bad, except to wish sometimes that her little brother had never been born. What was going to happen to her now? She was exhausted and wanted to sink down onto the floor, but remembering the soldier's warning, she shifted from foot to foot. Her legs felt like lead. She wanted to be brave but knew she wasn't. It would almost be a relief when the soldier came back, although the thought of what would happen next made her throat close up so that she could hardly swallow. How long were they going to keep her here? She wondered whether her mother and brother were still in the waiting room. What if the train arrived and they got on? How would she ever find them again? Her mother wouldn't just sit around, she'd know what to do.

Her mind drifted back to their life in Lwow. She remembered when her father's Russian boss in Lwow had urged him to leave the city. 'The Germans are coming. We're pulling out tomorrow,' he said. 'You're a Jew, you shouldn't stay. Come with us. We'll give you a truck, you'll be our driver. You can bring your family to Russia.'

Zygmunt thought it was a good idea. 'We should listen to him, Anechka,' he said. 'Hitler won't rest till he's killed every Jew in Europe.' But Andzia didn't want to hear about going to Russia. 'The Russians are savages. How can you suggest living among such primitive people? You must be mad!' Krysia's heart sank when she heard them quarrel. Her father's patient reasoning had no chance against her mother's vicious tongue. 'Go on, then, run away to Russia with your cronies,' she taunted him, adding, 'Go, but I'm not going with you.'

Andzia had got her way, but it wasn't long before she'd found out that the Russians hadn't exaggerated the cruelty of the Nazi regime. The terrifying screams of Jewish neighbours dragged out of their homes, loaded onto waiting trucks and later shot in nearby woods were testament to that.

In the midst of the horrors taking place around them, and the daily risk of deportation and death, Krysia had become ill. In her fevered state, bombs exploded, the earth shook, soldiers pointed rifles at her head, and demons leapt around her bed. The doctor said that only a blood transfusion could save her, but she had a rare blood group that was incompatible with either of her parents'. The chance of finding someone whose blood was compatible, and who would be willing to donate blood at a time when people were dying of hunger and needed all their strength, seemed very remote.

As Krysia's temperature rose and she lapsed into unconsciousness, they almost lost hope. There were no medicines, and hospitals were forbidden to admit Jewish patients. Andzia and Zygmunt were hovering around her bed, watching for any sign of life, when there was a knock on the door. In the entrance stood a young woman they'd never seen before. 'I've heard that you have a sick child in here,' she said. 'I've come to give her my blood.'

She had a round smiling face and wavy brown hair that cascaded onto her shoulders. While Andzia and Zygmunt stared at this apparition, hardly able to believe their ears, the doctor warned the young woman of the risks. In reply, the lovely stranger waved an impatient hand. 'Doctor, please stop wasting time, there's a dying child in there,' she said. 'Let's get on with it.'

Andzia and Zygmunt held their breath while the doctor took a drop of blood for analysis to see if her blood matched Krysia's. His shining eyes told them that they'd been granted the miracle they hadn't dared to hope for. The woman who had materialised out of thin air had the same rare blood group as their dying daughter.

When Krysia drifted out of her unconscious state and opened her heavy eyelids, she saw that she was connected by thin rubber tubes to a young woman she didn't know. They were linked by a slender thread of vermilion coursing between them. As she grew stronger, the doctor was jubilant. 'This is a child who came back from the other world,' he kept saying. On the eve of the annihilation of millions, everyone rejoiced at the survival of one little girl. But when Krysia had recovered, they discovered that the mysterious stranger had vanished as suddenly as she had appeared. 'I can still see her before me,' says my cousin Krysia fifty years later. 'She was about twenty-five, medium height, quite plump, with a lovely face and long wavy hair. To my everlasting regret, I can't remember her name.'

Now, trembling at Gestapo headquarters, Krysia wished fervently that some guardian angel would come to her rescue once again. Looking back, it seemed as if over the past year she'd lurched from one terrifying incident to another. After she'd recovered from her illness, there had been that terrifying incident with the Ukrainian guards. Her father had gone into hiding that day, and her mother had gone with him because the Germans were scouring every corner looking for Jewish men and women. 'You stay here and look after Fredzio. Don't let anyone in,' her mother had said.

Before Krysia had time to read Fredzio his favourite story, someone had banged on the door and a man's voice had yelled, 'Open up!' Krysia put her finger to her lips, took her little brother's hand and together they crept behind the door. The shouts and curses grew louder, then suddenly the door was flung open and two Ukrainian guards burst in, sinister in their navy uniforms with the yellow and blue circle. As the terrified children watched, one of the guards said, 'I know there's a gun in here somewhere.' He rummaged through their bedding and even poked his arm inside the tiled stove. They were about to leave when one of them paused on the doorstep and turned round to have another look. In that instant he lunged towards the table with a triumphant shout. He'd finally found what he was seeking. Lying under the table was a revolver. Krysia held her breath as she clung to her little brother. The guard pounced on the weapon, examined it and, a moment later, with a look of murderous rage on his face, hurled it across the room. It was one of Fredzio's toys. Now the guards would kill them both out of spite. But the men stomped out, slamming the door so hard that it almost fell off its hinges.

Not long after this they'd gone to live inside the ghetto, where there'd been that business with the Menashes. They were friends of her parents, a stiff couple with white faces and tight, unsmiling lips, who'd arrived breathless one morning and kept looking at the door. 'The Gestapo! They've just ransacked our flat! Oh my God, what are we going to do now?' Mrs Menashe lamented, her little letterbox mouth stretched into a straight line. 'Our documents and passports are still inside. Without them we're done for, but if we go back, we'll be caught.' Suddenly everyone was looking at Krysia.

To this day Krysia still doesn't know why her mother allowed her to go out and retrieve the Menashes' valuables. Probably they thought that no-one would suspect a child with such an angelic face. She pulled on the gloves which her father had given her a few weeks before. At a time when it was a struggle to obtain food, flour or fat, these gloves represented princely indulgence. Nobody had ever seen such gloves. They were fur-lined, smooth as butter outside, a lovely honey brown, and they came almost up to her elbow.

Even now, sitting inside the Gestapo station in Lwow, expecting a terrible fate to befall her, Krysia still felt a pang of regret when she remembered those gloves. Thrilled with herself in her new gauntlets, she had crept into the Menashes' flat and started opening drawers, exactly where she'd been told to look for their passports. Engrossed in her search, she didn't hear the footsteps behind her, until someone grabbed her shoulder and she spun around to see a soldier in a long grey-green coat with shiny gold buttons and military emblems. Then she saw the death's head on his stiff cap and knew she was looking into the face of an SS officer.

Without letting go of her, the officer said something which

she didn't understand. Then, without any warning, he leaned towards her and pulled the precious gloves off her hands. Then he waved his arm. 'Go on, *raus*, get out of here, quick!' he ordered. Krysia had sobbed all the way home. She'd never have such gloves again.

Andzia had taken one look at her daughter's puffy eyes and mournful expression, pulled on her overcoat, taken Krysia's hand, and led her back towards the Menashes' flat. 'Have a good look around and show me who took your gloves,' she fumed. Outside the Menashes' building stood the familiar figure in his long grey-green coat. 'That's him!' Krysia pointed, triumph overcoming terror.

Andzia planted herself in front of the SS officer. 'I believe you have my daughter's gloves,' she said. 'Please give them back to her.'

Fixing her with a cool gaze, the German replied in a polite tone. 'Unfortunately, *Gnadige Frau*, I am not able to do as you wish. My superior officer has taken the gloves and I no longer have them on me.'

While he spoke, Krysia's eyes were glued to the bulging pocket of his overcoat, where a bit of soft brown fur peeped out. She wanted to shout, 'Those are my gloves!' She longed to reach forward and pull them out, but Andzia was tugging at her sleeve. The officer was surveying them with narrowed eyes and her legs had begun trembling. Trying to appear calm, they walked away, trying not to quicken their step until they were out of sight. That's when it had hit them that they'd risked their lives for a pair of gloves.

Life inside the ghetto became tougher all the time. Krysia heard that in some houses so many people were crammed into one room that they didn't have enough space to lie down at night. Almost every day the Germans rounded up thousands of people and drove them away in covered trucks. Someone who managed to escape came back and told them that there was a place called Belzec where thousands of people were gassed in special chambers and then incinerated. No-one could believe him. Even now, with everything they had seen and suffered, people still refused to believe that the Nazis had designed a blueprint for genocide on a scale never seen before in the history of the world.

As Krysia's father had worked for a German car repair firm, he'd earned a little money and sometimes when he travelled on business to nearby villages, he occasionally managed to obtain an onion or some grain. Like that horrible millet flour which reminded Krysia of mud and tasted almost as bad. With her typical resourcefulness, Andzia had made a concoction by browning the flour on a pan then pouring water over it till it plopped and became like glue. Krysia hated the gooey stuff with its strange musty taste but there was little else to eat. Andzia had turned some of her flour into pancakes which she arranged appetisingly on a metal tray and sold for a few coins.

At least they hadn't been dying of hunger like some of the people with huge staring eyes and distended bellies who tottered around and dropped onto the street, too weak to move.

Not long before they'd decided to leave Lwow, there had been a rumour that the Nazis were going to hunt down and kill every Jewish child still alive. No hiding place in the ghetto would be safe. Krysia saw anxiety carved into her parents' faces. Where could they hide the children? Zygmunt's German boss came to the rescue. While the streets of the ghetto resounded with the despairing screams of mothers whose children were being torn out of their arms, and as lines of terrified boys and girls were herded at gunpoint and hurled into waiting trucks like slabs of meat, Krysia and Fredzio spent the entire day shivering in the trench where the mechanics stood when they repaired car chassis.

It didn't occur to the Nazis to search for Jewish children in a German workshop.

In the past there had always been some way of averting disaster, but alone in this Gestapo station, Krysia racked her brains in vain for some way out. If she tried to escape, the only place she could go was the railway waiting room, but they'd find her there and probably kill her mother and brother too. This was like the nightmares she'd had during her illness when demons had danced all around her, wanting her dead.

Death had been on everyone's mind for the past weeks. 'They're about to liquidate the ghetto,' she'd heard Uncle Henek tell her mother in a sombre voice. 'Time's running out. You must get Aryan papers, Andzia. Another week or two and there won't be a single Jew left alive in Lwow. Don't put it off any longer,' he'd urged in his quiet, forceful way.

After Andzia had obtained false papers, Krysia had overheard her father saying, 'Aryan papers will be enough for you, but a man has to have army papers and work cards as well. I'll get all the documents and join you later, but you've got to get the children out of here now. There's not a moment to lose.' Remembering how sad she'd felt saying goodbye to her beloved father, Krysia's eyes now filled with tears. Would she ever see him again?

She jumped with fright when the door opened and a German soldier with a triangular face entered the room. 'What are you doing here?' he demanded, seeing the girl. Her heart hammered under her blue knitted dress.

'I don't know,' she whispered.

'Are you Jewish?' he asked. She shook her head.

'Is your mother Jewish?' he asked. Again she shook her head.

'You'd better not lie to me,' he snapped. Then he leaned towards her and spoke in a softer tone. 'But if you tell the truth I won't hurt you.' Instinct warned her not to fall for this.

'Honestly, I'm Catholic,' she insisted.

'How come?'

'Because I was born that way,' she retorted, fiddling with her chain.

Peering at the cross around her neck, he asked, 'So how come you've got a brand new cross?'

'I've had it for years,' she argued, and thought in panic, Don't let him ask me to recite Our Father, because I'll get it mixed up and then he'll know I'm not Catholic.

Just then another German entered, and the two men spoke together, pointing at her and shrugging. No-one seemed to know why she was there. Finally the one with the angular face walked back to her. 'Go on, get out of here, I don't want to see you again. *Los!* Quick!'

Krysia raced back to the waiting room where her mother sat, a stricken look on her face. She seemed to have aged ten years in the past thirty minutes. She looked at Krysia and closed her eyes, unable to speak.

Finally their wait was over. The platform vibrated, a whistle shrilled, and behind thick funnels of black smoke and squealing pistons a pug-nosed train rumbled into the station. As Andzia hauled her bundles over her shoulder and lifted Fredzio into the carriage, she caught the eye of the soldier who'd grabbed him in the waiting room. He was looking at her with a mocking smile. 'Okay,' he seemed to be saying, 'this time you win. But next time . . .'

Inside the grimy compartment, Andzia wiped the worn seat so that their clothes wouldn't be smeared with soot. Exhausted, Krysia sank down and listened to the sound of the train. Unlike the trains she'd heard before the war, which went 'clackety-clack', this one made a sound that sent shivers down her spine. 'Watch out!' it seemed to be saying. 'Watch out!'

CHAPTER 20

Bitter winds had blown that March in 1942 when the Nazis had ordered all the Jews of Lwow to abandon their homes and move into a small area of town set aside for them near the railway line. My father had no illusions as to why they planned to squash the remaining Jewish population into an area so tiny that, in some cases, several families had to live in one room. People were only allowed to bring what they could carry or fit into a pram, and often even those few belongings were wrenched from them along the way.

'The Germans didn't care where people would go or what they would eat,' he wrote in his memoirs. 'In their opinion, Jews were only temporary citizens of this vale of tears.'

My father had managed to obtain permission for us to stay where we were in Lwow for the time being, but when the Germans began hunting down Jewish children with relentless savagery, he realised that we had to escape as soon as possible. The problem of where to go preoccupied him day and night. It was as hard for a Jew to find a hiding place in Poland in 1942 as for a deer to hide from a pack of wolves on a treeless plain. Our only hope of survival was to pose as Catholics, and while he was figuring out where we could possibly go without arousing suspicion, he arranged for my mother and me to travel to a small town near Krakow and wait there until he let us know where to join him.

My mother never spoke to me about her last days in Lwow, or about parting with her family. Her mother Toni, along with Hania and her family, had left for a nearby village where Hania's husband Dolek had found someone prepared to hide them in return for money. I wonder whether my mother had a premonition as she kissed them goodbye that she would never see any of them again. After the war all my mother was ever able to discover was that her mother, Hania, Dolek and their baby had all been killed in that village, after being turned in to the Germans by one of the villagers.

Several days after our departure, my father obtained false papers stating that he was Henryk Boguslawski, a Catholic dentist. In an attempt to alter his appearance, he'd cut his hair very short, parted it on the side and grown a clipped military moustache. For his ID photograph, instead of his usual affable expression, he'd assumed a cold, hard look.

Now that his new papers were ready, he needed to register with the Dental Board as all dentists were required to do. The only dentists exempt from this regulation were Jews, who had no right to practise dentistry or any other profession. Henek knew that he couldn't register in a false name in Lwow where he was known, so he decided to do so in Warsaw where nobody knew him.

The train to Warsaw was so crowded that there was only enough room to stand on one leg at a time. The train spent more time standing between stations than moving because the line was being used by army trains jammed full of German troops on their way to the Russian front. During the interminable stops, Henek tried to cheer himself up by thinking that even though the trains stood still, time was still moving on and every minute brought him closer to the end of the war. For a Jew to take off the armband and live on the Aryan side would be difficult and risky. He'd have to watch every single word for fear of giving himself away. But there was no choice. Staying in Lwow meant certain death and, no matter what happened, Danusia must survive.

He'd have to watch himself in Warsaw, too, look self-assured and walk purposefully to avoid the extortionists who hung around the railway station. These hyenas had a sixth sense for detecting Jews, whom they blackmailed and then turned over to the police. After what he'd gone through in Lwow, he wasn't afraid of dying, but he'd heard that when the Germans got their hands on a Jew with Aryan papers, they tortured him until he betrayed other members of his family. Outside the train window the countryside shimmered and farmhouse roofs poked up above fields of pale green corn. It looked so normal. Henek sighed. If it wasn't for Danusia, he wasn't sure whether he'd have the strength to go through with this dangerous masquerade.

As the temperature soared inside the stuffy compartment, and a musky odour of sweat drifted in the torpid air, Henek mulled over another problem. Where could he stay in Warsaw while registering? He'd cut out the address of a boarding house from the newspaper, but boarding houses were dangerous because Germans searched them for new arrivals.

Much later, when his legs felt like lead and his feet were numb, the compartment began to empty. Sinking into a seat, he almost laughed at the absurd relief of finally being able to sit down. At that moment he caught the sympathetic eye of the ruddy-complexioned woman sitting next to him. After they'd exchanged pleasantries and commiserations about the length of the journey and the privations of the war, Henek asked the woman whether she knew of a private home in Warsaw where he could spend one or two nights. She looked at him with a steady gaze for a moment and gave him an address. After they'd chatted for a while, he asked her name, realising that in these uncertain times she may not be willing to give it. But after the briefest hesitation she said, 'Tell them that Pani Kotowiczowa sent you.' Henek was overjoyed. Now he had a place to go and a personal recommendation as well.

When he rang the bell, a man came to the door. 'I ran into Pani Kotowiczowa recently and she thought you might let me stay for a few days,' Henek said, trying to give the impression that he knew her quite well.

The man stared at him. 'Who did you say sent you?' While he repeated the woman's name, my father felt uneasy. Something was wrong. The man's manner was guarded and he was looking at him with mistrust.

'Why didn't you register in Lwow?' the man wanted to know.

On impulse my father blurted, 'Because I don't like Ukrainians.' He must have struck the right chord because immediately the atmosphere changed and he was invited inside.

'Please sit down, I'll be back in a minute,' the man said. Again Henek felt anxious. Perhaps the man had gone for the police and he should run away while there was still time. On the other hand, if the man had alerted someone to keep an eye on him, bolting would look suspicious. He decided to sit it out.

When the man returned, he was accompanied by a woman who was also looking at him strangely. 'I'd like to introduce you to the real Pani Kotowiczowa,' he said, watching my father closely. Henek was confused, but when he described the woman on the train, the two exchanged knowing glances. It was obvious that they knew who she was. Suddenly he understood. The woman on the train had wanted to help him but she hadn't been prepared to give her real name or take any responsibility for him. She was leaving it up to her friends to make that decision themselves.

To his surprise, the man, who my father later learned was called Mr Warda, and the real Mrs Kotowiczowa burst out laughing. 'Our friend played a trick on you!' As my father laughed with them he felt a friendly complicity growing between them, as though they'd all been the victims of a practical joke. Mr Warda agreed to let him stay for a few days in his tiny flat and the circumstances of their meeting became a joke he shared with all his friends.

Mr Warda was the town hall caretaker but he was also engaged in selling food illicitly to Jews walled inside the Warsaw ghetto. It was a lucrative trade because those starving Jews who still had anything to barter were prepared to trade a fur coat for a loaf of bread, while those who had nothing slowly died of hunger along with their children. No-one had the strength to bury those who died of starvation, disease or just froze to death in the ghetto streets. My father avoided discussions about the plight of the Jews with his landlord, in case his outrage gave him away.

Next day, inside the large high-ceilinged offices of the Dental Board, my father saw the registrar writing at his desk. With a shock Henek realised that he knew him. Before the war, when my father had been on the executive of the Krakow Dental Board, Mr Laczynski had been the president, and they used to meet frequently at board meetings. Here he was coming to register as Boguslawski, a Catholic dentist from Lwow, and any moment Mr Laczynski would look up and recognise him as Baldinger, the Jewish dentist from Krakow.

Fortunately Mr Laczynski was concentrating on filling in a form and still hadn't looked up. Keeping his head down and muffling his voice, Henek pretended that he'd come to see the secretary. At this moment the registrar glanced up for the first time. Mumbling something about returning later, Henek turned and quickly left the office, leaving his application on the secretary's desk.

While limping down the corridor, he glanced in through

the registrar's window and saw Mr Laczynski frowning into the distance, his elbow propped up against his cheek, as if racking his brains trying to remember something. My father had no doubt that sooner or later he'd realise why his face was familiar, and he hoped that he wouldn't regain his memory too soon. Perhaps Mr Laczynski was a decent man, but in a world where neighbours and acquaintances had become betrayers, you couldn't trust anyone.

The following day, when Henek returned to collect his registration card from the secretary, he was careful to keep out of Mr Laczynski's way. Leaving the Dental Board with his document, he was so jubilant that he bought a loaf of rye bread and a ring of country smoked sausage on the way home. Mr Warda was expecting a visitor, and the three of them would have a feast to celebrate his success.

Mr Warda's friend Mr Bultowicz talked in the phlegmatic unhurried way of country folk, but when Henek said that he was looking for a quiet little place to practise dentistry, the visitor sat forward. 'That's a coincidence. My village needs a dentist. Why don't you go there?'

Although he'd never heard of Piszczac, Henek's heart started beating faster. Arriving in a remote village as the new dentist would reduce the suspicion if one of the villagers had recommended him. According to Mr Bultowicz, this was a remote hamlet close to the Russian border, so it was unlikely that Henek would come across anyone who knew him. Mulling it over during the night on the divan bed, my father decided that this was a heaven-sent opportunity. Piszczac would be perfect.

The wooden cart which jolted my father over the rutted country road from Biala Podlaska to Piszczac passed roadside shrines decorated with garlands of poppies, cornflowers and asters. He knew that Polish villagers were fervently religious and tried not to dwell on the problems of trying to pass himself off as a Catholic. Under a blazing July sun, sunflowers wilted in the potato fields, and in the orchards the branches of the fruit trees bent under the weight of apples, peaches and cherries. What fun the local boys must have running in the fields and raiding these orchards, Henek thought. Lost in the rural beauty of the scene he almost forgot his own predicament for a while.

The rumbling wooden wheels of the cart slowed down as they came to a few small houses where straggly tomatoes hung off the vines and chickens scratched in the dirt. 'Piszczac!' the driver said, waving a callused hand. My father knocked on the door of the Bultowicz house with some trepidation, but Mr Bultowicz had already told his family about the dentist's arrival and he was invited in at once.

Mrs Bultowicz's sister and her husband poured Henek a glass of vodka and, warmed by the spirits and their hospitality, he began to relax. They were having a pleasant conversation about life in Piszczac and the state of the war when the husband leaned across the table, pointing a bony finger. 'You can say whatever you like about the Germans,' he said in a confidential voice, 'but I reckon we should build Hitler a monument in gratitude for freeing Poland from the Jews.' My father's fingers gripped the glass tightly as he drained his vodka with what he hoped was an impassive expression. He had to remember that he was Henryk Boguslawski, a Polish Catholic, and had to steel himself to hearing such views.

The next day, when Henek called at the municipal office to see about being allocated a house, the town clerk pumped the new dentist's hand enthusiastically. 'Now we won't have to go all the way to Biala Podlaska every time we have a toothache!' he laughed and wrote a requisition on a piece of paper. 'Take this to the Judenrat and they'll find you a house.'

Henek pretended to look puzzled. 'Where can I find this Mr Judenrat?' he asked innocently. He knew only too well that in every town the Germans had set up a Jewish organisation forced to liaise between the Jewish community and themselves, to confiscate Jewish money, valuables and belongings, and ultimately to submit lists of Jews for deportation and death. Although initially many Judenrat members had believed that their intervention would save lives, my father felt that in fact they made the Nazis' task much easier. Although some members of the Judenrat committed suicide rather than cause the death of fellow Jews, many remained ensnared in the trap of collaboration, hoping to save themselves and their families. But nobody wins a deal with the devil, and after all the Jews had been deported or killed, the Judenrat members were killed as well.

On his way to the Judenrat office, horse-drawn carts heaped with newly cut hay rumbled past and farmers touched their battered caps in greeting. '*Szczesc Boze*! God bless you!' In front of their wooden cottages, women scattered seeds from their apron pockets for the chickens and staked up their tomatoes.

The President of the Judenrat gave a deep sigh when he read the town clerk's note, then asked my father to accompany him to a huddle of dwellings behind the market square where sad faces peered out of cracked windowpanes. The Jews had been thrown out of their homes and forced to live in a tiny area behind the marketplace. 'We're so short of room that we've already had to push several families into one house, and each hut is crowded to bursting point. But we'll cram more people in to find you a place to live,' his companion said grimly.

My father felt increasingly uncomfortable. 'I won't take a house at someone else's expense,' he said. The head of the Judenrat glanced at him with obvious surprise, and my father wondered whether he'd guessed the truth or just thought that he'd encountered an unusually decent Pole.

Still shaken from his meeting with the man from the Judenrat, Henek was crossing the marketplace when a young woman with a Jewish armband came up to him and said, 'You're the new dentist, aren't you? You remind me of a dentist I knew in Krakow.' With a dry mouth and the most innocent smile he could muster, Henek told her that she was mistaken. 'My name is Boguslawski and I'm actually from Warsaw,' he said and quickly walked away. To be seen talking with a Jewess in a public place would immediately arouse suspicion, and he hoped that no-one had overheard.

Back at the town clerk's office he explained that the accommodation offered by the President of the Judenrat wasn't suitable. After a moment's thought, the town clerk said, 'I'll ask Mrs Bogdanowa if she'll rent out part of her house. Things have been hard for her ever since the Germans deported her husband to Buchenwald, and she might be glad of some extra money.'

In the doorway of a gabled farmhouse by the Chotylow crossroads stood a kindly woman in her thirties whose plump body was covered in a faded shift. Showing him around, Mrs Bogdanowa explained that she and her ten-year-old daughter Zosia were the only ones at home, as her older daughter Anna was away at school at Biala Podlaska, so there was plenty of room for him and his wife and child, provided that Mrs Boguslawska wouldn't mind sharing the kitchen with her.

'We get water from the well outside,' she explained as he followed her into the yard to a well located in front of a woodshed and outdoor toilet. 'My poor husband built this house with his own hands only ten years ago,' she sighed. As he looked into her honest face, Henek felt instant sympathy for this hard-working woman and felt safe in the cosy atmosphere of her spotless house. The downstairs area was spacious, and it would only take a folding screen to separate it into a surgery and living quarters.

Now that accommodation was organised, Henek suddenly felt overwhelmed by the risks he was taking and remembered the woman who had approached him in the square. He'd assumed that no-one would recognise him here but he'd obviously been mistaken. Tomorrow someone else might recognise him. The villager's comment about thanking Hitler for getting rid of the Jews kept running around in his head. How was he going to pass as a Catholic when he'd never been inside a church before and had no idea what to do? How was he going to get Bronia and Danusia to Piszczac? He had very little money, how was he going to buy the dental equipment he needed? Even the thought of a new dental chair seemed too much to cope with. Suddenly a feeling of such total exhaustion swept over him that he fell onto the bed as if drugged. He lay on the bed incapable of formulating his thoughts or taking any action. And this was only the first day.

Three days later, when he felt stronger, he made inquiries about a dental chair and headed for the Jewish part of town where he'd heard there was one for sale. Inside a pitifully bare room lived an old man who showed him an old office chair with a square metal sheet fixed to the back and a piece of wood as a headrest. His son, who'd been a barber, had converted it for his clients, but the son had been taken away and the chair was all the old man had left to sell. Saddened by his plight, my father bought the chair.

Henek's first big test came on Sunday. If he was to pass as a Catholic, he'd have to go to church like the other villagers, but he had no idea how services were conducted or how worshippers behaved. So when his Warsaw acquaintance, Mr Bultowicz, arrived unexpectedly at his house, Henek breathed a sigh of relief. Now he'd have someone to go with, and see how things should be done. 'Are you going to church tomorrow?' he asked, and immediately flushed to the roots of his greying hair as he realised his mistake. The villagers didn't talk of going to church but of going to Mass.

Next morning, as he walked along the wide dirt road beside Mr Bultowicz, he noticed someone watching him from across the road. First he saw the armband, and then he looked at the face and almost stopped walking. It was his cousin Berta, his Aunt Johevet's eldest daughter. It was agonising not to be able to speak to her, but he couldn't take the risk. Berta understood his situation. Without saying a word or trying to approach him, she just looked at him with an expression he never forgot. Affection and hope for him shone from her eyes. He never saw her again.

In the vestibule of the small white church on the rise beyond the square, Henek stepped aside to let Mr Bultowicz enter first so that he could follow his lead. My father described this incident so vividly that I almost feel as though I was there that morning and watched the whole scene. Being a perfect gentleman, Mr Bultowicz also stepped aside, and they both stood there, like characters in some absurd slapstick comedy, each stepping back and urging the other to go first. Finally, in desperation, my father said, 'Please go first, Mr Bultowicz; after all, you know how they do things here.' His companion gave him an uncomprehending look. 'What's there to know?' he shrugged. 'A church is a church.' Henek kicked himself for his stupid comment. No Catholic would have said such a thing. But sitting on the wooden pew beside him, Mr Bultowicz gave no indication that anything was amiss.

Within a few days Henek was ready to hang out his shingle. He'd nailed the barber chair to a soap box so that he wouldn't have to bend down while he worked, had found a bucket as a spittoon and a kitchen cupboard to house his instruments. His only conventional equipment was a foot-operated drill sent from Warsaw.

So when he heard footsteps crunching on the dirt path leading up to the house, he hurried to the door, ready to greet his first patient, but the smile soon faded from his face. It was a German officer. Disaster already, my father thought, his face the colour of chalk.

But instead of arresting him, the German threw himself into the dental chair and demanded a gold crown. When Henek said that he didn't have any gold, his patient waved his hand dismissively. 'That's no problem,' he shrugged. 'I'll find some Jews and shoot them and knock the gold out of their teeth,' he said with as much emotion as if he was talking about going to the grocer to buy a loaf of bread.

Not trusting himself to speak, my father busied himself dabbing oil of cloves and mixing a dressing for the tooth. While he worked, he listened with growing incredulity as the German chatted about his civilian life. Only two years ago, this cold-blooded killer had been a jovial barman mixing cocktails for holiday-makers on a cruise ship. Henek was so deep in thought that he didn't notice that the village masseur had poked his head around the door.

'Dr Boguslawski, I've brought vodka so we can all have a drink,' he said flashing a servile smile at the officer in the chair. The masseur was one of the evacuees from Poznan and he considered himself more German than Polish. He'd even received a medal from the Kaiser in World War I.

'Ah, vodka, *zehr gut!*' the officer said.

Henek took out some glasses and a moment later the three

of them were sitting around the table drinking when they were interrupted by a peasant woman who'd come to see the dentist, but as soon as she laid eyes on the German, she fled. Henek was delighted that she'd witnessed this bizarre scene and hoped that she'd tell everyone about it. Drinking with a German officer would surely erase any suspicion that he was a Jew.

His next visitor was the district health officer who demanded to know why he hadn't registered yet and ordered him to do so immediately. My father had avoided registering for fear that once his registration form was circulated to Dental Boards around the country, one of his former colleagues would be bound to recognise him, but now he had no alternative. When he arrived at the office at Biala Podlaska, however, the health officer was away, and Henek got chatting with the talkative young clerk who complained that it was hard to obtain good country butter these days. When Henek returned a week later he brought the clerk a big pat of yellow butter wrapped in muslin. On this occasion too the boss was away, and he and the clerk chatted away like old friends. Suddenly the clerk changed the subject. 'You know, the district officer wants you out of here. I heard him say that Boguslawski has to get out of this district.' Henek's chest tightened. So the district officer already suspected that he was Jewish. But the clerk continued, 'Don't worry. He and I are both members of the A.K., only there I'm his boss, so nothing will happen to you!'

Piszczac was a hotbed of resistance activity with cells all over the region. Because of its location, trains carrying German soldiers travelling to the Russian front were frequently sabotaged by local activists. They were so successful in derailing carriages and delaying troop movements that a Gestapo unit was brought to Chotylow only three kilometres away, which made train travel especially dangerous in the area.

Now that he'd organised a house and started up in practice, my father arranged to meet my mother and me at Lukow Station and from there we were to travel to Piszczac together. Waiting on the platform, he consulted his watch for the tenth time in as many minutes. Not long now. Four minutes to go. Suddenly there was a commotion. Truck motors roared, tyres screeched, and helmeted German soldiers with rifles drawn were swarming over the station, blocking all the exits. With harsh voices and angry motions they began herding everyone in one direction. Craning forward, Henek could see the waiting trucks.

His heart was banging against his rib cage. Any moment now Bronia and the baby would arrive and he wouldn't be there to meet them. He could picture her scanning the platform, not knowing what to do or where to go. The thought of his wife and child being herded at riflepoint into a truck and deported to a concentration camp jolted him like an electric charge.

He never understood how he managed to hover back and forth between the waiting room and the platform and to evade the soldiers who were now rounding up the last of the people waiting for the train and pushing them into the trucks. Then the ground vibrated, a high-pitched whistle pierced the air, and Bronia's train was chugging into the station.

As her train was pulling into Lukow Station, Bronia's heart was thumping. She craned her blonde head anxiously up and down the platform but it was deserted and there was no sign of Henek. Just outside the station building, she could see German soldiers pushing people into trucks. She felt sick. They must have taken Henek away. What am I going to do now? she thought, holding Danusia tightly.

At the far end of the platform, Henek was hiding behind an untidy stack of wood and masonry when one of the soldiers spotted him, gestured threateningly with his rifle and yelled at him to go with the others. Suddenly Henek heard himself yelling back to the German, words he didn't know he knew, loud, commanding and guttural. He pointed at the oncoming train and kept uttering unintelligible words which were intended to sound like German. The German stared at him for a moment in disbelief and looked towards the exit. Everyone was already crammed into the trucks, and the rest of his unit was ready to leave. He turned on his heel and strode towards his companions.

As she climbed down from the train, my mother looked up and saw one lone figure standing on the platform. It was my father.

CHAPTER 21

Snowflakes glistened on the black cassock of the young priest perched on the edge of the cart which clattered towards his new parish. Squeezed in amongst villagers who had reluctantly made room for him, he watched the wheels spray slush from the dirt road. His boyish face looked unusually serious. He knew that he was supposed to be humble, but he couldn't help wishing that the bishop hadn't sent him to this distant village. As he flicked specks of mud off his soutane, he thought moodily about his unfortunate predecessors, both of whom had been arrested by the Gestapo and sent to concentration camps.

At thirty-two, Roman Soszynski was sharp, bright and ambitious. His dreams of a distinguished career didn't include a backward village of drunks, peasants and Ukrainians which had already proved unlucky for two priests. Bishop Sokolowski's warnings had done little to ease his apprehension. 'We live in dangerous times,' the prelate had cautioned. 'It's impossible to know which side people are on, so don't call on your parishioners. Let them seek you out. And don't get involved in resistance activities. Those villagers like their vodka, and while they're drunk they'll open their mouths too wide, as your predecessors found out to their misfortune.' The more he thought about this parish the more discouraged Father Soszynski felt. 'I feel like a naked man about to walk through a field of nettles,' he thought.

294

It didn't take long for the news to spread around the village that the new priest was friendly, young and good-looking, a big improvement on the others. The young girls blushed when they described Father Soszynski's twinkling blue eyes and bantering manner, while the young matrons cast their eyes down to conceal thoughts that were definitely not spiritual.

Henek listened with growing interest to village gossip about the new priest's sense of humour, keen intellect and passion for chess. Father Soszynski sounded like a kindred spirit. Ever since my father had arrived in Piszczac, the problem of making friends had been on his mind. Being newcomers made him and Bronia too vulnerable, because all new arrivals were suspected of being Jews until proved otherwise. He'd noticed that all the other newcomers in the village, who were Catholics, soon found mutual friends or church connections which made them accepted, but neither he nor Bronia could claim such links. He'd already asked the church organist to enter his certificate of baptism into the parish records. Although it was a false certificate, once it was entered it would appear genuine and he'd be able to make copies if he ever needed proof of baptism.

It was vital to make friends and become part of village life as fast as possible. The contact with the Bultowicz family had been helpful but it wasn't enough. They'd already befriended some of the other newcomers, most of whom had arrived here after being forcibly evacuated from Silesia when Germany incorporated their coal-rich region into the Third Reich. Amongst them was Jurek Zawadzki, a likeable young pharmacist, and his merry wife Danuta who soon became so attached to Bronia that she didn't go anywhere without her. Henek was delighted that the sociable Jurek played a good game of bridge, as did Dr Forycki, another refugee from Silesia, and the bridge game he organised became a weekly event which they all enjoyed.

A few weeks after the new priest had arrived, Henek was heading towards the post office. Fresh snow creaked under his shoes and flakes melted on his thickly quilted *fufajka*. He was about to post yet another letter to his sister Slawa. From what people said, he could see that it was important to receive regular mail from friends and relatives, but as most of his family were in hiding or on the run, regular correspondence was impossible and he and Bronia hardly ever received any letters.

Although he had to let his sister know how vital it was for them to receive frequent letters, he couldn't say so directly because it was rumoured that the postmistress read the mail. He hoped that this time Slawa would read between the lines and sense the urgency behind his words. He was about to walk into the post office when he heard a cart rattling along from the direction of Chotylow. The driver tugged the reins, the cart stopped, and out stepped the new parish priest, brushing the sleet off his black soutane. His heart beating at his own audacity, Henek hastened towards him and apologised for accosting him in the street. 'On the contrary, my dear Dr Boguslawski,' replied Father Soszynski with a disarming smile. 'I'm the one who should apologise for not having called on you, but I've been following the bishop's orders. What can we do, we live in such dangerous times!'

Heartened by the priest's friendly manner, Henek pressed on. 'This evening my wife and I have invited some friends over to our place. If Reverend Father would come and have a glass of tea with us, we'd be very honoured.'

Roman Soszynski looked with interest at this greying man whose neatly trimmed moustache and slight limp added to his air of distinction. He'd already heard about the new dentist from the organist, who'd reported the conversation about the baptism certificate with a look which had implied some doubt. But he liked Dr Boguslawski's sincerity and his direct gaze.

'I'll be delighted to come tonight and meet your good lady,' he replied.

When Henek told Bronia the good news, her forehead crinkled like a washboard. 'How do I know what to say to a priest?' she fretted.

'Don't worry about anything, leave the talking to me,' Henek said. 'Anyway, he seems very approachable.' As it turned out, the evening proceeded better than either of them could have hoped. Roman Soszynski was an entertaining raconteur with an easy flow of conversation, and although his observant gaze missed nothing, he knew how to put people at ease.

He loved to hear what was going on in the parish and laughed at jokes as loudly as anyone, but with his Jesuit training he also enjoyed arguing, debating and exchanging ideas. One of his regrets about coming to this sleepy hollow was that there would be little opportunity to sharpen his wits, so he was delighted that the dentist was a thinking man, well read and cultured. It was stimulating to find a parishioner with whom he could discuss the ballads of Mickiewicz, the epic canvases of Matejko, and the poems of Slowacki. Before leaving that evening, Father Soszynski told Henek that he'd welcome a game of chess in the presbytery. While they washed the glasses after their guests had gone home, Henek couldn't help smiling. 'Just imagine, the son of Reb Danil Baldinger playing chess with a priest!'

Year later, when my mother talks about her double life in Piszczac, I marvel how she managed to appear so cheerful and keep up a flow of light-hearted conversation when every single day situations arose which made her blood freeze with dread. 'Sometimes I wonder myself how I managed,' she tells me. 'There wasn't a day when I wasn't terrified in case I said the wrong thing and gave us away.'

While we talk about those terrifying days, sunlight dapples the ground beneath the bamboo palms in my courtyard and the scent of star jasmine fills my head. As she watches me spiking the lamb loin with garlic for our dinner, she comments, 'In Piszczac even cooking was risky. The first time that the Zawadzkis and Foryckis came to dinner, I served them chopped egg mixed with onion!' She puts her blonde head to one side and spreads her small hands in a gesture of wonder. 'It just didn't occur to me that this was a typically Jewish dish!' When she served roast goose rubbed all over with a garlic clove, the odour made one of her guests sniff suspiciously. 'Isn't that the way Jews prepare goose?' she asked. Bronia didn't hesitate. 'That's right,' she said. 'I learned to do it that way from one of my neighbours.'

Not a day passed without some traumatic incident which threatened to reveal their secret. One day their inoffensive landlady Mrs Bogdanowa held up something she'd found in the street. 'I've scrubbed it over and over but that funny writing won't come off. If I can clean it up, I'll use it as a doormat.' My father's face froze as he recognised the faded letters. It was part of the Torah scroll which must have been ripped up when the Germans had razed the village synagogue to the ground. With a voice that he tried to keep steady, he replied, 'I wouldn't bother. It's too flimsy for a mat.'

As if they didn't have enough to worry about, a few months later I became ill. In his memoirs, my father wrote, 'Poor little girl, she sat on the potty for hours, holding her stomach and moaning: "My tummy hurts, my tummy hurts." I'll never forget that sight. Her face was as red as a beetroot. All she could pass were tiny red drops which resembled blood cells under the microscope.'

Dr Forycki diagnosed gastroenteritis. 'It's raging through the whole district,' he said. 'Some of the children have already died.' The blood drained from Henek's face. 'There's an injection which might help, but we don't have any in Piszczac,' the doctor was saying. 'They might have some in Biala Podlaska.'

As soon as Dr Forycki left, Henek wired his brother Izio in Krakow and Mr Bultowicz in Warsaw, asking them to send the medicine immediately, even though he knew that it would take at least eight days to arrive and that I wouldn't last that long. While scrawling the messages with his neat, slanted writing, he noticed the postmistress glance up sharply when she saw the address on the telegram he was sending to Izio was Syrena.

She'd seen that strange name somewhere before, it was on the tip of her tongue. Then she remembered. Months ago, before they took all the Jews away, someone from that shop Syrena had sent parcels to one of the Jewish women who'd been transported here. So Syrena must be a Jewish firm! She gave Henek another searching look. She couldn't wait to share her suspicions with her family. Perhaps the new dentist wasn't what he claimed to be.

Although he was aware of her puzzled expression, Henek didn't have time to worry about the postmistress. He had to figure out how to get to Biala Podlaska which was twenty-six kilometres away. Travelling by train was too dangerous, but one of the villagers was setting out next morning by truck and agreed to drive him there and back.

It was late summer and clusters of tangerine rowan berries hung off the mountain ash trees which lined the dusty road. They passed wheat fields and barley fields, and orchard after orchard where large pink apples hung off the boughs. Brindle cows grazed beside sluggish streams, and every few minutes there was yet another wayside shrine garlanded with wreaths. Twenty-six kilometres had never seemed so long.

As soon as they arrived in the town centre, even before the driver had come to a complete stop, Henek jumped off the truck and rushed into the shop which displayed a mortar and pestle under the sign *Apteka*. Inside the pharmacy he blurted, 'I need to buy an injection for my daughter no matter how much it costs.' The woman in the white coat behind the counter raised her eyebrows so high that they almost touched her hairline. 'I wouldn't put it that way,' she admonished him, but in spite of the rebuke, he sensed some concern in her manner. She was warning him. Only a Jew would express himself that way.

The pharmacist was shaking her head. 'I don't have any of that medicine but there's another pharmacist in town, a Jewess. She's not allowed to work any more, but she might have some left. Otherwise, your only other hope is the hospital.'

The home of the Jewish pharmacist shocked Henek with its austerity. All they had left was a couple of old chairs and a crooked table. The woman was looking at him with frightened eyes. She wasn't allowed to sell medicine and was obviously afraid that he'd report her. Shaking her head, she quickly closed the door.

Beads of perspiration stood on his forehead. It was almost time to return to Piszczac but he still didn't have the medicine. He rushed to the hospital, cursing the stiff knee which slowed him down. 'My little daughter is terribly ill and our doctor said that without this injection she's going to die. She's only three years old. Could you let me have one phial? In a few days I'll be receiving some from Krakow and I'll let you have it as soon as it arrives,' he pleaded. After thinking it over, the hospital superintendent nodded. Tears of joy sprang to my father's eyes.

Henek heard the town hall clock striking noon as he rushed to the meeting place, clutching the precious medicine. He looked up and down the street, crossed the road, turned back and looked around again. No sign of the truck. There was no point waiting any longer, the driver hadn't waited for him. He'd have to catch the train after all.

The train wasn't leaving for several hours. Bronia would be frantic with worry, and Danusia would have to wait for her injection, but there was nothing he could do. Resigned, he bought a ticket and waited. Time seemed to stand still. He looked down so that the others in the waiting room wouldn't see the anxiety on his face. Finally it was five to three. Any minute now the train would arrive. Only one more hour and he'd be able to fetch Dr Forycki and give Danusia the life-saving medicine.

An unexpected noise made him look round. German boots were clattering along the platform and soldiers were ordering everyone to show their *Kennkarte*. Henek gripped his ID card tightly so that his hands wouldn't tremble, holding his breath while they scrutinised the photograph and stared at him with faces which seemed to be cast from steel. Then, without saying a word, they handed back his card and walked off.

Luckily the Germans were only looking for saboteurs. High-ranking German officers and troops often travelled along this line to the eastern front, and their train was about to pass. Relief at not being detained now turned to dismay as he realised what that inspection had meant. The train Henek was waiting for would be full of soldiers and wouldn't be picking up any passengers, and the next train wasn't due for another five hours. By the time he walked the three kilometres from Chotylow station to Piszczac, it would be too late to call Dr Forycki. Would Danusia be able to hold out until next morning?

As he sat in anguish in the waiting room, trying not to sigh or draw attention to himself in any way, he noticed that the others were all staring at him with such intent expressions that he had to look away. Perhaps it's because I'm a stranger, he thought. Or maybe they sense a Jew in their midst. To add to his apprehension, a Polish policeman in a navy uniform was coming straight towards him. He walked past all the others without even looking their way, but stopped in front of Henek and demanded to see his papers. Fortunately the light in the waiting room was dim, so no-one could see how white Henek's face was. The policeman checked his *Kennkarte* and walked on, but Henek couldn't even allow himself the luxury of breathing out in relief because all eyes were still fixed on him.

It was dark when he finally reached home. White-faced, the skin stretched taut over her cheekbones, Bronia sagged against him. 'I was sure that the Germans had caught you and I'd never see you again,' she gasped. He looked anxiously at the flushed, listless child lying in the iron bed. 'No change,' Bronia sighed.

They tossed in bed all night, unable to sleep. It was torture to have the drug yet have to wait till morning to fetch Dr Forycki, but they didn't dare disturb the doctor late at night. Early next morning, Henek rushed over to the doctor's house. As if by a miracle, within half an hour of receiving the injection, my temperature dropped and the stomach cramps ceased. My father wasn't surprised because he'd pinned all his hopes on this wonder drug but he was taken aback by Dr Forycki's comment. 'Dr Boguslawski, you have no idea how lucky you are, because that injection doesn't always work!'

In the meantime the postmistress hadn't wasted any time voicing her suspicions about the new dentist. Her mother added some observations of her own and, before long, rumours about the Boguslawskis were spreading through the village. Danuta Zawadzka told her friend Bronia with a cheery laugh, 'You'll never guess what our village is buzzing with today.

Some busybody at the post office has been saying that Danusia must be a Jewish child because she's got curly hair!' My mother made light of the rumour, and they both laughed, but there was no smile on Bronia's face when she reported it to my father.

Henek immediately called me to him. He sat me down on a chair and proceeded to brush my hair until not one wayward curl remained. Then he twisted the strands into tight little plaits. From that day on, this became our morning ritual. While I squirmed and wriggled, my father patiently straightened out my thick brown hair, brushed back the tendrils from my face, and braided them into tight plaits. Every single curl must be ironed out until not one suspicious kink remained. I had to look like a Polish Catholic girl.

He did this gently and lovingly, but with a child's sensitivity I must have sensed the desperation behind each stroke of the brush. I have a photograph of myself in Piszczac taking part in a church procession. I'm standing between two little girls, a tray of rose petals suspended around my neck. In spite of all my father's efforts, tendrils of soft hair have escaped from my plaits and form a soft aureole around my solemn face. My companions, on the other hand, have strands of almost white hair which hang straight, the way Polish hair should, and their giggling faces don't have a care in the world.

The fear that my curly hair was going to expose our Jewish identity and cause our death affected my father for many years to come. Long after the war was over, years after we'd arrived in Australia, when I was already fourteen, he still insisted that I keep my hair in plaits and refused to let me cut it. He was still terrified in case it looked too curly. I detested my old-fashioned plaits and decided to defy him and cut my hair, but while the hairdresser was snipping them off I sat on tenterhooks wondering if I was going to emerge with a mass of frizzy hair.

To my relief, and that of my father as well, I emerged with smooth, slightly wavy hair.

It's hard for me to grasp that in spite of all the traumas and the terror they suffered during this time, my parents were also leading an apparently normal social life. There were sleigh rides in the snow, walks in the woods, and the fun of picking earthy mushrooms and small dark blueberries which hid under flat wide leaves. While the men played bridge, my mother and Danuta Zawadzka became close friends and gossiped about the county secretary who was having an affair with the town clerk's wife. My mother was very fond of Danuta, but beneath the laughter and the confidences one niggling thought bothered her: would she still be her friend if she knew the truth?

Danuta had recently had a baby boy, Krzysztof, and the two women often talked about the trials and tribulations of child-rearing. One day Danuta came over and it was obvious that she had something on her mind. 'Bronia, I have something important to ask you,' she said. My mother's heart turned over. 'I'd like you to be Krzysztof's godmother.'

My mother was flattered because this was an honour that some of Danuta's other friends were longing for, but being a godmother meant taking on a religious responsibility and forming a lifelong relationship with the child. 'It was a dilemma. I had to lie in order to survive, but I couldn't deceive my friend,' my mother explains. 'The trouble was, I couldn't accept her offer but I couldn't tell her why. What reason could I give?' Finally Bronia figured out an excuse. Shaking her head regretfully, she told her friend, 'I'm terribly sorry but I can't accept because I bring bad luck. All the children I've been godmother to became sick.'

Henek's chess game with the priest became the highlight of the week for them both. Father Soszynski admired his opponent's strategies which always left him outmanoeuvred.

He thrived on the challenge and never lost hope of beating Henek one day. As they faced each other across the chess table at the start of a new game, the priest looked up at his opponent. 'Perhaps this time I'm going to win!' he chuckled.

While Henek was considering his move, Roman Soszynski sat forward with an expectant smile, waiting to see what the older man would do. There was an air of nobility about this man whose wit and impeccable manners the priest admired. Henek was an asset to Piszczac, no doubt about that. Father Soszynski had heard rumours about the Boguslawskis. Periodically someone raised a query about Bronia's origins. Someone said that she was a Jewess, others that she was a communist. And today someone had said something about Danusia, who was such a quiet, obedient little girl.

Before making his counter-move, the priest looked steadily at his opponent. 'At school today one of the children said that Danusia was Jewish,' he said casually. Henek's eyes were boring into his face. 'I told them it wasn't true,' Father Soszynski continued. 'I said I knew Danusia and that she couldn't be a Jewish child because she was so obedient and well brought up.' Henek breathed out again. Thank God. The comment about Danusia was a back-handed compliment, but he understood that the priest was letting him know that he was on his side.

Now Roman Soszynski swooped down on his queen's rook and his boyish face was beaming. 'Checkmate!' he cried.

A long shadow fell across the little girl tracing patterns in the dirt with a stick. After watching her for a few minutes, the stranger asked, 'What's your name, little girl?'

Without looking up, she replied, 'Danusia Boguslawska.'

'But what was your name before that?' he insisted.

Henek, who was standing by the open window, froze when he heard the last question. Instead of rushing outside and grabbing the child to prevent her from answering that insidious question, he was struck dumb and stood there helplessly awaiting her reply on which all their lives depended.

The child looked up, stick poised in her hand, and stared at the man's ingratiating smile. 'That's always been my name,' she said with a touch of impatience.

Henek breathed out in relief. This time there had been a reprieve, but what would happen next time? For the rest of the war, however long it lasted, their lives would hang in the balance of every single word they uttered.

Thinking back on this incident today, I don't know whether I'd simply forgotten our original name or whether I knew that it must never be mentioned. My mother's strained white face and my father's relentless patience as they repeated our new name over and over must have impressed me with their gravity. But whether it was my good memory or bad memory that saved our lives on that occasion, it's a revelation that our survival depended on me, as well as on my parents.

'Not long after we arrived in Piszczac, you said something that made my blood freeze,' my mother suddenly recalls while reminiscing about the war years. 'We'd just passed a Jewish woman in the street and you pointed at her armband and said loudly: "Look, Mummy! You used to wear one of those!" I nearly died!' We sit in silence looking at each other, balancing the horror of my innocent comment with the miracle that no-one had overheard it.

Several years ago in Sydney I attended a workshop based on reclaiming and healing the child within. During a guided meditation, I saw a little girl of about three or four crouching behind a door, watching me with eyes in which I sensed fear, apprehension and mistrust. This was a child who lived suspended between knowing and not knowing, who stifled feelings and suppressed reactions. Without understanding the significance of the situation, she knew that one wrong word from her would cause disaster, that there were secrets she must never tell because their lives depended on them.

For the first time in my life I came face to face with the child who still lives deep inside me.

CHAPTER 22

Four men sitting around a table wreathed in the smoke of a kerosine lamp scrutinised the cards fanned out in their hands. Realising that it was his turn to put down a card, one of the players sat forward. He seemed to be moving in slow motion as his hand hovered above the cards, seemed about to select one, then stopped in mid-air while he mulled over his choice for a few more minutes, and then moved tentatively towards another. The minutes ticked away. He closed his thumb and forefinger around a card but hesitated yet again. This time, however, the slim, tense man on his right sprang forward, plucked the card out of his astonished hand and rammed it down on the table with a thump. 'Wake up!' he shouted. 'Are you playing or dozing?'

Henek shot his brother a furious look. If Izio didn't curb his temper, he'd be the death of the whole family. Izio was known in the village by his Aryan name Jozek Orny, but a name wasn't enough to allay suspicion. Playing bridge every night with the phlegmatic Bultowicz brothers was excruciating for him too, but it was vital. He had to have a social network in the village so they wouldn't be regarded as outsiders. The brothers were good-natured men who arrived at ten every night after closing the shop in the market square which they'd taken over from the Jewish owners who'd been deported.

'Now, now, Mr Jozek,' one of them chided in his good-natured way, 'we mustn't get impatient! We don't have a train to catch, do we?' Beneath the mild words, Henek could sense disapproval. He'd always known that having his brother Izio with him in Piszczac was a terrible mistake. Ever since arriving in the village Henek had made an unremitting effort to blend in with locals, to speak in a more dispassionate way, to toss back glasses of vodka, and to behave like the others in church, but his brother's reckless behaviour was likely to undermine all his endeavours and put them in danger.

It was our second summer in Piszczac and my parents had just started to feel that they were becoming accepted as part of the community, when out of the blue a letter arrived from Izio saying that he was coming to join them. He'd just escaped from the Krakow ghetto by bribing a guard and had nowhere else to go. In the last months brutality in the ghetto had intensified, and during their lightning raids SS officers sank to new depths of cruelty as they set about their task of emptying the ghetto and deporting its inmates to Plaszow Concentration Camp.

Although the Germans kept insisting that they were only sending people to work camps, occasionally someone managed to escape and tell their gruesome story. They spoke of trains which sped through dark woods at night; of sealed waggons where hundreds of men, women and children were crammed for days in searing heat without food or water; of dead bodies which tumbled out when soldiers armed with rifles and savage dogs finally unhasped the doors; of the exhausted, emaciated people who'd survived the hellish journey only to be stripped naked, herded into bare cement rooms, gassed and shoved into ovens carefully designed to burn human bodies. They spoke about black smoke which poured out of tall chimneys day and night, and about the sweetish stench of burning flesh that hung in the air for miles around. They spoke of these things but nobody believed them.

Sometimes a card arrived in the ghetto, creased and grimy, dropped through the cracks of a cattle train and posted on by a farmer who found it fluttering among the daisies in his field. One day Izio received such a card. As he and I talk, the last rays of the harsh Californian sun drill through the window of his flat and I have to shout and repeat each question because his hearing aid is making a buzzing sound. What with that and his wife's pitiful condition, my uncle is maddened to distraction. His second wife Zosia slumps in her wheelchair like a rag doll, unable to speak or move, a dribble of saliva threading down her chin, her wasted legs agape but her eyes horribly alert.

'My poor Zosia used to be a dentist, she spoke six languages, now look at her!' Izio laments. 'How do you expect me to concentrate on your questions when I see her suffering like this?'

Eventually he calms down and returns to his story. 'Some time in 1942, while I was still in the Krakow ghetto, I received a tattered postcard.' I sit forward, anxious not to miss a single word. 'It said: "We are on a train bound for God knows where. Help us!" It was Karola's handwriting. The postmark was Belzec.' Too shocked to speak, I watch tears splashing down his furrowed cheeks. 'She wrote it in that cattle truck. Imagine it,' he shakes his head in wonder, 'she wrote to me while she was inside it, knowing what was about to happen to them. She threw it out of the train and some villager must have picked it up and posted it on.'

We sit in silence while the sun glares into his hot room. I think about that lovely, fun-loving young woman and her handsome adoring husband who both loved life so much yet had so little time to enjoy it. I recall my mother's words.

'Karola would have survived on false papers because she looked like one of Hitler's ideal Aryans with her tall slender figure and ash-blonde hair, but Stasiek refused to get false papers. He was too naive to believe that anyone would wish him harm, and poor Karola stayed with him.' When I ask Uncle Izio to show me Karola's postcard, he slumps in his chair. 'When I escaped from the ghetto, I didn't want the Germans to find anything incriminating on me, so I destroyed it. I shouldn't have done that. I should have kept it no matter what. I destroyed the last words that Karola ever wrote!'

When the last of the inmates of the Krakow ghetto were about to be deported to Plaszow, whose Commandant Amon Goeth used prisoners for target practice, Izio bribed a guard and escaped. As there was no place to hide in Krakow, he decided to come to Piszczac. 'When your father heard that I'd given Izio our address and that he was coming to stay with us, he could have killed me,' my mother recalls.

'How could you endanger us like that? How could you tell him where we were, when we agreed that nobody must know? He'll be the death of us!' Henek reproached her. Bronia bit her lip. She knew he was right, but she'd had no choice. 'Anyway, it's done now so there's no point in recriminations,' she said. 'Luckily Izio doesn't look anything like you so we don't have to say he's your brother.'

When Henek had calmed down, he figured out a way to prevent the villagers from becoming suspicious about Izio's sudden appearance. He advertised for a dental technician in the Warsaw newspaper so that when Izio arrived he could introduce him as his new technician. Izio was good with his hands and would soon learn the rudiments of dental work, but at the same time Henek would have to coach him how to behave so as not to attract attention.

But Bronia and Henek soon realised that no amount of

coaching would make Izio blend in with the locals. Although he'd changed his name to Jozef Orny, there was something about his cast of features and the melancholy expression in his fine dark eyes that looked Jewish. But his temperament was a bigger threat than his appearance. Hot tempered, impatient and argumentative, he didn't seem able to curb his tongue. Henek often warned him about the importance of sounding cool and understated, while my mother urged him to tone down the extravagant compliments he paid the village women whose hearts he set aflutter.

Now, glaring at his brother across the card table, Henek realised with a sense of foreboding that Izio seemed unable to grasp the danger to which his behaviour was exposing them. A few more outbursts like this and the villagers would soon know the truth.

Finally the interminable rubber of bridge was finished. It was past midnight when the Bultowicz brothers were draining the last of the vodka. 'We'll be seeing you at Mass on Sunday then, Mr Jozef,' they said.

'Not me!' Izio replied with a short laugh. 'I'm a believer but not a churchgoer.' Henek winced. He could envisage this bizarre comment making the rounds of the village, adding more fuel to the growing speculation about the newcomer.

They were still sitting around the table when a loud banging on the door made Henek start. When he opened up, he felt the colour draining away from his face and bent over, pretending to be searching for something on the floor so that the two hulking German police officers wouldn't see his terror. They strode inside, whips in hand, looked around, and when they spotted the cards they shouted, 'Where's the money?' After my father and his partners hurriedly explained that they were playing bridge, not poker, and there was no money involved, the Germans quietened down and turned to my father. They'd come to see him about some dental treatment.

That night, after everyone had left, Henek sat up for a long time, every fibre in his body throbbing and churning. We're walking on a gossamer tightrope flung across a deep abyss, he thought. How long can it be before it breaks? Anything would be better than living with this unremitting anxiety. Not a day passed without rumours about them, not a night passed without nightmares of Germans coming to take them away. Only that week a group of schoolchildren walking past their house had yelled, 'Jude! Jude!' Like all villages, Piszczac had its layabouts and drunkards who drank with the Gestapo officers in the taverns. They would denounce their own mothers for a bottle of vodka. How long will it be before they denounce us, he wondered.

In the cool moonlight that streamed into their room, Bronia saw her husband's furrowed brow and a steely glint shone in her eyes. 'They're not going to get us. We're going to survive. The war can't go on forever. The Germans aren't as invincible as they want us to believe.' For months now, illicit shortwave broadcasts from England had spoken of a general called Montgomery whose tanks had defeated Rommel's Afrika Korps at El Alamein. More recently, people whispered about the huge losses of Hitler's Sixth Army at Stalingrad. If those stories were true, how much longer could Hitler go on? All they had to do was keep going. One day the war would end.

Calmed by Bronia's optimism, Henek decided that the best way of dealing with the rumours would be to give a big party. At the same time it would be a good opportunity to widen their social circle. Poring over the guest list, they decided to include some new people and considered inviting the post-mistress as well, but since most of their friends didn't like her, they decided against it. It was a decision they were later to regret.

Vodka flowed freely, the sound of laughter and clinking glasses resounded through the house, and the guests devoured the herring canapes, jam doughnuts, *pierogi* filled with potato, and the cheese and poppy-seed cakes that my mother and Mrs Bogdanowa had spent several days preparing. Relaxed after a few glasses of vodka, Henek entertained the guests with his party piece, a mime of a bachelor trying to sew a button onto his shirt. His sharply observed movements came from personal experience, and he stretched his arm wide with an imaginary thread longer than his arm as he tangled the cotton, missed the holes, broke the cotton and then ended up staring in amazement at his hand. He'd sewn the button onto his finger instead! The guests laughed until tears rolled down their cheeks.

By now Henek had an admiring circle around him and, encouraged by the success of his mimic, he told one of his favourite stories. 'It happened at a party just like this,' he began. 'Marysia, the hostess, called her husband Wojtek out to the kitchen, and she was very upset. It was only midnight, the party was in full swing, but they'd run out of caviar to put on their canapes. Wojtek said, "Don't worry, there's some buckshot in the shed, we'll sprinkle it on the canapes. They're so drunk, they'll never know the difference." As you can see, they were both pretty sozzled as well, so she did what he said, and the guests caroused till dawn. Next morning, Marysia remembered what she'd done and panicked. Eating buckshot was dangerous, the guests might have dropped dead by now. With great trepidation she started ringing their friends. "Are you and Maciek all right?" she asked her neighbour. "We're fine," the woman replied. "Are you sure?" Marysia persisted. "Quite sure," said her friend, "but you know, something really strange happened this morning. When Maciek bent over to put on his slippers, he shot the cat!"' A roar of laughter exploded in the room.

'Ah, Dr Boguslawski, nobody tells jokes like you!' said Father Soszynski, his puckish face crinkled with laughter.

Despite the atmosphere of bonhomie, Henek noticed that some of the men had their heads close together and were whispering in low, intense voices, but whenever he approached them, they fell silent. He had the feeling that they were talking about him. One of the men, Stanislaw Lewicki, was the leader of the local cell of the underground. Although their activities were supposed to be secret, the villagers often discussed them amongst themselves but they never discussed them with Henek. They visited his home, drank his cherry vodka and laughed at his jokes, but they didn't trust him. No matter what he did, he was always the outsider.

As he circulated among his guests, offering them marinated mushrooms, herrings in sour cream and pickled cucumbers, Henek overheard Izio saying something scathing about Polish patriotism. 'Don't worry, we still have plenty of caviar! We don't have to serve any buckshot yet!' he quipped and tried to distract their attention with an anecdote about bottling cherry vodka. He'd have to speak to Izio yet again about his provocative remarks.

But before he had time to speak to him next morning, the first patient had already arrived. It was the postmistress. Bristling with indignation, she pointed at Izio who was sitting at his work table pretending to be making a crown. 'What is that man doing here?' she demanded in a tone sharp enough to shave the beard off a man's face. Henek pretended to take her question literally. 'Mr Jozek came from Warsaw to help me. We're lucky to have him, he's a first-class technician.' The woman didn't say any more about Izio but from her scowl my father could see that he hadn't heard the last of it. When she inquired about last night's party with a tight little smile, he understood why she was angry. Making an enemy of the most malicious gossip in town hadn't been a smart move.

Fifty years later, Uncle Izio still seems oblivious of the anxiety his presence caused my parents. His melancholy face brightens as he recalls life in the country, where he staked up tomato plants, planted cucumbers and brewed cherry vodka. He even learned to pickle pork. 'The peasants used to pay us with poultry, butter and cheese, but one day someone gave us half a pig. Naturally I had no idea how to pickle it but since my false papers said I was a farmer's son, I couldn't ask too many questions. So I asked my landlady, "How much saltpetre do you use?" and when she said one spoon, I replied, "So do I!"'

As he describes life in Piszczac, I close my eyes and once again breathe in the poignant scent of lilac which wafted in through the window on warm spring nights. In late summer, our house swirled with the spirituous almond smell of morello cherry vodka which my father and Uncle Izio used to brew. My mouth puckers at the memory of ducks roasting to crisp brown perfection, and of big pale pickled cucumbers stored in the cellar beside big wooden barrels of cabbage and small tart apples. I remember picking blueberries and mushrooms in the dewy woods.

Mushrooms grew abundantly in the woods around Piszczac and on damp autumn mornings the peasants filled their woven straw baskets and sold them in the marketplace. Bronia marinated them with bay leaves, fried them with eggs and thickened them with barley to make my favourite soup. Shortly after eating this soup one day, Izio blanched, staggered to a chair and clutched his belly. 'I'm going to die,' he groaned. They put off calling the doctor as long as possible, but when his cramps became so agonising that he couldn't straighten up, there was no choice.

My father held his breath while Dr Forycki bent over to prod his brother's abdomen. 'Pull up your shirt,' the doctor said. Henek and Bronia exchanged taut glances. Any second now the doctor would see that Izio had been circumcised. Izio managed to pull up his shirt without letting go of his trousers and Dr Forycki continued his examination without asking him to lower his trousers. 'It will pass,' he said. 'It's food poisoning from the mushrooms.' Izio never touched mushrooms again.

While my parents were trying to cope with the problems that Izio's presence created, my mother's sister Mania suddenly arrived on their doorstep. My father couldn't conceal his shock at seeing her there, and when my mother confessed that she'd given Mania their address, he stared at her as though she'd lost her mind. 'You might as well have placed an advertisement in the newspaper!' he shouted. But Bronia stood her ground. 'I had to tell her in case she was desperate for somewhere to go.'

Mania certainly was desperate when she arrived in Piszczac. She'd been blackmailed several times and everything she owned had gone in paying off extortionists. She had no money left and nowhere to go. Bronia, who had begun to look at people through the villagers' eyes, thought that Mania talked too much and was too sure of herself, and that the saucy tilt of her hat was a dead giveaway because most Jewish women pulled the brim down to the side *à la* Dietrich.

Aunty Mania used to love telling me about one incident that took place during her stay with us. Looking at me fondly with her lopsided smile, she said, 'I was supposed to be a friend of your mother's called Wanda Morawska. They warned me not to make too much fuss of you because we weren't supposed to be related, but after I'd been there for a few days I noticed you watching me with your big blue eyes. Then you came over and whispered in my ear, "Pani Wanda, can I call you Aunty?" '

Although I'd recognised her, I knew that I mustn't reveal that she was my aunty. Thinking about that four-year-old child, wary beyond her years, I can understand why for most of my life I've held my feelings inside, kept my thoughts to myself and been slow to trust others.

Mania didn't stay with us for very long. According to my mother, she left as soon as the villagers started gossiping that Mrs Morawska was Jewish. Before she left, my mother gave her most of our bed linen and a treasured gold bracelet she'd received from their mother, so that Mania would have something to sell.

Not long after her departure, Henek was bending over a patient, telling her an amusing anecdote from his student days, when he looked up to see Bronia's agitated face peering at him through the screen. Putting down the drill, he went over to her. 'Izio will have to leave Piszczac straightaway,' she gasped.

At the weekly market she'd run into Mrs Naimska, the agronomist's wife. 'People are saying that the gentleman staying with you has escaped from the Krakow ghetto!' she'd said. Fighting a wave of nausea, Bronia had retorted, 'What rubbish! Mr Orny is a Pole and comes from Warsaw. Anyway, as it happens, he isn't here any more, he left yesterday.'

Henek looked alarmed. 'But he's still here!'

'He has to leave while there's still time,' my mother whispered back. 'It's market day and they're all out shopping, so no-one will notice if he slips away to Chotylow and catches the train to Warsaw.' Henek returned to his patient who was waiting for the end of the anecdote, but my father continued drilling in silence.

CHAPTER 23

Clouds of steam almost hid the slender young woman with the hat turned down at a rakish angle as she clicked along the platform of Warsaw's Central Station, her slim hips swaying with a deliberately carefree rhythm. Chin tilted high, Mania Schwartz looked neither left nor right, avoiding the narrowed eyes of the men lounging against the wall. One thought pounded in her head. I must get to Misko before they catch him.

Misko had arrived in Warsaw a week earlier and, on his way to the tram, he had sensed that he was being followed. Turning around, he caught his breath as he looked into a face he knew. 'What are you doing here, Mr Schwartz?' It was the janitor from Lwow. His eyes slid down Misko's arm, lingered on the spot where the armband should have been, and stopped at his wrist. 'I like your watch!' he said. Without a word, Misko unclasped the watch and handed it over, but the man was still wheedling. 'I'm a bit short of cash at the moment, could you lend me some?' With only a few zlotys left, Misko had wired Mania for help.

After leaving Piszczac, Mania had moved to Krakow, but as her false papers described her as single, she was living on her own, and Misko had decided to try his luck in Warsaw by himself. When she received his desperate telegram, Mania was in turmoil as to how to help him. Desperate for cash, she went

319

through her few possessions. Picking out her suede ankle-strap shoes and some of Bronia's monogrammed bed linen, she headed for the pawnshop and was so relieved when the dealer handed her a wad of zlotys that she didn't even try to bargain with him. As the train clattered towards Warsaw, she wondered how she and Misko could possibly survive with so little money and nowhere to go.

As she quickened her step past the row of extortionists who staked out the station, she saw one of them tip the brim of his hat off his forehead, stub out his cigarette on the ground and blatantly start following her along the street. With him close on her heels, she didn't dare ask anyone directions to Nowy Swiat where Misko was staying, for fear of revealing that she was a stranger in town. As she stood at the tram stop, trying to look confident, the man was so close that she could smell the nicotine on his breath. With an insolent expression he looked her over from the tip of her little felt hat to her well-worn but stylish shoes. Suddenly he jabbed her with his elbow. 'Where are your manners?' she snapped. 'Can't you look where you're going? How dare you follow me!' Taken aback by her unexpected attack, he was momentarily lost for words. Just then a tram ground to a halt in front of her and, without a second's hesitation, she jumped on board. It didn't matter where it was going as long as she got away from that hyena.

As the tram clanged along Warsaw's wide streets, it seemed that, like the people, the buildings were sad and grey. Although it was spring, a smoky pall hung over the city and an acrid smell irritated Mania's nose. The woman beside her was saying to her neighbour, 'My place faces the ghetto, and a few days ago I saw a Jewess standing on a window ledge, clutching a child with flames all around them. I couldn't take my eyes off them. Suddenly she jumped and I watched them falling through the air.' From the woman's shocked expression, Mania could see that she still had the scene before her eyes.

Her companion nodded. 'They say those *Zhideks* fought like tigers in there. Who'd have thought they had it in them!' Then she turned to her small daughter and pulled a scarf over her mouth. 'Don't keep your mouth open like that, Jadzia, you'll be breathing in Jews.' Mania gritted her teeth and turned away.

She'd caught the wrong tram and by the time she reached Misko's room, it was almost curfew and he was in despair. They were trying to figure out what to do when she remembered that somewhere in her bag was a telephone number she'd been given back in Lwow several months ago. 'If you ever need help in Warsaw, call me on this number,' Mr Hening had said.

Each time she asked for Mr Hening, however, the same voice told her that she had the wrong number and hung up. She was about to give up when, on the tenth try, he said, 'The person you are looking for is staying at the Hotel Polski, on Dluga Street.'

At the entrance to the modest hotel, a Jewish policeman barred her way. 'Who are you and what do you want?' When she told him that she was Wanda Morawska, he burst out laughing. 'You can tell that to the Wojteks and the Wladeks, but you can't fool me! You're as Polish as I am!'

She flushed. 'What does it matter who I am? I just want to see my friend Mr Hening.'

The policeman shrugged and pointed upstairs. 'He's on the second floor.'

Mr Hening's room was full of people, some of whom Mania recognised from Lwow. It was comforting to see familiar faces, and she made her way over to Mr Hening, hoping that he'd be able to help them find somewhere to stay. 'Have you got plenty of money?' Mr Hening asked. 'Because these days without money you can't do anything.'

With the money he and his family had raised by selling jewellery and valuables, they'd bought Puerto Rican passports. Being citizens of another country, he explained, made them untouchable.

'How can I get one of those passports?' she asked.

'Money, only money,' he repeated. 'Without money, nothing can be done.'

Mania's heart sank. She walked slowly down the wooden staircase and headed down towards the courtyard where guests were sitting around wooden tables sipping coffee and enjoying the spring sunshine. When her eyes had grown accustomed to the light, she found herself looking into the face of a man she recognised from her carefree prewar days. Mr Donner had been the most sought-after dancing partner when she and Bronia used to kick up their heels in the nightclubs on Legionow Street. 'Well, if it isn't Miss Bratter!' he exclaimed. 'How are things?'

He listened intently as she described her predicament. 'Without money for a foreign passport, I don't know what's going to become of us,' she sighed.

'There's one possibility,' he said. 'I know a wealthy man who has helped a lot of people from Lwow. Mr Koenigel is a kind of liaison officer between us few remaining Jews and the Germans. He's been trying to get us special passports, because it looks as if the Germans won't touch anyone with foreign citizenship,' he explained.

Mania's meeting with Mr Koenigel went better than she expected. It turned out that they had mutual friends, and his confident personality and booming voice gave her hope. When she told him that she had no money, he immediately took out his wallet. She reddened and shook her head. 'I have enough to live on,' she explained, 'but I don't have enough to buy foreign citizenship.'

'Why don't you put your name down on the Palestine list?' he suggested. 'Just say that your parents are living there. They won't ask for proof, but if they do, tell them to speak to Engineer Koenigel. In the meantime, you and your husband should come and stay at the hotel and not budge from here. They're still scouring Warsaw for Jews who've escaped from the ghetto and this is the only safe place in town.'

The Hotel Polski was so overcrowded that many people were already sharing rooms so, along with the other latecomers, Mania and Misko sat on the stairs by day and slept on the hard floor by night. The overcrowding and discomfort didn't bother them. They were thrilled to have a safe haven, the patronage of an influential man and the prospect of migrating to Palestine.

Several days later, while sitting on the stairs, Mania saw a face that made her heart leap. Now their worries were over. Mr Furstenberg was a wealthy zinc and tin manufacturer whose merchandise her father had sold in Lwow. When war had broken out, the Furstenbergs had fled to Lwow where she and her parents had taken them in. Now that roles were reversed and Mr Furstenberg was staying in a spacious room and eating three meals a day, Mania was certain that he'd want to help them. 'But people have short memories,' my aunt tells me. 'He didn't lift a finger to help us.'

Mr Engel was in charge of the Palestine list. She'd seen him strutting around the hotel as if he owned it, this big boss from Lodz who traded diamonds for food and favours from the Germans, and charged people a fortune to be included on the list. 'So what have you got?' he asked her.

'I haven't got a thing,' she replied.

'How come? Lwow people are rolling in it!'

She tried to keep calm. It was devastating to be poor when money meant the difference between life and death. 'Well, we don't have any money, but Mr Koenigel said that he'd vouch for us.' At the mention of the liaison officer's name, the man nodded and, to her relief, added their names to the list.

Over the next three weeks Mania's bones ached from sleeping on the floor and she couldn't wait to have a bath. How much longer would they have to stay there? One morning her thoughts were interrupted by a commotion downstairs. Out of the window she watched as five lorries roared through the wide entrance and screeched to a halt inside the yard.

Out jumped a dozen German soldiers shouting out names. Straining to catch the names, she soon realised that those with South American passports were being summoned. They collected their belongings as fast as they could and rushed towards the waiting trucks. As they climbed eagerly inside, she caught sight of Mr Hening and his family amongst them. At last they were going to Vittel.

For the past three weeks they had talked of nothing but going to Vittel where they would be met by the Red Cross and sent to Paraguay, Nicaragua or Costa Rica. As the last truck drove away, Mania wandered into the Henings' empty room and slumped on the bed. All those lucky people were about to be transported to freedom while she and Misko had to stay behind in Nazi-occupied Warsaw. Misko tried to cheer her up. 'Perhaps the trucks will come back for those of us who are going to Palestine,' he mused.

About an hour later the trucks did come back. But this time she heard yelling in the courtyard and the sound of whips cracking. People were scattering, running in all directions to get away from the soldiers, but only a few managed to escape through the back gate. Watching from the Henings' room on the fourth floor, Mania had a hollow feeling in her stomach. Turning towards her husband, she spoke in a strangely calm voice. 'Let's stay right here. There's no way out. And if they come for us, let's jump out of the window together.' Misko nodded without speaking and put his arm around her slim shoulders.

Suddenly everything became quiet. Mr Koenigel had appeared. Taking in the situation at a glance, he started chatting to the Germans in his jovial way and invited them for a drink at the bar. Within minutes the barman was pouring schnapps, whisky and lager, glasses clinked in jovial toasts, and the sound of men's laughter resounded through the hotel. An hour later the Germans sauntered out of the bar with red faces and unsteady legs.

Even though they'd been saved at the last moment, the future looked bleak. They'd been staying at the Hotel Polski for three weeks without setting foot outside. With so many people crammed into a small space with no bathing facilities, the place has become infested with lice. Wherever they would go from here, they'd need to buy food, and Mania's money had almost run out. She wired Izio's wife Lola in Krakow asking her to send the rest of her belongings, a few clothes, the last of Bronia's sheets, and an eiderdown, but she knew that they couldn't survive long on the proceeds.

Several days later the lorries came back, but this time Mr Koeningel wasn't there to intercede for them. Along with the last occupants of the Hotel Polski, Mania and Misko were taken to the Umschlagplatz. 'We knew that this was the marshalling place from which trains took people to their deaths,' Aunty Mania tells me, 'but when we saw that these were normal trains with seats, and not sealed cattle trucks, we felt heartened. Perhaps they weren't taking us to a concentration camp after all.'

After chugging along regular railway tracks for about a day, the train turned off onto a single track surrounded by dense forests. A woman near Mania grabbed her arm. 'These secret tracks through the woods lead to death camps,' she said, her eyes wild with panic. 'I escaped from one of these transports a few weeks ago and I'm not going to sit here and wait for them to push me into a gas chamber.' Before Mania could speak, the woman snatched a capsule from her pocket, threw it into her mouth, tilted her head back and swallowed. Within minutes she slumped forward and they smelled the almond scent of cyanide. Some of the women broke down and sobbed but Mania felt a new strength course through her body. She was going to live through this.

After what seemed like days, the train pulled in at a small country station, and as they craned their heads out of the window, Misko was saying, 'If we're met by the Wehrmacht, we'll be all right, but if they're SS men, we're lost.' When Mania looked outside, her blood froze. Two men with death's-head insignias on their snappy peaked caps were awaiting them. The sign on the station said Bergen.

CHAPTER 24

While my parents were clinging to life by their fingernails in Piszczac, in other parts of Poland Jews were systematically being starved, tortured and killed. In a thousand birch woods and spruce forests, after the death squads had roared away, the ground heaved above hastily covered pits in which the desperate screams of the living were muffled by the suffocating shroud of earth and corpses, and the blood of grandmothers, mothers and babies stained the land.

At Stalowa Wola, a forced labour camp near Tarnow, a man and woman creep past the guard who patrols the Stahlwerke Braunschweig armament firm where they've been working. In the ongoing conflict between the Nazi principles of extermination and the Wehrmacht's need for exploitation, the Wehrmacht had won a temporary victory and was using Jewish labour to help the German war effort. Only a few days earlier, the man's German boss had called him into the office and told him to close the door. Even though this quiet employee with the misshapen ear was a Jew, he liked him so much that he offered to hide him. Jerzy's heart must have leapt at the prospect of being sheltered inside a German's home. But what about his wife Rutka? His employer shook his head. He would only hide one person. Now it was Jerzy's turn to shake his head. He wouldn't abandon his wife to save himself. Somehow they'd stay together.

Now, as they creep out of the compound gate, they're praying that the guard hasn't heard their ragged breathing. Only a few more steps and they'll be around the corner, out of sight. A gunshot explodes in Rutka's ear and Jerzy falls on the ground. Her scream hangs in the air long after the second shot has silenced it forever.

'Jerzy and Rutka were such a lovely couple,' my mother sighs. 'Out of all of Henek's family, I loved them most of all.' She walks into the large sunny bedroom which she has abandoned since my father died, opens a drawer, and carefully lifts out an old tablecoth. It's yellowed with age but the embroidered petals and intricate openwork are still intact. 'Rutka made this for us when we got married,' she says. As I hold it, I feel the love with which Rutka sewed these painstaking stitches. The tablecloth has outlived Rutka, the war, and the journey to the other end of the world.

It was Aunty Andzia who told me how Jerzy and Rutka died. It happened just after she'd left Lwow and was wandering from place to place searching for some safe corner for herself and her children. She had intended to go to Iwonicz, thinking that a spa town would be safer than a large city, but the man sitting next to her on the train from Lwow had looked aghast when she mentioned Iwonicz. 'Dear lady, what are you thinking of?' he said. 'The place is crawling with Germans!' Andzia was shaken. She had no idea where to go. 'My wife's a teacher and I work on the railways, so we need someone to take care of the baby,' the man had told her. 'Why don't you come and live with us? You'll have a roof over your heads and food in your stomachs.'

Andzia had been grateful for the offer but after a few weeks at his house she was worn out. By night she walked up and down rocking the baby, who bawled incessantly, and by day she cleaned, cooked, washed and ironed in return for their meagre food and lodging. She felt trapped until the day Mrs Skwara, an elderly neighbour, stopped her in the marketplace. 'Pani Sulikowska, why are you letting these people exploit you? Come and work on my farm and I'll pay you.' Andzia didn't need any prompting.

At the Skwaras' house she helped with farm chores from sunrise till past sunset. At night, when she fell exhausted onto the straw bed she shared with Krysia and Fredzio, her lonely thoughts turned to Zygmunt and she wondered whether she'd ever see her husband again. Reading between the lines of his guarded letters, each of which showed a different address, she felt his desperation in every word. He wrote that he'd been seriously ill and begged for help, distraught that he hadn't received a reply. 'I'm recovering slowly but need money for food and medicine. The weather here is extremely bad for convalescence,' he wrote in code from Lwow in October 1942. She knew he was referring to his slim chance of survival. That was the last letter Andzia ever received from him.

Life would have been bearable at the Skwaras' farm if not for their son who bullied Krysia and Fredzio mercilessly. Although Andzia knew that Zenek was always punching and bashing them when no-one was looking, the stakes were too high to place justice above survival. 'Keep away from him but don't ever hit back!' she warned.

At harvest time, when the golden fields shimmered and the farmhands were out scything the barley and tying it into sheaves, Andzia called Fredzio but couldn't find him. 'I saw him in Pani Skwara's cart with some of the boys heading for the fields,' one of the farmhands said. Andzia paced up and down. She knew that the village boys sometimes played games to see who could urinate the furthest, and she was terrified in case they saw Fredzio's penis. As she paced up and down, another thought struck her. 'What if Mr Skwara decides to check out whether Fredzio is Jewish?'

Krysia watched her mother anxiously. 'Let's not wait, Mama,' she said. 'Let's just go.'

Andzia's lips tightened. 'We're staying right here. If they turn Fredzio in, we'll die with him.' The hours dragged by until sundown when they heard voices and rushed outside. Sitting on top of a waggon piled with hay, Fredzio was holding the reins with Mr Skwara and jigging up and down with glee. 'Just look at him!' the farmer beamed.

No matter how exhausted she was, Andzia's mind never slept, and late one night she was awoken by murmuring from the other side of the wall where her employer slept with his wife and son in one bed beneath a big crucifix. Mr Skwara was whispering, 'Mother, can you hear me? I want to tell you something. I'm wondering about that woman we've got here with her kids. I've heard that the Germans are offering a bottle of vodka, five hundred cigarettes and fifty zlotys for every Jew.' Andzia pressed her ear against the wall. The man went on, 'After all, if we don't turn them in, someone else will.' A shiver ran down Andzia's spine as she realised that the man who had taken them in and treated them like family was willing to sell their lives for vodka, cigarettes and a few miserable zlotys. For the rest of the night her brain felt on fire as she tried to figure out how to get away before the Gestapo arrived.

As soon as wisps of light appeared in the sky and the cock crowed in the yard, she nudged Krysia. 'When we're all out in the fields, I want you and Fredzio to pick a fight with Zenek. Really let him have it so it shows!' Krysia stared at her mother with astonishment. At last they'd be able to pay the bully back. When Andzia came back from the fields that afternoon, her hair tied in a kerchief and her face red and sweaty, the children ran up to her, bubbling with excitement. 'We got Zenek into the barn and pummelled him so hard that his nose bled!' Krysia exulted.

Quickly Andzia untied the scarf, splashed water on her face at the pump, and hurried to the magistrate's office. 'I hope you'll help me because I'm very worried,' she told him. 'My children have had a fight with Zenek Skwara and I'm sure we'll be thrown out, but we have nowhere to go. Could you give me a certificate of residence saying that I come from here?'

The balding magistrate with the high forehead placed his shiny glasses on the desk and surveyed the flushed brunette. 'But how can I say that you're from Lomrzany? You've only been here six months!'

She looked beseechingly into his face. 'I know, but if I don't have the certificate, I won't be able to get the children's medicine.'

His face softened. 'Why didn't you tell me you needed medicine for the children?' he said, and filled out the form.

Andzia ran back to the farm, threw their belongings into a bundle, grabbed the children and headed for the station. She'd take the next train to Warsaw. It would be good to see her sister Slawa again. She kept repeating her sister's new name over and over, to make sure she didn't make the fatal mistake of calling her Fridzia. Mama and Rozia were living there too, so she wouldn't have to struggle all alone anymore. The station swarmed with German soldiers, but armed with her document of residence and false papers, she felt confident. She'd just settled into her seat by the window when a German soldier entered the compartment with his huge German shepherd and with a peremptory gesture ordered her to get up to make room for the dog. In the next compartment, however, a Pole from Poznan took Fredzio on his lap, while a German traveller gave her and Krysia his seat and she spent the rest of the journey chatting with a woman who admired her beautiful children. As they neared the outskirts of Warsaw and she began gathering her belongings, the woman whispered, 'Don't hang around the station. They're catching people all the time these days, not only Jews, so don't hesitate, just go.' The train was shuddering to a halt when Andzia broke into a cold sweat. She'd forgotten Slawa's address and there was no way of finding out because she'd destroyed her letter.

Remembering what the woman had said about loitering, she hailed the first *dorosky* she saw and climbed in with legs that shook because she didn't know what to tell the driver. Her mind was racing around in useless circles. Dear God, what's to become of us? Where can we go? The driver was looking at her, waiting for directions. Beads of sweat sprang out on her forehead and upper lip. She had to say something, quickly. Suddenly she heard herself say, 'Nowogrodzka, please.' As the driver tugged the reins and the horse clip-clopped away from the station, she sank back against the worn leather seat and let out a long sigh of relief. By some miracle the street name had come to her, but what was the number? Racking her brains, she thought of various numbers, but not one of them sounded right. Soon they'd reach Nowogrodzka Street. She couldn't wander from house to house with two children, knocking on every single door in the hope of finding her sister.

Aunty Andzia still remembers the panic of that *dorosky* ride, and the tightness in her chest as she scanned the stone-faced buildings. Leaning forward, she jabs her long red fingernail in the air between us. 'I could talk about it for a week and you will still never understand the despair I felt at that moment, knowing that if I didn't find my sister soon, we'd all be picked up.'

To this day she doesn't know what drew her towards a big wooden gate which led into a large courtyard with apartment blocks all around. At the first door in the large hallway, a woman looked her up and down, shook her head and shut the door before she had time to say a word. How many doorbells would she have to ring in this building, and how many in other houses, before she found her sister? And how long would it be before someone became suspicious and turned them in? Just as she took a deep breath and braced herself to press another bell, a door on her left opened centimetre by centimetre, a shadow fell across the hallway, and she was looking into her sister's face.

As soon as Slawa had found two vacant rooms in Warsaw, in a flat belonging to two elderly ladies, she'd sent for her mother and Rozia whom she introduced as her friends Mrs Marianna Popkiewicz and her daughter Karolina. The unexpected arrival of Andzia and the children meant that she'd have to hide the three of them in her small room. How could she conceal their presence from the landladies who lived in the same flat, who often dropped in for a chat? Pacing up and down her tiny room in a turmoil, Slawa stopped in front of the old-fashioned wardrobe with a mirror door.

For the next three weeks Andzia, Krysia and Fredzio spent most of their time in the space created between the wall and the wardrobe door, which they always kept open. It's hard to imagine a lively six-year-old boy spending entire days in silence behind a wardrobe door. Didn't the children get restless standing there day after day? 'No, they understood that our lives depended on it,' Aunty Andzia tells me. 'They were used to being hunted and living in terror. They were abused by life.'

My cousin Krysia still remembers standing behind the wardrobe, changing from one foot to the other, terrified of coughing, sneezing or making the slightest sound. 'After a while Aunty Slawa got us a little folding chair so we could take turns sitting down,' she recalls. 'We had to wait until the landladies weren't around before we could use the toilet, and we couldn't flush it too often in case it aroused suspicion. Mrs Makowska and Mrs Karasiewicz were deeply religious women who went to church every day, but if they'd known we were Jews, they would probably have turned us over to the Gestapo without a qualm. I remember being so terrified in case they came in and saw us that I hardly took my eyes off that door.'

'How do children cope with such terror?' I ask as we sip our coffee on a sunny terrace high above the Mediterranean Sea. For a few moments Krysia stares at the view below but I know she's not seeing the waves which slap against the ramparts of old Yaffa. 'In those times, children weren't children,' she says quietly. 'We stopped being children in the face of death.'

Within three weeks it became obvious that they couldn't conceal their presence in Slawa's flat indefinitely. Although Slawa tried to hide her bulging shopping bag as she climbed the stairs and although they crept around on tiptoe and hid every tell-tale sign, the old ladies had eyes like hawks and from the comments they made, it was clear that they were becoming suspicious. Andzia would have to find another room.

Sneaking out of the flat whilst the landladies were at church, Slawa and Andzia set off in search of a room, but at the first place the woman gave them a knowing look. 'I don't want to have to report you, ladies,' she said as she grabbed Andzia's handbag, opened it, pulled out a wad of zlotys, thrust the bag back into her hands and slammed the door in their faces. She knew that they couldn't take the risk of reporting her.

Until they found a room, Andzia and the children stayed in a small hotel which was even more frightening than staying with Slawa. Every night when the Gestapo searched the hotel, doors banged and blood-curdling screams resounded through the corridors as they dragged guests out. When they banged on Andzia's door, she hid Fredzio and handed over her papers in such a feisty manner that it allayed suspicion, but she knew her luck wouldn't last.

Little Fredzio often woke in the middle of the night to the sound of piercing screams in the street outside, or to the quieter, but infinitely more terrifying sound of his mother sobbing inside the room. For many years to come, those bloodcurdling yells resounded in his dreams. In those night-mares, smashed skulls lay on the ground with brains spilling out, streets split apart and turned into chasms beneath his feet, and menacing Germans chased him until he could run no further, and impaled him on barbed wire. Fifty years later, the vulnerable boy called Fredzio Rosenbaum has come a long way from those traumatic times. He has become a successful businessman called Fred Ross who lives in Maryland, has three brilliant sons, and enjoys an ideal retirement travelling all over the world with his wife Phyllis, but he still can't bring himself to talk about those dark war years. My cousin Fred is the only member of the family who refused to talk about his war experiences. He has broken his silence only once, to tell his sons what he went through, and locked the past in a drawer labelled 'Not to be re-opened'.

When Andzia called about a vacant room in Zlota Street, the landlady invited her inside and explained that she was letting a room because her husband, an army officer, had been killed. 'My late husband was an officer too,' Andzia said. Encouraged by their mutual woes, the woman said, 'Let me show you what a Jew did to my husband in Romania.' She unfolded a sheet of newspaper, pointed to an item in an unfamiliar language and, in a voice crackling with hatred, spat out, 'My husband's superior, Colonel Goldberg, was a Jew and he shot my husband. Someone sent me this article from Bucharest.' Sitting so close that Andzia could taste the hatred on her warm breath, she said with hypnotic intensity, 'Pani Sulikowska, if you ever see any Jews anywhere, you must turn them over to the Gestapo straightaway.' Andzia was wondering how to get away from there as fast as possible when the widow's next words took her by surprise. 'So when would you like to move in?'

Once she and the children had a roof over their heads, Andzia had to find some means of earning money and once again Slawa came to the rescue. Ever since arriving in Warsaw she'd embarked on a new industry—making cigarettes. She bought bags of tobacco on the black market and learned to roll cigarettes with a special gadget, tapping them to smooth out any bumps. When they were ready, she arranged them in the flowered Morvita boxes she saved from the cigarette papers. Most people only bought one or two cigarettes at a time, but with her cheery manner and attractively presented boxes, she had built up a regular clientele.

Andzia and the children became involved in Slawa's lucrative enterprise. With her nimble fingers, Andzia boosted the cigarette production; Krysia sometimes went down to the shadowy wharf to buy a sack of tobacco, while Fredzio sold the cigarettes to kiosks and passers-by who found it hard to resist his cherubic face.

April breezes were blowing leaves around the city footpaths when Krysia wrinkled her nose, sniffed, and called her mother over to the window. 'Mama, come quickly!' Columns of thick smoke were blackening the sky and flames crackled high above buildings in the distance.

By April 1943, almost all of the 400 000 Jews of Warsaw who had been walled inside the ghetto since 1940 had been killed. Many died of starvation, frost, disease or from the brutality of guards who terrorised them. Most were deported to Treblinka, a death factory whose gas chambers and crematoria consumed thousands of men, women and children every week. When the remaining Jews in the ghetto found out that the Germans were planning to totally destroy the ghetto during Passover, they resolved not to give up without a fight. In one of the most heroic episodes of the Holocaust, twelve hundred young ghetto fighters armed with hand grenades and Molotov cocktails, seventeen rifles and a few pistols opened fire on a force of German soldiers and SS troops with heavy artillery, machine guns, howitzers and tanks. For the next two weeks, to the rage of the Germans and the admiration of the citizens of Warsaw, the defenders of the ghetto held the Germans at bay, while buildings crashed and crumbled, and despairing mothers leapt out of blazing buildings with their children to their deaths. The ghetto fighters knew that the outcome was never in doubt, but they were going to die fighting and make the Germans pay a high price for their lives.

Outside the ghetto walls, a hurdy-gurdy was playing, fair-haired children rode painted horses on a carousel and Warsaw went about its business. 'The ghetto is fighting,' people said. 'The *Zhideks* are burning.'

Standing at the window, Andzia watched the flames and tears poured down her face. Standing beside her, the landlady clucked her tongue and tried to console her sobbing tenant. 'It's dreadful that we have to witness such a shocking sight but, really and truly, it had to happen.'

Not long after the destruction of the Warsaw ghetto, Andzia's brother Izio suddenly appeared on her doorstep. In spite of his harrowing flight from Piszczac and the long, tense journey to Warsaw, he still managed to look the picture of elegance, the crease in his trousers razor sharp, and the small hunting hat with the feather tilted at a jaunty angle. It would be hard to hide him in her room with the landlady coming in and out, but Andzia didn't hesitate. She pulled most of the stuffing out of the mattress she shared with her children for him to sleep on, and made him swear never to leave the room.

Each day Izio waited impatiently for her to return. He listened intently to her stories about the cigarette business and with his shrewd business mind helped her and Slawa double their productivity and increase their sales. The days dragged for him until he felt that if he didn't get out of the room, he'd explode. While Andzia was helping her sister roll cigarettes and Krysia and Fredzio were accosting passers-by to buy them, he waited until the landlady went out, put on his hunting hat and crept downstairs. As he hadn't been out for several weeks, he was wobbly and he'd only taken a few gulps of fresh air when his legs gave way under him and he fell on the footpath. His eyes travelled up a pair of shiny black boots, khaki trousers and a leather holster. He'd fallen at the feet of a German soldier deep in conversation with a pretty blonde. Uncle Izio chuckles as he tells the story. 'You'll never guess what happened next. He helped me to my feet and then turned back to his girlfriend!'

Encouraged by this stroke of luck, Izio sneaked out again a few weeks later. This time he was shopping for a hat. 'The hatter across the road advertised the best quality Austrian hat for only one zloty because it was all he had left to sell. Naturally I couldn't resist it! It might have been made for me and I put it on straightaway, but when I came out of the shop, I almost collided with a member of Colonel Roehm's SS Brigade with the red armband and the death's-head insignia on his cap. Before I had time to get out of his way, he bashed me over the head so hard that I reeled, but what upset me the most was seeing my beautiful new hat rolling into the dirt.

As soon as he lost interest in me and strode on, I ran back to pick up the hat, but it was stained and I never wore it again.'

As time went on, Andzia realised that the caretaker fancied her. She'd seen him watching her with an insinuating half-smile. He was always asking whether she needed any help and paying her clumsy compliments. 'A good-looking woman like you must get lonely at nights,' he'd wink. Several times he'd followed her up the stairs and she'd had to slip inside quickly to get away from him. 'Why don't you send the children outside so I can come in and talk to you?' he'd say. He was becoming a problem but she couldn't risk antagonising him because already some of her neighbours were gossiping that her daughter Krysia had sad Jewish eyes.

To make matters worse, Izio suddenly became ill. He shivered with fever, his eyes looked glassy, and perspiration drenched the sheets. Occasionally he lost consciousness and mumbled in his delirium. Andzia told Fredzio to make a lot of noise to drown out Izio's mumbling and he used to shout the multiplication table over and over again. To this day he can still recite the multiplication table in Polish. Andzia was frantic because the landlady, who liked her company, often came into their room and sat on the bed where Izio lay groaning and mumbling. Whenever the landlady came in, Fredzio had to jump around on the bed and ruffle it so that she wouldn't see the figure under the eiderdown. Somehow Andzia managed to maintain a normal conversation and stopped her eyes from darting to the shape that bulged beneath the bedclothes. 'I'll tell you something really strange,' Aunty Andzia said, a smile playing around her mouth. 'In spite of his fever, whenever the landlady came in and sat on the bed, as if by magic Izio always stopped twitching and moaning, and never uttered a single sound!'

Slawa managed to find a doctor whom they could trust. He

was the doctor from the Pawiak Prison who sympathised with their plight because he had a Jewish wife. He diagnosed typhoid fever but said that apart from cold compresses and fluids, all they could do was hope and pray. Their prayers were answered because Izio recovered. When he was strong enough, he moved into a room of his own across the street.

Slawa was still living at Nowogrodzka Street with her mother and sister, Rozia. She discouraged her mother from going out in case she forgot the words of Our Father, and warned Rozia not to pray aloud or leave her Siddur lying around in case the landladies saw it. Snow had been falling steadily throughout December and Slawa's woollen coat was covered in white flakes when she rushed upstairs with the black bread and cottage cheese she'd bought them for dinner. She'd just taken off her threadbare sodden shoes and was rubbing her frozen feet when one of the elderly landladies appeared at the door, twisting a handkerchief in her arthritic fingers. 'The caretaker has just told me that we have some Jewesses here,' she told Slawa, gesturing towards the room occupied by Lieba and Rozia.

The next day Slawa started looking for new accommodation for them. She'd heard about a Mrs Wiatrak and her friend Mr Zawoda who were said to let rooms to Jews with Aryan papers. When Slawa said that her friends, Miss Popkiewicz and her mother were looking for a room, Mrs Wiatrak explained that as it happened, she did have a vacant room, as her Jewish tenants had recently left for Hungary. To be on the safe side, she asked Slawa to meet her at the letting office, so that it would look as though they'd never met before.

Slawa understood that Mrs Wiatrak had to be careful, and agreed to meet her the following day at the letting office on Marszalkowska Street, as if by chance. Mrs Wiatrak would come in ostensibly to advertise a vacant room, and Slawa would take it then and there. The landlady insisted that Slawa's name wasn't to be mentioned, only the name of the ladies renting the room, so that in case they were ever denounced, no-one would ever find out that she'd known their identity beforehand. It was only much later that my aunt understood why Mrs Wiatrak was going to such lengths to protect herself.

January is a sad, bleak month in Warsaw, but the beginning of 1944 brought hope that the war wouldn't drag on for much longer. From illicit broadcasts and information obtained by the underground, news about the unstoppable Bolshevik army sweeping towards Poland aroused the hope that if only they could hold out a little longer, they would live to see the Nazis defeated. One group, however, viewed the Bolshevik advance with growing apprehension. Many members of the right-wing underground army mistrusted the motives of the Russian Politbureau and foresaw that one struggle would end but another would begin.

A chilly mist rose from the Vistula River and seeped into the grey buildings of Warsaw's Praga district that frosty January day in 1944 when a middle-aged woman fussed nervously over her stooped, grey-haired mother as they looked through the window of Mrs Wiatrak's flat, waiting for Slawa to arrive. Lieba and Rozia rarely went out these days and Slawa's visits were the highlight of their week.

As soon as they heard the familiar knock, Rozia hurried to the door and hovered over her sister with their groceries. As Slawa bustled around the room, unpacking the bread and cheese and trying to make cheerful conversation, she noticed that Rozia didn't take her eyes off their mother who'd become greyer and more shrunken. 'I don't want to stay here any more,' Lieba shivered. 'I feel I'm going to die here. Last night I had a terrible dream about your father. Usually I dream that he's alive and his spirit is protecting us, but last night I dreamed that he was dead. That means he won't be able to help us any more. This is the end.' Thirty years earlier, Lieba's own mother had had a similar presentiment of death. Slawa looked helplessly at her mother. They both knew that there was nowhere else for her to go.

As the months dragged on, Lieba's face sagged and her shoulders became more hunched. Spring came late that year. The buds had begun to swell on the rose bushes and sap was coursing along the boughs of the lime trees when Slawa set off for her weekly visit to her mother and Rozia. Hidden under the laundry, groceries and boxes of cigarettes in her shopping bag was a packet of jewellery she'd been asked to sell. As she hurried along the street, the only sound was the clicking of her heels. Turning into Wolominska Street, she almost ran into a group of German soldiers who were pistol-whipping their captives as they pushed them into a waiting truck. She flattened herself against the cold stone wall. One minute earlier and she too would have been in that truck that was speeding towards the Umschlagplatz.

Pale and trembling, she climbed the wooden staircase to her mother's flat. She was about to knock when she saw something that made her hand freeze in mid-air. Her heart stopped beating. The door was padlocked.

CHAPTER 25

With the image of her mother's padlocked door seared into her mind, Slawa flew down the stairs and rushed across town to find the landlady, Mrs Wiatrak. But when she ran up the stairs to the Standtortverwatungstelle, the German firm where the landlady worked, to her astonishment it was not Mrs Wiatrak but her friend Tadeusz Zawoda who came towards her, and there was no smile on his usually benign face. The words spilled out of Slawa's mouth in panic. 'I was bringing Miss Popkiewicz and her mother some food but I don't understand what's happened, there was a padlock on the door.'

Surveying her with cold disdain, Mr Zawoda reached for the food in her shopping bag and said, 'Well, they won't be needing this any more.' The floor swayed under Slawa's feet as she tried to grasp what he was saying. 'They've gone. I must say, they were pretty brave. They were taken away at midnight.'

Her thoughts were spinning around so fast that Slawa thought the top of her head would lift off. Since he knew so much about it, Mr Zawoda and his friend must have denounced them, a couple of jackals posing as helpers of the Jews. She wanted to spring forward and claw his treacherous face.

He'd already taken out the bread, butter and eggs, and his grasping hands were already on the cigarettes. Any moment now he'd discover the small parcel of jewellery she'd been given to sell. 'Get your hands off my things!' she shouted.

His eyes became malevolent slits. 'Don't get on your high horse with me. If you don't get out of here this instant, I'll turn you over to the first policeman I see.'

Realising that he had her in his power she stumbled out of his office. There was no point asking about her mother's things. Mrs Wiatrak had the key to the padlock and the two of them would divide up the spoils. 'There was no doubt in my mind that I only got out of his clutches because there wasn't a policeman around at the time,' she wrote in a report she sent to the Polish authorities after the war.

On her way to the tram stop, Slawa tried to grasp what had happened to her mother and Rozia. Now she understood why Mrs Wiatrak and her friend had gone to such lengths to set up their supposedly chance meeting at the letting office, and realised how the previous Jewish tenants had come to vacate the flat. She longed to sit down and collect her anguished thoughts, but lingering in the street was dangerous and she walked on, trying to look confident in spite of the panic she felt.

At Izio's place she sank into a chair and just looked up at her brother, eyes full of despair. When she was finally able to tell him what had happened, he paced around the room, his face white and drawn, fists clenched. They had to find out where their mother and sister had been taken before it was too late, but even making inquiries about missing Jews was risky.

They could hear the ticking of Izio's watch as they sat in clammy silence in the tiny room. Then Izio looked up, trying to remember something. He'd heard that a lawyer called Pawlowski had good contacts with Germans in high places. Perhaps he'd be able to locate their mother and sister if they were still alive. Thanks to their thriving cigarette business, they'd be able to pay his high fees.

Within one week the lawyer had good news. Lieba and Rozia were being held in Warsaw's Pawiak Prison. Slawa closed her eyes and let out a deep breath. They were alive! 'Please do whatever you can to get them out while there's still time,' she said.

While awaiting news from Mr Pawlowski, they sent bread and sausage for their mother and Rozia, and felt reassured when a brief note arrived confirming that the parcel had arrived. Finally, at the end of July, Slawa heard the news that made her dance around the room like a jubilant schoolgirl. On 1 August her mother and sister would be released.

But on that day Warsaw had an appointment with history. The underground army rose up against the German occupation. The Warsaw Uprising had begun. For Lieba and Rozia, however, the timing was disastrous. On the first day of the Uprising they were marched into the prison yard with other inmates, lined up against the wall and shot.

It was only after the war that Uncle Izio found out what had happened, when he ran into the doctor who lived near the prison, the one who'd come to see him when he'd had typhoid fever. After telling me this story, he lapses into heavy silence. He's eighty-seven now, physically fit, mentally alert and sartorially immaculate. All his life he has tried to suppress the memories which I'm now trying to revive, and they plunge him into deep depression. At the risk of arousing his anger and opening old wounds, there's one more question I have to ask: 'Do you feel bad that you survived and they didn't?'

He looks at me, his eyes tired, faded and full of pain. I have to sit forward to catch his tremulous whisper: 'Yes, I feel guilty.'

For Slawa, too, her mother's death remains an unhealed wound. 'I've been to Warsaw hundreds of times but I can never bring myself to go near the house where they used to live. I'll never forget how Rozia used to stand behind the door with her prayer book so the landlady wouldn't see her, murmuring prayers in her intense way. But God didn't hear her. She and Mama perished together.' Tears roll down my aunt's plump cheeks.

Pawiak Prison has now become the Museum of the Resistance. It's closed the day I visit, but I can picture my grandmother and aunt being pushed through that forbidding wrought-iron gate topped with barbed wire. As I peer over the wall to see the yard, I think of those two women who loved me standing there, and wonder what they said to each other before those bullets killed their world. I wonder whether Lieba's life scrolled before her as she sank to the ground, whether she thought of Daniel, or smelled the scent of pine trees as she fell.

CHAPTER 26

On 1 August 1944, unaware of her mother's fate, Slawa restlessly awaited her release. To fill the long hours, she decided to sell some cigarettes in the city. Near Zlota Street, however, the rat-tat-tat of gunfire made her run for cover. 'Get off the street, the Uprising's started!' people were shouting, and she started running and didn't stop until she reached her sister Andzia's place and collapsed on the bed out of breath.

The shooting continued and a few days later bombs started to fall, but Slawa was in such a state of shock that she refused to go down to the cellar with Andzia and the other tenants. Stretched out on Andzia's bed, she continued to read her novel as though the bombardment had nothing to do with her. Planes flew low overhead and bombs were falling terrifyingly close, but to Krysia's amazement her aunt hardly looked up.

Slawa doesn't know to this day what it was in the droning sound of the bombers flying directly overhead that made her leap to her feet and rush upstairs to the washroom where Krysia was standing in her thin nightdress, washing herself over the wide enamel basin. Throwing an overcoat over her niece's shoulders, she grabbed her hand and hissed, 'Run!'

When they reached the ground floor, Slawa suddenly ran out into the yard, stopped dead, and started counting the fighter planes. Krysia counted with her, both mesmerised by the surreal nature of the scene. In broad daylight, on a bright summer afternoon as the sun beat down on the city, bombs were falling all around them. They counted twelve before they suddenly came to their senses and tore down to the cellar just as a bomb hit their building and blew up the room where only a minute earlier Slawa had been reading.

They pressed themselves against the stairs as the whole building shook. With a clarity of mind that surprised her, Krysia counted five separate explosions. Five bombs hit their apartment block, and as everything around them shook, she expected the whole building to collapse on her head. 'I didn't know whether I was alive or dead,' she recalls in her slow, resonant voice. 'Those bombs weighed a tonne and reduced the building to rubble. I don't know why the cellar didn't collapse on top of us. It was used for storing coal, and the floor was blanketed with coal dust which billowed up with each blast. The air became so thick with soot that people couldn't breathe; they were coughing, choking and suffocating. The soot soaked into our skin, blinded our eyes and settled in our lungs. Everyone's faces, arms and legs were black. Suddenly I had the strange feeling that I'd been turned upside down and was standing on my head in the coal dust. I could hear muffled voices coming from far away, but had no idea whether anyone was still alive.'

Just then one last bomb struck the house. This one ripped through the wrecked building and landed in the cellar, but by some miracle it didn't explode. As it pierced the rubble, it created a hole through which they later crawled out.

Slawa was bewildered by the sudden silence. Her hearing was damaged by the blast, and for the rest of her life she was to remain deaf in one ear. Stunned, disoriented and covered in soot, she looked like a startled golliwog. 'Coal dust had penetrated my skin from head to toe, and my blackened hair stood on end. Tears were streaming from my eyes, carving two white paths down my sooty cheeks. Through the tears, I saw a tall aristocratic man looking at me. He took a handkerchief out of his pocket and gently wiped my face.

'And that's how I met my future husband Mietek and fell madly in love,' she says, as dewy-eyed as a teenager. 'I knew by then that my husband Jerzyk, from whom I'd been separated for the past two years, had been taken to the woods and shot together with his parents in 1942.' From the walnut sideboard which had belonged to her sister Karola, Aunty Slawa takes down a framed photograph of a sternly handsome man with gaunt cheeks and a craggy nose. Mietek, who was Catholic, had been caught by the Uprising while visiting his family. He told her that his family were descended from the *szlachta*, the Polish aristocracy, but that he worked on the railways. From the moment they met, she had looked adoringly up at him and hung on every word he uttered, intrigued by his reserved, laconic manner.

When it was safe to venture out, they crept out of the cellar. Warsaw had become a war zone and their building was in the centre of the battlefield. Dead bodies were lying all over the street, while injured people lay bleeding from their wounds, some moaning for help. What had been a neat city street was now a heap of smoking rubble. Gunshots sputtered from a nearby street, guttural German voices yelled orders, boots clattered on cobblestones, and flames licked the ruins.

For nine weeks the residents of Warsaw lived below the ground in a state of siege, while above ground members of the underground army fought for their city street by street. Day by day food became scarcer, and before long there wasn't a cat or a dog left alive. As the water pipes had been bombed, obtaining drinking water was the biggest problem. A few blocks away from their building stood an underground well, but to reach it they had to pass under what became known as the Gate of Death because German soldiers were shooting at anyone who passed through. Once they reached the well, they often had to queue all night for their turn to dip the bucket into the water, but whenever they heard the peculiar high-pitched mooing sound of rockets, they rushed back to their shelter empty-handed.

It didn't take long for Slawa's resourceful mind to become active again. Remembering that she'd left a cache of cigarettes upstairs, she and Mietek stepped gingerly up the rickety stairs and over the rubble to retrieve them, while the whole building wobbled around them as though hanging together by a thread. Through a hole in the wall they crawled into what was left of Slawa's room and picked up cigarettes which lay scattered amongst crumbled plaster, splintered shards of wood and broken bricks.

Once they'd stuffed them into their pockets, they looked around for something to eat. In one room Slawa found a big bag of bread crusts which were hard and blackened, but she rejoiced as though she'd unearthed buried treasure. 'We were so hungry that we didn't even brush off the soot. Our fingers shook as we lit a fire, made coffee and dipped those hard crusts into the bitter liquid and devoured them. There was such a terrible famine during the uprising that we used to go through rubbish bins, picking out rotting carrots and mouldy onions, whatever we could find. When some of the people in our street came across a horse which had died of gunshot wounds, they swooped on it and within minutes hacked it into chunks. I got a piece too and cooked it into a marvellous broth. It tasted just like goose!'

As she had hoped, the cigarettes saved them from starvation. When the resistance fighters heard about her supply, a brisk trade began. They used to raid abandoned shops and bartered slices of bread, coffee, sugar or buckwheat kasha for a few cigarettes.

As the struggle for Warsaw intensified, the Polish losses mounted. At first the Germans were bewildered by urban guerrilla tactics for which they hadn't been trained, but in the end, might and modern weapons defeated daring and patriotism. Some of the Jews who had survived the ghetto uprising now fought side by side with the resistance to liberate their devastated city.

But instead of putting Warsaw in Polish hands, the uprising became yet another of Poland's heroic defeats. The underground had counted on assistance from their western allies, but they weren't aware of the agreement in Teheran the previous year which had precluded their help. Britain and America had promised the eastern part of Poland to their ally Stalin. Although the Red Army was already close to Warsaw, on the east bank of the Vistula, Stalin was waiting for the defeat of the patriotic, right-wing members of the underground army, many of whom loathed communism even more than fascism. In the bitterest moment of his life, on 3 October 1944, General Tadeusz 'Bor' Komorowski capitulated to the Germans. About 150 000 Polish civilians had died during the uprising.

When Hitler ordered his soldiers to blow up every building in Warsaw so that the advancing Russian army would have no winter quarters, the mass evacuation of civilians began. The roads leading out of Warsaw were choked with refugees fleeing the doomed city on foot, lugging whatever they could carry. Izio, who had survived the bombardment in his cellar, joined his sister Slawa and Mietek, who were heading for Mietek's family home at Piaseczna. When Slawa saw that Izio was wearing his jaunty hunting hat, she advised him to change it for Mietek's railwayman's cap so that he'd draw less attention to himself.

Along the way they were so famished and exhausted that they knocked on a village hut, asking an old couple for food and shelter. 'When we said we'd come from the Uprising, they let us in, but all they had to eat were onions which the old woman sliced into a large white bowl. I was so ravenous that I couldn't stop eating them and burned the skin inside my mouth so badly that I could hardly eat for weeks,' Aunty Slawa recalls.

At the family farm, Mietek didn't tell his relatives that Slawa and Izio were Jewish. 'They wouldn't have agreed to have us there if they'd known,' my aunt says. For the next three months Slawa raked and planted in the garden, Mietek chopped wood and Izio looked after the piglets which ran after him like puppies. In January 1945, when the Germans had retreated and the Russian army had taken over, they decided to return to Krakow. 'While crossing the Debnicki Bridge, I saw a German soldier who had been crushed beneath a cement post. One of his feet stuck out and I noticed that the boot was missing. People were so destitute that someone must have pulled it off, hoping to trade one boot.'

Slawa and Mietek married as soon as they'd settled in Krakow. Then she started searching for the man who'd denounced her mother and sister to the Gestapo. The new socialist government had announced its intention of prosecuting those who had turned Jews over to the Nazis and she'd written a detailed report describing what had happened. Nothing could bring Lieba and Rozia back, but at least she'd have the satisfaction of bringing their betrayer to justice. She found out that Mrs Wiatrak's previous Jewish tenants had met a similar fate, while later ones barely escaped with their lives. When they returned to claim their possessions, the landlady had warned them that if they ever darkened her doorstep again, she'd set the Gestapo on them.

When Slawa found out that Tadeusz Zawoda was in Lublin, she travelled there, nervous but determined to confront him. She found him at the Army Commissariat of the Polish People's Republic, the image of a Polish patriot, self-assured in his captain's uniform. Her heart was thumping as she took a deep breath and accused him of denouncing her mother and sister.

Aunty Slawa will never forget the menace in his expression as long as she lives. Even now, the memory of it makes her tremble. 'The murderous hatred in his eyes terrified me more than his words. If looks could kill, then I would have died that instant. "Don't you ever dare say that again," he hissed, "Or I'll see that you regret it." I fled from Lublin, glad to have escaped with my life.'

CHAPTER 27

Winter had come again, and Piszczac nestled under its mantle of snow. Inside the house Danusia gazed at the fanciful patterns etched by the frost while her warm breath dissolved them before her eyes. The room was fragrant with the sharp, pine scent of the fir tree decorated with shiny baubles and paper cutouts, and like all the children in the village, Danusia was impatiently awaiting the arrival of St Nicholas.

This child is a mystery to me. I don't know what she thinks or feels, how much she knows or suspects. She scatters rose petals in church processions, kneels in church on Sundays and hears children saying that the filthy Jews killed Our Blessed Saviour. Does she also despise Jews? Or is there a corner of her mind where she conceals a secret she hasn't even told herself?

By now Henek and Bronia's foothold on life was becoming as slippery as the ice that glazed the roads. Although the village was buzzing with rumours that tens of thousands of German soldiers lay dead on Russia's frozen land, that the Wehrmacht was being thrashed by the Red Army, and the war couldn't last much longer, rumours about the Boguslawskis were still gathering momentum. It seemed as though they were fighting two wars simultaneously: one against the Germans and the other against their neighbours, and of the two, the latter was far more threatening.

More anxious than ever to be included in all the village activities, my parents went for sleigh rides in air so crisp that you could almost crush it in your fingers. Sleigh bells jingled merrily and the sound of laughter echoed through the spruce forest while Henek chatted with Jurek Zawadzki whose wife Danuta hooked her arm through Bronia's. 'Want to hear the latest gossip in our little backwater? Someone told Mrs Forycka that you walk like a Jewess!' Bronia tried to make fun of the accusation but there was no mirth in her laughter.

Despite the fact that the end of the war was imminent, our lives were still in danger. Only a week ago some children had run past their house shouting 'Jews! Jews!' My mother sighs in the midst of reminiscences she'd rather forget. 'They never let up. We never had a moment's peace.' Suddenly my mother recalls that Mrs Forycka, the doctor's wife, was such a gossip that one of the villagers had made up a song about her, to the melodious tune of 'Carnival in Venice', and she begins to sing it. After all these years, she still remembers the words. 'Her mouth stretches to heaven, to heaven flies her mouth, if only you could measure, it stretches north to south!'

My parents were living on top of a volcano. They heard its rumbling, saw wisps of smoke, and felt the eruption building up beneath their feet, but they couldn't flee from its path. 'How did you keep going?' I ask. 'Didn't you ever feel you couldn't go on?' My mother shakes her head with that definite motion of hers. 'Never. When the day finally ended, and we'd survived one more day, I felt on top of the world.' I look at her, still pretty with her porcelain complexion, immaculately set fair hair now as fine as cotton wool, and eyes that still look unflinchingly at the world. 'Having you kept us going. I never allowed myself to think even for a moment that we wouldn't survive.'

After Izio had fled, Henek had organised a new bridge game

with Jurek, Dr Forycki, and Mr Grochowski, who worked at the agricultural supplies store and was a member of the underground. While they were playing a rubber in Jurek's pharmacy one night, a German policeman walked in, glanced at each of the players in turn, locked eyes with Mr Grochowski, and walked out without saying a word. No-one said a word about the German's visit, which was obviously connected with Mr Grochowski's underground activities. It bothered Henek that they never spoke about these matters in front of him, not even Jurek whom he regarded as a close friend.

He'd just finished taking an impression for dentures for one of his regular patients when she looked at him with a serious expression. 'Dr Boguslawski, I feel I ought to tell you, people are saying that your wife is Jewish.' Henek's heart almost jumped out of his chest. It was the first time that anyone had made the accusation to his face.

Several days later, just before Christmas, Jurek drew him aside and there was no smile on his usually friendly face. 'Danuta and I have just received an anonymous letter. It said, "Don't have anything to do with the Boguslawskis. Their life hangs by a thread."'

My father could see us sliding towards disaster. Pretending to be outraged, he told everyone that he was determined to find the culprit who'd dared to malign them. He'd heard that most of the gossip originated from the postmistress. Ever since they'd neglected to invite her to their first party, she'd become their enemy, but people hinted that the priest's sister was also spreading rumours.

When New Year's Eve came round, Henek was relieved that they'd been invited to the Grochowskis' party. Mr Grochowski had always surveyed him with a sardonic expression which made him feel uncomfortable, so he assumed that the invitation indicated some level of acceptance. But when they arrived at the Grochowskis', they sensed a strained atmosphere. People glanced their way and quickly looked away again as though they weren't there. Only one person was watching them, and it was a man my father didn't trust. A week ago this man had suggested in a snide voice that they should go to the Turkish baths together, and Henek had no doubt that his aim was to check out whether he was Jewish.

Realising that they were being ignored, Henek was relieved to see his friend Jurek chatting with a few men near a table loaded with canapes. But as soon as he came up to them, the conversation came to an abrupt halt. 'I think you should go away because we're discussing things that aren't for your ears,' Jurek said.

Henek flushed from his neck to the top of his head. Humiliated, he longed to get away as fast as possible but he couldn't afford the luxury of hurt feelings. He had to ignore the insult and brazen it out to the end. He put on a smile and, together with Bronia, moved from group to group, pretending to be unaware that no-one was speaking to them.

At the stroke of midnight, glasses were filled again, people who had until then addressed each other in the third person linked arms and drank Bruderschaft and hoped that 1944 would bring peace. Henek and Bronia were leaving when the man who'd suggested a visit to the Turkish baths stepped over to them. Through fumes of the machorka tobacco he was smoking, he sneered, 'I'm planning to pay you a visit tomorrow, Dr Boguslawski, at six in the morning,' he said.

'That's too early, I'll be in bed,' Henek replied pleasantly.

'That's exactly where I want you to be,' the man replied.

Henek and Bronia trudged home in the snow in silence, their heads bent. Millions of stars trembled in a black and brittle sky, and the moon lit up boughs that drooped with snow. The air was so pure and cold that it speared Bronia's heart. Finally she spoke in a firm, strong voice. 'They're playing a cat and mouse game with us, but they won't win.' She looked up into the starlit sky and breathed in the frosty air. 'God won't let us perish.'

Henek's mind was churning. He and Bronia had planned a New Year's Day party and now he wondered whether anyone would turn up. If they boycott our party, that will be the end, he thought. He decided to swallow his pride and visit everyone they'd invited, to make sure. First he called on the Bultowicz brothers. After they confirmed that they'd be coming, Henek broached another subject. 'I wonder who's been spreading these stories about Bronia,' he said. He deliberately focused on my mother as the butt of the rumours, because it should have been very easy to prove that he himself wasn't a Jew.

Bogus Bultowicz shifted in his chair and sat for a few moments without speaking. 'Grochowski reckons that Bronia is definitely Jewish, but as for you,' he cleared his throat, 'he says he'll have to check you out.'

At the doctor's house Mrs Forycka made excuses. She was too tired, she didn't feel like going out, and anyway her husband was away and she had no idea when he'd be back. 'Do come, it won't be a party without you!' Henek urged. To his relief, she nodded. 'All right, I'll come, and I'll leave a note for Jozek to come over as soon as he gets back.' Feeling as triumphant as Napoleon after one of his victories, Henek braced himself to call on the Grochowskis. Mrs Grochowska refused point-blank, but her husband said that since he'd promised to come, he'd keep his word.

All day Bronia prepared for the party with Mrs Bogdanowa, who never involved herself in village gossip. They roasted ducks to crisp brown perfection, prepared marinated mushrooms and cabbage rolls, and baked cheese pancakes. But all day a black cloud hung over them. What if no-one turned up?

They were relieved to see the cassocked figure of Father Soszynski standing at the door, followed by their neighbour, Mrs Podobasowa. But as neither of them had been at the Grochowskis' the previous night, they mightn't be aware that their hosts had been ostracised. Henek and Bronia tried not to glance at the door. Half an hour passed and no-one else had arrived.

Suddenly young Krajewski, the Lewickis' son-in-law, poked his head around the door, saw the priest deep in conversation with Henek and Mrs Podobasowa, and disappeared, soon to return with the whole Lewicki family. Another five people. Before long Dr and Mrs Forycki arrived, followed by the man who'd threatened to visit Henek before he'd had time to dress. Henek had never imagined he'd be so happy to see his sardonic face.

Jurek and Daunta were there too, but Henek noticed that they were more reserved than usual and kept their distance. Circulating among the guests, Henek kept filling up glasses with cherry vodka and telling the jokes for which he was famous. Soon the atmosphere lightened and people started to laugh. Henek felt like a prisoner on death row, reprieved at the last moment.

The party was in full swing when the sound of angry voices made everyone stop and turn around. Mrs Forycka was shouting at Mrs Lewicka. While the guests stared in horror, the older woman reached out and slapped the other hard across the face. The combatants then took their husbands by the arm and hurriedly left, which soon broke up the party. Henek wasn't sorry about this turn of events. A juicy scandal in the village might divert attention away from them.

The following day Mr Lewicki came over, ostensibly to ask Henek to try and settle the quarrel between his wife and Mrs

Forycka, but he had another agenda. In his forthright manner, the resistance activist said, 'For heaven's sake, Boguslawski, clear yourself of this slur about being Jewish once and for all!'

Henek's reply was swift. 'Don't worry, I'm making inquiries to find out who's casting these slanderous rumours about Bronia.'

Before he had time to mull over Stanislaw Lewicki's warning, there was another knock on the door. Mrs Forycka had arrived. Henek assumed that she too had come to discuss the fracas of the night before, but her words took him by surprise. 'Everyone is saying that you're Jews,' the doctor's wife was saying. 'If you are, then you should leave as soon as possible. I don't like Jews, but I'll help you to get away in my brother-in-law's car.'

After she'd left, Henek's face was ashen. 'Things have come to a head. Maybe we should take her up on her offer and get away while we can.'

Bronia was staring at him with disbelief. 'You must be mad!' she cried. 'Leave and admit that we're Jewish? How far do you think we'd get before someone runs to the Gestapo? And where would we go? Wherever we go, people will guess that we're Jews. Running away is the worst thing we could do. Our only hope is to sit tight and keep denying the rumours. You remember what Father Soszynski said when someone told him that Danusia was Jewish. At least here we have a few friends. And as for Mrs Forycka, I'll tell her I'm as Jewish as she is!'

Henek couldn't let it go any longer. At the post office he confronted the postmistress and her mother. 'I've been told that the slander about my wife being Jewish started with you,' he said in a voice that was deadly calm. While the women stared at him, he continued, 'If that's true, I demand an apology or you'll find yourselves in big trouble. If the Germans find out that you take money out of people's letters, they'll arrest you. As you know, they throw people into jail first and ask questions afterwards.' He was bluffing but the guilty look on their white faces told him all he needed to know.

After a few moments the postmistress found her voice. 'Dr Boguslawski, we've also heard the rumours about your wife,' she said. 'But we didn't start them, they came from the presbytery, not from us. We've heard that Mrs Boguslawska serves chopped egg and onion, and goose rubbed with garlic, the way the Jews do. Of course we wouldn't know about these things, since we've never been to your place.' Henek apologised for the oversight. 'You must come over for a glass of tea very soon,' he said.

The presbytery was next. In the village square some of the layabouts were lolling under the chestnut trees, still under the influence of *bimber*, the rotgut they brewed in their illicit stills. In the modest living room of the presbytery, under the priest's alert gaze, Henek's voice was reproachful. 'People in Piszczac are saying that we're Jews, and I'm shocked to hear that these dangerous rumours have been spread by your own sister.'

Clearly upset, Father Soszynski asked his sister whether this was true. She denied it and blamed Mrs Podobasowa. Determined not to let the matter rest, my father knocked on his neighbour's door and his implacable gaze made it clear that excuses would be useless. But Mrs Podobasowa shook her head. It wasn't really her, it was a friend of hers who'd started those stories. 'Unless your friend turns up at my place by four this afternoon to apologise and retract the slander, I'm going to report both of you to the police,' he said.

Back home, he paced around the room like a caged tiger, glancing out of the window every few minutes. What if they called his bluff and refused to come? What if they decided to pre-empt his threat by going to the Gestapo first? As the minutes ticked by, he became convinced that they wouldn't come. It was childish to think that such a ruse could work.

But when he looked out of the window yet again, he couldn't believe his eyes. Mrs Podobasowa and her friend Mrs Jorucka were walking up the path.

The two women sat on the edge of their chairs, their eyes darting around uncomfortably. 'I never actually said that Bronia was Jewish,' Mrs Jorucka stated. 'All I said was that when she's out with Danusia, she walks very fast and drags her along just like a Jewess.'

Henek had a deadpan expression. 'If that's all you said, then I don't have any problem with that, because in my opinion, you talk like a Jewess.' Mrs Jorucka reddened. She came from Silesia and spoke Polish with a strong German accent. Henek thanked her cordially for coming to clear things up and suggested that she refrain from making dangerous accusations in future.

CHAPTER 28

From Bergen–Belsen station Mania and Misko staggered with their belongings for several kilometres until they reached the camp, which was enclosed by barbed wire. In the grim watchtowers, helmeted soldiers held their fingers on machine gun triggers. Someone thrust a pair of heavy wooden clogs and a red enamel bowl into Mania's hands, yelled instructions and gestured towards one of the barrack huts. Numb with shock and exhaustion, she slumped onto a narrow two-tiered wooden bunk covered with a few handfuls of hay.

Much later, when she was able to raise her head, she was surprised to see a few familiar faces. She was looking at the wealthy holders of South American passports whom she'd envied so much a week before. Among them were the big bosses who'd charged a fortune to be included on the lists. Instead of going to Vittel, they'd been sent to Bergen–Belsen.

In the adjacent barrack, the huge glassy eyes staring out of cadaverous faces and the skeletal bodies of the prisoners filled her with foreboding. When guttural voices ordered them out to the Appelplatz for rollcall, and thousands of phantoms waited to be counted, she saw that Belsen was a grotesquely sprawling township of starving Jewish, Polish, Russian and Greek prisoners of war.

She'd been there one week when they were ordered to have a shower. A deathly silence descended over the barrack.

No-one could bring themselves to voice the unthinkable. They were marched into a cold cement washroom, men told to stand on one side, women on the other. Avoiding one another's eyes as they were forced to strip naked, they shivered on the cement floor. As the first jet of water hit her body, Mania clenched her eyes and murmured a long-forgotten prayer.

When the water was turned off, she looked around in amazement. They were still alive. Thanks to their foreign passports, Mania and Misko's group at the Hotel Polski had been sent to this camp which had no gas chambers, instead of to Auschwitz or Treblinka where most Jews were being deported. If you didn't starve to death or die of typhus, and managed to avoid the sadistic eye of the SS men and the phenol injections of camp doctor Karl Jager, you had a slim chance of surviving at Bergen–Belsen.

'While summer lasted, things weren't too bad, but in winter I couldn't warm myself up from the inside or the outside. I was starving, nothing but skin and bones, and had no warm clothes to wear,' Aunty Mania reminisces. 'And those interminable rollcalls. In snow or rain, we had to stand in the Appelplatz until they'd counted over two thousand people. If they made a mistake, they started all over again. But you know what's really strange? Hardly anyone got sick.' She looks at me with her bemused gaze. 'Can you understand that? At home I was such a weakling, but at Belsen I wasn't sick once!'

While Aunty Mania is describing life in Belsen, I can hear my mother's disapproving footsteps in the flat above. Her assertive footsteps are telling me that I'm spending too much time with Mania. Why didn't I come up and see her first? My mother's resentment seeps through the ceiling and hovers around us. Normally she would have knocked on her sister's door by now, but she's not talking to Mania at the moment, so she's trapped upstairs by her own anger.

In October that year, when Commandant Adolf Haas ordered them out to the Appelplatz after rollcall had been completed for the day, everyone was on edge. As the guard started calling out hundreds of names, Mania realised that they all belonged to those with South American passports.

Mania's friend Lilka whispered, 'Look over there, they've got lorries waiting, they're going to take them to Vittel after all. I'm going to say that I've got papers for Paraguay too, so I can go too,' she said and stepped forward, holding her little daughter's hand. For once the Germans didn't check anyone's papers, so she joined the several hundred who climbed happily onto the lorries. The group included the Henings and most of the wheelers and dealers, all thrilled that they were going to South America at last. Mania felt depressed after so many of her friends had left. 'People with money always manage to save themselves, while we're left here to rot,' she grumbled.

As more and more prisoners arrived in Belsen, the barracks were soon bursting at the seams and typhus raged through the camp. 'Lice were eating us alive but there was nothing we could do. We were only allowed one hot shower a week and they wouldn't give us any soap,' Aunty Mania recalls.

It's hard to imagine this fastidious woman, always perfectly groomed and dressed in the latest fashion, wearing clogs and living in filth, so I'm not surprised when her friend Irka recalls with a fond smile, 'Even in Belsen Mania tried to look elegant. No matter what was happening, she always looked her best and she never lost hope.'

'All the time we were in Belsen, your aunt never stopped talking about you,' Irka continues. 'I've never met an aunt so obsessed with her niece. "My Danusia had lovely curly hair and big blue eyes, she's so clever, she knows the names of all the animals ..." On and on and she went. It was almost as if she believed you were actually her child. She talked a lot about your mother too. Bronia this and Bronia that. She couldn't wait to see the three of you again. Especially you.' Tears fill my eyes when she adds, 'I think the thought of seeing you again kept her going.'

Every day more prisoners were crammed into the camp, most of them exhausted, starving women from Flossenburg, Plaszow and Auschwitz. Among the transport from Auschwitz were two teenage sisters from Amsterdam who clung to each other—Anne and Margot Frank.

Among the latest arrivals from Auschwitz was my father's cousin Rozia Johannes with her fourteen-year-old daughter Wisia. When this dignified old lady tells me her story in Tel-Aviv, her calm, matter-of-fact narration seems incongruous with her experiences. Not long after Krakow had been occupied by the Germans, Rozia and Wisia, her only child, were interrogated at Gestapo headquarters in Pomorska Street in Krakow. 'They thought that I was very wealthy and that I was working for the underground, so they imprisoned me with the political prisoners. I did have some jewellery but I managed to hide it among the coal in our fireplace before they took us away. They separated us at Pomorska Street but an SS man took a fancy to Wisia and let her visit me in my cell every evening. They interrogated me for a whole week,' she says and adds: 'I've been through a lot in my life.'

After Pomorska Street, Rozia and Wisia moved to the Krakow ghetto and when that was liquidated, they were taken to Plaszow concentration camp. 'That was a tough place,' she says. 'If you wanted to turn over in your bunk, all the others had to turn too. When I got pneumonia, the woman next to me was also drenched with sweat. Luckily one of the officers liked Wisia, so we were allowed to work at the Kavla tile factory.' Wisia was Rozia's good-luck charm because her earnest little face and long fair plaits melted even hard hearted guards.

Wherever they were, some Ukrainian guard or German overseer took pity on Wisia and smuggled her an extra ration of bread or made sure that she and her mother weren't separated.

From Plaszow's tile factory they were transported to Auschwitz. 'They told us that we were destined for the *Himmelkommando*, or death,' Rozia recalls. 'Only two crematoria were functioning by then, the others had been bombed. We arrived in a shocking downpour and stood there soaked and shivering while Dr Mengele carried out the selections at the railway station. He was an extremely handsome man. With a disarmingly courteous manner he decided whether people would live or die. We were among the few who were allowed to live. At Auschwitz they cut off Wisia's plaits.'

Rozia tells her story with as little emotion as if she were describing an interesting but not particularly involving movie she has seen. Like many survivors, she has erected a high protective wall between herself and her experiences, and I don't dare to penetrate her defences, especially as Wisia, her only child, has recently died of cancer. So Rozia continues her story, from Auschwitz to Buchenwald and then on to Bergen–Belsen in December 1944.

Aunty Mania recalls that, with the influx of prisoners, food rations became so small that the flesh was dissolving off people's bones, and anatomy students wouldn't have needed skeletons to learn about body structure. In the mornings they were given brownish water which tasted like acorns and a small piece of bread which had to last all day.

She gives a short, bitter laugh. 'It was terrible bread but it tasted so good! Nothing tasted so good as that bread. I longed for a whole loaf with butter to spread on it, or even a chunk of bread without butter, but to have so much that I couldn't eat any more. You know what we talked about all day? Food. Cooking. Recipes. We exchanged recipes. We argued whose chicken soup was better, whose *matzoh* dumplings were the lightest! To avoid thinking about the terrible things around us, we escaped into a world of delicious cakes and elegant clothes. We talked about what we once had and hoped one day to have again.

'At home I was a fussy eater and turned my nose up at most of the food that my mother put in front of me. I wouldn't touch fruit with the slightest blemish, or meat with a morsel of fat. Only cakes from the best patisseries were good enough for me. My mother used to shake her head and say, "One day God is going to punish you for being so fussy." When I was so hungry that I would have devoured anything, I remembered my mother's words.'

But no matter how hungry she was, or how many people were dying around them, Mania never gave up hope. 'We have to stay alive to see the Germans defeated,' she used to tell those who were weak and in despair. 'We have to survive so we can see them crawling in the gutter.' Having Misko there boosted her morale. 'Whatever we had, we shared between us. I saw that those who had someone to care for, or who cared about them, did better than those who were alone,' she told me. 'The first to die were the single men.'

She recalls that by pressing against the barbed wire, they sometimes saw Germans riding bicycles, carrying shopping bags and leading normal lives. 'Later those people said they knew nothing about Belsen.' Her voice rises with anger. 'How could they lie like that?

'By 1945 the real horrors began. Tens of thousands of prisoners on death marches from other camps poured into Belsen in a pitiful condition, but nothing was provided for them, no roof over their heads, even though it was winter, and no food, not even water. By then we were no longer living: we were slowly dying,' my aunt recalls. 'Hunger gnawed at me day and night, it made me cry. People were as transparent as ghosts, you could count each bone, and the flesh had disappeared from their buttocks. Those who could still walk stumbled around like grotesque skeletons, others were too weak to move and lay dying in their own excrement. The first sign that someone was about to die was that they turned yellow. We called them "*Mussulmans*" because of the colour of their skin. They just lay there and lost interest in everything, even food. In a few days they were dead. I really don't know how I survived,' she muses in a drained voice. 'Sometimes I wonder, was it me or was it someone else?'

It was from one of the new arrivals that Mania found out what had happened to the Henings, Lilka and her little daughter, and all the others with South American passports who'd looked forward to going to Vittel. They'd been taken straight to Auschwitz and gassed.

Although the inmates didn't know what was going on outside, sometimes while queueing up for their rancid turnip soup, they could hear the guards talking and they began to realise that the war wasn't going well for the Germans. By the beginning of April, when they saw allied planes flying overhead, they knew that the war must be coming to an end.

On a fine spring day in 1945, two years after Mania and Misko had been transported to Belsen, the guards rounded up those few who could still walk and herded them to the station and onto the waiting train. Cheered by the rumour that they were going to Switzerland, Mania and Misko found themselves on a train speeding through Germany. Past Hanover, they heard gunfire but didn't know who was shooting.

At Madgeburg, the firing became so intense that the train couldn't go any further and stopped beside the River Elbe. While it was stationary, one of the prisoners overheard that their guards planned to take all of them down to the marshes

369

and shoot them. Hearing this, one of their group tried to persuade the German commandant to reconsider. 'How will it benefit you to kill us?' he said. 'You know you've lost the war. The Americans will be here any moment. If we tell them that you let us go, they mightn't kill you.' But the American column had already caught up with them and when the soldiers found out that the guards intended to kill those ghostly survivors of Bergen-Belsen, they shot them.

It wasn't until Mania reached the nearby town of Hillersleben that she realised that the war was over. She could hardly believe her ears when she heard the Americans announce to the German residents, 'Get out of your flats and make room for the Jews!'

I'm looking at a photograph taken several months later, on a sunlit street in Brussels. A slender young woman in a check jacket and high-heeled shoes leans against a handsome balding man and smiles lopsidedly for the street photographer. Aunty Mania and Uncle Misko look like any carefree young couple on holiday.

CHAPTER 29

By the early summer of 1944 while Mania and Misko were still languishing in Belsen, it was clear that the Russians would soon enter Piszczac. Everyone was speculating about what would happen and some said that the village would be caught in the crossfire between the two armies, and that there would be fighting in the streets. Like some of the other Silesian refugees, Jurek and Danuta Zawadzki were planning to move westwards. But Henek and Bronia saw no need to flee from the Russians. In fact they couldn't wait for them to arrive.

Even now, on the eve of German defeat, my parents still couldn't relax. Henek overheard Stanislaw Lewicki talking about someone his underground colleagues had caught in the woods. They'd checked him out, found out he was a Jew, and shot him. 'One of these days we'll have to get you into the woods and check you out too!' Mr Lewicki told my father with a meaningful look. To the villagers Mr Lewicki was a resistance hero, but to my parents he posed a constant threat. Although the rumours had quietened down after their New Year's Day confrontation, my parents knew that they were still in danger. 'If the war had gone on any longer, someone would have turned us in,' my mother used to tell me. 'We were hanging on by our fingernails.'

But when the German retreat became imminent, the atmosphere grew tense. No-one knew what to expect and people feared the lawlessness of the retreating and advancing armies. As my father was packing our belongings, ready to leave the village if necessary, a sturdy peasant woman in heavy boots and a thick headscarf walked into his surgery and asked him to make her a bridge. Pointing to the suitcases and bundles piled in the centre of the room, he explained that he'd already packed his instruments. 'The Russians are about to move in,' he said. 'This isn't the time to be starting dental work.'

She explained that she wasn't worried because she lived deep in the woods, safe from marauding armies and gun-happy soldiers. Henek was intrigued at the thought of a community living in the forest. 'If you want me to do this dental work, you'll have to take me with you!' he joked. To his astonishment, she nodded. 'Be ready to leave early in the morning with all your things, and I'll pick you up.'

The sun was rising in the wintry sky when a rickety cart with rough-hewn sides clattered along the dirt path leading to our house. As soon it was loaded up with suitcases, my small iron bed, bundles of eiderdowns, the dental chair and boxes of instruments, we clambered up beside the peasant woman as she picked up the reins and whistled to the horse to get moving.

We were just about to swing out of the yard when a long German supply column of foot soldiers, lorries and armoured vehicles appeared in a cloud of dust and rolled along the street. As we waited for the endless cavalcade to pass, they suddenly came to a dead stop outside our house, blocking us in. 'Now what do we do?' Bronia whispered. 'We're stuck.' Henek didn't dare ask German soldiers to move on during their humiliating retreat; besides, the last thing he wanted to do was to draw attention to the cart, our belongings and ourselves.

Henek slid down from the cart and drew closer to the

column. Perhaps he'd be able to find out how long they were planning to stay. As he strained to hear what the soldiers were saying, he realised that they weren't speaking German at all. He was listening to a language he recognised from his boarding school days. They were Hungarian soldiers in German uniform. Addressing the platoon commander in Hungarian, he asked for help to get the cart across the road.

Astounded that someone in this godforsaken place could speak Hungarian, the commander looked at the distinguished greying man with the military moustache who spoke to him in his own language with such an authoritative manner. 'He must have thought I was a high-ranking espionage officer stationed close to the border to pass on information,' my father wrote in his memoirs, 'because he clicked his heels, snapped to attention, and gave a sharp salute.' Out of the corner of his eye Henek saw one of the villagers staring at this extraordinary scene. 'I'll see to it immediately, sir,' the commander replied in Hungarian and ordered the soldiers to move on so that we could pass.

As the cart trundled on towards the woods, my father marvelled at this turn of events. 'You see, nothing in life is ever wasted,' he used to tell me. 'If it hadn't been for the fact that I spoke Hungarian, we wouldn't have got out of Piszczac that day, and who knows what might have happened.'

Deep in the woods where she lived in a little community of eleven families, the woman gave us a room in her hut and my father started work on her bridge. For the first time since the war had started, Henek felt calmer and tossed less in his sleep. In this peaceful forest where mushrooms sprouted in moist loam and blueberries grew in patches laced with sunshine, he went to bed without feeling afraid.

He was fast asleep when the glare of a lantern shining into his face made him sit bolt upright. When he jumped to his feet and lit the kerosine lamp, Henek saw a thick-set soldier in Russian uniform with a younger one standing behind him. Although he'd been waiting for the Russians to liberate them, he felt uneasy wondering why these two had come to see him in the middle of the night. When the stocky one demanded who he was and what he was doing there, Henek stiffened. 'I'm waiting for the war to end,' he replied. Immediately, the older of the two Russians gave a triumphant shout: '*Aha, ty udral z Germancem!*' 'You're a German collaborator!'

Henek's heart was thumping. He knew that the vanguard of any army dispensed summary justice, and if these two decided that he was a German collaborator, they would shoot him. Cold sweat was trickling down his back. Surely after surviving the Nazis, he wouldn't be shot by his liberators. When he tried to explain who he was, they stared at him with impassive faces and he tailed off, resigned to the fact that they couldn't understand him. Suddenly they burst out laughing and thumped him on the back. They'd known all along that he wasn't a German collaborator. They knew he was a dentist and had come looking for alcohol.

Well aware of Russian soldiers' reputation for heavy drinking, rape and robbery, Henek couldn't get them out of the hut fast enough. 'Vodka *nyet,*' he kept saying in the few Russian words he knew. '*Nie ma* vodka.' Hearing this, the older man made menacing gestures, 'Get some food ready because we're coming back with our own vodka!' he shouted.

The sun had barely risen and light was slanting through the slender mottled trunks of the birch trees when the Russians returned with a big bottle of vodka which they slammed down on the wooden table. They sat down heavily, sprawled out, and shouted '*Dawaj stagan!*', pointing to two big tumblers in the cupboard. Pouring vodka up to the brim, the older soldier tilted his head back and proceeded to swallow one quarter of a litre of vodka without stopping to take breath.

When his glass was empty, he poured himself another full tumbler with a steady hand, but for his younger companion, who had also drained his, he poured only half a glass. Henek watched astounded as he drank one tumblerful after another as if it was water. Still sober, the soldier asked my father to make a crown for one of his teeth. After Henek had taken an impression of his tooth, the old soldier propped his large head against his meaty hand and slept for an hour. Henek fitted him with the crown and the two left, thumping his back in gratitude.

Later Henek found out that he'd had a lucky escape. These two had been wandering around the countryside conning the peasants. The first soldier would go into a peasant's hut and trade an army blanket for a bottle of vodka, and a short time later the second would arrive and, pointing accusingly at the blanket, would threaten the peasant with imprisonment for being in possession of army property unless he returned it immediately. Within a few days, however, the regular army caught up with these entrepreneurs and ended their alcoholic marauding.

When we returned to Piszczac several days later, it was already in the hands of the regular Russian army. It was March 1944 and for this part of Poland the war was over. For five years my parents had lived on the razor's edge. They rejoiced with their Piszczac friends, wept tears of joy as they sang the national anthem, and linked arms in toasts of Bruderschaft. Now that the Nazis had gone, Henek began to relax. 'Finally I can tell them that we're Jewish,' he told Bronia.

She stared at him in dismay. 'You can't be serious,' she said. She still sounds indignant about it even after almost fifty years. 'After all you've heard them saying about Jews, how can you even think of telling them? Do you expect them to say "Isn't that wonderful?" You don't live in the real world!' She shakes her head in tight-lipped disapproval. 'Sometimes your father wasn't very realistic. Luckily, he listened to me that time.' Not long after my parents' argument, Piszczac buzzed with news. Some Jews found hiding in the forest had been murdered. Bronia flashed Henek a meaningful glance.

We stayed on in Piszczac for another nine months, posing as Catholics to the end. Lolling around the camp fires every night, Russian soldiers drank vodka, slapped their legs in boisterous Cossack dances, and sang melancholy songs of the Steppes in soulful Russian voices which boomed through the village.

Winter had ended but spring hadn't yet begun when my parents went to say goodbye to the priest and their Piszczac friends. I was lifted into the back of a truck which was covered by a khaki tarpaulin and saturated with acrid fumes of gasoline which bit my throat. It was March 1945 and we were returning to Krakow.

On the way, we stopped in Lublin. While queuing for bread, Bronia looked up and screamed with delight. Coming towards her was Henek's cousin, Janek Spira, and his wife Maryla. Janek's usually lively brown eyes filled with tears when he told them that his mother Salomea and younger brother Karol had been killed. Salomea Spira, who had Aryan papers, was on a train when German soldiers entered her carriage and asked her name. She was so petrified that she couldn't remember her false name. Realising she was Jewish, they shot her on the spot. Janek's brother Karol had managed to survive on false papers, but one week before the war ended, someone denounced him to the Germans.

Maryla and Janek, who didn't have a zloty to their name, were expecting a baby. 'How can I bring a child into the world at such a time, how will I manage?' Maryla lamented.

'Don't worry, things will work out,' Bronia reassured her. 'You'll never regret having a baby.'

For the rest of their life, Maryla and Janek were grateful for my parents' moral support at that difficult time. Not long before she died, Maryla wrote to me. 'When Anne was born, your father gave me a beautiful doll for the baby, saying that each baby brings its own luck.' Anne, who inherited her parents' warm and hospitable nature, became a doctor and lives on a religious communal settlement in Israel with her husband and three children.

As they travelled to Krakow my parents occasionally saw Russians leading groups of conquered German soldiers through liberated towns. No longer immaculate and invincible, they looked scared and shrunken while bystanders jeered, cursed, spat and hurled rotting tomatoes, yelling, 'Let the bastards have it!'

My mother watched in silence. 'I couldn't bring myself to join in with them,' she told me. 'Maybe among those soldiers there was one decent man.'

The war was over.

CHAPTER 30

Down in the street, people hurried along cobblestones glistening with melted snow, their chins buried deep inside their upturned collars. Occasionally a tram, an angry pillar-box red, splashed the street with colour as it ground its way towards St Florian's Gate. Although I was sitting by the window, I wasn't interested in the activity outside. Already at the age of six I'd discovered the pleasure of escaping into the world of books and was engrossed in *The Golden Slipper*, a historical novel set in medieval Krakow which Aunty Andzia had given me on St Nicholas' Day.

'A gift for Chanukkah,' she'd said holding out the book. I squirmed. I didn't know what Chanukkah was but I didn't like the sound of it. Although I didn't ask, and nobody explained, I noticed a quick glance pass between my mother and my aunt. I was a bit scared of Aunty Andzia whose eyes stabbed you like pins, not like Aunty Slawa who had a merry laugh. Aunty Slawa hadn't said anything about Chanukkah. 'This is for Christmas!' she'd said, handing me a doll's tea set.

After six long years, we were back in Krakow. In months to come, like bruised birds returning from faraway places, Jews drifted back from concentration camps and gulags. Some had spent years squeezed into recesses behind walls; others had been bent double in holes beneath barn floors, or stooped in freezing pits in the forest. There were children who'd forgotten how to smile and play, youths aged before their time, and adults whose pasts had been snatched away.

They came back to a city which felt like an empty shell. Kazimierz, once the heart and soul of a vibrant culture, had become a ghost town. Streets and marketplaces which had bustled with life and colour for five centuries had now fallen into an uneasy silence. Broken tombstones littered ancient cemeteries, synagogues lay in ruins, and prayer houses, Talmud–Torah schools and community halls were taken over by people who didn't mourn the destruction of Jewish culture. They hadn't yet discovered that they too would be impoverished by the loss.

Day after day Jews clustered around the noticeboard in Dluga Street and ran trembling fingers down the lists of survivors posted by the Jewish Committee, hoping against hope to find the names of their missing loved ones. Gradually they discovered the bitter truth. The Nazis and their willing helpers had almost succeeded in wiping the Jews off the face of the earth. Out of 225 000 Jews who'd lived in Krakow in 1939, only 15 000 had survived. Out of over three million Jews who'd lived in Poland before the war, only 250 000 remained, and most of them had survived not in their native land but in the Soviet Union. In concentration camps, death camps, extermination camps, labour camps, ghettoes, forest groves, hillsides, villages and cities, six million innocent people had been gassed, shot, hanged, beaten, tortured, mutilated, set on fire, buried alive and starved.

And these atrocities hadn't been perpetrated by some pagan tribe in a remote and primitive land centuries ago. They were committed by the obedient citizens of the most progressive and cultured nation on earth. Much of the savagery had taken place in devoutly Catholic Poland, among rustic villages, rustling forests and meadows whose innocent beauty made your heart ache.

But there were those whose courage and humanity had been a beacon on that black night of the human soul when compassion almost vanished from the earth. They were the feisty nuns who took in Jewish children, the devoted nannies and housekeepers who passed their Jewish charges off as their own children, the stout-hearted peasants and compassionate town-dwellers who risked the malice of their neighbours as well as the revenge of the Germans by offering sanctuary to their own countrymen destined for extinction.

In this atmosphere of grief and restrained optimism we rented a flat on Florianska Street, a long cobbled thoroughfare running from the Glowny Rynek to the medieval gate of St Florian's which led to the Planty Gardens. The crumbling eighteenth century facades of the houses in our street were decorated with heraldic emblems, cherubs and statues of saints. I remember climbing the curved staircase in the dark entrance hall to our high-ceilinged flat on the second floor. My father had his dental surgery in one room, while we lived in the other. My iron bed stood against the wall, near the white tiled stove in the corner, and we ate my mother's tasty dill-flavoured potato soup and *bigos* stew at a small wooden table with a single bulb dangling above our heads.

My father's brother, Uncle Izio, was a frequent visitor. As Vice-president of the Jewish Committee, he brought my mother the news that Mania and Misko had survived Bergen–Belsen and were living in Brussels. By then Bronia knew that, apart from Mania, her entire family had been wiped out. Dozens of aunts, uncles and cousins had been consumed in the flames of the Holocaust.

When all efforts to find her relatives had failed, Bronia travelled to Lancut to claim her grandfather's land. It took weeks to process her application, the loneliest, coldest, most miserable weeks she could recall. When her claim was finally approved, she sold the land for two hundred US dollars, a considerable sum at the time, especially for my parents who had nothing.

Not long after Bronia returned to Krakow, an angry letter arrived from a cousin she thought was dead. Moniek, the only member of his family to survive, had just returned from Siberia and accused her of grabbing the inheritance to which he was equally entitled. 'I had no intention of cheating him,' my mother tells me. 'Chaim Goldman and Breindl Faust were his grandparents too. But before I had time to do anything about it, Henek got so upset about the letter that he sent him the whole two hundred dollars!'

'Why didn't you just split the money with Moniek?' I ask. She waves her small hand in that impatient gesture of hers and utters a short, exasperated sound. 'Because as usual your father rushed in and didn't ask my opinion,' she retorts. 'He couldn't stand someone thinking that we'd taken advantage of them, so he gave him the lot, finish! You know how impulsive he was. I had such a hard time in Lancut and then Moniek got all the money, but then I thought, let him have it. He had a hard time in Siberia, and then came back to find that his two sisters had been killed.'

Now that the war was over, the euphoria of having survived had faded and the problems of peace began. Andzia was depressed because Zygmunt hadn't come back, and the prospect of bringing up two children on her own weighed her down. 'Don't worry,' Henek told his sister. 'I haven't got much, but whatever I have, I'll share with you. If I have two crusts of bread, I'll give you one.' A few days later, my mother was strolling with me in the Planty Gardens when she overheard Andzia complaining to her friend, 'I can't rely on anyone to help me. All I can expect from my brother is a crust of bread!' My mother admired her sister-in-law's courage but she couldn't stand her vituperative tongue. 'Andzia is like a cow that gives you a bucket full of creamy milk but suddenly for no reason kicks the pail over and spills the lot.'

Izio and Lola's wartime separation had become permanent. During the war, she'd fallen in love with another man and she married him as soon as her divorce from Izio was finalised. My mother was an inveterate matchmaker who couldn't bear to see her good-hearted, good-looking brother-in-law remain single, and before long she'd found someone for him. 'I've met the perfect woman for Izio,' she told my father one day. 'Zosia Guttentag is intelligent, cultured and very attractive.' They hit it off immediately. Izio was impressed by this refined woman who was a dentist, spoke six languages, and looked at him with eyes that glowed like dark pansies. Before they married, Zosia set one condition. She'd survived the Holocaust by working as a maid for a German, but Izio was never to ask her about her war experiences. 'They shared everything and were extremely close, but there were things my father never knew about her,' their daughter Lee tells me in Los Angeles many years later.

One of Izio's duties as Vice-president of the Jewish Committee was to distribute the aid parcels which arrived from the United States. I remember the excitement of unpacking the big boxes of United Nations relief rations stamped with UNRRA labels. The packets, cans and powders inside mystified us. There were boxes of crisp yellow flakes that no-one knew what to do with, packets of sugared crystals called Jello, and thin grey sticks which turned into rubber when you chewed them. My cousin Fredzio, who always seemed to know things, taught me to stretch the gum out without breaking it, and to save it for the next day by sticking it onto a plate.

Fredzio, who was four years older than I, was like a brother to me. Together we took the tram to the Glowny Rynek, went to the Pantechnikon where we peered through special glasses at pictures which changed before our delighted eyes, and rode my red wooden scooter in the Planty Gardens. Fredzio was unhappy because the other boys at school taunted, tormented and bashed him for being Jewish. For six years he'd been terrified of being killed by German soldiers, but now he was frightened of going to school with his own countrymen.

Many years later, when we meet again, my cousin Fred tells me that the time he spent with me in Krakow was the only part of his childhood he recalls with pleasure. 'You were my favourite playmate,' he says. Although we hadn't seen each other since 1948 and had only corresponded about family events and personal milestones, from the moment Fred arrived in Sydney in 1987 with his wife Phyllis, it was as though we'd never been apart. Our childhood bond had survived a separation of forty years and separate lives on far-flung continents.

Although the war had ended, and most of Poland's three million Jews had been wiped out, those who'd survived still felt insecure. It wasn't paranoia. There were many incidents of Jewish survivors being ambushed and murdered, and between 1945 and the end of 1947, over 1500 Jews were murdered by fellow Poles.

But it was the pogrom in Kielce that made my parents realise how deeply-entrenched anti-Semitism was in their country. One hot July day in 1946, in the town of Kielce, a little Catholic boy returned home after being missing for two days. Frightened of being punished for running away, he told his parents that the Jews had kidnapped him. Before long, the town was buzzing with rumours that Jews were kidnapping Catholic children and using their blood for making *matzohs*, an anti-Jewish slander which had been the excuse for pogroms back in the Middle Ages. Most of the Jews of Kielce, who by then numbered less than two hundred, lived in Planty Street, and that's where the boy's father headed, along with a mob of angry townspeople brandishing clubs and crowbars, followed by policemen armed with revolvers.

What happened next resembles the medieval pogroms in Krakow and the wartime barbarity of German soldiers. In an orgy of bloodlust, the mob, aided by the police, butchered every Jew they could lay their hands on. They threw tiny children through the window of the third floor *cheder*, ripped open the wombs of pregnant women, battered old men and teenagers to death, and then beat the corpses to an unrecognisable pulp. One man was so disfigured that the only thing which identified him was the number the Nazis had tattooed on his arm at Auschwitz. Forty-two Jews were murdered on that beautiful summer's day in Kielce. They'd survived Hitler only to be massacred by their fellow countrymen.

I was discussing life in postwar Poland with Aunty Andzia in Tel-Aviv when she shocked me by saying, 'It was because of the antisemitism that your father had you baptised after the war.' This came as a shock—I had no idea I'd been baptised— and I thought that she'd made a mistake, but when I questioned my mother about it after my return, she nodded. 'When it looked as though we'd be staying in Poland, your father decided we should be baptised so you'd never have to suffer what we went through. I was totally against it. Being baptised didn't help Jews during the Holocaust, but he was adamant that it would make your life easier.'

Even now, after all this time, it's hard for me to think about being baptised without feeling uncomfortable. The idea of baptism bothers me even though I understand why he did it and know that my father felt intensely Jewish all his life and never denied who he was.

As a pupil at a Catholic school run by the Prezentek order of nuns, I learned to draw poplar, plane and chestnut leaves, copied the letters of the alphabet onto my slate, and learned the difference between cumulus and rain clouds. Whenever our attention strayed, the nuns made us kneel on dried peas in the corner of the classroom. No matter how much you shifted and wriggled, those peas bored into your knee joints.

Like my father, I wasn't good at sums, but I excelled in religious education, according to the report card which my father kept all his life. During church services, I was beguiled by the odour of incense which wisped from the censer, and by the perfume of full-blown roses whose petals spilled onto the white altar cloth like splashes of blood.

In fact, I was so steeped in religious teaching that one afternoon, after I had walked home by myself, I horrified my parents by announcing that I hadn't looked to see whether any cars were coming because I had a holy picture in my pocket. 'Sister Cecilia said that if I always kept Jesus Christ with me, he'd look after me,' I explained. My mother looked horrified, while my father said, 'Sister Cecilia is very wise but you still have to look both ways before you cross the street.'

Sister Cecilia is no longer alive when I return to visit the convent in 1989 with my husband Michael and daughter Justine, but the headmistress, Sister Fabiola, is eager to show me around. The highly polished linoleum corridors of the school and its old-fashioned wooden desks look familiar. In one of the classrooms girls in navy skirts and blouses with sailor collars, just like the ones I used to wear, jump to their feet when we enter. 'This is Pani Diane Armstrong from Australia who was a pupil here once and has come back to see her old school,' Sister Fabiola tells them.

I don't tell Sister Fabiola that Danusia Boguslawska who attended the school from 1945 until 1948 was a Jewish child whose parents had been too apprehensive to reveal her religion.

There isn't time to delve into the murky waters of Jewish-Catholic relations and my chest tightens at the very thought of it. After so many years, I still feel uneasy about revealing my religion in Poland.

My mother and I were walking towards the Glowny Rynek one fresh spring morning in 1946 when shots rang out. People were screaming, shouting, running. Without saying a word, she grabbed my hand and pulled me along the cobbled street until we came to a church. She swung the door open and we sank into the nearest pew, gasping for breath, our hearts almost jumping out of our chests. I leaned against her, trembling as I listened to the shots and yells.

Long after the tumult had subsided, we crept out of the church. Quickening her step, my mother tightened her grip on my hand. We hurried home along empty streets which echoed with our footsteps. It was May Day, and a demonstration of workers' solidarity had turned into a riot as rabble-rousers stirred up the crowd with a call to get the communists and the Jews.

In July, along with the other pupils at the convent, I spent the summer holidays at Jordanow. It was the first time I'd been separated from my parents and I clung to my mother like a limpet, but she insisted that the country air and wholesome food would build me up. I think the holiday also had another motive. After the trauma of the past six years, my parents must have longed to have time to themselves.

It was the longest month of my life. Each afternoon after our nap, we had to slurp down a raw egg. The slime slipping slowly down my throat made me gag. 'Raw eggs will give you a beautiful singing voice,' the nuns used to say. It didn't work. Every evening we had to line up for a dose of cod-liver oil whose fishy flavour and thickly viscous consistency I can taste to this day. But the worst thing of all was our daily cup of goat's milk. In the mornings we walked in pairs to a barn where a plump girl planted on a low stool pulled on the long teats of the tethered goat, squirting milk rhythmically into a bucket. The goat stank, the liquid was hot and frothy, and its rank odour and musty taste made my stomach heave.

When winter came round again, my parents took me to Zakopane in the Tatra Mountains. Bundled up in my thick woollen coat and knitted hood, I breathed in air which stabbed my lungs like shards of crystal, and crunched thick snow under my little boots. I awoke to the sound of cocks crowing and the guesthouse owner calling to her chickens. In the distance, saw-toothed peaks zigzagged the sky. It was an Alpine world of untouched beauty and tranquillity where cruelty, violence and hate seemed far away.

My father and I were strolling through the hamlet on our usual afternoon walk when I tugged at his hand and pointed. On an ornate pine fence someone had scrawled an ugly-looking word I'd never seen before. *Jude*. 'That's the German word for Jew,' my father explained. 'Somebody wrote that because they don't like Jews.' For some reason I felt uneasy, but neither of us said any more about it.

Letters began to arrive with unfamiliar stamps. The uninteresting ones with the head of the English king came from Aunty Mania who'd recently migrated to Australia when Uncle Misko's cousin had sent them a permit. Write to Aunty, my mother used to say. 'When I grow up I'm going to be an author,' I wrote one day. Looking back, I realise that even at the age of seven I was already silently observing, interpreting and assessing, detecting the mood behind the expressions and the meaning behind the words.

Although over a year had passed since the war had ended, people were still searching for lost relatives. Occasionally a Jewish child would be found at a convent or a lone boy would emerge from the forest. Such reunions were becoming increasingly rare, so my mother couldn't understand the reaction of my father's cousin Hela when she was told that her niece Polusia had been located at an orphanage not far from Krakow. Instead of being overjoyed at the possibility that her dead sister's child might still be alive, Hela showed no interest in seeing her. 'My niece died along with my sister Stefa and the rest of the family,' she insisted.

Hela had lost most of her family during the war. Her father Ignacy had been bashed by thugs who broke into his office and demanded money and typewriters. Ignacy, who'd been a supply officer in the Austro-Hungarian army, had insisted on a receipt. In reply, they beat him so savagely that he died. Of Ignacy's five children, only Hela and her brother Jakub had survived. Hela's sister Ludwika had perished with her husband and small daughter, and only their son Olek had managed to survive by hiding in the forests. Her other sister Stefa had been killed together with her husband and little son, and she assumed that their daughter Polusia had perished with them. On the memorial that she and her husband Jozek erected in the Jewish cemetery in Krakow, they'd included Polusia's name.

Even after her friends had prevailed on her to visit the child, Hela maintained that she couldn't tell whether it was her niece or not. My mother was shocked. 'It was terrible that it took her so long to acknowledge her sister's child,' she tells me. 'I don't think she wanted the responsibility.' Then she becomes pensive. 'But you shouldn't judge. After what people went through during the Holocaust, it's a wonder that anyone was normal.'

Like my father, Hela's husband Jozek had also left Krakow for Lwow as soon as war was declared, while Hela and their five-year-old son Marian had remained in Krakow. From the Krakow ghetto they were sent to Plaszow Concentration Camp from which Hela had managed to escape by bribing a German guard with a piece of jewellery. With her little son she fled to Lwow to join Jozek, who in the meantime had been interned in the dreaded Janowska Camp. By the time they arrived, he'd escaped, been recaptured, and had escaped again.

As soon as they reached Lwow, Hela placed Marian in the care of her housekeeper Janina Mikolajewicz who was Catholic, and she told him to call her 'mother'. Janina became the housekeeper of a high-ranking German officer in charge of the Wehrmacht's fleet of armoured cars in Lwow. Marian was a sweet-natured child with a mop of brown hair and melting brown eyes and he soon became a favourite with the German soldiers at 10 Kopernika Street who had no idea that he was Jewish. 'They treated me as if I was their own child, gave me sweets, and let me sit behind the wheel of their cars and pretend to drive them,' he emails me from his home in New York.

The good times ended when a Gestapo officer arrived looking for Marian. A neighbour reported that Janina was keeping a Jewish child but her boss sent the policeman away, refusing even to discuss the matter. Several weeks later, however, the Gestapo returned with a warrant for Janina and Marian's arrest issued by the Governor of Lwow.

Marian and Janina were taken to Lwow's Lackiego Prison, where my father and grandfather had been beaten the previous year. In his quiet, understated but chilling way, my cousin Marian describes his recollections of his ten-month stay in jail as 'slides' which have been engraved in his mind forever. 'As soon as we arrived, the German guards tried to separate me from Janina. I was terrified and clutched her with all my might, I cried and kicked and screamed, "Mother! I want to stay with my mother!" until a man in a white coat came out, the prison doctor I suppose, and talked the guards into letting me stay with her.'

The next slide shows him in a small cell with about forty women, standing beside the small window covered by a heavy iron grille. 'The window is level with the ground and outside I see a huge yard. The yard is a stage where different things happen every day. Sometimes the guards arrange people into groups, they separate the men from the women, the women from their children. Then they load them all onto big trucks and drive away. The women in my cell say they've been taken to Piaskowa Gora to be shot with machine guns. Sometimes the people resist. I hear their screams while the guards are beating them. Sometimes they beat them to death. Sometimes they shoot them on the spot. I see hundreds of people being shot in that yard. This is a bloody and unforgettable entertainment.'

During the interrogations, his nanny insisted that she was an Austrian Catholic and that he was her own son. She concocted a story to explain why the boy had been circumcised, similar to the story my father had invented in his 'document'. She said that her husband had been Jewish, and when she'd left Marian with him as a baby, he'd had him circumcised without telling her. In their determination not to leave a single Jewish woman or child alive, the Gestapo continued their thorough investigations in Vienna. When Janina's sister corroborated the story, Marian and his nanny were released. 'He was one of the few Jewish children who ever left Lackiego Prison alive,' his mother Hela tells me.

While Marian was in prison, his parents were being hidden by a brave Catholic woman whom Jozek had found after his second escape from the Janowska Camp. My mother's eyes sparkle when she describes Jozek. 'He was such a good-looker! Better looking than the film actor Tyrone Power, and so charming. He swept women off their feet.' His new-found landlady was no exception and within a short time she fell passionately in love with him. When Hela arrived in Lwow, the landlady agreed to hide her too, on condition that her relationship with Jozek continue.

'It must have been unbearable for Hela to sleep in the same room as her husband and their landlady until the war ended, but what could they do? It was a choice between life and death,' my mother clucks her tongue. 'No wonder she had a nervous breakdown after the war. But when it was all over, she still had her husband and her son, and I just couldn't understand why she didn't want to acknowledge her niece. I went to see the child myself and was amazed by the resemblance to her dead mother. Polusia clung to Hela's side like a puppy at a pet shop who longs to be taken home. "I don't know how you can be so hesitant," I told Hela. "She even has Stefa's rounded forehead!"'

Hela was finally persuaded to take the child home for a trial period. From the way she tells me about it in Tel-Aviv fifty years later, it's obvious that although she gave Polusia a roof over her head, she had little feeling for her. When I come to visit them, Jozek is waiting for me in the street, his eyes moist with nostalgia as he wraps me in a long hug. His handsome features have blurred with age, but the warmth and charisma are still there.

Inside their European-style apartment with its polished floor, bookshelves and porcelain, Hela's unlined face and carefully groomed blonde hair show that she is still proud of her appearance. Her words flow easily and evenly but without emotion, as if she is telling an interesting story about somebody else. 'How could I know it was Polusia? I hadn't seen her since she was a baby. She was terribly neglected when we brought her home,' Hela recalls. 'Her hands were rough. And she was plain. A very plain child. I took her straight to Michalewska's shop and bought her some decent clothes.'

As Hela still wasn't convinced that Polusia was her niece, someone suggested she should go and see a fortune-teller. 'As soon as I sat down, the clairvoyant said, "You have a problem surrounding a child, you're wondering who she is. She is related to you."' Hela sat stunned. 'Bit by bit I saw that she did resemble my sister Stefa. She certainly had her father's flair for maths. At school in Krakow she won medals and prizes and her teacher used to say, "If Polusia doesn't know the answer, then nobody does." She's been a top student everywhere and ended up with enough gold medals to make a bracelet!'

'And she's been a marvellous daughter,' Jozek adds softly. His are the first words which show any feeling for the girl they brought up.

One year later, I meet my second cousin Polusia for the first time, in San Francisco. She has reverted to her original name, Tamara, and is a prominent tax consultant in California. I wonder what she'll be like, this woman with the painful history of abandonment, isolation and rejection. Tamara has short black hair cropped over her rounded forehead, jet-black eyes which shine with intelligence, and a strong voice. She's warm and forthright, and I feel as if I've known her all my life.

Polusia's mother, Stefa Richter, was my father's cousin, one of Ignancy Spira's five children. Stefa had fled with her family from Krakow to the township of Strij in 1939 when Polusia was one year old. When the Germans occupied Strij, Polusia was sent to live with one Polish couple while another Polish family, Mr and Mrs Jarosinski, hid her parents and little brother in a recess under the house. Her father paid the Jarosinskis for doing this, and arranged for them to pass on money each week to the couple looking after Polusia.

Although she missed her family, Polusia felt safe with her

foster parents until the night she overheard them arguing. 'You have to get rid of her,' the man was saying. 'They're not paying us any more, the money's stopped, so the devil take her, we're not going to throw good food away on a Jewish brat for nothing.' Now the woman was talking. 'Well, what do you expect me to do, cut her throat?' Polusia almost stopped breathing, terrified of making a sound. The man cleared his voice and spat. 'The Gestapo are searching for Jews everywhere. Do you want to get us killed on account of a lousy Jew? Kill her or take her to the Germans, but I don't want to find her here tomorrow when I get home.'

The following morning, before dawn, Polusia's teeth chattered while the woman bundled her up in her coat and knitted stockings and pulled a woollen cap low over her curved forehead so that her huge black eyes glowed in her white face. Taking the child's mittened hand, she took her to the convent. 'Don't move from here until morning,' she said and, turning on her heel, walked away, leaving Polusia shivering outside the convent gate.

Sister Michaela, the director of the convent, took her in and called her Michasia. Nazi regulations required that each child admitted to the convent had to be reported to the authorities, and the Gestapo checked out each child to make sure that no Jewish children were given refuge.

When the Gestapo officer arrived, he questioned Polusia for several hours, asking about her mother, father, where she used to live, and whether she used to go to church or synagogue. To every question she replied that she didn't know or couldn't remember, but the policeman still wasn't convinced. He wanted the child taken to Lwow for further interrogation and a blood sample to prove whether she was Jewish, but the principal managed to talk him out of it.

Although Polusia felt secure at the convent and liked the

nuns, she guarded her secret and kept mostly to herself. She'd been at the convent for several months when two new girls arrived who kept staring at her and whispering. 'She's not Michasia at all. Her real name is Polusia and she comes from Strij,' they told the headmistress. 'Her father's name was Jozef Richter, he was a Jew. He used to show us photos of her.'

By a chilling coincidence, it was their parents who had hidden Polusia's family until the day when someone reported that there were Jews living in their house. The Germans arrived and killed everybody—the Richters, their little son, and the Jarosinskis as well, for hiding Jews.

Despite the girls' insistence, Polusia maintained that she was Catholic for the rest of her stay at the convent. After the war had ended, when a Jewish woman came searching for Jewish children to reunite with their families and questioned Polusia about her parents, the little girl was still too frightened to admit that she was Jewish. After hearing Polusia's story from the nuns, however, the woman began making inquiries which led her to Hela and Jozek.

My cousin Tamara has been telling me the story of her childhood in a strong voice, without any trace of sentimentality, but in the depths of her large dark eyes, I see a five-year-old girl in thick woollen stockings, heavy coat and woollen cap stamping on the iced-up doorstep outside the convent gate where her foster mother had abandoned her on a dark, deserted street.

When I ask about her life with her aunt and uncle, she hesitates. It's clear that she doesn't want to criticise them or dwell on past hurts, but it's equally clear that she wasn't overwhelmed by love and warmth. 'I've always been grateful to Hela for taking care of me,' she says, 'but as far as she was concerned, I was never a daughter. Jozek was much warmer. But I accepted that's how it was. My childhood has made me tough and self-reliant because I learned from an early age that I couldn't expect anything from anyone, I had to rely on myself. Until I met Arieh.' And she smiles at her husband who has been looking at her with love and empathy while she tells me her story.

This is a Cinderella story. The painfully shy, withdrawn little girl who was orphaned so young and rejected so often, and who learned that nobody could be trusted, became an outstanding student, received a scholarship to study in the United States and won enough gold medals to make that bracelet Hela was so proud of. At eighteen she found out that she had inherited some money which her father had deposited in an American bank before the war. While studying in the States, she met Arieh Zahavi, a handsome, caring man who still adores her. 'When our children Shirley and Joseph were born, I tried to give them the warmth and security I never had,' she says.

One afternoon my mother came home from Hela's place, where she'd gone to see how little Polusia was settling in, to find my father and me sorting chestnuts and arranging them in rows. While she was preparing dinner, my father sat down on the edge of my narrow iron bed and looked into my face. 'Do you remember your grandparents?' he asked. When I shook my head, he said, 'You know, my father was Jewish.' I looked up. 'My mother was Jewish too,' he continued. 'So were Mummy's parents.'

We sat in silence while I processed this, aware of my mother hovering around in the background. Finally I spoke. 'If your parents were Jewish, then you and Mummy are Jewish. So I must be Jewish too.'

My father braced himself for my reaction but I wasn't even surprised. It was as though I'd always known, as though one corner of my seven-year-old mind had always sensed that there was something different about us. A missing fragment of the puzzle had neatly dropped into place.

As reports of violence against Jews increased, my father read Mania's glowing reports about religious tolerance in Australia with ever-increasing interest. But it was the comment of a Catholic friend that was the deciding factor. Whenever they'd discussed the situation in the past, Mr Wrablec had always insisted that these attacks were isolated incidents which didn't mean anything. 'You're lecturing at the dental school, you've got such a good reputation in Krakow, you shouldn't think of leaving,' he used to say. But when my mother ran into him in the Glowny Rynek one afternoon, his words shocked her. 'It makes me sad me to say this, Pani Bronia, but I really don't see any future for you here. I think you'd be better off making a new life for yourselves elsewhere.'

When my father's cousin Janek Spira sent my parents a permit for England, they were tempted to accept. England recognised my father's degree, so he could have started working immediately, but something held him back. England was too close to Europe with its prejudices, blood-stained past and uncertain future.

The solution to their dilemma came in the form of a telegram from Australia. 'Misko gravely ill,' it said in English. Not long after their arrival in Brisbane, Uncle Misko had contracted kidney disease and had undergone emergency surgery. I couldn't understand why my parents looked so sad. 'It only says he's ill, he'll probably get better,' I said, but my father shook his head.

'We decided to go to Australia because Mania was left alone after Misko died,' my mother used to explain, and often added that our life would have been much easier in England. But I know that Australia appealed to my father far more. At our small table in our Florianska Street flat, my father would open the Romer Atlas, flick past Europe, South America and Africa, and point to the strangely-shaped pink blob called Australia. 'It's the end of the world,' my mother used to sigh. 'That's why I like it,' he used to retort.

My father knew that if he wanted to practise his profession, he'd have to study all over again. But as he was forty-seven years old, had no money and spoke no English, he felt that studying was out of the question. He'd have to go into some kind of business. Someone must have told him that Australia was short of buttons because he bought a special machine, ready to embark on a button-manufacturing career in Australia.

We weren't the only members of the Baldinger family planning to leave Poland. Andzia had recently married Idek Cyzer whose wife and children had been killed in the Holocaust, and they'd decided to emigrate to Israel where Lunia and Berus had already settled. Izio and Zosia were migrating to Canada. Of all the Baldingers, only Slawa remained in Poland to watch over their father's grave in an ancient cemetery of broken tombstones.

CHAPTER 31

My little cousin Aline, a roly-poly three-year-old, is jumping up and down, her beguiling brown eyes brimming with excitement as she tugs at my arm and repeats words I don't understand. I can't understand her mother, Tante Rolande, either, although she speaks French slowly and looks as though she understands how embarrassing it is to be eight years old and not understand what a baby is saying. My father's brother Janek, whom everyone now calls Jean, gives me a reassuring smile. 'Aline wants you to go to the park with her,' he says in Polish.

It was March 1948 and my father, mother and I had recently arrived in Paris where we were staying with my aunt and uncle, waiting for a passage to Australia. Bored and lonely in their high-ceilinged apartment near the Champs Elysees, I couldn't wait for our occasional trips to Neuville where Aline's older sister lived with her grandparents in their old gabled farmhouse. I envied Danielle's carefree existence in the country among farm animals, rolling meadows and cherry orchards, unaware that she was at the centre of a storm raging around her.

When France had capitulated in 1940, and Nazi uniforms had darkened the boulevards of Paris, Jean and Rolande had left Danielle with Rolande's parents, the Guyots, and fled south to Rodez. They knew that their daughter would be safe with her Catholic grandparents. When Rodez also became dangerous for Jews, my aunt and uncle escaped to Andorra, but the Nazis were never far behind, and when they occupied the tiny mountain state, Jean and Rolande returned to France and hid in the farming valley of Le Puy until the war ended.

Five years had passed by the time they returned to Neuville, eager to be reunited with their little daughter, but they met with an unexpected obstacle. Rolande's parents refused to hand back the six-year-old they'd brought up since she was a baby, and Danielle didn't want to leave their side.

To complicate matters even further, Rolande, who'd converted to Judaism to marry Jean and who took her conversion seriously, found that the Guyots had baptised her daughter who now wore a cross around her neck and prayed to Jesus. While the tug-of-war continued, to increase the pressure on them, an anonymous letter arrived which threatened that if they took Danielle away, it would kill Madame Guyot.

My cousin Danielle and I are back in Neuville the day she tells me about her confused childhood in this farming village. On this summer afternoon the meadows are splashed with scarlet poppies and big dark cherries hang lusciously in the orchards. Danielle has Rolande's features and tawny coloured hair, as well as her vivacious though rather detached manner, and her Gallic matter-of-factness. Independent and entrepreneurial, she deals in pianos in Paris, but today she's left her business, her husband Jean-Pierre and children Anne and Julien to spend time with me in Neuville. About the custody battle which raged around her as a child she says little. 'It was a difficult part of my life so I forgot it. Perhaps we forget things that are painful for us to remember. But I do remember my grandmother telling me, "Your mother was so beautiful, so clever, she could have married anyone she wanted, why did she choose a little Jew from Krakow?"'

The Guyots won. Seeing that Danielle didn't want to leave her grandparents, my aunt and uncle decided to leave her in Neuville for the time being. While Jean found work and Rolande looked after their new baby, Aline, they visited Danielle frequently and brought her home for the holidays, hoping to win her over.

From the moment she was born, Aline lived with her parents in Paris as if she was an only child, although she knew that her older sister lived in Neuville. Aline was a bubbly child who brightened their lives with her ceaseless chatter. In looks and temperament she took after the Baldinger side of the family.

When at the age of eleven Danielle finally came to live with her parents in Paris, she and Aline became very close. 'But I think that the problems my sister and I are having now probably originated when she came to live with us,' muses Aline, who is more emotional and more introspective than her sister. At the time of my visit, the two sisters had been feuding ever since their mother's death several years earlier.

During our six-month stay in Paris with Uncle Jean and Tante Rolande in 1948, we also spent a great deal of time with my other uncle, Marcel. Unlike Uncle Jean, who had a trenchant wit, a quiet twinkle, and a reserved manner, Uncle Marcel filled the room with his booming voice and high spirits, but he had a short fuse and scared me with his sudden outbursts of anger. Marcel had a Gallic passion for good food and thought nothing of trundling to the other side of Paris for the ripest brie or the most buttery croissants. He had no patience with the listless way my mother and I picked at our meals and used to badger us to taste some slimy shellfish or sloppy cheese whose smell turned my stomach. These reluctant attempts usually ended, to his disgust, with me rushing to the bathroom, hand clamped over my mouth. 'Marcel has a heart of gold,'

Aunty Slawa and Uncle Mietek with their son Mario in Krakow, 1956.

Aunty Slawa's dining room in Krakow, 1989. Left to right: Justine, my cousin Mario with his son Tomek behind him, his wife Gosia, me and Slawa in front of Aunty Karola's walnut sideboard.

Uncle Janek (Jean) as a young man in Krakow.

Uncle Marcel (left) in the French
Foreign Legion in Tunisia, 1940.

Uncle Marcel in his country house
in Neuville, 1990.

Photograph of the family in Paris taken in 1960. From left to right, standing: my cousins Danielle and Aline, Uncle Marcel, Aunt Rolande, Aunt
Jako and her daughter Edith (Poussy). Seated: Uncle Jean.

Aunty Mania and Uncle Misko in Brussels in 1946, not long after the end of the war.

Aunty Mania's wedding to Bronek Ganc in Sydney, January 1951. Left to right: Bronek, me, my mother Bronia, Mania and my father Henek.

My father as a young man in Krakow.

My father's ID photograph during World War II.

My mother, Krakow, 1938.

My parents, Krakow, 1946.

My mother and I in Krakow, July 1939.

Piszczac, 1943. I'm standing between two village children, taking part in a religious procession.

Piszczac 1944.

With my cousin Krysia, in Krakow, 1946.

Michael and his family, taken in Sydney in 1979. From left to right: my mother-in-law Aida Armstrong, sister-in-law Carole Solomon, father-in-law Ben Armstrong and husband Michael.

Justine and my father Henek, taken at my parents' home in Sydney, 1975.

My father on graduation day, Sydney University, 1952.

Jonathan graduating in Science, University of New South Wales, 1993.

Our wedding day, 20 December 1959, taken on the steps of the Great Synagogue, Sydney.

Jonathan and Susan's wedding day, Sydney, 5 April 1998. (Photo courtesy of Jennifer Gilmour)

From left: Justine, Jonathan, Susan, me and Michael, taken at Jonathan and Susan's wedding. (Photo courtesy of Phyllis Ross)

Top: With my father Henek at my parents' home, Sydney, 1975.

Left: With my mother Bronia, Sydney, 1989.

Below: With Father Roman Soszynski at his home in Biala Podlaska, 1995. (Photo courtesy of Justine Armstrong)

my mother used to say. 'He'd give you the shirt off his back.' I just wished he wouldn't insist on giving me oysters and camembert.

By a strange coincidence, Marcel had a similar heartache with his daughter Edith France as his brother Jean had with Danielle. Marcel and Jako's only child, who was two years old at the time we arrived in Paris, was living in the southern town of Rodez with her Catholic grandmother who also refused to give her up.

In the modern living room of the country house he loves in Neuville, Uncle Marcel tells me that he arrived in Rodez during the war. 'That was after I was discharged from the French Foreign Legion. Did you know that I was a Legionnaire?' He chuckles and his amber eyes twinkle in his fleshy face. Now that I'm no longer frightened of my uncle's explosive temper, I enjoy the easy way he tells a story, leaning forward and smiling into my face, creating a feeling of camaraderie that shuts out the rest of the world. Of all my uncles, he most reminds me of my father, and I love his generosity, warmth and vulnerability.

Encouraged by my astonishment, my uncle backtracks to the beginning of the war. 'As I was a foreigner, they didn't let me join the regular army so they sent me to the Foreign Legion at the other end of the world! I had to learn to ride a horse. My horse and I made a pact: once I'd ride him, and the next time he'd ride me! But he didn't keep to the arrangement, and always ended up on top of me!' He's laughing so heartily that his corpulent body is shaking while he shows me a photo of himself in Tunisia, a round-faced young man with a shy smile under the legionnaire's cap.

While we're talking, in the kitchen Jako is scouring, dusting, mopping, sweeping. Uncle Marcel shakes his head in irritation and I can see that he takes her activity as a personal affront.

'She never stops. I wanted us to enjoy this house together but she can never relax.'

The French Foreign Legion evokes exotic images of adventure, but Uncle Marcel's life in Tunisia was relatively uneventful. He only remembers one skirmish. The Italians in the Legion were always stirring up the Arab villagers to attack the Jews, and his regiment was sent to restore order. But instead of fighting the locals, my uncle, ever a gourmet, used to sneak out with another comrade and steal chickens from a farmyard. 'It didn't do me any good, though, because I was stupid,' he chuckles. 'When we divided up the chickens, I took the biggest one, not realising that it would be old and tough!'

Not long after he arrived at the Legion, he was taken to a bunker along with some other soldiers. 'It was just as well that Tunisia was never attacked,' he says. 'They left us there for a week with an ultra-modern cannon no-one knew how to use and they'd forgotten to provide us with ammunition!'

After nine months with the Foreign Legion, Marcel obtained a work certificate from a friend in Rodez and was discharged. It so happened that a businesswoman in town needed a furrier, and she arranged work and accommodation for him. At first life was peaceful in this sunny southern town, but in 1941 the Gestapo arrived and rounded up the Jews. No-one turned him in but after that, he obtained false papers in the name of Marcel Faire, grew a luxuriant moustache, and dressed in sabots and a cloth cap to pass as a local farmer.

As food was scarce and available only through ration cards, and as there were several Jews hiding in Rodez, his employer's attractive daughter Jacqueline used to cycle fifty-two kilometres for meat, sugar and flour to a neighbouring village, and then cycle all the way back with her provisions, flashing the Germans a cheeky grin as she rode past. My uncle's eyes light up when he recalls the spunky brunette who wasn't afraid of anyone.

Jako, as she was called, had inexhaustible energy and an effervescent personality that lifted his spirits like the finest champagne. She was always pealing with laughter, mimicking the Germans or the locals, or pulling faces. As soon as the war ended, one hundred guests toasted the newlyweds at their wedding breakfast.

Marcel and Jako had already moved to Paris by the time their daughter Edith France was born, but soon after the birth, Jako was diagnosed with ovarian cancer and had a hysterectomy. For several months she hovered between life and death, exhausted and emaciated. At the same time, Marcel was suffering agonies from kidney stones, so there was no-one to take care of the baby who cried so pitifully that they nicknamed her Poussy. They sent her to Jako's mother in Rodez but when Jako finally recovered, her mother refused to return the child.

Uncle Marcel shudders as he talks about his mother-in-law. 'That woman had a Machiavellian streak. *Oh là là!* She could have taught the Borgias a few tricks! She's a character straight out of a Balzac novel. She ruined us twice. We had a business together but when she sold the merchandise she never paid us.'

My cousin Poussy, who has kept her childhood nickname, still remembers the terror of being kidnapped by her parents. She is tall, chic, mannequin-thin and typically Parisian, with a gamin haircut which accentuates her high cheekbones and huge opalescent eyes which survey the world with the haughty remoteness of the vulnerable. Heads turn when she walks along the street with the slow self-conscious saunter of a model on the catwalk.

'I hated my father for taking me away from my grandmother, and I was scared of him because of the things she had said about him,' she says. It wasn't a good start, and set the pattern for their lifelong conflict. Poussy, who is a psychiatrist, has spent a great deal of time analysing their relationship. 'It wasn't just the initial trauma. My father never asked what I wanted. He just treated me like a doll, not a real person with ideas and feelings. I was told what to do and how to be. At thirteen I became anorexic as a reaction against my parents and their expectations, and I've had a horror of being fat ever since. I only studied medicine to prove my father wrong because he used to tell me I was stupid.'

Family relationships are as fragile as egg-shells and as complex and unfathomable as the universe. As Poussy speaks, I recall Uncle Marcel's face glowing with pride on so many occasions while he showed me her photographs and marvelled that a self-educated furrier from Krakow like him had managed to produce such a beautiful and accomplished daughter.

In spite of her grandmother's anti-Jewish views, her lifelong conflict with her father, and the absence of any Jewish education, my cousin feels Jewish. 'That's really odd, because my father wasn't religious and never pushed me to become Jewish,' she says while we pick at our antipasto in a cosy Italian restaurant near her apartment. 'One day I just walked into a jewellery shop and bought myself a Star of David.'

Poussy is striking, sexy and intelligent, but the men in her life have all been unsuitable, impossible or unavailable. 'I won't every marry,' she says. 'I'm content knowing that I'm developing my own potential. I never wanted to have children anyway.'

My cousin Aline, however, has found happiness comparatively late in life in marriage and children. 'I'm glad I started psychoanalysis when I was an adult, otherwise I would never have had kids,' she says with a loving glance at her daughter Judith. While we sprawl on the floor of her rustic home beside the Marne, baby Charlotte on her lap, Aline's expressive eyes light up when she talks about her romance with her husband

Eli which resembles *La Bohème* with a happy ending. 'We were living in adjoining garrets and got talking over the balcony. I was pregnant when we met, and our romance began when he came to visit me in hospital when I had Judith,' she recalls.

As we sift through the trunkful of family letters, photographs and memorabilia which her father kept all his life, she says: 'My father rarely talked about the past. He kept in touch with his brothers and sisters but never spoke about those who had died. I think he felt guilty that he left Poland and survived, and they didn't.' Uncle Jean was witty and charming but Meniere's Disease affected his hearing and as his deafness increased, he felt increasingly isolated and depressed. As Aline talks, I recall the letter that he wrote to me after my father died. 'Hardly a day passes that I don't think with sadness about my father and our family life in Krakow before the war.'

Aline has become pensive. 'Although I always knew that I was Jewish, I didn't have any Jewish education whatsoever. My mother said it was because of what happened to Danielle. How could they bring me up to be Jewish when my sister had been baptised as a Catholic?' she says in her deep, calm voice. Aline, who has kept the Baldinger surname along with her married name Achour, keeps a Jewish home, observes the traditional holidays and is a social worker with a Jewish community organisaton. She has recently written an informative handbook about Judaism, Christianity and Islam which will be published shortly. 'To me, being Jewish means being part of the story of my people, and I am very proud of that,' she says. Although there has been a rift between her and Danielle ever since their mother died, when Aline's daughter Judith celebrated her Bat Mitzvah recently, Danielle and her family were invited to share the occasion. Shortly afterwards Aline invited them over for Seder night. The long rift was over.

Before I leave Neuville, Jako takes me to the flower-filled

little cemetery where Jean, Rolande and the Guyots lie buried. She bustles about, filling a watering can, sprinkling the flowers she has planted, and pulling out weeds. I'm fascinated to learn that although Jean had been totally disinterested in Judaism, at the end, when he lay dying, he asked for someone to say Kaddish for him.

Today, Uncle Marcel is buried near the brother he loved, with whom he often fought and feuded. Unlike Jean, Marcel didn't want anyone to say Kaddish. 'My God died at Auschwitz,' he told me one day. Daniel Baldinger's youngest son derived more comfort from the Masons than from his father's religion, and when he was dying of cancer, he asked for the Masonic emblem, a sprig of acacia, to be carved on his tombstone. 'Just the same, if I'd been a man, I would have said Kaddish for him,' Poussy said.

After waiting in Paris for six months for a passage to Australia, we sailed from Marseilles on a scorching August day in 1948 with six hundred other refugees. On humid nights when the air in the cabin was like pea soup, we all slept on deck, on khaki canvas deckchairs. The women tied their hair in scarves, fanned themselves, hitched up their skirts, and sat with their legs wide apart to capture each tentative breeze. Around us hung the viscious smell of tar and sump oil, and the sharp smell of the sea as the ship rolled up and down on dark waves. Inside the ship, my nostrils recoiled at the mouldy, wood-rot odour of the slimy wooden slats of the communal washroom, the rank smell of too many bodies in one airless cabin, and the sour odour of the dining room where everything was cooked in tomato paste and served with salty pickled vegetables.

The SS *Derna* was a rusting, clapped-out vessel whose Panamanian flag concealed a life history as tumultuous as that of many of its passengers. Built in 1915 for the German-owned East Africa Line to carry cargo and nine passengers, it was seized by the Allies after World War I and given to France in war reparations. After the fall of France, the United States Shipping Administration took it over as a transport ship. When Greek shipping magnate Livanos bought it in 1948, he had it registered in Panama, changed its name, and converted it to carry the maximum number of passengers in minimal comfort.

The *Derna* was a perfect example of the sailors' adage that changing a ship's name brings bad luck. Only two days after leaving Marseilles, the chef dropped dead and we had to return to port. That was only the beginning of the misfortunes which dogged this vessel. We hadn't long put out to sea when the refrigeration broke down, all the meat rotted, and we watched incredulously as the crew jettisoned putrid carcasses overboard. For most of the voyage we lived on tomato soup, macaroni and pickled vegetables.

In the course of the voyage which lasted eleven weeks, boilers broke down, water became scarce, and to make matters worse, at Aden, the locals filled the tanks with brackish water. Then one of the engines caught fire. Although we were at sea, they couldn't put out the flames because it turned out that the fire hoses had holes in them, so the fire raged unchecked. The captain's pleas for assistance went unheeded by other boats, and for a time it looked as though we'd have to don life jackets and jump overboard, but eventually the fire burnt itself out. Finally, the navigation equipment failed, and we drifted off course, adding days to an already interminable journey. Many of the passengers muttered that they'd survived the war only to die on this acursed ship.

My mother hated every moment of that voyage, and if she'd known that it was going to take almost three months, I doubt whether she would have walked up the gangplank on that August day. For anyone who loathed ships as much as she did, this overcrowded vessel was purgatory. My mother and I shared a stuffy cabin with a single porthole, with ten other women. The bathing facilities were primitive, most toilets had no doors, and the shortage of water made washing clothes difficult. From the moment my mother boarded the *Derna*'s scuffed decks, leaned over its scabrous rails and felt the rolling sensation of the ship, her stomach knotted itself into a tight fist. She felt seasick most of the time, couldn't eat the food, and her creamy complexion sallowed in revolt.

To add to her misery, she felt neglected. My father, who didn't feel seasick and wasn't bothered by the food, spent most of his days playing bridge or studying English grammar and didn't seem concerned that she was unwell and unhappy. I suppose they were both reacting in their own way to what they'd been through. She needed care and attention while he was desperate for some respite from anxiety and responsibility. For him, this voyage provided a relaxing lull between the harrowing past and the uncertain future; for her it was a miserable existence, aggravated by what she perceived as his selfishness.

The disasters of the *Derna* together with the tensions of the passengers created a combustible atmosphere. The ship was a floating microcosm of refugees from Poland, Czechoslovakia, Latvia, Hungary, Estonia and France. The current Australian immigration policy, in response to anti-Semitic attitudes voiced by some politicians and journalists, restricted the percentage of Jewish immigrants on any one ship to twenty-five per cent, and the *Derna* carried an explosive ethnic mix of Jewish survivors who had lost their entire families, as well as some Nazi sympathisers. In these overcrowded, tense conditions, tempers flared and fights broke out. Some of the

Baltic passengers accused some of the Jewish teenagers of spreading communism. One of the Ukrainians on board boasted that he'd killed Jews during the war. One moonless night, he vanished and was never seen again.

In spite of all the turmoil, there were shipboard romances, illicit liaisons and bitter-sweet love affairs. Planted on their deck chairs, self-righteous matrons gossiped about the immoral single women who were seen emerging from the officers' cabins. My mother spent most of her time chatting with other Polish refugees, mostly with Sophie Frant who, with her husband Dr Herman Frant, became my parents' lifelong friends. The Frants had been appointed chaperones to the sixty-one Jewish orphans on board. They had survived by jumping out of the train taking them to Treblinka, while their daughter Christine owed her life to a courageous Catholic woman called Helcia who took her out of the Warsaw Ghetto and pretended to be her mother. For the next few years, Christine wore sunglasses whenever she went out, even to school, claiming that a rare eye condition made it necessary to protect them from the light. Their real purpose was to conceal her suspiciously dark eyes.

Everyone on board had an epic story to tell. My mother admired a young woman called Topka, who looked after her brood of younger sisters like a mother hen. Before their parents had been killed by the Germans, Topka had promised their mother that she would always take care of the others. She kept her word, and even after she got married in Australia, she decided not to have children of her own so that she could devote her life to her sisters.

Together with Mrs Frant, my mother helped a young couple look after their baby girl. Only teenagers themselves, Sam and Esther Fiszman had been orphaned during the Holocaust. At the age of twelve, Esther had been deported to Auschwitz where her mother was killed. If it hadn't been for an older woman who had taken care of her, she wouldn't have survived, but after liberation, they were separated and Esther despaired of ever seeing her guardian angel again. Out on deck one day she looked up and couldn't believe her eyes. It was the woman who had saved her life. Esther's hot-headed young husband Sam had smuggled arms into the Warsaw Ghetto and had crawled out through the sewers just before it was burnt to the ground. Esther was so violently seasick that she spent most of the voyage in sick bay, and my mother and Mrs Frant helped Sam find food for little Maria.

As for me, there was little to relieve the monotony of the voyage. I spent most of my time on board reading, knitting clothes for my doll or playing with the other children. One night my mother woke me up and took me out on deck where all the passengers were craning over the rails, staring at something burning in the distance. Lifting me up so that I'd have a better view, my father said: 'This is something you only get to see once in a lifetime.' Mt Etna was erupting and the terrifying red-hot lava flowed down its slopes like a river of blood.

In eleven weeks, there were only three ports of call. At Port Said, the Jewish passengers weren't allowed to disembark because the Arabs had declared war on the newly created state of Israel, and all Jews were regarded as enemies. At Aden we were beseiged by a flotilla of bobbing wooden boats whose vendors loaded up hands of bananas and dozens of coconuts into buckets which were pulled up on board. It was the first time any of us had visited the Orient or seen such a profusion of tropical fruit or exotic palm trees which grew on the shore. My father called me over to see men with white turbans and mahogany skin climbing up the ropes, and pointed to their sinewy thighs, no wider than his arm. It distressed him that human beings had to work so hard for so little. Although the crew instructed the passengers not to give them anything to eat, my father, along with many others, surreptitiously dropped food into their baskets.

In Colombo, we were finally allowed ashore. In a small lighter that skimmed the cobalt sea, we landed in a bustling, dusty town planted with lush palms and milling with women in bright saris and men in loose white tunics. Women with fat bejewelled arms sat in rickshaws pulled by men with bare legs and gaunt cheeks. On the pavements, hawkers with glittering eyes offered ivory elephants, wooden monkeys and silver bangles for sale. An old man with a bushy white beard selling wooden figurines of Hindu deities smiled at me approvingly and offered to buy me from my astonished parents.

The thought uppermost in everyone's minds was food. After the privations of shipboard cuisine, we longed for a hearty meal. Our mouths watered when, in a restaurant decked out in textured crimson wallpaper, the waiter placed a whole chicken on the table. It was roasted to perfection, its skin an appetising reddish brown, its aroma a tantalising blend of unfamiliar spices. We couldn't wait to bite into it but within seconds, we were all coughing, spluttering, gasping and choking. No-one had warned us about Ceylonese curries. The appetising colour of the chicken was due to chili and although I drank enough water to put out the fire on the *Derna*, the inside of my mouth felt as though it had been scalped. It was almost a relief to return to the macaroni and sour pickles on board ship.

Shortly before we reached Melbourne, while the *Derna* was pitching and tossing in the Great Australian Bight, Halina Kalowski, one of the Jewish women on board, gave birth to a baby she named Jennifer Derna. The birth lifted everyone's spirits. It seemed a good omen for starting life in a new land.

It was drizzling when we finally docked in Melbourne on 5 November 1948. Our odyssey was over. As we stepped ashore on this unfamiliar and remote continent for the first time, we wondered what the future would bring. As for the *Derna*, her long career soon came to an end. Unfit to sail, she was sold for scrap metal and demolished at the shipyards of Blyth.

PART III

CHAPTER 32

Coral trees blazed, banana palms rustled in the breeze, and the sun lay gently on my shoulders like a benediction. From the moment we arrived in Brisbane, I felt as though I'd stepped through a magic mirror out of a wilting world of pastel hues and apologetic skies into a fantasy land exploding with light and colour, a land that seemed innocent of hate and history. No halftones diluted the triumphant colours, no twilight deadened the dazzling day.

In this enchanted place, fruit tasted like flowers and flowers smelled like fruit. My head whirled with the delicious scent of gardenias, frangipani and jasmine on warm summer nights. Like the flowers, the fruit also belonged to a world of make-believe. Bright orange pawpaw, with its hollow filled with black peppercorns, repelled and attracted me with its musky odour of sweat and tropical perfume. The scented, slimy pulp of passionfruit and the luscious flesh of mangoes made my tongue quiver.

Our house, too, was strange. A box on stilts, with a dark, cool verandah running all the way around it. Every night Mrs Black, who owned the house, grilled a slab of beef under a high blue gas flame, filling the whole house with the mouth-puckering smell of steak, crisp on the outside and juicy pink inside.

By day, my mother worked in a house for orphaned Jewish

boys run by the Jewish Welfare Board. In return for a small wage, she looked after the boarding house and cooked their meals, while my father spent his days at the university, discussing the possibility of studying dentistry again.

The button-making machine he'd brought from Krakow had been stolen from the wharf along with most of our belongings when the *Derna* had docked, and my father took this as an omen. He gave up the idea of becoming a businessman and decided to continue being a dentist. My mother supported his decision whole-heartedly. 'Your father is as much a businessman as that cat is a brain surgeon,' she used to say. 'He's too straightforward to succeed in business.'

On my first day at school I feel anxious because I can't speak English and everyone will think I'm stupid. How will I find my classroom? On my new leather satchel my father has printed my name in bold capitals. DIANA BOGUSLAWSKI. Finally I can revert to the name he always wanted me to have. But at school the teacher calls me Diane, so I hastily turn the A into an E, assuming this must be more Australian. I don't want to be different here too. That's why I hate my schoolbag. The kids at school carry bags resembling small suitcases which they call ports, not leather satchels which look foreign like mine.

It's hot and steamy, and sometimes we have lessons in the schoolyard, in the shade of the wattle trees whose yellow flowers resemble fluffy balls of cotton wool. I can't understand what anyone is saying. It's like trying to find your way around blind-folded, but more embarrassing. Everyone smiles at me but the days seem endless. In class the teacher points to a little boy and says, 'Next.' I deduce that this must be his name, but a moment later she says it again and points to another boy. What a peculiar country, so many boys with the same name. Then she says 'Next' once again, but this time a girl stands up to answer. I've learnt my first English word.

Every day I walk to school and back with Beverley, the girl next door, and on the way home we stop at the corner shop which is plastered with signs for Kinkara Tea and Mother's Choice Flour and sells emerald-green ice blocks for one penny. Before I reach home, I've sucked all the lime colour out of it, and all that's left is a tasteless cylinder of marbled ice that numbs my tongue.

One day Beverley is sick, and I walk home alone. Suddenly the sky darkens, thunder crashes above my head, rain lashes my shoulders, and I can't remember the way home. In the thunder and blinding rain, I run into a side street looking for the movie poster with the woman with red hair cascading onto her bare shoulders whose name seems to be Tap Roots. I run on, panicking now because I'm all alone, don't know where I am, and have no idea how to ask. I try not to cry when suddenly I heave a huge sigh of relief. There's Miss Tap Roots and I'm in Upper Moray Street where we live.

Sometimes we visit Aunty Mania in her small room which smells of perfume and cigarettes. She shows me her jars of creams and bottles of make-up, dabs perfume on my wrist and chats to me as if I was grown up. We've come to Brisbane because Aunty Mania was alone after Uncle Misko died. They migrated here because of his relatives, one of whom has a little daughter called Maxine. She's always chattering, jumping and running, and even giggles when she gets into trouble. For her, life seems so light and easy, while to me it feels so complicated.

Even the grown-ups in Brisbane seem light-hearted. My favourite is Uncle Misko's cousin, Bernard Rapaport whom I've nicknamed Uncle Furry because his short simian arms are covered in thick black hair. This short, balding man is the most charismatic person I've ever met. The moment he strides

417

into a room, the air is charged with electricity. He talks rapidly, has an opinion about everything, a joke for every occasion, and everyone regards him as their best friend.

Bernard, his wife Tosia, and Maxine's parents Gina and Bert all treat us like close family. During school holidays Maxine's parents invite me to their weekender at Palm Beach. Standing on an Australian beach for the first time, feeling the sun-warmed sand squishing between my toes, I let the Pacific Ocean lick my toes, and listen to the waves as they slap, suck and whoosh endlessly against the shore. Unbroken waves crest to a peak as crisp as the crease on my father's trousers, curve over, and tumble down in a joyous eruption of spray and foam. Uncle Bert, who has the kindest blue eyes and the softest voice I've ever heard, teaches me to jump the waves. 'One, two, three, jump!' he calls as he lifts me over the crest or shows me how to dive underneath. He's whooping, laughing and having fun like us. I never realised that adults could play.

While I'm discovering the joys of the beach, my father is falling in love with Australia and its friendly, tolerant people who smile at strangers in the street for no reason and say, 'How are you?' which is a greeting and not a question. After the stiff hierarchical relationships of Poland, where age, education and occupation created an unbridgeable gap between people, and where you could know someone all your life and still address them in the third person, he likes the informality of Australians who call him Henry as soon as they are introduced.

Soon after we arrived in Brisbane, my father wrote to Father Soszynski, describing life in our new country. This was a land of opportunity where even labourers owned their own cottages, where bank loans were accessible to everyone, food was plentiful, and no-one seemed hungry or homeless. The Prime Minister, Mr Chifley, was a genuine working man, and journalists were free to criticise the government without fear of censorship or reprisal.

My parents often wondered why the priest never replied.

From the safety of our gate, I watch children crowding around the bonfire, their faces glowing from the flames. Every few minutes they jump back shrieking as something sputters and rockets towards the sky with a flash of light. 'Give us a sparkler, Dad!' a small boy lisps through the gap in his front teeth, and soon there are shrieks of glee as loops of light circle against the night sky. One of the men letting off the fireworks comes over to me and holds out a sparkler which crackles with points of light. 'Would you like one, love?' he asks. Mr Knight has a kind face and a soft English burr in his voice, but I shake my head and shyly edge away.

It's Cracker Night, Empire Day 1949, and we've just arrived in Sydney because here my father will only have to study for three years instead of four. In deference to his twenty-five years' experience as a dentist and university lecturer in Poland, the dental faculty has agreed to credit him with the first year of the course. We're renting a small semidetached cottage in Bondi Junction. Like all the others in the street, it has a curved roof over a narrow verandah whose floor is covered in a mosaic of maroon, blue and beige tiles, and is hidden by a privacy hedge in front.

My parents have never lived in a cottage before and are ignorant of the finer points of house maintenance, like trimming hedges and mowing lawns. Occasionally my father borrows Mr Knight's clippers to trim the unruly bushes in the front, but no matter how hard he tries, the hedge always ends up bulging out at one end and nipped in at the other like a lopsided bird's nest.

But gardening isn't very high on my father's list of priorities.

Every night he sits hunched in the front bedroom, a blanket draped over his shoulders for warmth, poring over notes and textbooks while my mother brews cups of coffee to keep him awake. Becoming a student again at the age of forty-eight is hard enough, but studying in a language you don't understand is like trying to decipher a secret code. Every evening when he returns home from university, he takes out his lecture notes and looks up all the unfamiliar words in the dictionary, but that's not as simple as it sounds. During lectures he jots down what he hears, but English isn't a phonetic language so he can't find many of the words in the dictionary.

In spite of his difficulties, my father never complained or criticised the system which obliged him to study all over again after so many years of dental practice. Henry, as he came to be called in Australia, had most in common with the mature-age students, ex-servicemen who were admitted to the course after the war. One of them was John Levitt, a sandy-haired Aussie with a whisper-soft voice and dry sense of humour who became our friend, along with his large warm-hearted family.

As dentistry was a full-time course, my mother had to find a job to support us. For a woman who could hardly speak English and had no employment skills, the choice was limited. Bronia became a finisher at a dress factory, and at the end of each day she would lug piles of skirts and toppers to hem at home to earn extra money. Long after I'd gone to bed, she was still sitting under the single-bulb lamp, thimble on her finger, stitching and hemming until the small hours of the morning.

In the late afternoons I used to hear the sound of her heels clicking on the pavement long before she turned the corner into our street. Footsteps are as unique as fingerprints, and as revealing as hands and voices. Her short, rapid steps crackled with energy and tapped out a message of optimism for the future.

When I think about my parents at that time, I marvel at their strength and resilience. They appreciated the kindness of their neighbours, work-mates and fellow students, and liked being called New Australians. It made them feel accepted. But although they never complained, I became an emotional antenna, acutely aware of all their difficulties. I didn't realise how much of their anxiety I'd absorbed until many years later when their friend, Max Brenner, was reminiscing about our first few years in Sydney. 'You hadn't been in Australia very long when I asked you what you'd like for your ninth birthday. I never forgot your answer. You said that the only thing you wanted was for Daddy to pass his exams.'

Dr Brenner, a Jew from Lwow who'd arrived in Sydney before the war, was our first contact with Sydney's Jewish community. An energetic man with a shiny bald head and probing dark eyes in a round face, he became our advisor, doctor and friend. My parents never forgot his kindness. Soon after we moved in, he arrived lugging a sack of coal over his back so that we could heat our chilly cottage.

Walter Street was a tightly-knit but open-hearted community where the children called the neighbours aunty and uncle. Whenever we were asked to run down to the corner shop to buy a few slices of devon or a jar of Kraft cheese spread, we were always given threepence to spend. The corner shop was plastered with advertisements for Craven A cigarettes, Bushells, the Tea of Flavour, and Peters Ice Cream which was touted as The Original and Best. The term original as applied to ice cream always made my father chuckle. 'I suppose Moses brought the recipe down from Mount Sinai,' he would joke.

The food we ate at home made me acutely aware of how different I was from the other children. Every afternoon when our neighbour's daughter Anne came home from school, her mother, a kind, grey-haired woman we all called Aunty Tessie, took out a loaf of bread which resembled two white breasts billowing on either side of a deep cleavage. On each soft, spongy slice she smeared a thick layer of amber-coloured spread called Golden Syrup whose malty odour made my mouth water, so much more enticing than the dry rye bread speckled with caraway seeds which my mother always bought. In the evening, while my mother braised beef goulash in her pressure cooker, Aunty Tessie fried lamb chops with their crisp collar of fat, and their tantalising smell wafted over the fence into our kitchen.

On rare occasions I was allowed to have dinner with the Knights, a cause for great jubilation, as lamb chops, peas and mashed potatoes followed by jelly and ice cream seemed the epitome of gastronomical indulgence. Before we started eating, Uncle Reg always said grace. Everyone closed their eyes while he thanked the Lord for the food and blessed everyone, saying: 'For what we are about to receive, may the Lord make us truly thankful.' I knew that he was praying to Jesus, but I closed my eyes out of respect to my hosts. My father had put Jesus into a historical and social context for me, as a Jewish rebel with a social conscience, an early socialist whose disciples formed a new religion.

The Knights were kind-hearted, tolerant people who included me in most of their activities, even church outings. Although Uncle Reg sometimes discussed theology with my father, our religion caused him no problems, while my parents saw nothing wrong with me attending Baptist church picnics at Bronte Beach or physical culture in the local church hall.

Ever since moving to Sydney to be with us, Aunty Mania put her love of hats to good use by becoming a milliner. Every Friday evening she handed me two shillings pocket money which she used to call my 'wages'. 'Fri-die is pie die!' she'd say, exaggerating Australian vowel sounds. 'I'm becoming a real Aussie,' she would laugh, 'Even if I was on my last legs, I'd crawl to work on Friday to be paid!' On Monday afternoons, clutching my precious two shillings, I used to go with my best friend Mary Zantis to buy our favourite girls' magazines, *The Schoolfriend* and *Girls' Crystal*.

Occasionally Aunty Mania took me with her on a date with one of her boyfriends, none of whom ever met with my mother's approval. 'Mania should be more discriminating,' I sometimes overheard her say to my father. She disapproved of the current boyfriend who went to the pub on Fridays and to the races on Saturdays. Les was a slow-talking, laid-back fellow with a brown hat pushed back from his forehead. Horrified that I'd never been to the Easter Show, he took me and bought kewpie dolls, fairy floss and sample bags filled with treasures like Captain Marvel comics, colouring books, Jaffas and Violet Crumble bars.

Before long, Mania met Bronek Ganc, a Polish Jew from Lodz who had survived the war in Romania. Bronek had large pale blue eyes, a ready smile, and traces of moisture in the corners of his mouth. He didn't drink or gamble, but he worked in a factory and didn't have a penny to his name. What he did have, however, was a devoted, loving nature. A bachelor in his early forties, he idolised Mania and lavished love on me for the rest of his life.

Although they hadn't been in Australia very long themselves, and my father was still studying, my parents were always ready to help and advise newly arrived migrants. On Sunday afternoons, my mother would run to and from her tiny kitchen where she baked cakes in a small stove with a kookaburra on the door, and kept drinks cool in an ice chest, serving coffee, yeast cake and encouragement to the guests.

Among our regular visitors were my mother's second cousins, Srulek and Aron Kestecher. She was delighted that the sons of her mother's favourite niece Balcia had survived the Holocaust and had migrated to Sydney.

But the joy of finding her cousins alive was mingled with grief when they told her what had happened to the rest of their family. Shortly after Srulek and his father and two brothers had been exiled to Siberia, one brother jumped off the train and returned to Poland but was later caught and shot by the Germans; the other brother disappeared never to be found, and his father died of a fever. All alone in the harsh Siberian gulag for two years, Srulek was frostbitten and hungry, but there was something appealing about this skinny teenager with large grey eyes and shy smile, and the Russians often gave him extra rations.

After two years, along with many other Polish prisoners, Srulek was released but he had to remain in the Soviet Union. Fending for himself among tens of thousands of other homeless refugees, he had nowhere to go and nothing to eat for days except a raw cabbage he'd brought from Siberia. Pickpockets flourished and most travellers had valuables stolen. 'I lost nothing because I had nothing,' he wrote in his succinct style. 'That was one time it paid to be poor.' When he arrived in Tashkent, he lived in filth and squalor at the railway station which was crammed with refugees, many of whom became ill with dysentery and typhus. When the war ended, he was taken to an orphanage where he learned English, played sport, discovered an aptitude for nursing, dreamed of being reunited with his mother and other brothers, and longed for news from home.

Out of the blue, a letter arrived. 'When I saw my home address on the back of the envelope, I became so agitated that I couldn't get myself together to open the letter,' he recalled in his memoirs. 'When I finally read it, the sad news struck me like an electric shock.' The letter was from his younger brother Aron, the only member of the family who had survived.

While Srulek with his father and two older brothers were travelling east, his mother Balcia and two younger brothers had remained in Budy Lancutskie. They were hiding in a barn when armed German soldiers found them but Balcia managed to cover twelve-year-old Aron with straw so that he couldn't be seen. From inside the barn he could hear the shots and watched as his mother and brother fell to the ground. My mother was heartbroken when she heard about Balcia's fate. 'Poor Balcia,' she kept saying. 'She was so good-hearted and pretty with those huge blue eyes and masses of dark hair. But she didn't have any luck in life. She married an unbending man and wasn't happy with him.'

For the remainder of the war, Aron lived by his wits, moving from one village to another, hiding in forests, barns and wheatfields. Once a farmer took pity on the boy and hid him in his barn until the neighbours grew suspicious and Aron had to find yet another place to hide. While he was hiding in a potato field, he was caught in the crossfire between Russian and German soldiers. Just as he lifted his head, he was spotted by a German soldier who opened fire. Making a dash towards the Vistula River, Aron jumped in and stayed submerged while the soldier searched for him. When night fell, the boy swam across the river and joined a group of Russian partisans with whom he stayed until the war ended.

In the memoirs Srulek wrote many years later, he mused about what enables people to survive in seemingly impossible situations. 'You never know when something terrible might turn out to be a lucky break,' he wrote. 'Like Siberia. I thought we were unlucky to be exiled there, but as it turned out, we were the lucky ones. You must never give up. Once you give up, you're dead.'

No-one who met these neatly-dressed, gentle, well-spoken

young men in Sydney in 1949 would have guessed what they'd been through. Young though I was, however, I could see that the brothers were very different. Srulek had a warm nature but he had a coiled-up intensity that made him difficult to be with. With the restlessness in his large grey eyes and his vulnerable expression he reminded me of a deer, continually looking over his shoulder in case he had to flee at any moment. It was difficult to make arrangements with him. He would promise to come for dinner but then failed to arrive without letting us know, and we wouldn't hear from him for months. 'He's a good-hearted chap but his nerves aren't right,' my mother used to say. 'It's the war.'

Because of his elusive personality, we saw little of Srulek, and gradually lost touch with him over the years. It was only recently, after he had died, that his daughter Michelle sent me his memoirs. Reading them, I was moved by his lyrical descriptions and the heartwrenching recollections of his family, and regretted that I'd never got to know my cousin's sensitive and poetic soul.

Aron was stronger, calmer, and more down-to-earth than his brother. At the age of nine, I was flattered that a young man of twenty-one was interested in what I was doing and talked to me as an equal. He often brought me records to build up my small collection. As we talked, a wide smile would split his face, revealing protruding front teeth that were separated by a gap. His religious devotion fascinated me. He always wore a *yarmulka*, kept strictly kosher, and walked for miles on Saturdays rather than catch a tram. It mystified me that after being orphaned at such a young age and living by himself in fields and forests, he still maintained the lifestyle of his orthodox parents. But to Aron, it was the most natural thing in the world to follow his parents' example. In his quiet, patient way, he would explain: 'I was brought up in a very religious home and that's what I want to continue in my life.'

Every morning I walk to school with the other children in Walter Street. In the shady playground of Waverley Public School, my school friends and I skip rope, bounce balls, and drink small sun-warmed bottles of milk which we have to shake to blend the thick layer of cream at the top. At midday two pupils are chosen to bring the lunch orders. Stacked on a tray are brown paper bags with spreading patches of grease. When the lucky children bite into the pies, brown sludge oozes out. I can never convince my mother to let me buy one. 'What's in those pies?' Her forehead creases like a concertina. 'How do you know what rubbish they put in them?' So I continue to bring rye bread sandwiches with egg and tomato which cement into a paste in the summer heat.

My mother's ignorance of Australian food is sometimes an embarrassment. Birthday parties are frequent celebrations in our street, and the gifts, games and party food never vary. Guests arrive with their hair freshly brushed and braided, fastened with coloured clips and tied with crisp ribbons. The gifts are always practical: hair ribbons, socks, handkerchiefs or panties. We play blindman's buff, pin the tail on the donkey, and hide and seek, eat crustless triangles of white bread coated with brightly coloured hundreds and thousands, clusters of crisp brown mounds called chocolate crackles, tiny cocktail frankfurts dipped in tomato sauce, and sponge cake smothered in cream and topped by the appropriate number of candles which have to be blown out with one breath or your wish won't come true.

When it's my turn to have a party, I explain the mandatory menu in great detail to my mother. She nods until I come to the frankfurts. 'But what do you eat with the frankfurts?' she wants to know. My reply, tomato sauce, doesn't satisfy her. 'What about potatoes?' she persists. 'Pickled cucumbers?' I impress on her that frankfurts don't need any accompaniments.

Finally my birthday comes around and my new friends and I are sitting around the table, munching fairy bread and chattering about the new Jane Powell and Errol Flynn movies showing at the Coronet, when my mother triumphantly places a large platter in front of us. A neat mountain of cocktail frankfurts are sitting on what resembles a lake of translucent frogs' spawn. Twenty eyes widen with disbelief. 'What's that?' my friend Wally whispers to her older sister Robyn, wrinkling her little freckled nose. 'Breakfast Delight!' my mother beams, delighted with her solution. My guests are too polite to comment but they push the offending semolina as far away from the frankfurts as possible while I wish I could sink through the floor. I can imagine them telling the kids at school about this gastronomical faux pas. But later, when I blow out the candles on the cake in one go and all my friends chorus 'Happy birthday, dear Disy!', my embarrassment is forgotten as I feel a surge of happiness. Now I really belong!

But every day there are reminders that I live in a different world from these children for whom life is so uncomplicated and free. There are so many things I'm forbidden to do. When rain buckets down in winter torrents, they simply take off their shoes and walk to school barefoot, but I have to stay home in case I catch pneumonia. When I catch a cold, I also have to stay home. In winter I'm not allowed to eat ice cream.

My surname is a constant source of embarrassment. Whenever I have to stand up in class and say my name, the others stare and titter and their eyes bulge with incredulity while I spell it out for the teacher syllable by syllable. 'B-o-g. U-s. L-a-w. S-k-i.' So when my parents discuss the possibility of changing our surname, I can't wait to have one that won't need spelling out. One possibility is to revert to my father's real surname, Baldinger, but when I mention this to one of my friends, she promises to nickname me Baldy, which is hardly an improvement. I wade through my magazines in search of Anglo-Saxon surnames: Barnett, Beresford, Bourke. In the end, my parents decide to keep Boguslawski. 'After all, this name brought us luck during the war,' my father argues. For the rest of my single life, I cringe each time I have to say my name. My husband Michael still teases me that I only married him so that I'd finally have an Anglo-Saxon surname!

The worst thing is that I'm not allowed to play outside like everyone else. The pavement in our street is chalked with hopscotch shapes, we throw tors and hop into heaven or into hell. In the vacant lot behind our street we re-enact the stories we've seen at the Saturday matinee, dividing ourselves into goodies and baddies while we rush around with make-believe swords or declaim heroic lines from swashbuckling movies. Sometimes in the midst of a dramatic scene, I glance guiltily towards our house to catch my father's flinty look and see his imperious finger beckoning me inside. 'Nice children don't play in the street like larrikins,' he says. Even though he suffered so much as a boy because of his own father's rigid rules, that doesn't stop him from inflicting similar restrictions on me.

The dance between the generations never ends. I always thought I was a very liberal, permissive parent until my daughter commented recently that she had felt restricted as a child because I had been overprotective and had forbidden her to do some of the things her friends had been allowed to do.

In time my parents discovered that although Australians were more friendly and polite than Europeans, they weren't as forthright. The stranger who appeared at our door one day was a health inspector. Someone in the street had reported that our back yard was overgrown and unsanitary, a breeding place for rats. After poking around in the spindly grass, the inspector advised my father to keep it cut. When he said that the complaint had come from our next door neighbour Mrs Leckie, my parents were amazed. This benevolent-looking old lady in the neat apron chatted to them over the fence every day, and her duplicity shocked them. My father was un-Australian enough to ask her why she'd gone behind their backs. 'Why didn't you tell me?' he asked. She couldn't answer and went inside.

At home my parents spoke Polish to each other, but soon I was replying in English. Changing your language in childhood is not just a linguistic loss. Apart from losing a world of subtleties, nuances and connotations of the words themselves, you also lose part of yourself. Language and culture influence the way you form thoughts and express feelings. English is more concise, blunt and matter-of-fact; it has a larger vocabulary but a smaller range of emotional expression than Polish, which is the language of affection. Nowhere is this contrast more obvious than in people's first names. While in English we truncate them into impersonal monosyllables devoid of tenderness, in Polish names are lengthened by endings which in themselves are endearments. Danuta, for instance, became affectionately softened to Danutka, Danusia, Danushka and Daneczka.

I wasn't aware of going through a linguistic transition process any more than a butterfly remembers emerging from a cocoon. It seems as though one moment I spoke no English, and the next I was suddenly writing compositions which were being read out to the class as examples of good writing. 'Diane is a New Australian but she can spell better than most of you,' the teacher sometimes said, but when I repeated this to my father, he looked doubtful. 'It's not good to be too clever.

The other children won't like it.' He thought that foreign children, especially Jewish ones, shouldn't draw too much attention to themselves.

It seems that I'm always destined to be in a minority. In Poland I was a Jewish child in a country of Catholics, and here I'm a Jewish Polish child in a country of Protestant Australians. On Sunday mornings the children in our street go to Sunday school and come home with pictures of Baby Jesus, similar to the ones I had been given by the nuns in Krakow. The religious tolerance of Australians delights my parents, but Aunty Mania says that's because the Protestants are too busy hating the Catholics to worry about the Jews.

On Sundays the clanging of the ice cream van draws all of us out into the street to buy chocolate-coated bats or tubs of frozen fruit salad. My friend Kay, whose father works on the Snowy River Hydro-Electric Scheme, plants herself in front of me, arms akimbo, eyes glinting with secret knowledge. 'Anyway, the Jews crucified Jesus!' she announces. Suddenly I'm surrounded by a ring of silent, accusing faces. 'No they didn't,' I protest. 'The Romans did.' Kay tilts her head to one side. 'The Jews killed Jesus,' she repeats. 'Our minister said.' Someone starts chanting over and over, 'Nebuchadnezzar King of the Jews sold his wife for a pair of shoes.' I try to say that Nebuchadnezzar wasn't even Jewish, but some of the others have taken up the chant and drown me out.

Just then Aunty Mania turns the corner into our street, and I see her walking towards me with a smile. She mustn't hear any of this. I know that she's been in something called a concentration camp, and although I have no idea what that means, I sense that she'd be very upset. Leaving my friends, I skip towards my aunt and steer her towards our gate. She gives me a shrewd glance. 'What were they saying?' she asks. 'I thought I heard them saying something about Jews.' I shake my head. I don't want her to be upset, but I don't want her to think badly of my friends either. They never bring it up again.

After having gone to Mass in Piszczac, attended the convent school in Krakow, and joined in the activities run by the Baptist church in Sydney, I knew more about Christianity than about my own religion. I'd never been inside a synagogue, heard Hebrew prayers or learned anything about my religion until Jewish scripture classes at primary school, when the flustered young teacher tried to teach us Hebrew songs while the boys threw paper aeroplanes and the girls whispered behind their ink-stained hands. I knew that it was now safe to admit that I was Jewish, but whenever I had to state my religion in public, I felt a weight pressing on my chest.

My parents didn't go to synagogue or observe religious holy days, although my mother bought *matzohs* at Passover and fasted on Yom Kippur. My father didn't believe that you needed synagogues or rabbis to commune with God. When a letter arrived inviting me to join a Jewish youth group called Habonim, I showed it to him, eager to join. To my dismay, he crumpled it up and tossed it into the wastepaper basket saying, 'You don't need Habonim.' He looked so angry that I didn't pursue the subject. He still hadn't lost his fear of belonging to an identifiable Jewish group.

About other things, however, my father treated me as an adult and took my questions seriously. One day, watching him light up yet another cigarette, I asked why he smoked. After considering this for a few moments, he replied, 'It's a dirty, stupid habit. It stains your fingers, yellows your teeth, gives you an unpleasant breath and damages your lungs.' That was the last cigarette he ever smoked. Years later he told me, 'How could I expect you to respect me if, after telling you all that, I kept on smoking?'

All the children in our street had a pet but my mother was adamant that she had enough to do without having an animal to look after as well. One afternoon, when 'Uncle' Reg Knight came home from work on his motorbike, he had a passenger. Attached to the handlebars was a letterbox, out of which peered the bewildered black face of a kitten miaowing piteously. 'It's for you,' he said.

Beside myself with joy, I ran inside, cuddling the trembling ball of fur. 'What's that?' my mother demanded. 'A kitten. Uncle Reg brought it home for me! Look, isn't he sweet!' Her frown made it clear that she didn't share my admiration. 'I need a cat like a hole in the head,' she grumbled. 'Thank Mr Knight but tell him we don't want a cat.'

By now I was wailing and pleading, and my mother was shouting and gesticulating.

Above our altercation, we heard my father's limping footsteps. 'What's going on here? How can I study with you two quarrelling?' As I sobbed out the story, he tickled the white triangle on the kitten's throat until it purred like a little motor. 'I have enough to do without a cat,' my mother repeated.

'Mummy is right,' my father replied. 'But you're a big girl. Maybe you can look after the kitten?' I nodded gratefully. Now I too had a pet.

Flip, whom my father named after a comedian from the silent movies, had idiosyncratic notions of hygiene. An unpleasant odour emanated from the bathroom, a musky, rancid smell we could not identify until my mother caught the culprit in the act. Flip had scrambled down the side of the bath and was peeing down the plughole. 'You can write that down in your notebook,' my father laughed.

For some time I'd been recording my feelings, experiences and impressions in a notepad, and at the age of twelve I wrote my first short story and submitted it for publication. My imagination must have been overheated by my mother's novels, because 'The Scorpion' was about a relationship ruined by ambition and duplicity. A young woman who longed to become an actress was offered the starring role provided that she could prove to the theatre director that she could act. He set her an unusual test. If she could convince a complete stranger that her life was in danger and induce him to rescue her, she'd get the part.

My heroine boarded a bus, sat next to a handsome young stranger, and sobbed that she was in the clutches of a sinister man known as the Scorpion. Unless someone accompanied her to his hideout to protect her, she'd be murdered. The smitten hero fell for the damsel in distress and for her story, but when they arrived at what was supposed to be the scoundrel's lair, it turned out that she'd brought him to the theatre instead. She got the part but lost the man!

After making sure that the manuscript was written in my best writing, I mailed it to the *Australian Women's Weekly*. Each day I rushed out to the letterbox as soon as I heard the postman's whistle awaiting their reply. Several weeks later, Mary and I were playing jacks on the verandah when the whistle shrilled.

When the postman handed me a large manila envelope, I saw that it was addressed to me and, with an author's instinct, knew that my story had been rejected. Without saying a word I ran inside and pushed it into a drawer out of sight, but Mary's quick eye had spotted my name on the envelope. I insisted that she was mistaken. Mary and I were soul mates and rivals. We had the same taste in books, film stars and games, longed to beat each other at school and shared the frustration of restrictive European parents, but I wasn't going to tell her that I'd had a story rejected. At the age of twelve, I was too embarrassed to admit literary failure.

It was to be another thirteen years before I submitted anything for publication again. Once again I submitted my story to the *Women's Weekly*, but this time it was accepted. My writing career had begun.

The bright summer sun of 1951 gilded the sandstone buildings of Sydney University and slanted through the stained-glass windows of the Great Hall when my father, attired in a graduate's black gown and mortarboard, shook hands with the Dean and received his degree as Bachelor of Dental Science. But although his studies were over, for the rest of his life he had a recurring nightmare about sitting for exams that he hadn't prepared for. Even at the age of seventy that dream would fill him with such panic that he used to wake up covered in sweat. It's not surprising. After all, so many times in his life, survival had depended on passing some test whose rules he didn't know.

In his dentistry year book, his entry is headed 'Is it so?' which must have been a phrase he often used. It goes on to say:

> *One of the older men in our year, Henry commenced his studies in 1949. At first, Henry had difficulties with our language, but has mastered it so quickly that statements such as 'I will borrow you my knife' are becoming rare. In fact, he has been heard to use the expression 'It fits like a bomb.'*
>
> *Henry has a very keen sense of humour and is able to appreciate a joke at his own expense. This, coupled with his ability and philosophical outlook, ensures him a happy future in the dental profession.*

By 1951, I too was assured of a happy future: in my last year at Waverley Primary School, the headmistress had astounded me by appointing me school captain. At the end of the year I was the only one in my class who was sent to Sydney Girls' High School, which was then fully selective.

My parents applied for Australian citizenship as soon as they were eligible. When I was going through my father's papers after his death, I found the copy of a letter he'd written to the then Minister for Immigration, in reply to his formal letter of congratulation.

> *Dear Mr Holt,*
>
> *Although I know that I am not expected to reply, I feel that I should take the opportunity of expressing my very sincere thanks and gratitude on my own and my family's behalf, in being accepted so thoroughly into the Australian way of life, and can assure you and my fellow-Australians of my wholehearted co-operation in my new responsibilities.*

Hirsch Baldinger, now Henry Boguslawski, had become a proud Australian citizen.

CHAPTER 33

While in Sydney my father was poring over his lecture notes, in Rio his eldest brother Avner was packing his bags. Avner's nightclub, like his previous ventures, had failed. 'My oldest brother ran a nightclub on Copacabana,' my father used to say with a mixture of wonder and pride at Avner's entrepreneurial flair. It sounded exotic, but the image was more glamorous than the reality. At first the restaurant had been a success but problems with the clientele soon emerged. The refugees wanted to sit and gossip all afternoon over one cup of coffee, which was unprofitable, and to make matters worse, the wealthy Cariocas didn't want to patronise a restaurant filled with impoverished expats. Eventually the refugees became offended and spread rumours that Avner was arrogant and didn't want them to patronise his club. To add to the dissension, some nights the son of President Vargas swaggered in drunk, kept drinking, and started firing his pistol as if he was in a wild west bar, which frightened off some of the regular clients. And on top of all that, Avner wasn't making any money because the chef was robbing him blind. Avner closed the restaurant.

There was nothing to keep him in Rio any longer. He'd never belonged in this hedonistic city where mulatto exuberance, African rhythms and Carioca poverty pulsed beneath the predatory European lifestyle. What's more, so many Germans had found refuge in this pro-Nazi corner of South America after the war that Jews felt uneasy. So when in 1949 their daughter Wanda gave birth to her first son, Peter, the prospect of seeing their first grandchild was the impetus that Avner and Hela needed to leave Brazil.

For the fourth time in his life Avner, at fifty-five, found himself in a new country, broke, and once again facing the dilemma of how to earn a living. Dependent on their daughter and son-in-law in Connecticut for a roof over their heads, he and Hela struggled to earn a pittance. Avner's first job in America was selling baking powder door to door. Slumped in a chair at the end of a demoralising day, he told Wanda, 'Every customer would have to buy ten containers of baking powder every week for me to make a living out of this, but unfortunately one box lasts for two years!' The only job he could find was operating an elevator. For a time the two of them packaged candies in Wanda's cellar. For a man of grand visions and big ideas, life in the United States was dispiriting.

By then Wanda had been living in the United States for three years. When she arrived in New York from Rio in 1947, she was twenty-five, stunning and single. Like so many bright, beautiful and temperamental women with a stormy relationship with their fathers, she tended to choose unsuitable men, and her relationships in Rio had been unsatisfactory.

Although she'd come to the States for a holiday, when she was offered a job as secretary with the Chilean Delegation at the United Nations in New York, she jumped at the opportunity of staying. Freedom beckoned. As it turned out, her inde-pendence was short-lived because before the year was over she was married. She met Max Matt through some Baldinger relatives she'd located through the telephone directory. At the turn of the century, Daniel Baldinger's youngest sister Eva had migrated from Poland to New York and although Eva had died before Wanda's arrival, her daughter Esther introduced Wanda to the intense young man whose soft voice and strong character won her heart.

When Avner and Hela arrived in Connecticut, Max was managing a chain of grocery stores. He felt it was his duty to help Avner get started, but couldn't see what an unqualified man in his fifties without assets or capital could possibly do. From the moment they met, Max was fascinated by his sophisticated, cultured father-in-law and his gift of the gab. 'Avner could charm the shirt off your back,' he recalls. 'If he drew a castle in the air he could convince you that it was solid marble. If only he'd arrived in the United States during the twenties or thirties, he would have made a fortune, but by 1950 the opportunities were dwindling.'

Wanda shakes her head impatiently. 'Father didn't make it anywhere because he was profligate. They both were.'

'I don't believe so,' Max counters in his husky voice. 'Perhaps in Europe, but not in America, anyways.'

There's something elfin about this octogenarian whose whiskery grey beard, blue denim jeans, and quirky cap pulled over his bald head make him look like an eccentric intellectual. He is strong and centred, looks at the world with curious eyes and an open mind, and gives others space to be themselves.

Later that afternoon, as we hike along a steep path that leads to a mountaintop, Max talks about his own childhood in a Ukrainian village, and it strikes me that privation forges stronger character than plenty. Max was five years old when he and his siblings were orphaned in 1915 and they were taken in by their aunt and uncle who could barely feed their own five children. One of his first memories was being chased by Ukrainian boys who threw stones at him because he was Jewish.

By the time he was nine, he knew that being Jewish meant

death. During a pogrom, one of his aunts and her daughter were raped and killed by hoodlums whose catchcry was 'Kill the Jews and save the Ukraine'. Not long afterwards his aunt and uncle tied their meagre possessions in bundles and the whole family fled to Romania on foot. Max still remembers the terror of crossing the Dniester River by night. The river was iced over, their feet kept slipping, and they couldn't see where they were going, but they knew they mustn't utter a sound in case the border guards heard them. Suddenly Max's little sister Hilda started crying. Shots rang out. Any moment now the guards would shoot them. Swiftly their uncle picked Hilda up, muffled her crying with his hand and carried her for hours across the slippery ice.

When they reached Bucharest, their uncle couldn't find work, so Max and Hilda were sent to an orphanage. 'To this day I have nightmares that I'm back in that soulless place. Nobody cared about us and hunger gnawed at me night and day.' He used to sneak out at dawn with some of the other boys to ambush farmers on their way to market and steal apples and melons off their carts. One memory from those days still makes Max tremble. 'I was walking with Hilda through a park, tailing a man who was eating an apple, just waiting for him to throw away the core. The moment he did, I swooped down on it and started devouring it. My little sister was tugging at me, crying with hunger. She wanted some too.' In a voice that's barely audible, as though he doesn't want to hear what he's saying, he whispers, 'But I didn't share it.' Tears are running down his furrowed cheeks. He still can't forgive himself.

When the Hebrew Immigrant Aid Society arranged for Max and his sisters to set sail for Canada along with two hundred other Jewish orphans, he was overjoyed. They were told that they'd be adopted by farming families who needed help on the land. Max knew nothing about Canada or farming, but he longed to get away from that orphanage and get enough to eat.

Soon after their ship docked, the adoption process began. The farmers and their wives looked over the children as if they were apples on a stall and selected the ones they fancied. By the afternoon most of the orphans had been taken to their new homes, but no-one chose Max or his sister. The day was almost over when a couple of latecomers looked Hilda over and took her with them. Max was left standing forlornly in the hall.

When Max was told that he'd have to go to the Montreal Hebrew Orphans' Home, he went berserk. An orphanage meant hunger, cold and misery, which he'd have to face all alone as his little sister had gone. Max became a wildcat. He screamed and yelled, bit and scratched, kicked and fought, and they couldn't calm him down.

In the midst of this rampage, Max looked up and the shout died on his lips. Running towards him was his little sister. As soon as Hilda had realised that she was going to be separated from Max, she also screamed and yelled so much that the couple became alarmed and brought her back. The children clung to each other, overjoyed to be together again. No matter how bad the orphanage was, at least they'd be together.

But when Hilda and Max entered the Montreal Hebrew Orphans' Home, they couldn't believe their eyes. It was a big and beautiful building with bright rooms, clean bathrooms and food in abundance. For the first time in years they were well fed, clothed, given books and treated with kindness, but Max didn't believe it could last. There had to be a catch.

Not long after they arrived, he got up at night and crept down to the kitchen where they kept a basket of apples. Although he wasn't hungry, he grabbed three, ran upstairs and hid them under his pillow. Next morning the headmaster called Max into his office. A kitchen hand had seen him take the apples. Max's knees trembled as he faced the headmaster, dreading the punishment to come. But Mr Goldie looked into his face with such compassion that Max had to look away. 'If you take three apples, two other children will miss out on theirs,' the headmaster explained. 'But if you're really hungry, you can keep them.' Red-faced, Max handed back two apples. He never stole again.

Long before I met him, I'd heard from my parents that Max was a remarkable man who became the supervisor of his orphanage at the age of nineteen and, shortly afterwards, was appointed director of the Montreal Hebrew Orphans' Home. Ten years later, however, he realised that it was time for a change. He was twenty-nine and he had no social life or interests outside the orphanage. When he found out that he had a relative living in Connecticut, he moved to Hartford and worked in his cousin's grocery business until he was drafted in 1941.

As we climb a steep leaf-strewn mountain path that smells of spring in New England, Max, who is eighty-two and has had bypass surgery, forges ahead of me. 'The effect of war on a soldier cannot be explained,' he muses in his soft, husky voice. 'Self-preservation takes over, and you do things you don't believe you'd ever do. You don't give a damn about anyone or anything. All you know is, if you don't protect yourself, you're going to get killed.'

He served in North Africa, Italy and Germany. 'You know, we Americans believe that we are angels, but ugly stories come out of every war. When we got to Civita Vecchia we wanted to place our anti-aircraft guns on top of the plateau but we knew that the Germans had planted mines and booby traps. So the army selected some town dignitaries and made them lead the way. If they made it, we knew we could use the same route. Of course often they didn't make it. I don't think I felt bad about it. At that time the Italians were the enemy. I was in anti-aircraft—we'd see a plane and shoot it down. We had a battery of four big guns and maybe twenty or thirty calibre machine guns. Whenever we saw injured American soldiers, we lusted for revenge. That's what war does to people.'

The hardships he'd suffered making his own way in the world made Max admire Avner's resourcefulness and tenacity. He also liked Hela's genuine, down-to-earth attitude. But Wanda and her parents had never got along, and before the year was over, conflicts escalated between them. 'They spoiled the baby rotten,' she reminisces. 'They couldn't say no to him. When Peter picked up a penknife one afternoon, my father ran into the kitchen shouting for me to come quickly so that he wouldn't have to be the one to take it away from him!' She was astonished that Avner didn't know how to play with his own grandson. 'I still remember the wistful look on my father's face when he told me, "I never learned how to play because my father sent me to *cheder* when I was three years old."'

Apart from arguments about the baby, Wanda resented the way her parents ordered her around and sided with Max against her. 'Whenever Max and I argued, my mother would say to him, "Only you would tolerate a person like Wanda!" I just couldn't see myself spending the rest of my life with my parents after I'd travelled 5000 miles to get away from them!' she says. Things came to a head when she and Max were about to move into a new home. 'I was willing to help them financially but not to live with them,' she says. Musing about her relationship with her parents, she says: 'Life isn't fair. The pleasures that parents give children are brushed away like crumbs, but the pains are absorbed into the psyche like inkblots.' Once again, my cousin's insight resonates in my mind for a long time to come.

Avner and Hela moved to New York to live with their son Adam and his new wife Margot, and continued to live with them for the next eight years. Having in-laws living with you for years in a cramped apartment sounds like a recipe for disaster, but Margot's affection for her parents-in-law never waned, not even after she and Adam parted.

Even now, twelve years after Avner's death, this seventy-four-year-old woman's eyes brim with tears when she talks about her father-in-law. It seems to me that Margot appreciated Avner and Hela better than their own children did. 'Papa was a wonderful man, he had such charisma. I still miss him. He kept me spellbound with those marvellous stories. Adam used to roll his eyes, but I could listen for hours,' she reminisces during her recent holiday in Sydney.

Soon after arriving in New York, Avner started working as a diamond broker, a business he'd learned in Antwerp. According to Adam, he was unlucky from the start. He made a sale of industrial quality diamonds but as the customer didn't pay, he couldn't pay the supplier and lost the business. His next venture was costume jewellery, but that didn't work out either. Neither did his attempts to sell real estate.

Adam has come to Connecticut to meet me. Again, it's disconcerting to realise that this elderly white-haired man with the stroke-slurred speech and stiff gait is the cousin who has always been referred to in the family by the childish form of his name, Adash. Unlike his sister, Adam doesn't analyse his parents or himself. When I ask why so many of his father's enterprises didn't work out, he shrugs. 'You have to realise that for many people of that generation, life didn't go in a straight line. Your father was a dentist so he remained a dentist, he didn't have to keep trying to figure out new ways of earning money. But my father didn't have any trade or profession, so he had to keep finding new businesses. Finally he hit on the idea of making pâté. He loved fine food and felt that there had to be a market in the United States for the chicken liver pâté he used to buy in Antwerp before the war.'

It was in Margot's tiny kitchen, with a benchtop barely big enough for one person, that Avner began experimenting with the recipes which would finally lead to success. Every night, when Margot came home from hospital where she worked as a laboratory technician, there were pots bubbling on the stove, mixtures sizzling in frypans, and dishes piled up on the table. As soon as she walked in the door, Avner and Hela would hold out a spoon for her to taste the latest version of their recipe.

Margot adored Adam, and when, not long after they were married, she discovered that he was unfaithful, she poured her heart out to her mother-in-law. Hela consoled her. 'Don't worry,' she said. 'Most men stray from time to time. It doesn't mean anything.' Then she flashed her daughter-in-law a mischievous smile. 'You know, it's not made of soap, it won't wear out!' Margot took Hela's advice and stayed with Adam for another twenty years, but she realises this was a mistake. 'Adash should never have married. He was overindulged by his parents, never applied himself to anything and had a foul temper. I loved him and made allowances for him, but basically he was a spoiled little boy who never grew up.'

When they finally got the pâté recipe right, Avner realised that the mixture would have to be sold in cans. He leased a dialpidated room in a condemned building in the Bronx and Max bought him a second-hand canning machine. Margot still marvels how hard her in-laws worked at their age. For eighteen hours a day Hela cooked in huge vats while Avner put the pâté into cans, using the old-fashioned foot-operated machine. 'They came home exhausted but never complained. Papa never lost his sense of humour or his optimism,' she recalls.

The turning point in their pâté-manufacturing career came when they discovered that it only cost a few cents more per tin to have someone else produce it. Soon their pâté was stocked on the speciality shelves of all the supermarkets and did so well that they were able to move into a nice apartment and hire a maid. 'Papa bought Mama a diamond ring and a fur coat. It was lovely to see them finally doing well,' beams Margot, who never resented the fact that she kept her in-laws for eight years. Before long, Kraft wanted to buy Avner's recipe for $5000, but he refused to sell it. By then, he was close to seventy. Finally, in his old age, he'd found the recipe for success. Baldinger's Chicken Liver Pâté is manufactured to this day. One tin of it stands on a shelf in my kitchen in Sydney, a tribute to my uncle's indomitable spirit.

Hela didn't live long to enjoy their new affluence. In 1977, while on a draconian diet, she had a massive heart attack. 'My father was devastated when Mother died,' Wanda recalls, 'but it wasn't long before the widows in his apartment block started visiting.' At eighty-two, Avner was stooped with osteoporosis but he still had an appreciative eye for a good-looking woman, a ready compliment and a never-ending supply of enthralling stories. Within a short time he formed a relationship with a much younger woman who brightened his last years. 'But Adam and I always said that if he had died first, Mother would not have gotten over it,' Wanda remarks.

It surprised everyone who knew him that, after turning away from religion throughout his life, Avner began studying the Torah again in his old age and joined an orthodox synagogue. When he died in 1985, at the age of ninety, he had an orthodox funeral which would have gladdened his father's heart.

Avner's brothers Marcel and Izio didn't attend his funeral because they were angry with him over money or whatever emotional issues the money represented. 'My father had a strange attitude to money,' says Adam. 'He was generous in his own way but he didn't repay loans and that caused a lot of bad feeling.'

The last time I visit Uncle Izio, he has become disillusioned with his eldest brother, but by then he is sunk in misery about his wife's debilitated state and disillusioned with the whole world. 'Avner was the most powerful character in our family and we all idolised him. But much later I realised that he was selfish, ruthless and dishonest. He had a formidable brain and a photographic memory but he took advantage of people, even our parents. I can remember him saying to me one day, "There's only me, me, me and then, a long long corridor away, there's you." That's how he was.'

When people realise that they've been worshipping a false god, their disappointment with their own judgment makes them turn on the object of their idolatry. Once Izio began to see his brother's faults, he couldn't accept that he was a human being with good and bad qualities. 'Ten years ago I suddenly saw that this is how he's been all his life, and I couldn't forgive him,' he says.

The only one of Avner's siblings who was with him when he died was his youngest sister. By a strange coincidence, Slawa had come to visit him in New York for the first time shortly before he became ill. Sitting by her brother's bedside, Slawa had time to reflect over her life which had diverged from the rest of the family and left her isolated in her native land.

CHAPTER 34

By the flickering light of the candle in her dimly-lit room on Urzednicza Street, Slawa picked up each thread of the laddered nylon stocking with her needle. The candlelight made her eyes feel as though they were about to drop out, but she forced herself to continue mending until the whole pile was done. Life was tough and every zloty helped.

Gusts of wind as sharp as knives still blew over Krakow that April of 1952, and spring seemed far away. Of Daniel Baldinger's eleven children, only Slawa had remained in Poland, while her seven surviving brothers and sisters were now dispersed all over the globe. Like a handful of sand tossed up in the air and blown about by the wind, they'd settled in Tel-Aviv, Montreal, Sydney, Paris and New York. Although her brother Henek had suggested that she and her husband should migrate to Australia, an offer she'd found tempting, Mietek, who wasn't Jewish, hadn't wanted to leave his native land.

From the top of the walnut sideboard, Aunty Slawa picks up her wedding photograph with a sigh. The bridegroom's severely handsome face suggests a self-contained man who didn't waste words. She, on the contrary, beams out of the photograph, her eager face framed by wavy brown hair. That smile hasn't changed, but her grey hair is now cropped short around her plump face.

Looking adoringly at Mietek's photo, she says, 'It's twenty years since he died. The most wonderful husband in the world, sensitive, kind-hearted, obliging. We complemented each other: he was introverted and laconic and I was the lively, energetic one.' She still has so much energy that it's hard to believe she's eighty. Every day she walks for miles in search of the best veal or the juiciest oranges, and then lugs them up four steep flights of stairs. 'Mietek treated me with great respect,' she reminisces. With a twinkle she adds, 'But not in bed!'

Mietek worked on the railways until he retired. 'That's why I have a pension, a rail pass and coal coupons,' she says, 'but who's going to haul bags of coal up four floors now that Mario's moved out?' Mario, their only child, was born nine years after they married, long after she'd given up hope of ever having a baby.

She interrupts her story to slip on her well-worn dog-brown shoes and gabardine belted jacket, and continues talking while we walk to the market. Stout women in blood-stained aprons hack veal shoulders with cleavers, and babushkas in headscarves crouch on the pavement, holding posies of lilies-of-the-valley. Aunty Slawa buys me a bunch of these white bells which tremble against spear-shaped leaves of forest green, and I bury my nose in their sweetly delicate fragrance which always reminds me of Poland.

Scrutinising a scrawny chicken held up by a hawker in a cloth cap doesn't interrupt my aunt's flow of memories. 'Life was tough when the communists took over,' she says, shaking her head at the price the man's asking for the chicken. Life is still hard now that the communists have been trounced, and her widow's pension can't keep up with escalating prices. But like all the Baldingers, she has a joke for every occasion. 'Life in Poland is just like the unhappily married woman who went to have her fortune told. "You're going to have ten terrible years," the clairvoyant predicted. "And then?" the woman asked eagerly. "And then you'll get used to it!"'

When Slawa and Mietek set up house in their one-room flat on Urzednicza Street, all they had was Karola's walnut sideboard and the bedroom suite which my parents had given them before leaving Krakow. Her present flat, in which she has lived for over thirty years, is a repository of family furniture. I sleep on Lunia's old divan bed, take dishes out of Jerzy and Rutka's painted kitchen cupboard, and look at Karola's sideboard while eating breakfast. That link with the past is exciting but it saddens me that furniture is all that remains of my uncles and aunts.

I don't think that Aunty Slawa has ever thrown anything away. The blue woollen dressing gown which I wear during my stay arrived from Australia forty years ago. 'Your parents sent me that even though they had to struggle themselves at the beginning,' she says. I remember that as soon as my father had saved up a few pounds, he used to send skeins of Australian wool and warm clothes to his sisters Slawa and Andzia. 'Your father has always been good to his family,' my mother used to say. She was right. While he was sending parcels to his sisters overseas, we had so little money to live on that my mother used to cut and glue Kromite rubber soles onto our shoes to make them last longer because we couldn't afford repairs.

Aunty Slawa is thrilled that I've come to Poland to see her. Every morning she brews a pot of coffee and brings it to me in bed with great ceremony. This precious French coffee, which she keeps for special occasions, has come from her brother Marcel who sends her parcels filled with delicacies several times a year. Like a squirrel, she stashes the treasures away and makes them last. But when I ask whether she feels close to these brothers who have helped her all her life, she shakes her large head. 'I never felt close to any of my siblings except Jerzy who used to cuddle me,' she says. 'Just once, after Father died, Izio put his arm around me. Other than that, I don't recall any of them showing me any warmth or even being interested in me. Being the youngest, I didn't count.'

Resting her plump cheek against her hand, she reflects on her life in Poland after the rest of the family had left. Mending nylons strained her eyes, so when she saw an advertisement for tourist guides, she applied and became a guide for the government tourist agency, Orbis. The work suited her friendly, energetic personality and enabled her to travel overseas at a time when political restrictions made this very difficult. Sighing with nostalgia she says, 'I adored my work. I met interesting people and visited fantastic places like Turkey and France and Egypt.'

Supplementing Mietek's small salary was essential because Mario, who was seven years old at the time, developed a worrying cough and had to be sent to a sanatorium. 'The treatment was so expensive that we virtually lived on dry bread for two years. After that I took him to the seaside every summer and he grew strong, but he was highly strung as a child. He still is. Mario was afraid of his father. Mietek was terribly strict. Most of our arguments were about the way he disciplined the child.'

I always knew that I had a cousin called Mario, but the little boy with the Slavic face and smooth blond hair whose communion photograph Aunty Slawa sent us many years ago never really seemed part of my family. Although I knew that his father was Catholic, my aunt's next words take me by surprise. 'For most of his life Mario didn't know I was Jewish,' she says. 'I never told him.'

From the way her face sags, I can see that it's painful for her to talk about this. 'Although almost all the Jews had been killed off during the war, anti-Semitism here never stopped.

In fact, it got much worse during the sixties,' she explains. 'Jews were bad. Anything Jewish was bad. When people opened up, you felt their consuming hatred, as if they wanted to eat Jews alive.'

In 1967, when Israel's victory in the Six-Day War provoked a wave of anti-Semitism in the then pro-Arab communist bloc, Poland's communist government followed suit. Jews were vilified, accused of causing all the country's problems, persecuted, and fired from their jobs. Aunty Slawa didn't lose her job because they didn't know that she was Jewish. 'Ever since the Occupation I've had a complex about admitting I was Jewish and the events of 1967 proved me right. I never said I was Catholic, but I didn't say I was Jewish either, not unless I was asked outright. To this day I don't advertise it,' she says. 'That fear stays with you all your life.'

To Aunty Slawa's horror, Mario used to repeat the anti-Semitic comments he heard at school. 'You can't imagine how it hurt me to hear him say those things, but I just didn't have the courage to tell him the truth,' she tells me. 'I couldn't bring myself to tell him that I was Jewish, and that he was Jewish too. I tried to explain that people envied Jews because they were successful, educated and wise, and that for centuries Jews have been persecuted and discriminated against for being different. I told him that one day he'd read books and understand.' She gives a long sigh. 'But nothing I said made any difference. He didn't want to know.'

How strange life is. Growing up in the city where his devout grandfather once prayed in synagogue every morning, Mario was ignorant of his heritage. 'I felt terrible about it, but I had to deal with the world I was living in,' Aunty Slawa shrugs. 'To this day, being a Jew is considered a disgrace in this country. If someone wants to discredit a politician, they spread rumours that there's a Jewish skeleton in his closet. Either he had a Jewish mother, or he's a converted Jew. I wanted to spare Mario the pain of belonging to a despised minority. I didn't want him to go through what I did.'

Mario didn't find out the truth until he was twenty-five years old, and only then because his mother was being blackmailed. A Catholic acquaintance threatened Slawa that she would tell her son she was Jewish unless Slawa gave her a piece of jewellery she wanted. In a panic, Slawa rushed to Lola's place for advice. Izio Baldinger's first wife, who was also widowed after the death of her second husband, was her closest friend. Lola, who was always level-headed and objective, saw the crisis as an opportunity rather than a catastrophe. It was time that Mario knew.

I ask my cousin how he felt when he discovered the truth. At the age of twenty-five, I imagine that he must have been horrified to learn that he was half-Jewish. Mario's reply is so swift and matter-of-fact that I can't conceal my surprise. 'I wasn't shocked at all,' he says. 'It was perfectly all right, it felt fine. Things I'd never understood before suddenly fell into place. I used to wonder why my mother cried sometimes, why she got so upset about things which didn't seem important. Naturally I wondered why she hadn't told me sooner, but I understand that she was worried about how I'd react.' Talking to Mario about this, I recall that I too once faced the same revelation and that, like him, I'd always known deep down that my family was different.

When he fell in love, however, Mario also lacked the courage to tell his fiancée about his Jewish blood. He was so much in love with Gosia, a sensual blue-eyed blonde with a dreamy manner, that he was terrified of losing her and didn't tell her until after the wedding. 'She accepted it,' he says, 'but said that I should have told her sooner.' His bride's parents, however, found it so difficult to cope with the fact that their son-in-law was Jewish that for a long time their relationship with the young couple was very distant.

While he talks, Mario's ash-blond hair falls across his forehead. It's hard to imagine that this tall, handsome man of thirty-five was once a sickly child. With his regular features, thick moustache and slightly sardonic expression, my cousin looks typically Polish, but beneath the Polish charm, the explosive Baldinger temperament lives on. Eloquent, knowledgeable and intense, he overwhelms me with a torrent of facts and figures. 'All they understand here about capitalism is putting up prices,' he scoffs. 'Every merchant in Poland has to become an instant millionaire.' The words tumble out thick and fast, and when he's finished, I feel I've been run over by a truck.

As Mario and I wander around the Kazimierz district together, he is a lively companion, peering into windows, pushing open gates, darting down alleys. When we peer through the grimy windows of the temple on Miodowa Street, across the road from our grandparents' first home, he hoists me up so that I can see the impressive colonnaded interior with the Star of David on the wall, the vaulted ceiling, wooden gallery and the thick tomes stacked on dusty shelves.

Walking along these twisted lanes, I'm aware of the ghosts of the past all around us. The patina of every building seems imprinted with untold stories and vanished lives. Invisible eyes are watching me and phantom fingers clutch at me as I pass. There's a brooding stillness here. Everything seems poised, watching, waiting. The cobbled lanes twist, widen and narrow, and grasses push up between the paving stones. Some buildings have the tell-tale elongated, curved windows of old synagogues and *shtibls*, some facades still have traces of old Yiddish signs. Children with pale faces and flaxen hair stare at us from doorways. It's strangely silent here, like watching a movie with the sound turned off.

As we walk through the sad overgrown alleys of the Jewish cemetery, Mario explains the symbols on the graves: lions, deer, candelabra, hands clasped together. He reads books about Jewish history and traditions and studies Hebrew tombstone inscriptions. With the hushed voice and shining eyes of someone about to disclose an exciting secret, Mario confides, 'I'm really glad that I have a Jewish background, because that means I belong to the chosen people!'

It takes me a while to realise that he's speaking from the perspective of his new religion. In an effort to resolve the dilemma of his religious identity and reconcile the Christian and Jewish worlds, he and Gosia have joined an evangelical Protestant sect which accepts the Old Testament alongside the New and gives him permission to be proud of his Jewish heritage. His mother marvels at his interest in religion. 'You should see how he pores over the Old Testament!' she says.

Aunty Slawa has joined us outside her old family home in Sebastiana Street. It's a shady street, where the boughs of the chestnut trees let little sunlight through. Inside the entrance to number twenty, I take in the curved ceiling, the ochre and maroon geometric patterns on the tile floor, and the fragments of royal blue glass set into the semicircular pane above the door that leads to the back of the house. Outside, the paving is broken, the paint is peeling and the walls are crumbling. Aunty Slawa is shocked. 'It never looked like that when we lived here!' she exclaims. Then she points to the shed at the far end of the courtyard. 'That's where my father had his workshop. I remember him standing there in his overalls, pottering around, tinkering, soldering and making his first prams.'

My aunt is prowling around like an animal which has caught

the long-lost scent of home. She calls me over, her voice trembling with emotion. 'Look!' she points. On the fence, I can discern the faint imprint of some old structure. She's almost dancing with excitement. 'This is where we used to have our Sukkah! We ate our meals together there on Sukkoth, under the awning that Father erected.'

She runs over to the ground floor balcony which is heaped with old boxes and rusting scraps of metal. 'We used to keep our fridge there. And over there, against the shed, we had a pear tree. It had big yellow pears. We children weren't allowed to pick them, but I was such a tomboy, sometimes I climbed the tree and raided it!' As she speaks, lost in happy nostalgia, I recall her brother Izio's account of those same pears which he coveted as a boy. I can still hear his resentful voice saying: 'I used to look at those big pears which my father placed on brown paper to ripen and longed to have one, but they were only for the visitors. If I wanted one, I had to steal it.' It amazes me that these two siblings who grew up in the same house react so differently to the same incident. The memory that makes her smile brings a hurt expression to his face. Then it strikes me that no two children ever grow up in the same way in the same family or remember their childhood in the same way. Personalities affect perceptions and filter memories.

Aunty Slawa and I knock on the door of the ground floor flat where my grandparents used to live, and as she presses the key-shaped bell, she stares at it in disbelief. It's the same one. The woman who opens the door lets us in, and I stand in a long, sunny room facing the street. This used to be the sitting room, where the piano used to stand with the embroidered shawl thrown over the well-polished top. It was from this window that my cousin Krysia used to peer on Saturdays, quaking with fear as she watched the Chassids walking to synagogue in their large black fur hats.

Aunty Slawa is chuckling. 'I used to climb through that window when I came home after a date so my parents wouldn't know how late I was!' As she talks, my mind is whirring. This is the house where my father grew up, where eleven strong-minded children lived with their religious father and overworked mother. I imagine my father, running around outside and kicking a cloth ball in the yard until Daniel calls him inside. Overwhelmed, I long to sit here by myself, alone with my thoughts and feelings, to give the phantoms of the past enough time to emerge from the shadows. But we only have a few rushed moments, so I press the shutter, take one final look, and leave.

Later, over iced coffee and strawberry ice cream in the Glowny Rynek, a troupe of folk musicians in red boots and streaming ribbons serenade us with nostalgic melodies of old Krakow and a hawker pushes a barrow with the crusty salt-encrusted bagels called *obwarzanki* which my mother used to buy me after school. Aunty Slawa has become pensive. She feels isolated and misses the family. Apart from her brothers Jean and Marcel whom she sometimes visited while escorting tours to Paris, she hasn't seen much of her family in the past fifty years.

She used to long for her sisters to invite her to Israel. 'I hadn't seen Lunia since 1939 and wanted to see her and Andzia so much, but I couldn't afford to go to Israel. I was thrilled when Lunia invited me to come a few years ago, but at the last moment she withdrew the invitation, claiming she was ill. She was probably ashamed of the way I looked. Or else she didn't want me to see how she'd aged.' Slawa got her wish when her niece Krysia, Andzia's daughter, invited her to Israel for a holiday several years ago. But the attractive, elegant young women she remembered now resembled ancient ruins. 'I would never have recognised Lunia,' she shakes her head in dismay. 'She was so old and frail in her wheelchair but her mind was as sharp as ever. She recognised me straightaway but Andzia had no idea who I was.'

All around us, Glowny Rynek is bustling with activity. A flock of pigeons swoop down in front of the Mariacki Church and take off again over the stalls of roses, carnations and gladioli, their wings flapping above our heads. A hawker in bright red boots and embroidered jacket is plying tourists with peacock feathers. Sharp-eyed gypsies accost tourists with wheedling voices while their probing hands are tugging at their bags. With a loving smile my aunt says: 'My darling Danusia, I can't tell you how thrilled I am that you've come to see me. I always loved the whole family, and I miss everyone so much.' She lapses into silence. Suddenly the smile vanishes and the happy facade is stripped bare as lifelong resentments spill onto the piazza. 'After Mietek died, not one of my brothers or sisters made any effort to get me to join them. I was left here all alone.'

CHAPTER 35

In 1950 Slawa was struggling to make ends meet in Poland, Avner was struggling to make a living in America, and my father was struggling to pass exams in Australia, but their eldest sister Lunia had already established a sewing school in Tel-Aviv. When she and her husband Berus had arrived in Palestine in 1940, she bought three sewing machines, turned her living room into a classroom and Madame Stella's Sewing School was open for business. A lifelong fascination with fashion, along with her satiny charm and steely confidence, ensured her success.

'All I knew about tailoring was from the brief sewing course I did in Bucharest on our way to Palestine. At first, I was only one step ahead of my pupils,' she tells me in the garden of the Beth-Hadekel Nursing Home outside Tel-Aviv. 'I often had to dash into the bedroom and close the door so that they wouldn't see me looking things up in my notebook! But eventually my school was so successful that when Krysia arrived in Tel-Aviv, she came to work for me.'

On the drive back to Tel-Aviv, past fields of watermelons, olive groves, and flat-roofed buildings on dry, dusty streets, my cousin Krysia talks about her decision to migrate to Israel forty years earlier. 'You'll probably find this odd,' she says, 'but in 1950 the idea of living in a country full of Jews terrified me.' Deep in her heart, she was still a frightened child peering out of her grandparents' window at shadowy men in black beards, black hats and long black coats, still the hunted girl who knew that being Jewish meant death.

That evening in Tel-Aviv I meet other cousins who also found it difficult to be Jewish again after the war. We've all gathered at Alina Erlich's. Everyone is talking at once, Polish and Ivrit, glasses are clinking, and we're all trying to work out how we're related. 'My father and your mother ... no, my grandfather and your uncle ...' Alina and Dov's grandfather Ignacy and my grandmother Lieba were brother and sister. Their father Kuba Spira, was my father's cousin. He and Hela Kwasniewska were the only two of Ignacy's five children to survive the war.

After spending the war years on Aryan papers, Alina found it difficult to adjust to being Jewish again. 'I didn't feel Jewish and I didn't want to be Jewish,' she says. 'It wasn't until Israel became a nation in 1948 that I started feeling proud of being Jewish. My parents had permits for Australia, but I thought, why go to Australia when we have our own country?'

Krysia's husband Marcel Ginzig is nodding in agreement. While Krysia had been reluctant to live in a nation of Jews, Marcel couldn't wait to reach the Promised Land. Marcel was an idealist who'd been educated at Krakow's Hebrew Gymnasium which imbued its pupils with a love for Palestine. When World War II broke out, Marcel at sixteen was already familiar with the geography of Palestine, the concept of a kibbutz, and the inspiring songs of the pioneers.

Forty years after their arrival in Israel, he is still an idealist, a retired school teacher with a deliciously dry sense of humour. He speaks with a quiet intensity, and often ends his sentences with a bemused questioning 'Hm?' In their flat which is decorated with Krysia's paintings and sculptures, I list all the places I'm going to visit in Israel: Haifa, Kinneret, Safed,

Jerusalem, Ein Gedi, Masada, Beersheva ... With a deadpan expression, he asks, 'And what will you do in the afternoon, hm?'

The only son of indulgent, loving parents, Marcel had led a charmed life in Krakow before the war. He had a shiny new bicycle, a real leather football, and a father who bought whatever he wanted. His friends nicknamed him 'Daddy-Will-Pay Ginzig' because whenever he bought anything, he used to tell the merchant breezily, 'Daddy will pay.' At the thought of those happy, far-off days when there were still mothers, fathers, sisters and school friends, Marcel sighs. 'There were fifty-two pupils in my class when war broke out. Only six of us survived.'

Bursts of laughter and guttural conversations float up to Krysia's small balcony which overlooks the street. While she puts out herrings, pickled cucumbers and cheese for our supper in their cosy little flat, Marcel takes out a small, faded photograph with bruised edges. He handles it like a priceless talisman, and that's exactly what it is.

It's the only photograph he has of his mother Frederyka, his father Dawid, and his twelve-year-old sister Halinka. 'I kept that photograph with me all through the war,' he says, 'Even in the camps when we weren't allowed to keep anything, I folded it up and slipped it between the sole and the heel of my shoe, and that's where it stayed through all the years I spent in concentration camps. The photograph survived: the people on it did not.'

By night Marcel often revisits Auschwitz in his dreams, and after all these years he still screams in his sleep. As he starts talking, the large crimson sun slides down the cloudless sky and melts into the Mediterranean. Night falls quickly in the Levant and soon it's dark outside, but the darkness that closes in around us has nothing to do with the time of day.

In his understated way, Marcel begins. 'We were evacuated from Auschwitz in January 1945. Our March of Death had begun.' In that bitter winter, when they could already hear the artillery of the American army in the distance, the Nazis forced their emaciated captives to flee at gunpoint from those who were coming to rescue them. Camp survivors, who were so weak that they could hardly stand on their wooden clogs wrapped in rags, had to take care not to stumble on the icy ground because anyone who fell was shot. 'There were over three hundred in our group when we started, but they shot so many along the way that soon only about twelve remained.'

Shuffling alongside Marcel during the forced march was Henek, his old school friend from the Hebrew Gymnasium who had been with him in Plaszow, Ostrowiec and Auschwitz. 'If we hadn't had each other, we both would have perished,' he says. 'We kept each other going. I wouldn't eat a bite without giving him half, and he did the same.' Marcel grimaces. 'Conditions at Auschwitz were so dreadful that some fathers and sons tore scraps of food out of each other's mouths, but somehow my pal and I kept each other going.' There were times when Marcel had felt so desperate that he was ready to hurl himself against the electrified fence to end the suffering, but each time his friend had managed to give him enough hope to keep him alive one more day.

'He was staggering beside me when a guard shot him,' Marcel recalls. 'The bullet went straight through his jaw. He was covered in blood and couldn't close his mouth. When we passed a well beside the road, I took his hand and somehow led him to it. They'd posted an SS man to guard the well to make sure that we couldn't drink any water, but I wasn't going to let him stop me. Supporting my pal with one hand, I grabbed the German's sleeve with the other, and pushed him away from the well. He could have shot me on the spot, but he was probably too startled. I took off the rotting blanket I'd wrapped around me against the cold, tore off a strip, soaked it in water and tied it around Henek's head.

'For the next three weeks he walked on with my filthy lice-infested blanket over the gaping hole in his face. Believe it or not, by the time we reached Karlsbad, his wound had healed, and all he had to show for it was a small scar and one missing tooth. By some miracle, the bullet had missed all the nerves that connect with the brain!'

When I ask how his friend managed to eat like that, Marcel widens his eyes in mock amazement. 'Eat? Eat what? Who ate? Did you think we were at a party? One day the German guards tossed rotting potatoes into the ditch and laughed to see starving people flinging ourselves on food. My pal was just about to join them but I held him back. "Keep away, that one rotten potato isn't going to save your life, but it could kill you," I hissed in his ear. And that's how it turned out because as soon as people started running for the potatoes, those guards started shooting at them. They were bored and wanted a bit of fun.

'The next thing I remember is opening my eyes and thinking that I must have died and gone to heaven because angels with white haloes were hovering around me. I was in a Czech hospital staffed by nuns. I'd been lying in a ditch, left for dead among a pile of bodies, when an American tank stopped to see if anyone was still alive. Luckily one of the soldiers noticed a spark of life and brought me to the hospital. One of the nuns picked me up and carried me as easily as if I was a child. I was twenty-two, weighed thirty-eight kilos and my bones ground against each other.'

That hospital was to be Marcel's home for six months. He points to the scars which still indent his jaw and forehead.

Blood poisoning had reached the brain and he had to undergo six operations to drain out the pus. While he was lying in bed, weak and in pain after surgery, he was grief-stricken because, after all they'd gone through together, it seemed as though his friend hadn't survived the death march. Suddenly he looked up and his heart almost burst out of his chest. Walking towards him was Henek. The Americans had taken him to a different hospital and he'd just been discharged. Marcel smiles. 'To this day we always call each other on the date when the Americans found us, because that's our real birthday, that's when we were born again!'

When Marcel was well enough to leave hospital in October 1945, he made his way back to Krakow to begin the sad search for surviving relatives. The last time he saw Krakow, he had a mother, father and sister, and life bloomed with promise. Now, at twenty-two, he was alone and disoriented in a meaningless world which had allowed his parents to be murdered along with his twelve-year-old sister. Exhausted and depressed, he wondered why he'd returned. He found work as a turner in a factory and soon learned that vodka was a good anaesthetic.

Although his boss helped him obtain a government scholarship so that he could study at night, Krakow had too many sad memories, there was nothing to anchor him there. When the State of Israel was proclaimed in May 1948, Marcel felt something stirring in his blood.

By then he'd met Krysia and wanted to marry her. Looking fondly at his wife, he says, 'She looked the image of the Madonna. I fell in love with her the moment I saw her.' Krysia smiles with embarrassment but looks pleased. At sixty she still has that serene face, the almond-shaped grey-green eyes and the slow, resonant voice. As Krysia was still at school when they met, Marcel used to write absence notes for her after she skipped classes to go out with him. They married before her nineteenth birthday.

When they arrived in Israel in 1950, Haifa dazzled them with its golden sand, wooded hills, and vistas of dark blue ocean. Their accommodation, however, was less enticing. They were staying at a transit camp consisting of hundreds of American canvas army tents and corrugated iron huts.

Within a few months Marcel was appointed to a school in Tiberias, where their little daughter Ronit was born in 1953. Although Krysia thought that she'd been prepared for the hardships of life in this new land, she was shocked by the rough conditions and the heat. 'Do you have any idea what Tiberias is like in summer?' she shudders. 'An inferno.' Apart from the heat, which sapped her energy day and night, everything was in short supply in this new land which had been forced to fight for its existence from the moment it had come into being. Apart from bread, tomatoes and oranges, everything was rationed. They were entitled to two or three eggs and a hundred grams of chicken per week.

But Israel was refreshingly friendly and informal. This was a nation of refugees who understood one another and shared a common past and similar goals. Possessions were unimportant. Marcel owned two shirts, a white one for Saturdays and a khaki one for everyday. 'We all had ration books with coupons. If one of us needed a pair of shoes, we both had to save our coupons.'

But that didn't matter, Marcel says. 'Don't forget that everyone was equal. No-one was living in penthouses. My boss was my mate. And it was the same in the army. Jews worked as bricklayers, carpenters, plumbers. Before I got a teaching job, I worked as a fitter and turner.'

With a pioneer's passion, he says, 'It was tough but there was a joy in living and a joy in the land. Today I can order

French delicacies at a five-star hotel, but life was far better and people were more honest in the days when all I could get was three eggs per week on the ration card. On Yom Hatzma'ut, our independence day, we danced in the streets, rejoicing at what we were building up. I don't see that simple joy any more. Now there are formal balls where people go to show off their outfits, furs and diamonds, so their friends should burst with envy.'

Marcel describes life in those first years with the dreamy nostalgia that distance confers on even the toughest times. 'I used to lug ice for our ice chest up the hill on my bicycle. Who dreamed of owning a fridge? In winter we were happy to find fuel for our little kerosine heater which smoked more than it heated. Every morning I used to run downstairs with a saucepan so that the milkman could pour milk into it from his churn. Sometimes I was in such a hurry that I got on the bus with a saucepan of milk in one hand and my briefcase in the other!'

Twelve years after they'd arrived, life in Israel was still hard. Marcel didn't earn much, and now, with their little son Igal as well as Ronit to support, it was a struggle to make ends meet. For the past few years Krysia had been employed by Aunty Lunia, giving lessons at Madame Stella's Sewing School. The memory of working for her aunt twists my cousin's placid face into a grimace. 'Uncle Berus wanted me to become their partner but she kept stalling. I didn't earn much money and wanted to leave, but my mother always sided with Lunia. Never mind that I was unhappy and struggling, that didn't count. "You can't let Lunia down," she used to say. Even though she and Lunia fought like cat and dog, Lunia was her guru. So I kept working there, on the understanding that one day the business would be mine.'

'Imagine my shock the day Aunty Lunia came over to see

me and said in that honeyed tone of hers, "You know, Krysia, I've sold the school!" I was struck dumb. After twenty-five years I was left in the lurch without even a pension. Berus was compeletely different. He was an angel, I've never met anyone like him,' she sighs. 'When he was dying the last thing he said to me was, "Don't abandon Aunty." If not for that, I wouldn't have put up with her all these years.'

Krysia's dissatisfaction with life in Israel came to a head in 1962 when she travelled overseas for her brother's wedding to Phyllis Pomer in Connecticut. Fred had been strong enough to get away, while Krysia felt trapped in this impossible land, shackled to her demanding aunt and distrustful mother who alternated between generosity and vitriolic criticism.

So when her friend in Canada organised a work contract for Marcel, Krysia returned home fired up with enthusiasm to migrate to Canada. 'Let's go for one year and see,' she pleaded. 'We won't risk anything. They're even going to pay for our flights. We can always come back.' But Marcel was adamant that he wouldn't leave Israel.

Sooner or later in the life of every marriage, an issue surfaces which tests the strength of the relationship. 'It was serious, because Krysia wanted to go at all costs but I said not at any price,' Marcel recalls. 'No power on earth could make me leave Israel. Maybe this sounds funny, but I was afraid of being a Jew again. Here among Jews, I was an Israeli. I wasn't going to become a Canadian Jew. Maybe I would have been better off in Canada. Certainly I would have led a quieter, safer life without wars, hostile Arabs and intifadas, and my granddaughters wouldn't be going into the army.'

In the warm Tel-Aviv night we discuss what it means to be Jewish when you don't go to synagogue or observe religious laws. In his quiet, compelling way Marcel says something which resonates in my mind for years to come. 'We are descended from a long chain of people who started with Moses a few thousand years ago. They were persecuted and hunted, but they didn't abandon their faith or their Torah. The Assyrians, Sumerians, Hittites, Babylonians and all their gods have come and gone, Pharaohs, emperors, sultans and chancellors have tried to annihilate us, but we're still here, hm?'

Outside, some of those Jews are shouting to each other in the sultry night, and a bald man with a Yiddish accent pokes his head over the balcony. 'Is my building a conference hall?' he shouts. 'Go have your meeting somewhere else.' They laugh and move away, and their voices fade in the dark night as we sit around the table and muse about our Jewish legacy.

Krysia has been deep in thought, her head propped up on her hand. 'I didn't put down roots in Israel until 1967,' she says. 'During the Six-Day War, when our very existence was in danger, our soldiers conquered the armies of the Egyptians, Jordanians and Syrians in six days, broke through to Jerusalem and kissed the Western Wall. I thought I'd burst with pride. That's when I knew that I belonged here, that this was my land.'

CHAPTER 36

On her way home from her brother's wedding in the United States in 1962, my cousin Krysia stopped over in London and stayed in the high-ceilinged Edwardian flat that Michael and I were renting in Maida Vale. Judging by the size and self-important air of the solid houses which lined Elgin Avenue, this must have been a prestigious address at the turn o the century, but by the time we arrived it had come down i the world, and most of the houses were divided into draughty, inhospitable furnished rooms let to impecunious Commonwealth visitors like ourselves. My reunion with Krysia was much warmer than our accommodation, and even the frosty weather and foggy nights didn't dampen our pleasure at seeing each other again for the first time since we'd parted in Krakow fourteen years before.

Michael and I had been living in London for two years. A trip to England after graduating was considered an indispensable part of your education, and Michael, who'd recently finished studying medicine, was keen to work in London hospitals. Most Australians in the predominantly Anglo-Saxon society of the sixties referred to England as 'back home', but in his case, this was actually true.

Michael was born in London in 1935 to Ben and Aida Armstrong, both of whose parents had migrated from Russia to the UK during the pogroms at the turn of the century.

How a Jewish immigrant from Kiev came to have a Scottish surname was a mystery that not even my father-in-law could satisfactorily explain. Ben was a tall man with a loping stride, thick glasses over myopic eyes, and a hearty laugh. When, on arrival in Britain, his father had told the immigration officer his long Russian name, it must have sounded like Armstrong, which is what the man wrote down, and that's how it remained ever since. I must admit a sneaking feeling of gratitude towards that immigration official whose laziness saved me from having another unpronounceable surname!

In his lilting Welsh accent, my father-in-law told me that his father had started off as an itinerant peddler, and later became a ships' chandler in Cardiff. 'My father was a huge man with a long red beard, so strong that he could lift up brawling sailors with one hand and throw them out of his store which smelled of candle wax, hemp, paint and tar,' he reminisced.

Ben's parents were an ill-matched couple who waged unremitting war against each other. His mother was a difficult, embittered woman whose parents had pushed her into marriage with a man she detested all her life. They had seven children, the youngest of whom sat too close to the fire one cold winter's night and her long thick hair caught fire. Ben's mother never got over her terrible death and the quarrels grew even more acrimonious. Although the parents finally separated, they still didn't stop fighting and embroiled the six children in their on-going battles. 'We weren't brought up, we were dragged up, us kids were shunted from pillar to post,' Ben often said.

Desperately unhappy at home because of the bitter rows, Ben stowed away on board ship at the age of thirteen and worked his passage as a cabin boy. As the ship pulled away from the port in Cardiff, he watched his mother running along the quay, her long skirts flying as she vainly tried to catch up with him before it was too late. In one hand she held his boots, in the other, a packet of *matzohs*. It was Pesach.

In Canada and America Ben led the kind of colourful, rambunctious existence that fills adventure books. 'I bummed around for years, got into all sorts of scrapes,' he used to laugh, waving the large hand with the short middle finger in a disparaging motion. He left that bit of finger behind in a lumber camp in the Yukon. After working as a lumberjack, he smuggled liquor over the border during Prohibition, and later made a living as a boxer in a seedy part of New York, although it always puzzled Michael how, with his poor vision, he ever managed to land a punch.

When Ben returned to England in the early thirties, he was twenty-nine, a tall impetuous man with an expansive nature and a fund of exciting stories. He had intended to return to the United States but fell in love with a woman who impressed him with her refinement and class. Aida Kleiman was his opposite in every way. Frugal where he was extravagant, restrained where he was emotional and reserved where he was extroverted. Intelligent and well-spoken, she was very proud of the fact that her father, a Russian immigrant tailor from the East End of London had sent her to Clark's College to become a secretary while her three sisters, like most of the daughters of immigrants at the time, had gone straight from school to the workroom.

Because of his unhappy childhood, and the misery he'd seen at home, Ben longed to have a happy home life but having chosen a woman so different from himself guaranteed considerable marital friction. But there was one aspect of their life on which they both agreed and that was their devotion to their children. Ben and Aida had migrated to Australia in 1949 mainly to give Michael and Carole a better life. When Michael and I started going out, Carole was a shy, thoughtful twelve-year-old who preferred to listen than to talk. She had an infectious laugh and a quiet strength far beyond her years.

Michael was in fourth year medicine and I was a wide-eyed Arts freshette when we met on the steps of Mitchell Library and began a conversation which has continued ever since. To my father's disappointment I'd chosen to study arts instead of dentistry. In an era when most parents saw their daughters as future wives and mothers, my father believed that women should be financially independent, and he urged me to become a dentist. 'You never know what life will bring,' he used to say. 'You can't count on a man supporting you all your life. You might be divorced or widowed. As a dentist, you can always support yourself. What will arts give you?'

Although I had no idea how I would earn a living with an arts degree, my father's practical arguments didn't sway me. English and history were the only subjects I was passionate about, and when it turned out that I was one of the top English and history students in the state in the Leaving Certificate, I felt that my choice was vindicated.

As soon as we met, Michael knew that I was the girl for him. He had an unexpected ally. My mother, who usually made withering comments about my other boyfriends, could find no fault in him. 'Michael is a mensch,' she told me, using the Yiddish word which denotes a decent, caring, reliable human being. In years to come, she often gloated that she'd been the first to recognise his fine qualities.

Although Michael was Jewish, I had been allowed to go out with boys who were not, unlike many of my friends. Religion was never an issue and all my friends were equally welcome. 'Marrying someone of the same religion is no guarantee of happiness,' my mother used to say. 'These days so many Jewish couples don't get through one sack of flour together.'

Ours was not a religious household. My parents never lit candles on Friday nights or went to synagogue. When in my first year at Sydney Girls' High I announced that I was going to fast on Yom Kippur with my friend Liliane, my father nodded approval. 'Fasting is good for the system,' he said. It was with Liliane that I went to synagogue for the first time. We sat upstairs with the women and looked down at the boys who were always glancing up to catch a glimpse of their girlfriends. I didn't understand a word of the Hebrew prayers, but when the cantor's full-throated voice sang ancient Jewish melodies, those haunting cadences tugged at my heart. Deep in my unconscious, something stirred in recognition.

Although the religious affiliation of my boyfriends was never an issue, my father and I clashed about dating. In many ways my father was far more up-to-date and open-minded than any of the other fathers. My friends were always impressed that he discussed sex, religion and politics with me, and that he always knew who was the latest pop star, who we used to 'swoon' over, and which songs were top of the hit parade.

But where dating was concerned he turned from an understanding pal into a Victorian patriarch. He had two fixed beliefs, both of which I found archaic and unreasonable. He was convinced that going out with boys would distract me from my school work, so while I was at school I wasn't allowed to go on dates. As all my friends had boyfriends and talked about them incessantly, I rankled under this injustice. In his armchair beneath the bay window which often vibrated with the screech of buses hurtling down towards the beach, my father would take off his glasses, put down the book he was reading, and say, 'You want to go out with boys? So leave school and get a job, and you can go out every night.'

After I'd matriculated and was finally free to go out as much as I liked, the second rule came into operation. No going steady. According to my father, who'd been my age back in 1917, a girl who went out exclusively with one boy for more than three months was compromising herself. 'How does it look if you break up after going out so long with one boy?' he'd say, his face red with irritation at my protests. 'After a few months people know how they feel. Either get married, or stop going out,' he'd pronounce. He couldn't understand that in 1957, the year the Sputnik had been launched in space, it was acceptable for young people to go steady, that three months was considered insufficient time to form a lifelong commitment, and that going steady wasn't perceived as a sign of loose morals. My mother didn't share his mid-Victorian views, but once my father had made up his mind, it was impossible to budge him.

My mother had a biting turn of phrase and often demolished my boyfriends with comments which were invariably apt. 'That fellow looks as if he's swallowed a stick,' she once said about one of my less relaxed suitors. So when she started praising Michael, I was taken aback. 'If you like him so much, why don't you go out with him?' I teased her, but Michael soon swept me off my feet. He rang several times a day, brought flowers every time he came, found my thoughts riveting, and said things which made me laugh until my sides ached. I'd never had so much fun. He was witty, playful and sensitive but also protective, strong and very determined. I didn't realise until much later that in many ways he resembled my father.

We became inseparable. In the mornings he used to pick me up in his blue Mini Minor and drive me to lectures. By day we sat side by side in the Fisher Library without ever turning a page and later had romantic picnics in the park. At night we went out for coffee, dinner or a movie, and then spent several more hours talking on the phone until past midnight. 'I've never seen anything like it,' my mother used to grumble. 'You'll wear out that telephone.'

Two years later, just after sitting for our final exams, we married in Sydney's Great Synagogue. I was so thrilled to be marrying Michael that my wedding day passed in a haze of euphoria. Feeling like a fairy-tale princess, I walked down the aisle on my father's proud arm, and stood under the *chuppah* in front of Rabbi Israel Porush whose stern gaze reminded me of a biblical prophet. After I'd taken a sip of wine from the sacramental goblet, Michael stamped on the glass in memory of the destruction of the Second Temple and as a symbol that the silken thread of life is interwoven with joy and sorrow.

A year later we set sail for England. Never having been separated from my parents before, I was reluctant to leave, but Michael argued that he needed to work in London hospitals and we needed to stand on our own feet and learn to depend on each other. Although we'd intended staying for about eighteen months, we enjoyed the theatre, the concerts and the English countryside so much that we stayed for almost four years. While Michael worked in hospitals, I did the last thing I thought I'd ever do. I became a teacher.

Having lived with our respective parents until we married, we revelled in our freedom in London. Living in England enabled me to meet some of the family I'd heard about for so long. We came to love my father's cousin, Janek Spyra, his wife Maryla and their lively, warm-hearted daughters Anne and Shirley. Janek's charming brother Albert and his delightful wife Gertrude were wonderful to us and often invited us to Covent Garden and Sadlers Wells, luxuries we couldn't afford on our meagre salaries.

Occasionally Uncle Marcel came from Paris to visit us. We adored this bearlike man with a heart of gold and eyes that shone with warmth and humour. Marcel, who loved good food, always returned to Paris with a leg of lamb and a side of smoked salmon under each arm. During one of these visits he gave Michael a Practika camera. 'I found it on top of a rubbish bin in Monte Carlo,' he explained. 'I looked around and asked, "Does anyone own this camera?" No-one replied, so I took it.' Then he added with a booming laugh, 'I have to admit I didn't ask very loudly!'

During our four years in London, while I was teaching English at a blackboard jungle school in West Ealing, Michael had a meteoric rise in medicine. After working as junior resident at Willesden General Hospital, he was appointed Senior Medical Registrar. While working there, he wrote *A Systematic Method of Interpreting ECGs*, which has been translated into five languages and hasn't been out of print since 1965.

Before returning home, we toured Europe for six months in a campervan. While we were travelling, I became obsesssed with recording every detail of our trip and wrote down everything I saw, heard, bought, ate and thought every single day. Without realising it, I'd become a travel writer. That trip also marked another, more important beginning. Our daughter Justine was conceived.

Nine months later at Sydney's Royal Hospital for Women, Michael sat beside me holding my hand during a long and exhausting labour which I thought would never end. My hands shook when I finally held the perfectly formed baby that was my own flesh and blood and yet distinct from me, and tears streamed down Michael's face. As Justine nestled into my arms like a warm possum, I felt overwhelmed at the thought that we'd created a whole new world, a new human being.

My writing career, which had a much longer gestation period than the baby, was born in the same year as Justine. My first magazine article about the trials and triumphs of teaching at a difficult London high school was published in the *Australian Women's Weekly* while I was still in hospital. From the moment I saw the story splashed across two pages of a magazine that was then read by almost every woman in Australia, I became hooked. Writing had entered my bloodstream.

Two years later, when Justine was a delightful toddler with a mass of fair curls, an extraordinary vocabulary and a mind of her own, our second child Jonathan was born. After the nurse had said, 'It's a boy!' there was an ominous silence during which I held my breath. Then his triumphant cry resounded in the delivery room, the most wonderful sound I'd ever heard. 'He's the image of Henry,' my mother-in-law commented as soon as she saw her new grandson. Jonathan inherited my father's finely shaped head, intellectual mind and individualistic personality. Many years passed before I realised that I'd unwittingly chosen a name for him that was similar to that of my ancestor, the famous Krakow scholar Natan Spira.

CHAPTER 37

Summer had ended and the autumn sun shone weakly through my parents' dining room window, casting long shadows on the wall. At one end of the table Justine was deep in conversation with my father. Their heads were close together as they bent over a sketch pad, and her long thick hair, the colour of polished teak, fell across her eager face as she showed her grandfather her latest drawing. If it had been sketched by a famous artist, he couldn't have given it more attention. He admired a flowing line here and suggested more shading there, while she nodded, glowing with pleasure. From time to time, his comments were interrupted by a short, dry cough.

Jonathan, a ten-year-old whose motor rarely ceased revving, was growing restless so Michael took him outside to play catchings. As usual my father brought out his camera to capture the occasion, fiddling with the settings until we moaned at having to hold the pose until the smiles froze on our faces. 'Hurry up, Henek, I have to make the coffee!' my mother protested. Now in her sixties, she still had that flawless ivory complexion. With her fair hair, sparkling smile and ramrod straight back, she reminded me of a daffodil.

Before we sat down to Aunty Mania's chocolate roll, my father stood the children against the doorway to the dining room, told them not to stand on tiptoe, and pencilled a mark to record their height as he did every year so we could see how much they'd grown. Years after he'd died, this remembrance of the passing years remained on the architrave like a memorial.

On every wall of my parents' flat hung the landscapes, abstracts and portraits which my father had recently painted. Late in life he'd begun attending art classes and discovered a new talent. 'Maybe I'll become a Grandpa Moses,' he used to joke. The first portrait he ever painted was of his father.

At the other end of the table my mother was arguing with her sister. 'You're talking just so your saliva doesn't dry up!' she scoffed. It was a safe bet that if my aunt said that the sky was blue, my mother would immediately find ten reasons why it wasn't. If Mania bought something, it was never the right thing, she'd paid too much, and she shouldn't have bought it anyway. Her smoking was a constant irritant too, because Mania had rheumatic heart disease and had been told to quit.

Aunty Mania usually dismissed her sister's criticisms with a shrug and a lopsided smile to prevent minor skirmishes escalating into major battles. War meant that my mother would refuse to speak to her for weeks and these prolonged hostilities took too much out of my aunt. Mania lived downstairs, and whenever I visited her during these feuds, I could always hear my mother's assertive footsteps stomping in the room above. This meant that she'd already seen my car and knew I was consorting with the enemy.

My mother and her sister were enmeshed in a relationship that puzzled me all my life. I couldn't understand my mother's generosity to my aunt on the one hand, and her criticism on the other. When my mother had suggested that Mania could live in her building at a very low rent, my aunt had accepted, but close proximity only made things worse. Indebtedness neither engenders gratitude nor improves relationships.

Whenever I questioned my mother about their arguments,

her mouth became a minus sign and her eyes became flame-throwers. 'You always take her side! You don't know her like I do!' she would rage. 'She's an arch-manipulator. You have no idea what misunderstandings she's caused all my life!'

It sometimes seemed as if my mother envied her sister, although I couldn't see what she could possibly be envious about. She was much better looking than Mania, who had become more round-shouldered with age and whose complexion had become more blotchy. Financially, too, my mother was far better off. Mania and Bronek had started off selling underwear at the markets and gone on to make plastic raincoats, but their cottage industry had come to an end when plastic raincoats started being mass-produced. For a time Bronek worked as a travelling salesman, but for the past few years they'd lived on my aunt's war pension.

Aunty Mania received a pension from Germany because she'd been interned at Bergen–Belsen concentration camp. My parents were also entitled to some compensation on account of their experiences and losses during the Holocaust, but my father had refused to lodge a claim. 'I don't want to accept blood money,' he insisted. 'They can't compensate me for what I went through or for the relatives they've murdered. I don't want the Germans to think that because they've paid me a few marks, their conscience is clear.' My father was always rather quixotic but I admired his high principles.

If it wasn't envy that soured my mother's attitude towards her sister, perhaps it was jealousy because I loved spending time with my aunt who was a sympathetic listener and had a good sense of humour. Because she couldn't afford to buy the clothes she loved, she taught herself to make them. Soon she was sewing for me as well, so we spent a lot of time together, discussing styles, chosing fabrics and having fittings.

Family relationships are harder to untangle than skeins of

wool. One day when I dropped in to see Aunty Mania during one of their feuds, her face looked drawn and sad, and her back was very bent. She must have been thinking about her early life because she suddenly said, 'I know it isn't nice to say this, but my parents didn't love me. That's what I always felt.'

Now, as we all sat around my parents' table drinking coffee and chatting, Aunty Mania was looking out of the window where a jacaranda tree brushed against the pane, but by the bitter twist of her mouth and the cloudy expression in her olive-green eyes, I knew that she was looking at some bleak landscape of the heart. Finally she murmured, as if to herself, 'Sometimes a person goes through life just looking for some sign of love from her brother—or sister.'

It was 1978, three years after my father had sold his dental practice. When he'd retired, his devoted patients had felt that they hadn't only lost an extraordinarily talented dentist, but also a caring friend who was never too busy to listen to their troubles or to share a joke. He had begun going to art classes, had taught himself carpentry, and had been reading history books. After one of our Saturday lunches, he handed me a sheaf of typewritten notes stacked in a folder. 'I've written my memoirs,' he said. 'One day you and the children may want to know what happened.' There were one hundred neatly typed pages written in Polish and divided into periods. Thrilled to have his memoirs, I hadn't asked him for more details. The questions only occurred to me when it was too late.

As we sat together that day, I noticed that my father looked paler than usual. When he coughed again, Michael repeated his earlier comment, 'You really should get that seen to.' As usual my father shrugged it off. 'It's nothing. Just a cough.' At seventy-seven he was fit, trim and energetic. He ate moderately, just as Daniel had taught him, and went for a stroll every day.

When he had started developing a paunch, he'd dieted until he lost it; when his teeth had yellowed, he'd had them capped.

Finally he agreed to have a chest X-ray. When it didn't reveal anything, Michael urged him to have further tests. Like most strong-minded, determined individuals, they sometimes clashed, but they understood and respected each other. Henek had a high regard for Michael's diagnostic skills and his compassionate nature, but was sceptical about the medical profession in general. 'Once specialists get their clutches into you, you never get away from them,' he argued. I think that deep down my father already knew what the tests would reveal.

Several weeks later, when the pain in his hip was so severe that he couldn't go for his daily walk, he agreed to go into hospital for tests. 'Since I asked for a medical opinion, I have to follow the doctor's advice,' he said to me. 'If you say A, you have to say B.' Winter light was slanting through the bare branches of the jacaranda tree, highlighting the whiteness of his hair and the pallor of his face. Then he made a deprecating gesture with his hand and said in an angry voice, 'This is the beginning of the end.'

I was shocked. I don't know whether it was his negative attitude that shocked me so much or the possibility that he was seriously ill. 'Why are you so pessimistic?' I asked, angry in turn. 'You're just going for some tests, that's all.' He shot me a look that said I didn't know what I was talking about, but didn't say any more. I glanced at my mother. She was looking away and every muscle in her face seemed clenched.

When she left the room to brew coffee, he turned to me, calmer now. 'You know, Diane, I'm not afraid to die,' he said. 'I've made my peace with God. I just don't want to suffer.' A jumble of frightened, confused feelings stumbled about in my head, but over them all one short clear word kept repeating itself. No. No. No.

The first time I visit him at St Vincent's Hospital, his face seems carved out of tallow, and the whites of his eyes are as yellow as if an egg yolk had burst. But although he is jaundiced, he is in good spirits and entertains us with anecdotes from Poland, about the conmen of Warsaw who used to accost gullible peasants, and 'sell' them the city's trams. While Jonathan giggles I can't stop looking at my father's waxlike feet poking out of dead-white sheets.

Back home we watch television together and talk about trivia to avoid the topic that is on all our minds. Justine suddenly goes over to kiss Michael who gives her a hug. It strikes me that I never did that with my father. We were very close, had similar ideas, and shared a love of music, literature and ideas, yet we were never demonstrative. My father was reserved and now I realise that I was too.

Next day, he is drowsy and listless. His eyes are a stranger's eyes, and their dullness alarms me. I reach forward to pat his hand. Touching has never been our way of showing emotion so it feels awkward. When I look down, I'm shocked by the contrast between my pink hand and his yellow one. On top of the building across the road, a huge plaster Christ with outstretched arms seems to be looking right into this room. For the first time I know that my father is going to die.

That night Jonathan looks searchingly into my face. 'Is Grandpic going to die?' There's a lump in my throat the size of a grapefruit as he says, 'I'm sure Grandpic's going to be all right. But if it was you, I don't know what I'd do.' This boisterous ten-year-old with dancing eyes and front teeth that cross over, who is always running, jumping, shouting or bragging, squeezes my heart.

Later, Justine puts her arms around me. 'It's natural that

you're upset, but Grandpa has had a good life,' she says. The sensitivity of my children touches me. Sometimes it seems that they are far wiser and more mature than I am.

At the hospital my mother sits miserably at the foot of my father's bed, drowning inside her bulky winter coat which she refuses to take off even though the hospital is overheated. Her optimism has deserted her and she seems to have shrunk, swallowed up by her own unhappiness. She can't bring herself to talk openly about his illness, and I can't face the thought of his death or her grief.

To relieve her pent-up anger, she wages war with one of the nurses, the one my father jocularly calls 'The Duchess' because she has such regal bearing. It irritates my mother that this woman has long conversations with my father and walks past her as if she wasn't there, as she does right now. 'She's got a nerve. Now she'll disturb him,' my mother bristles. Later, when we go into his room, his eyes have a dreamy look. 'The Duchess sat beside me, held my hand and kept saying, "You'll be all right, my dear, you'll be all right." It was so comforting.' It's touching and painful that this stranger understands what he needs better than we do.

Next morning, the tall specialist with wavy hair carefully combed across his bald scalp asks me to step outside. Everything about him, from the concern in his eyes, the breathless voice and the way he stoops towards me, tells me what his message will be. Not taking his eyes off my face, he gives me scientific information about sedimention rates, liver function tests and white cells. He says something about a blocked bile duct and a tumour. 'We can operate to relieve the blockage,' he says.

Later Michael explains it to me gently, several times, because there's a humming in my head and I keep tuning out. My father has cancer of the head of the pancreas which has spread. It's not curable. Surgery can relieve the blockage but it won't alter the outcome. I feel numb. Death is the down payment we make on life, but it's always too soon to discharge that debt.

Michael told me that when they were alone, my father had said, 'I'm not afraid of dying. My conscience is quite clear. I've never knowingly hurt anyone. But I don't want to suffer, linger or become dependent. What do you think about surgery?'

In a voice he tried to keep steady, Michael replied, 'I don't think that it will solve the problem. You don't have any pain. If it was me, I wouldn't have it. I'd go home.' My father nodded. He'd made his decision.

When he returned home, he looked so serene and was in such good spirits that I wondered whether the doctors were mistaken after all. Perhaps he'd get well, I thought, ignoring the fact that he spent most of the day in bed and that even shaving exhausted him. We never talked about dying. I lacked the courage to bring it up, and he probably didn't want to upset me, so we spent the precious last days of his life talking about things that didn't matter, to avoid the only thing that did. He didn't discuss his approaching death with my mother either. The only person he talked to openly was Michael.

Not long after he came home, as we sat talking, he suddenly said, 'Jews should never become complacent, even in a tolerant society like Australia. All Jewish children should know that anti-Semitism can occur anywhere at any time so that they're prepared.' He must have been reviewing his life. Several years later, when Sydney synagogues and Jewish day schools were fire-bombed, and more recently, when a Queensland politician with a racist platform started whipping up hatred against ethnic groups, his words came back to me.

After saying goodbye to my father one afternoon and promising to return the following day, I was on my way home when something made me decide to go back and see him again. On the way, I did something I'd never done before. Stopping at a florist's, I selected one perfect crimson rose for my father. When I handed it to him, his face lit up as if his dearest wish had just been granted.

A few minutes later Justine arrived, as she did every afternoon after school. I didn't expect Jonathan to come that day as he had soccer practice, but to my surprise the doorbell shrilled and there he was. Like me, he'd come on impulse. 'I was already on the bus to go straight home, but suddenly I got off and caught the other bus to see Grandpic,' he explained.

'Am I very yellow today, Jonathan?' my father asked.

Jonathan scrutinised his face. 'A bit,' he replied.

'Oh well, green or yellow, what's the difference, as long as you feel all right,' my father quipped. 'Because apart from this illness, I'm really perfectly well!' he smiled, and asked whether he'd like to watch television.

Jonathan, who usually jumped at the chance, because at home we rationed the viewing, shook his head. 'I've come to keep you company, not to keep the television company,' he said.

Glancing at my mother, who was sitting on the edge of the bed, her knuckles as white as her face, my father turned to Justine, 'Look at Nana, she's so upset, she takes everything too seriously.' My mother hadn't even told their closest friends how ill he was. My father hadn't wanted anyone to see him weak and ill, dreading the pity in their faces. And she, always accustomed to bearing her burdens silently and alone, didn't know how to accept compassion or share her pain.

'Don't come in to check on me tonight,' he told my mother when she came to say goodnight after we'd gone. Ever since his illness, she had slept in the spare bedroom so that he wouldn't be disturbed, and had placed a little bell on the bedside table in case he needed anything. 'The floorboards

486

creak and wake me up when you come in. Just go to bed. Don't come in till I ring the bell,' he said.

Next morning, after Michael had left to see my father, I was washing my hair when the telephone rang. Michael's voice sounded strange. 'Leave everything and come,' he said. I didn't ask any questions. Twisting a towel around my sopping hair, I gathered the children and we sped towards my parents' place, cursing every red light. One thought kept drumming through my mind. I hope I'm in time to say goodbye, to hold his hand and see a spark of recognition in his eyes. I didn't realise that I'd already said goodbye with my rose.

We ran up the two flights of stairs. The door was open, and I heard the jerky, heart-breaking sound of Michael sobbing, the loudest, most heart-wrenching sobs I've ever heard. The five of us stood with our arms wrapped around each other. My mother had tears in her eyes but she didn't cry then, or later. Aunty Mania put her arm around her while she sat on the lounge suite, crushed and white, like a piece of crumpled paper, her chin trembling with the effort not to weep, staring at my father's books on the walnut table beside his armchair. Many years later, my mother surprised me by admitting that she used to cry for him, alone at night. She had perfected the art of invisible grief during the Holocaust and it had become a habit.

I rose and walked slowly towards the bedroom. The demarcation line between life and death is clear and shocking. The person who lay in my father's bed was a wooden statue of my father, stiff and set. His jaw had dropped open and the light had gone from his eyes. When I stroked his cold head, even his hair felt dead. Michael moved forward and with a movement as gentle as a butterfly's wing, closed his eyes.

Later I asked Michael, 'Why did he call you back yesterday when we were leaving?'

'To remind me that he wanted to be cremated,' he replied. Although the Jewish religion forbids cremation, my father had a horror of burial ever since the Holocaust, because the Germans used to dig up Jewish graves and wrench gold out of the mouths of the dead.

My father had discussed his funeral arrangements with Michael. Although he felt profoundly Jewish, read Jewish authors and studied Jewish history, he hadn't said anything about Kaddish. He was strong enough to need neither tradition, ritual nor organised religion. His faith was a private matter between him and his maker and he didn't need intermediaries to pray for him. 'It doesn't make any sense for someone who doesn't know me to talk about me. But if the family would like a few words said, then I'd like it to be you,' he told Michael.

Among the mourners inside the crowded chapel of the Eastern Suburbs Crematorium, one close friend is absent. My mother's cousin Aron, who loved my father and often visited him, couldn't bring himself to attend the cremation which our religion doesn't permit. Bodies must be returned to the maker in their original shape so that they can be resurrected when the Messiah comes. Although he was clearly distressed at the pain his decision was causing, Aron wasn't prepared to compromise his principles. 'I cared too much for your father to participate in something I believe to be wrong. But I'm going to say Kaddish for him every day for a year.'

Inside the crematorium chapel, I try not to look at the coffin, try not to think about my father lying inside it, or about the flames that will soon reduce his body to a handful of ashes. I try to think how lucky I am to have had a wonderful father for thirty-nine years. Michael stands in front of the assembled mourners and clears his throat. Several times he has to stop speaking while he weeps aloud. I admire his courage in making this tribute and exposing his grief. 'In death as in life, Henry knew what he wanted. He was an independent thinker who didn't like ceremony or hypocrisy, what mattered to him was genuine feeling. "I feel at peace," Henry told me. "I've done nothing I regret, and I don't regret leaving anything undone." '

I don't know whether my father believed in a creator as taught by the Torah, but he never forgot what his father had taught him—to marvel at the beauty of the world and all its creatures and to be grateful for the faculties that enabled him to enjoy it. My father died on his own terms like his own father had done almost exactly thirty years before. He didn't suffer, didn't linger, but died with dignity, all his faculties intact. And he'd died on the Sabbath, when souls go straight to heaven. The best gift that parents can give their children is their own life fully lived, and that's the gift my father gave me. There was a feeling of completeness about his death. I didn't understand until much later, during my mother's last years, that my father's death was perfect, just as he had planned it.

CHAPTER 38

Standing in front of the Ark at Sydney's Temple Emanuel, Jonathan was chanting the Hebrew words of his *parsha*, the section of the Torah which Bar-Mitzvah boys and Bat-Mitzvah girls read during their coming-of-age ceremony. As our son's uneven boyish voice rose and fell with the traditional cadences, Michael squeezed my hand and I felt tears pricking my eyes. Jonathan had become part of that spiritual river which has so often changed its course, been obstructed, and sometimes reduced to a trickle, but which has continued flowing for thousands of years.

While Justine and Jonathan were growing up, Michael and I faced a dilemma. How do parents who are not religious, and do not keep a kosher home, impart a sense of Jewish identity to their children? My identity had been forged in the flames of the Holocaust. I didn't need to learn Hebrew, observe kosher laws or light candles on Friday nights to know that I was Jewish. Michael, too, had a strong sense of Jewish identity, even though his parents hadn't been religious, but we realised that our children were growing up in a country where assimilation was a greater threat to Jewish continuity than anti-Semitism.

Although we didn't want our children to lose their heritage, we hadn't done much to nurture it. Going to synagogue twice a year, attending Sunday school reluctantly once a week, and gathering for festive dinners on Pesach and Rosh Hashana wasn't enough to imbue them with a strong sense of Judaism.

In an effort to create more Jewish feeling at home, we introduced Friday night dinners. Not having learned Hebrew or attended Sunday school, I had to learn the blessings from a book. Justine and I lit the Shabbat candles together and thanked God for the gift of the Sabbath; Jonathan said the blessing for bread over the plaited *challah*; and Michael, who remembered the prayers from his Sunday school days, said the blessing over the wine.

It wasn't belief in God, but belief in tradition, heritage and continuity that motivated me. Within my lifetime, six million Jews had died because of their religion and I too had been destined for death. It was a sacred trust to carry the flame forward to the next generation.

Together with my mother, Aunty Mania and Bronek, and sometimes with Michael's sister Carole, her then husband Ron, and their three high-spirited sons, we gathered around the Sabbath table. My mother loved Carole and her family. 'There's never a dull moment with Paul, Jeffery and Antony around!' she used to say as she laughed at their jokes and riddles and marvelled how caring and considerate the boys were. My mother's stories made them laugh too. Although she'd been widowed for three years, and found life desolate without my father, she hadn't lost her spirit and always had an amusing anecdote for every occasion.

One of the highlights of our Shabbat dinner was my mother's potato pie and sugar cake. Ever since my father had died, she had been eating with us several times a week, and always brought delicacies that she'd prepared. Whenever she arrived early, she always felt bad for holding me up. 'You probably want to write your articles, and I'm a bloody nuisance, taking up your time,' she used to say. Fiercely independent, she was determined not to become a burden. 'I have to get used to living alone,' she used to sigh. It brought tears to my eyes whenever she told me that she'd dreamed about my father again. 'He was standing right beside me, telling me that everything was all right, and patting me. His hand felt so warm and firm and I could still feel it on my shoulder when I woke up. I know he was there, she used to say.'

I thought that, with time, she'd adjust and start a new life, but time only made her more acutely aware of her loss. Her friends bored her and Aunty Mania irritated her more than ever. The only activity she enjoyed was bridge which she played three times a week. 'I love bridge because while I'm playing, I can't think about anything else,' she often said.

Not long after Jonathan's Bar-Mitzvah, Aunty Mania was admitted to St Vincent's Hospital with a massive heart attack. She'd often been in hospital with heart problems but had always bounced back and we didn't suspect that this would be any different. She was connected to a cardiac monitor, had an IV drip attached to her vein, huge bruises on her arms like ink stains, and was breathing with an oxygen mask. Like an injured butterfly, her exhausted heart fluttered between this world and the next, her eyes flickering occasionally as Bronek sat by her bed from morning till night trying to get some response out of her. 'Come on, kitten, Danusia has come to see you, what are you going to tell her?' he would coax.

At the end of that week the specialist told Bronek that Mania would not come home again. He wept, and his thin shoulders shook as he shuffled along the hospital corridor in his beige raincoat, a frail old man whose heart was breaking. 'Doctors don't know everything,' I said. 'They often make mistakes.'

And that's how it turned out. Two days later, when the specialist came to see her, accompanied by students and residents, Mania was sitting up looking at them. The doctor gazed at her as if she were Lazarus back from the dead. 'So you are better today, Mrs Ganc!' he exclaimed.

The woman who had been at death's door the day before gave him a lopsided smile and quipped, 'Well, would you believe it!' The entire entourage burst out laughing.

One day when I was alone with her, she was gazing at me with a loving expression. 'People don't get to choose their children,' she whispered. 'But I did. You are my chosen child.' I picked up her slim hand with its tapered fingers and almond-shaped nails, and for the first time in my life told my aunt that I loved her.

My mother came to the hospital every day and sat at the foot of her sister's bed with a worried face, saying little. One day, after my mother had left, Aunty Mania seemed to be staring into the distance, but she was really examining the past. 'You know, the wrong sister died during the war,' she whispered and there was a wistful look on her thin face. She meant my mother's favourite sister Hania. 'I know what I'm talking about. Your mother never forgave me that I was the one who survived. She would have been able to love me much better if I had died.'

Although Aunty Mania was very weak and couldn't walk unaided, she insisted on coming home. I was waiting for her when two ambulance officers carried upstairs a gaunt woman with hollow cheeks, dishevelled white hair and bloodless lips. My heart ached for my aunt, who hadn't looked like that since the day she staggered out of Bergen–Belsen. Bronek looked ashen and his hands shook. He sank into an armchair under the window, unable to get out a single word.

When Mania had settled down at home, we took the children to the South Coast for a week's holiday, but after a few days my mother rang. She sounded frantic. 'Mania is very ill, she's back in hospital, she can't breathe properly. I don't understand how you could have gone away. Can't you do something?' Michael called the hospital, prescribed something to ease my aunt's suffering and we threw our belongings into a suitcase and rushed back to Sydney.

Without waiting for Michael to park the car, I ran into the hospital. In Aunty's room Bronek sat slumped in a chair, alone, staring into space. 'Aunty isn't here any more,' he said. 'She passed away.' I stared at him. It couldn't be true. She must have been so ill, so frightened. I was her chosen child, I should have been with her when she died. Why do we let people we love just slip away from us? We look away and they're gone, taking so much love with them.

After Mania died, Bronek resembled a sad shadow flitting on the edge of life. From the moment she died, the sun ceased to shine for him. For hours he sat on the settee, holding a cigarette with trembling fingers, his cup rattling on its saucer as he stared blankly into the distance. One day he turned his big vacant pale eyes on me, his mouth turned down with a shiny snail-like trail of saliva in the creases, and said in a barely audible voice, 'She was a great woman.' Then he sobbed. 'What for should I keep living now? How will I ever survive this?'

My mother's reaction was terse. 'Don't worry, he'll survive.' But he didn't. Three weeks later he died. The doctors said that his kidneys and his heart had packed up, but they were wrong. Bronek died of a broken heart.

It took me several years to summon up enough courage to ask my mother about the day that Mania died. I knew that she was with her at the end, and wondered whether there had been any reconciliation between them. My mother shunned sentimentality and found it difficult to express emotion, especially where Mania was concerned. I asked whether she'd made peace with her sister at the end. 'I held her hand,' she replied.

'Did you love Mania?' I asked.

She looked at me as if I was talking nonsense and, with a finality that made further conversation impossible, said, 'Of course I did!'

CHAPTER 39

The moment I walk into the room, her face lights up. I'm in time to see the exercise class, and as I watch her wiggling her fingers and shaking her toes in response to the teacher's instructions, I feel as proud as any parent at a school open day.

But this time I'm not the parent. She is. Six months ago, when I left my mother at the day centre for the first time, she looked so forlorn that I spent the whole day in turmoil, just as I did when I took my children to kindergarten on their first day. This, however, has been far more painful. At kindergarten children begin to gain independence, but attending this centre means that my mother is losing hers.

It's hard to watch someone you love grow frail, lose confidence and become frightened of life; hard to see a strong mother become a clinging child. With each day her past recedes, and eighty years of courage are blurred by one year of confusion. It's hard to realise that this is the woman who sparkled like a mountain stream in sunlight, who defied Ukrainian militia, Nazi soldiers and Russian border guards. These days when we cross the street, my mother grips my hand and tells me with the same sense of wonderment that my hand feels just like her mother's, that she feels as if she is holding her mother's hand again. And in a sense she is, because we've now switched roles in this bitter-sweet reversal.

After exercises at the senior citizens' centre, there's a discussion about immigration. Evie, the group leader, asks whether my mother felt alienated when she first arrived in Australia and couldn't speak English. My mother shakes her head vehemently. 'Never! I always made friends at work, and we had wonderful neighbours. I think Australian people are tops!' she says in her Polish accent.

Evie turns to me. 'How are you two related?' she asks.

Too late, I hear myself saying, 'I'm Bronia's mother.'

Bronia has become a frail little woman in a neat suit who shuffles with a slow, unsteady gait and beseeches me to take her to the toilet in restaurants because she's afraid she'll lose her way. She riffles endlessly in her handbag to make sure that she has her wallet and her key, because she no longer trusts her once legendary memory. All my life I've thought that my mother was indestructible, just as she did, and the first intimations of her mortality have shocked us all.

It happened while I was overseas, travelling to the United States, Israel, Poland and France to gather information about the family, a project I'd been thinking about for a long time. Although I'd felt uneasy at being away for six weeks, Michael, Justine and Jonathan had reassured me that they could manage without me.

When I stepped off the plane in Sydney with a suitcase full of cassettes and a mind buzzing with reminiscences, a pale, thin woman I hardly recognised stumbled towards me. During my absence, my mother had gone into acute heart failure, and if Michael hadn't rushed over immediately and resuscitated her with oxygen and intravenous drugs, she wouldn't have survived. Although she had been taking medication for high blood pressure for several years, there was no doubt in my mind that anxiety about my prolonged absence had pushed her heart over the edge. I had become her anchor in an increasingly insecure world. 'You have no idea what Nana's like when you're away,' Justine used to tell me, and I don't suppose I ever understood the depth of my mother's despair. Perhaps I didn't really want to know. It seemed to me that my entire life had belonged to others, and now that I had finally carved out a career for myself and gained some independence, I didn't want to be restricted by my mother's insecurity.

I had become a freelance journalist, and my articles about personal experiences, social, medical, ethnic and women's issues, were frequently published in leading newspapers and magazines. Working freelance gave me the freedom to research whatever interested me, but after I'd received the Pluma de Plata, a prize awarded by the Government of Mexico for an article about that country, I became increasingly channelled into travel writing. As trips to exotic destinations kept being offered, I embarked on an enviable lifestyle which enabled me to combine the two things I loved doing: writing and travelling. By then Michael had developed his own creative talent, in photography, and had held several one-man exhibitions in top Sydney galleries, so we were often invited to travel as a team. For my mother this was a mixed blessing. Although she was proud of my success and showed my articles to all her friends, she felt insecure when I was away and dreaded my absences, especially when Michael and I travelled together. Whenever I told her that I was going away, she'd sigh and exclaim, 'Again!'

She became ill after I'd been away for four weeks. Although Michael and the children had told me that she was unwell whenever I telephoned, they had concealed the serious nature of her illness so that I wouldn't cut short my trip. Michael's care of my mother had been heroic. Not wanting to admit her into hospital where she'd be among strangers, he had brought her to our place and taken care of her with Justine and Jonathan's help. He came home during the day to check on her, cooked schnitzel to tempt her to eat, and kept finetuning her medication, while the three of them stayed with her as much as they could and made chicken soup to build her up.

Bronia trusted Michael's medical judgment implicitly. She had diabetes and adhered religiously to her diet; the only time she broke it was on Friday nights, when Michael looked at her over his glasses with the expression that made her call him The Professor, and said that she could have a small helping of ice cream, her favourite dessert. It was as though with his permission, and under his watchful eye, nothing could happen to her. 'The Professor said I could have some!' she would laugh, relishing every mouthful.

After she'd recovered from that episode of heart failure, I noticed that she held her right hand with her left so that no-one would see that it had begun to tremble with the onset of Parkinson's disease. 'I always imagined I'd take after my grandmother who lived to ninety-five and never even had to wear glasses,' she sighed one day. After her illness she lost weight and lines appeared on her lovely, smooth face. 'I can't bear to look at myself in the mirror any more,' she often said.

My mother always said that once a branch snaps off the tree, goats jump up and down on it until it breaks, and that described her own decline. When she'd recovered sufficiently to resume her bridge game, she found that her partners had replaced her with someone else. She was devastated. Those games were the highlight of her week, they provided her with structure and social life. My heart broke for her, but I realised that her cronies had used her absence as an excuse because my mother's powers of concentration had begun to fail.

A year after this, when I return home from a travel assignment, her face has become immobile and she can't focus on what I'm saying. When we ask a question, she stares into the distance and doesn't answer, as if some connecting switch has been turned off. Her lifelong optimism has also been extinguished. 'You are the only worthwhile thing I ever did,' she tells me, and when I demur, she says, 'What else have I ever done in my life?'

'Are you depressed?' I ask.

'Why shouldn't I feel depressed? she counters. 'Look at my life, I can't walk, I can't do anything.' Her hands shake, she can't cut her meat, it takes all her concentration to feed herself, to stop food from falling off her fork. She is so wobbly on her feet that I can hardly hold her upright when we walk along the street, and once she almost topples over in a cafe.

She's become agitated and forgetful. 'So you're picking me up at three?' she asks four or five times, and then calls several times to confirm our arrangement.

'There's something wrong with my watch,' she keeps saying, so I give her a watch with a big face and big numbers but she still can't work out whether it's five-thirty or six-thirty. She's confused and depressed; there's a painful diabetes-induced ulcer on her foot, and her hands shake so much that I have to pencil in her eyebrows for her.

When I call to pick her up for lunch on Sunday, she is wearing her nightie. 'What are you doing here so early?' she asks.

'It's one o'clock, I've come to take you home for lunch.'

She shakes her head in distress. 'I don't know what's happening to me, I'm such a pain in the neck to you.'

I help her on with her smart red and black check suit, brush her hair and wait while she goes to the bathroom. Ten minutes later I find her standing in the kitchen beside the stove, holding a box of matches in her hand. 'What are you doing with those?' I ask.

'I'm just going to make myself some porridge,' she replies.

Invisible icy fingers are pinching the back of my neck. When I bring her back home later she says, 'I'm worried I won't be able to light the match to warm up my dinner.'

'Of course you will, just keep trying. If you don't do it the first time, you'll do it the second or third,' I say. I don't want my mother to be in this state and I don't know what to do. I can't bear to think how strange and terrifying her world has become.

To help her, I summon social workers, counsellors, occupational therapists, geriatric psychiatrists. I want someone to wave some magic psychological or medical wand over her so she can revert to what she was. 'Ring your friends,' I urge her, 'get some new interests, go for little walks.' Michael thinks she's sliding into this apathy because she doesn't do anything, and he insists that unless we push her to do the few things she can still manage, she'll vegetate completely. I want to stop pressuring her but he's the doctor and I always defer to his judgment in these matters.

It is the incident with the cake that finally makes us all understand that there is no point pushing her to do things any more. On Friday nights she always used to arrive with a bag full of goodies she'd prepared for our Shabbat dinner: asparagus mornay, braised brisket and the chocolate roll which melted in our mouths. Although she used to love cooking for us, these days she makes excuses. 'When are you going to make your sugar cake, Nana?' Jonathan asks. 'I've forgotten how to bake,' she says. Finally one Friday she bangs a baking tin on the table and tears off the wrapping with a defiant look. 'Now you'll see that I can't bake any more!'

I can't meet her eyes. Instead of the usual handsome cake with its crisp sugary crust, there are only bits of crumbled, half-cooked dough.

But in spite of her decline, she still has a witty Yiddish saying for every occasion. When I suggest that she'll feel better if she attends a day centre for the aged because she'll have some company, she gives a sardonic laugh. '*Es vet helfen vi a toyten bankes.*' 'That'll be as useful as putting cupping glasses on a corpse,' she scoffs. At the centre she meets a woman she hasn't seen for a long time. 'So you had a pleasant time?' I comment. She shrugs. 'You know the only time a hunchback smiles? When he sees another hunchback!'

Instead of going to the day centre, she'd like to spend all day with me. 'The only thing that cheers me up is seeing you,' she often says. If I say that I can't see her that day, she says beguilingly, 'I know you won't let me down,' and ensnares me in a silken web of guilt. All my life she always did whatever she could to help me, so how can I refuse her now? Sometimes when I hear her voice on my answering machine, I sigh, anticipating another request. Then I remind myself that the time will come when I'll wish I could hear her voice again.

Now when I look back at my mother's last two years, I see a clear downward progression; but at the time I was only aware of unrelated problems, each one of which shocked me. Life is a huge mosaic, fragmented and incomprehensible from close up. Only distance gives perspective which enables us to take in the whole picture at a glance. But it wasn't just that I lacked the distance: I didn't want to see that each scene was leading to the inexorable finale.

We are never prepared for the roles that life throws at us. This situation reminds me of another of my mother's poignant Yiddish sayings: when a father gives his son money both laugh, but when a son has to give his father money, both cry. Although looking after my every need was never too much trouble for her, the responsibility and worry of taking care of her weighs me down. 'You made a big mistake years ago when

I asked you if you'd like a brother or sister!' she chuckles one day. 'You didn't want to hear about it, so now you have the burden of looking after me on your own!' I still remember how outraged I felt at the idea of sharing my parents' love and attention with another child. Now I am living with the consequences of having had my wish.

One afternoon, when I call to take her out to her favourite cafe in Double Bay, she doesn't open the door. The silence makes me panic. My heart is racing as I rush from room to room looking for her. I find her lying in the bath looking at me, as rigid and white as a marble statue. She'd got in to have a bath at night but hadn't been able to climb out. We can't tell whether she's had another small stroke or an acute episode of Parkinsonism.

Several weeks later, when she doesn't answer the phone, Michael and I rush over to find her confused and semiconscious. I wonder whether she has mixed up her medication when I hear her mumble, 'So I'm still here. I thought I'd finish it all. It would have been better if Michael hadn't got to me in time that night while you were away.'

As we bundle her up to take her to hospital, the thought that my mother has attempted to end her life paralyses me. At a moment when words are inadequate and unnecessary, and only love counts, I am only able to say, as if she were a troublesome child, 'You know we love you, how could you do such a thing?'

After she had recovered sufficiently to go home, it was obvious that she could no longer live alone, and I found a wonderful Polish woman to live with her. Zosia was the embodiment of caring, and if Bronia had been her own mother she couldn't have treated her with more affection and respect. They played cards together, told each other their life stories and my mother began to smile again.

But one Sunday several months later, when Zosia was visiting her daughter, my mother didn't open the door when I came to take her out for lunch. With a sense of foreboding I unlocked the door and found her sprawled out on the floor. She'd fallen over during the night and hadn't been able to get up.

A brain scan revealed that she'd had a stroke. She couldn't stand up, walk or feed herself. When we visited her in hospital, we fed her with chicken soup and tried to help her walk with a frame. All we could elicit in reply was a snarling yes or no, but the anger on her face spoke louder than words. It was a horrible existence for such a proud, independent woman, and we wondered whether she would ever walk or talk again. From St Vincent's, we transferred her to a private hospital. Every morning, long before I reached her little room, I could hear her shouting over and over again in an angry monotone, 'I'm sick! I'm sick!' as if a needle had stuck in the groove. Sometimes she shouted the names of the male nurses every few seconds in an expressionless voice. Whenever I came in, she glared and hardly spoke, yet the male nurses told me that when they sat beside her, she used to tell them stories about her life.

When she finally stopped repeating the same words and began to converse again, communicating with her became a minefield. She started to say something, then lost the words. She would start: 'Take me ... I want you to take me ...' Then her mouth would purse and tremble with the effort, but nothing more came out.

'Take you where?' I'd ask.

'Don't make fun!' she'd rebuke me.

'I wouldn't make fun of you,' I'd say, stung by her accusation. 'I love you, I want to help.'

'Don't take it so seriously,' was her response.

When I asked her how she was feeling, she snapped, 'Why

can't we talk about normal things?' When I wheeled her outside into the garden, and stroked her arm, she said, 'Can't you touch me the proper way?'

My mother's deteriorating condition was painful to see, but the change in her personality was even harder to cope with. I felt hurt and angry, and then I felt guilty for feeling angry. For the first time in my life I went to see a counsellor. Felicity had a soft voice, a kind face, and so much empathy that I couldn't stop crying as I told her about my mother's condition and her whole life. 'You feel bad because you want to make things better for her, but you can't make this better, can you?' she murmured. 'Perhaps she just needs you to acknowledge what she's going through.'

We brought her home for Mother's Day. In her wheelchair she looked like an angry, rigid doll, head down, calling, 'Orange juice!' or 'I'm sick!' Justine said gently, 'I know. What can I do for you, Nana?' Later my mother said, 'Justine! Hold me!' Justine put her arm gently around her shoulder. That was the first time I'd ever heard my mother ask for physical affection.

When I asked Justine how she was coping with her grandmother's deterioration, she said, 'At first I couldn't stand watching her like that. Then I realised that I had to let her be how she was, and not fight it, even though it was distressing. I know she has always loved me and I love her too, but she never really knew who I was. She idolised you, but she didn't value my ideas. Whatever I said, her response was always: "Ask Mummy." So I have mixed feelings. Your relationship with me comes into it too. I keep hoping that you can resolve your feelings with her so that we can become really close.' My mother didn't always think I was so clever, but the more dependent she became, the wiser I grew in her eyes. In fact, I valued Justine's ideas far more than my mother ever valued mine when I was young.

When my mother was ready to leave hospital, Zosia could no longer look after her as her visa had run out. We all cried when that angelic woman came to say goodbye. I had started looking for another woman to take care of my mother when she surprised me by saying that she didn't want to go home. She didn't feel secure there any more, even with a companion.

The problem dominated my every waking thought. While we were trying to figure out what to do, I brought my mother to stay at our place, but she needed attention day and night. I had always promised myself that she would never go into a nursing home and although this now seemed the only option, it felt like betrayal. Every day I went looking at nursing homes and came home depressed. No matter how the nurses' aides bustled about making cheery comments, they couldn't disguise the smell of urine and disinfectant, or hide the accusing resignation of people marking time before they died.

When I found a sparkling, newly built home with sunny rooms, open spaces and a sympathetic Irish matron in whose office I broke down and wept, I was overjoyed and brought my mother to see it. A group of people were sitting on the terrace having a barbecue, while others were about to leave for an excursion. 'Maybe it will be good to have company,' my mother mused. I felt a stirring of hope. Perhaps she'd enjoy her life here.

But the day I brought her there with her little suitcase, she sat stiffly on a chair, not saying a word. I couldn't bear to leave her, and when I finally did, I cried all the way home. During her stay there my mother never went on any outings and she rarely mixed with the other residents. She kept herself apart, remote and depressed. Every day when I came to see her, instead of being in the lounge room with the others, she was usually sitting in her room, dressed in one of her smart suits, just waiting for me. Whenever I left, she shuffled out to the glass door with me and stood there, waving to me bravely until I drove away, her face a small white triangle which haunted me for the rest of the day.

Seeing my mother look so beaten, so forlorn, like an abandoned elderly waif, I understood why she thought that it would have been better if Michael hadn't saved her life, although I never brought up this painful topic again and neither did she. I thought my mother couldn't cope with the knowledge that her powers were failing, but the one who couldn't cope with it was me. Throughout this ordeal my sister-in-law Carole often sat beside my mother and listened sympathetically while she spoke about her wish to die, and then she would gently try to help me come to terms with my mother's feelings and my own.

It hurt me to see my once dynamic and positive mother become a pale shadow for whom flowers no longer had any perfume and sunshine had no warmth. But whenever I came in, she always greeted me with a smile which, like a lone match struck on a gloomy night, lit up her lovely face for an instant and she invariably said with endearing wonderment, 'How wonderful that you're here. I was just thinking about you!' And then she'd introduce me yet again to the nurses and other residents. 'This is my daughter, meet my daughter,' she used to say.

Although my mother was anxious and unhappy, in the months that followed she seemed to accept her new existence and her condition seemed stable. Ever since she'd become ill, I'd reduced my workload considerably and refused most of the travel assignments I was offered, but now Michael and I felt that it was safe to accept a short trip, although we decided to say nothing about it to my mother until closer to the time.

Several days before we were due to leave, my mother didn't

smile when I came in or give any sign of recognition. She didn't even look at me when I spoke. After I'd asked several times why she didn't answer, she finally turned towards me. She fixed on me a piercing gaze of such intensity that I felt as if I'd been stabbed, even though I couldn't decipher its meaning.

Whether it was sorrow, accusation or despair, I cannot know but I'll take that knowing expression with me to the grave. It was as if I were looking at myself through her eyes and confronting the truth about life. Perhaps she knew that she was fading away, and that's what her look intended to convey. She'd always told me that I was a wonderful daughter, but maybe now she was thinking that this is how life ends, and that one day I too would learn how painful it is to realise that children have such a limited capacity for loving their parents.

The look on her face alarmed me so I returned to see her that afternoon and found her lying in bed, asleep. 'She's been very tired today,' the sister told me. As I sat beside her bed, I knew that I couldn't go overseas. I cancelled the trip.

On the very morning that we had been due to leave, the matron rang. 'Your mother's condition has changed. You should come in.'

She was lying in bed, but although her eyes were closed and she was barely conscious, she knew that we were there and answered in monosyllables which sounded as if they were coming from far away. Her breathing was laboured. With horror I noticed that her mouth had shrunken—they hadn't put her teeth in. 'She would hate that,' I told the nurse, 'couldn't you put them in for her?'

The nurse and Michael exchanged glances. 'It's better like this, it's more comfortable for her,' Michael said gently. Even then I was telling myself that she was just feeling weak and that it would pass and soon she'd sit up and be appalled at the way she looked.

We sit beside her, Michael and I, the curtains drawn around us. Occasionally a nurse parts the curtain, checks her pulse and leaves softly. This should be a time of deep thoughts and healing words but I can't summon up a single coherent thought, or word, or action. I look at the small, thin shape under the blanket and silently stroke my mother's arm. Only afterwards it occurs to me that she may have preferred me to put my arm around her.

'Is there anything you'd like?' I ask from time to time.

'No!' she replies in a surprisingly definite voice.

'Do you like me stroking your arm?'

'Yes!'

Michael leans forward. 'Would you like some ice cream?' he asks.

'Yes!'

When the nurse brings it in, he spoons her favourite dessert tenderly into her mouth. 'How is that?' he asks.

'Beautiful!' she replies. This is the last word she ever utters.

When my mother died, people told me that I should be grateful that I'd had her for so long. Others contrasted her past vitality and independence with her recent debility and depression. 'Her quality of life had gone, you wouldn't have wanted her to linger on like that,' they said.

They didn't seem to know that the longer you have parents you love, the harder it is to part from them. She was such a big part of my life that, when she died, she took such a big part of mine with her. When I was young I always thought that I was closer to my father, and perhaps at that time I was. But now I was attached to my mother in a thousand different ways, and her death tore me apart in a way that his had not. Perhaps because he had been more self-sufficient, while she had become so vulnerable. For the past few years I'd been convinced that she was dependent on me, but after she died I realised that it was I who had been dependent on her.

I'm grateful that we were with her when she died, that I was holding her small sparrow-like hand, so like my own, when her tired heart beat for the last time. But I feel cast adrift. She's been here all my life, and I can't imagine the world without her love and support. As long as she was there, I was still the younger generation, but now that the last custodian of my past has gone, I'm in the front line.

The day after her death, Michael, Jonathan, Justine and I sit together around the kitchen table trying to evoke the essence of the remarkable and unique person that Bronia had been. As Justine and Jonathan reminisce about their Nana, about her generous heart and her sharp tongue, her wisdom and her wit, I am grateful that they had the chance to know her so well.

Burying someone you love on a brilliant summer day is doubly poignant. On a day when fallen jacaranda leaves formed a thick violet carpet on the pavements, and the air smelled of honeysuckle and jasmine, we gathered at the Eastern Suburbs Crematorium. I must have been averting my mind from what was about to happen because seeing my mother's coffin in the chapel startled me like a sudden blow to the head.

With Justine's comforting arm around my shoulders, I listened to Michael's heartfelt words.

'My mother-in-law Bronia was a remarkable woman,' he began. 'She was different from anyone else I've ever met—which is why we are here at a cremation, instead of a conventional Jewish funeral.

'She had so many different aspects to her character that it

took four of us—Justine, Jonathan, Diane and myself—to sort out how to do justice to all her qualities.

'Like her late husband Henry, she thought for herself, said exactly what she thought, and wasn't influenced by what anyone else said or did. She was down to earth, and you always knew where you were with her.

'She was an extraordinarily wise woman.

'Material things meant nothing to her and in fact her greatest pleasure was in giving things away to those she loved. She gave love, money, jewellery, gifts, and never asked for anything in return—apart from one instance when she gave Justine and Jonathan her little green Datsun, on condition that Jonathan got rid of his motorbike! She always said that she preferred to give things with a warm hand, while she was alive, so that she could have the pleasure of giving.'

While listening to Michael's tribute, I imagine my mother saying, 'You see, I always told you that Michael was a *mensch*!'

Although having a Jewish funeral hadn't been important to my mother, I arranged to have a *minyan* at our place that night and asked Rabbi Jeffery Kamins from the Temple Emanuel to conduct the service. Mourning didn't feel complete without the comfort of the traditional rites and the Kaddish prayer. Friends held me, cried with me and wished me 'Long life', our traditional greeting to the bereaved. I'd never realised how comforting the rituals of death can be, even when you're not religious.

As friends streamed into our home to share our sorrow, I looked up and stared in disbelief. There in the corner of the room, watching me from a distance with sympathetic eyes, was my mother's cousin Srulek Kestecher, too shy and self-effacing to approach me. Now that his brother Aron had died, Srulek was my mother's only living relative but I hadn't seen him for many years, and now with a shock I realised that I'd forgotten all about him and hadn't let him know that my mother had died. Seeing him, so frail and vulnerable, reminded me of the times he used to visit us in Walter Street so many years ago when my mother was young and energetic, my father was still alive, and all my life was still in front of me. While Srulek apologised for imposing and disturbing me, I broke down and sobbed on his shoulder. When the prayers were over, I looked for him but, like a phantom, he had slipped away.

Several days after the funeral I walk alone along a deserted, windswept beach and watch the rhythm of the sea which has no beginning and no end. Waves roll and break, sands shift, and the wind whips my face. At night I gaze at the moon, luminous and ethereal, like a spiritual lamp shining in space. In our perpetual galactic dance, the earth pivots, stars beam across the heavens, and moons wax and wane. The eternal mystery of our existence comforts me. Everything in the world is interconnected, everything moves and changes, but nothing ever vanishes.

CHAPTER 40

As Justine and I buckle our seat belts in preparation for take-off, I steel myself for three weeks of emotional upheaval. Two years after my mother's death, we're on our way to Poland and Ukraine to trace our roots and walk in the footsteps of our ancestors, although I realise that this might prove to be a fruitless quest. Most Jewish documents were destroyed during the war, and after so many years I'm not likely to find any traces of my family.

But there's another aspect of the journey that makes me feel apprehensive. In recent months I've heard many reports about the resurgence of anti-Semitism in Eastern Europe, and even my friend Teresa, a Polish Catholic, has warned me about it. 'It's not pleasant for me to say this,' she said in her musical voice, 'but you need to know so that you'll be prepared. Instead of going forward, the Poles have regressed. The economic situation is bad, the church is struggling to regain power, and they're blaming Jews again, even though there are hardly any left!'

While I mull over her words, I glance at Justine who has pulled a book by an American Jewish feminist out of her backpack. I was glad when my daughter agreed to come with me on this pilgrimage. Our relationship over the past few years hasn't been smooth, and I hope that searching for our roots together will forge a stronger bond between us.

Sydney has receded into the distance and only the pale sandy crescents on the edge of the dark sea are visible when Justine looks up from her book to tell me about a workshop she recently attended about Holocaust survivors. 'It helped me understand some of the dynamics in our family a bit better,' she says.

I'm intrigued that she attended such a seminar because for the past few years she hasn't been much involved with the Jewish community. 'So how do you think the Holocaust has affected us?' I ask.

'Enmeshment, for one thing,' she replies. 'I always felt pressured to be close. You were also intensely overprotective and often fearful of something happening to me.'

It's an interesting point. I never thought of myself as being overprotective and wonder whether this was due to the Holocaust or normal parental concern.

On the Lot Polish Airlines flight from Bangkok to Warsaw, a male flight attendant with an unsmiling angular face hands me a Polish newspaper. Past the political and economic reports in the *Warsaw News*, a short item catches my eye. From his pulpit in Gdansk, Lech Walesa's priest and confidant, Father Henryk Jankowski, equated the Star of David with the swastika and the hammer and sickle, and stated that satanic Jewish greed had caused the Holocaust. My heart hammers in my throat. Teresa was right. Nothing has changed.

We touch down in Warsaw on a drizzly grey morning. The Grand Hotel doesn't live up to its name. Our cell-like room has two single beds whose mustard-coloured blankets peep through the diamond-shaped cut-out of the cover. The window, which doesn't open, faces a grim inner yard. It's seven-thirty on Sunday morning and we have two whole days in Warsaw before flying on to Lwow in the Ukraine. That sinking feeling has returned and I feel suffocated in our oppressive room.

Finally we rouse ourselves and set off towards the old market square. As we cross a side street, the name leaps to my eye. Nowogrodzka Street. 'This is the street where my grandmother Lieba lived with her daughter Rozia when they came to Warsaw from Radlow in 1942,' I explain, and tell Justine how Aunty Andzia spent several weeks standing behind the wardrobe with Krysia and Fredzio so that the landlady wouldn't find out they were there. Walking along the street, I try to imagine my aunt's desperation when she couldn't remember the number of the house and had to knock on these very doors in the hope of finding her sister.

It's a long damp walk to Stary Rynek, but after sitting in a plane so long, it's a relief to stretch our legs. In the spectacular square which resembles an eighteenth century street scene, burly *dorosky* coachmen groom their horses while they wait for passengers. At their easels, artists paint vignettes of the cobbled square with its boxes of scarlet geraniums, vine-covered cafes, and the baroque facades covered all over with paintings of mythological characters and eighteenth century scenes. In between the looming clouds, the sun is struggling to emerge.

A yeasty aroma draws us to Gessler's window where a bleached blonde in a floppy baker's cap wraps our doughnuts and morello cherry slices in coarse paper. As we sit under a striped umbrella, drinking espresso coffee and relishing our pastries, Justine suggests writing up our diaries, and we sit together in friendly silence in the centre of Warsaw, recording our impressions in an area that was razed to the ground fifty years ago.

Sitting here in Warsaw beside my daughter, I'm overwhelmed by a rush of gratitude. 'I feel so lucky that I had parents who were able to put the horror of the Holocaust behind them and get on with their lives, that I was able to grow up like other girls, and that you and Jonathan could live in a country where you were free to be Jewish without any fear.'

Justine nods sympathetically, then says in an impassioned voice. 'Many Jews have never expressed their anger about this. They've intellectualised and rationalised their feelings. What happens to all the anger that isn't let out? It must affect people and their children. If you're not in touch with how you feel, you can't be in touch with your children's feelings either.'

Maybe she's right. My mother always suppressed her feelings. It was only in the last years of her life that I realised she'd never expressed her anger or grief about losing her family. I don't suppose she had the time or the opportunity, or perhaps it was too painful to deal with. There were too many people to cry for, too much savagery to forgive. Only by clamping the lid tightly over that seething cauldron of anger and grief was she able to keep going.

I look at Justine with interest. She is much more questioning and confronting than I have ever been. While I've always longed to be part of the mainstream, she has often turned her back on it. Perhaps she has taken on the anger that I've suppressed, just as I took on the grief that my mother buried deep inside.

After strolling around the square and chatting with the artists, we go to the Karczma Restaurant which resembles an old country inn with rough-hewn walls, shiny wooden benches and oak tables worn by thousands of elbows. Blackened iron cauldrons of mushroom soup are simmering on the open stove and to my surprise there's a silver candelabra on the counter. 'This was originally a Jewish tavern in Biala Podlaska,' explains the gangly young waiter.

At the mention of Biala Podlaska I become excited. 'That's

near the village where Nana, Grandpa and I spent several years during the war,' I tell Justine. At first it seems wonderful to be sitting in what used to be a lively Jewish tavern, until it hits me that the last Jews who sipped cherry brandy, argued and drank at these tables were all dragged away to concentration camps.

By late afternoon the sun has finally peeped through the clouds in time for the Sunday concert in Lazienki Park. A large woman in loose black culottes and hair piled on top of her head sits down at the piano and, with a majestic nod to the audience, begins to play. With hundreds of other music-lovers, we soak up the fragrance of the rose gardens and the delicacy of Chopin's nocturnes whose yearning always makes my heart ache. Now they tug at my heart more than ever. Turbulent and tender, passionate and poignant, these etudes, nocturnes, polonaises and mazurkas are the very soul of the Polish people. Chopin was my mother's favourite composer, and each poignant note, like an invisible silver filament, binds me closer to her spirit.

Next morning we meet Jacek, our guide for the day. He's an intelligent, educated man with a distinguished head of greying hair and a disarming smile. We start our tour at the site of the Warsaw ghetto. The air around me is so dense with tragic and heroic stories that I drag my feet and feel too choked to speak. So I'm thrown off balance when, standing on ground that is sacred to the memory of those who perished here, Jacek suddenly says, 'It irritates me when I hear people saying that Hitler put so many concentration camps in Poland because Poles are anti-Semites. Why do we hear so much about Polish anti-Semitism? Why don't we hear about French anti-Semitism?'

'But we do hear about French anti-Semitism,' I protest. 'Only a few weeks ago, there was a documentary ...' I've

517

allowed myself to become sidetracked. The issue that needs to be discussed in Poland is not French anti-Semitism.

Pointing to the perimeter of the ghetto, Jacek gathers momentum. 'They say that people living around the ghetto walls didn't help. How could they help when the walls were so high? Anyway, helping Jews was dangerous.'

Justine, for whom I translate our conversations as fast as a simultaneous translator at a conference, is becoming distressed. 'We should have come here alone,' she says. 'Instead of acknowledging what happened here, he's making excuses for the past. I want to be able to feel my grief without having to listen to his dismissive comments.'

Nearby, at the site of the Umschlagplatz, thousands of names are engraved on the wall. From this station Jews were jammed into cattle trucks and left for days without water in scorching summer heat, on their way to Treblinka and Bergen–Belsen. The paving stones I'm standing on are the same ones that Aunty Mania trod when they brought her here from the Hotel Polski. Instead of a visa to South America, she got one to Bergen–Belsen.

At Pawiak Prison there's little left of the original jail except for the iron gate that's topped with barbed wire. Past the brick wall I peer inside at the courtyard where the exercise yard used to be and wonder whether my grandmother and aunt had been lined up against that wall. Looking up at the apartment blocks nearby, I wonder from which window the doctor watched them being shot on the day of the Warsaw Uprising. 'No-one could have seen the yard from there,' Jacek argues. This is his only comment.

Our last stop in Warsaw is the Jewish cemetery whose sagging gravestones are still riddled with German bullet holes, and whose spongy loam contains the mass graves of thousands of nameless dead. In front of the memorial to the million dead children, I break down and cry. I could so easily have been one of them.

It's a relief to leave this sad, grey city and drive along a straight country road that skirts neat market gardens planted with cabbages and carrots, and hothouses nurturing pencil pines, until we come to the flat farming land of Ozarow which stretches from horizon to horizon. Somewhere around here my cousin Tusiek fell in one of the first battles of the war. 'The battle was on the western side of the town,' Jacek explains. I think about the fair-haired young man whose teasing comments made my parents laugh, and wonder how he must have felt on the eve of the battle where his regiment rode on horseback, armed with lances, to face a juggernaut armed with cannons, tanks and howitzers.

As we walk along reading the inscriptions on the graves, Jacek resents the distinction between Jewish and Catholic war casualties. 'They were all Poles,' he says. I understand his desire to homogenise and sanitise the past. It's not comfortable to face the fact that this has always been a country of Jews and Poles, a very clear distinction. He wants to ignore the fact that the Jews were always regarded as aliens, especially when they were singled out for annihilation. He is angry that, to people like us, this country has become a vast cemetery, that instead of touring the countryside and visiting castles and museums, we come to find traces of our dead.

It's been a heavy day and we end it at a Silesian restaurant where dancers with fixed smiles and vivid costumes stamp booted feet in time to rousing folk tunes. Jacek and I toss back several glasses of Chopin Vodka the Polish way—without stopping for breath. Soon he's regaling us with tales of Polish gallantry and patriotism and quoting stirring ballads about spilt blood and scarlet poppies. Now that I've downed three glasses of vodka, I feel relaxed enough to acknowledge that he's as obsessed with Polish heroism as I am with Jewish persecution. 'You might feel angry about the past,' he says suddenly, 'but you're still closely linked to Poland. You can't deny that there's a bond. It's like a family feud: you feel anger because you also feel love.'

CHAPTER 41

As the aeroplane begins its descent over Ukraine, Justine and I look down on a patchwork of sage-, ochre- and cinnamon-coloured fields dotted with hay stooks and edged with dark forests. Then I stare at the date. It's 25 July. By a strange co-incidence, we have arrived in Lwow on the anniversary of my grandfather Bernard's murder in this bloodstained city.

My father's account of the brutality of the Ukrainian militia is vivid in my mind as we land. Since 1991 Ukraine has been an independent nation whose government erected a monument in honour of a military unit whose members helped the Nazis murder Jews and Poles. Today they're being hailed as patriots because they fought the Bolsheviks; their atrocities against civilians have been overlooked. My heart is beating fast as Justine and I step onto the tarmac. This is going to be a painful pilgrimage.

Inside the airport building of this city now called Lviv, I seem to have entered the pages of a John Le Carré thriller set during the iciest era of the Cold War. Sitting inside his flaking wooden booth, a flint-eyed official scrutinises newcomers with an expressionless stare. Finally he waves us towards a long table where a woman with an aggressive black fringe snaps something unintelligible. On the wall a patriotic mural depicts people in folk costume marching behind triumphant flags.

Outside, in the glaring sunshine, a smiling youth with a

boyish face introduces himself as our guide Oles, and ushers us towards the dinted turquoise Lada whose driver sprawls behind the wheel. Sasha has a foxy face and eyes that give little away. He has a macho style of driving and we bump along cobbled streets and lurch in and out of ruts and potholes until Justine and I are tossed around like rag dolls.

Oles suggests a stroll around the city but I'm impatient to visit the state archives. We only have five days in Lviv, and I'm determined to find out whatever I can about my mother's family. Sasha and Oles lead us through a shady park, along streets lined with lime and chestnut trees, and stop to show us the ruins of the Temple of the Golden Rose, a medieval synagogue. To save her community from death, the rabbi's beautiful daughter married the ruler of the town, but three hundred and sixty years later no-one was able to save the Jews of Lwow. Not even the intercession of Metropolitan Sheptitsky, the head of the Ukrainian Church, was able to stop the savagery of the militia gangs. The synagogue was burned down in the summer of 1942, at about the time when my parents and I fled to Piszczac.

'Life is not good in Lviv,' Oles explains in his earnest, halting English. 'Since independence, we have a lot of unemployment and crime. You can tell that it is bad here because there are not many Jews. My father says, when things are bad, Jews leave. They go to places where they can live better and make money.'

After all that the Jews have been through here, Ukrainians think that they have left simply to look for better pastures. Through clenched teeth, I ask, 'What makes you say that?'

'Oh, I just know it is so,' he replies.

'Do you know any Jews?'

'Only one,' he says. 'My science professor. Nice man.' Suddenly he asks, 'Why are you so interested in Jewish things?'

'My family were murdered in Lviv because they were Jewish,' I tell him. 'My grandparents, an uncle who was about your age, and my young aunty, together with her husband and baby daughter. I don't know where, when or how most of them died, and I don't even have a photograph to remember them by. It's as if they never existed. That's why I've come to find some trace of them.'

Oles looks upset. 'I am sorry,' he blurts. 'I am very sorry.'

I'm certain that he has no idea that 60 000 of his compatriots volunteered to join the militia who speeded up the Nazi carnage, but I don't want to give him a history lesson in the street, and anyway he probably wouldn't believe me. 'It isn't your fault,' I say gently. 'I just wanted you to understand why I've come.' By now a friend of his has joined us, and while we sit in an arcaded cafe sipping small cups of freshly roasted black coffee, Oles tells him why we've come to Lviv.

Through a weathered oak portal we all enter a medieval building which houses the state archives. I've brought a letter from my local mayor in Sydney, translated into Ukrainian, asking for permission to access information about my family. Climbing up a curved staircase of wooden steps sagging from centuries of use, we enter the archive office. Our three young companions are fired up with zeal and so keen to help us that they push past the couple sitting there, wave my letter of introduction at the director, and all talk at once, explaining why we've come.

Orest Matschiuk has thick grey hair which rests on the collar of his short-sleeved check shirt. After scanning the letter, he leans towards me. 'Are you the Armstrong who went to the moon, or the one who played . . .' He puts an imaginary trumpet to his lips and laughs, showing silver teeth. Then he becomes serious. 'We have thousands of ledgers, kilometres of records here. You don't have enough time to research them and you don't read Ukrainian. You cannot do it alone.' He calls out, and a slender young woman with glossy brown hair and a tip-tilted nose comes into his office. 'Galina will be your researcher,' says Mr Matschiuk. 'Tell her what you are looking for and come back in two days' time.' I feel heartened by the helpful attitude of our young companions and the director's co-operative manner. For the first time since leaving home I feel that there may be a chance of finding some traces of the relatives I never knew.

Now that business is over for the day, Oles wants to show us around Lviv. As we stroll along avenues lined with lime trees with their dense canopy of dark, heart-shaped leaves, I can see why Aunty Mania and my mother used to talk about their beautiful city. Like an impoverished duchess, Lviv retains traces of its Habsburg grandeur. Its opera house wouldn't look out of place in Paris or Vienna, nor would the city buildings with their elaborate plasterwork, carvings of mythical figures, and graceful iron balconies overlooking leafy streets.

Oles suggests a hike to Castle Hill. Towards the summit, as the path grows steeper, Sasha slings my camera bag over his shoulder. From the summit we look down on a city of green cupolas, square towers and baroque domes surrounded by tracts of dark forest. Standing on the parapet, Justine and I put our arms around each other while Oles clicks the shutter. It's a lovely moment.

Next morning, when the trees in Kosciuszko Park shimmer with sunlight and swallows twitter in the branches, I explore Lviv on my own, but the phantoms of the past are never far away. Students mill around the university which refused to admit my mother's brother Izio. The town hall over there, facing the pretty square where statues of Neptune and Diana spout jets of water, was where my father was taken for questioning. Two attractive Bratter sisters, Bronia and Mania, used to meet their friends in cafes along this avenue leading to the opera house. For an instant briefer than thought, I imagine the thrill of telling Bronia that I've visited her city and walked along the streets she knew so well. There are so many ways of feeling the loss of a mother.

Sasha and our new interpreter Dan can't wait to show us the countryside and suggest an excursion to the Carpathian Mountains. With his clean-cut features and knee-length shorts, Dan could be an Ivy League student, but Sasha has donned electric blue lycra shorts, iridescent hexagonal sunglasses, a T-shirt advertising World Freestyle skiing, and a baseball cap back to front on his blond hair. He brings a box of pirated cassettes, and as the car lurches, bumps and grinds over ruts and potholes, Dan, Sasha and Justine tap their feet and sing the chorus of the Sting song 'I'm a Legal Alien'.

While Sasha hurtles along, overtaking everything on the narrow winding road, Dan tries to teach me the Cyrillic alphabet so that I can read the road signs. We discover that we have something in common. His father is also a dentist who wanted him to follow in his footsteps, but Dan chose economics instead.

As we approach the mountains, the air becomes cooler and forests of spruce, fir and pine replace stands of beech and ash. Our destination is Tessovets, a ski resort which Sasha often visited when he was an international cross-crountry skier. It's deserted now, and the two ski lifts are idle. The sporting complex consists of dim corridors with crumbling walls, broken flooring and desolate spaces. Loud crackling music blares from a defective loudspeaker.

While we eat pickled cabbage and veal with mushrooms in the cavernous dining room, Dan says proudly, 'For the first time in five hundred years Ukraine is a free nation.' Later he tells us that Ukrainians do not like Jews. When I ask why, his eyes harden. 'In Ukraine people should speak Ukrainian, don't you think? The Jews speak Russian.' A feeling of despair washes over me. It's as if a malignant gene has entered these people's bloodstream. Anti-Semitism seems to be a free-floating cancer in search of a cause. Since they can no longer accuse Jews of being communists, the patriots have come up with a new reason for hatred: language.

'After all that's happened here, it's distressing for us to hear anti-Semitic comments,' Justine says. 'Most of my family were killed here. It seems that not many people in Lviv actually know what happened. I think it's important for all of us to know our history—or herstory—even if it is uncomfortable.'

But Dan doesn't want to hear about it and changes the subject to the famine of the thirties. He tells us that several million Ukrainians died. I don't want to compete with him for pain and suffering and I should commiserate about his loss, but how can I feel his pain when he doesn't want to know about mine? All it would take to heal my wounds, and enable me to hear his, is for him to acknowledge what happened instead of dismissing it. The four of us sit in uncomfortable silence while Dan seems to be struggling with something. Then he says slowly, 'There has been so much killing in this country for so long. Perhaps we are so used to violence that we are no longer sensitive to it.' I feel as if a burden has dropped off my back.

After this heavy interchange, it's a relief to leave the oppressive hotel and start hiking up the mountain. As the sun beats on our heads, Dan wades waist-high in a grove of frilly leaves as big as dinner plates, and picks them for us. Justine and I wear them like bonnets and double up with laughter whenever we catch a glimpse of each other. Sasha has stripped down to a skimpy scarlet swimsuit and marches ahead of us, toting my bag as usual, while Dan picks wildflowers to take home for his girlfriend.

At the summit we stretch out on soft grass sprinkled with buttercups and daisies, and lift up small round leaves to pick blueberries which resemble swelling drops of dark ink. I feel like a child again as I eat the fleshy little globules which leave a blue-black coating on my teeth and a bittersweet taste on my palate. For the first time since we arrived in Lwiw, I feel light and free, and I'm grateful to Dan and Sasha for the gift of this beautiful day.

After this interlude I'm anxious to return to my search. To help me find my way around the Lwiw of the past, I contact Leon Plager, whose name I was given in Sydney. Mr Plager was born in Lwow and was one of the few Jews who returned after the war. He is a stocky man of seventy-four with tufts of white hair springing out on either side of his bald head, pouchy eyes, a fleshy protruding lower lip and some teeth capped with silver. Although it's early when he arrives at our hotel, the sun is already hot, and he mops his brow with a big handkerchief.

As we walk towards the state archives, he tells me his story. 'I lost two hundred relatives during the war,' he says in his Russian-Polish accent. 'I joined the Russian army as a volunteer when the Nazis occupied Lwow in 1941. When I returned after the war, there was no-one left. My brother, sisters, parents, grandparents, uncles, aunties, in-laws, cousins, all dead. I decided to stay. Someone had to become a guardian of the past, a witness of what happened to the Jews of Lwow.'

Upstairs in her office, Galina, the archive researcher, holds out a sheet of paper. It's a page from Lwow's 1930 business directory, with one entry underlined. My heart leaps when I read: 'Bernard Bratter, wholesale steel merchant, Sloneczna Street.' It's the first time in my life that I have seen my grandfather's name recorded anywhere. I'm so overcome with joy that I don't realise until later that the listing gives no street number, so I won't be able to find the house.

Out in the street, Leon Plager whispers, 'I'll take you to another office.' We cross a courtyard, climb a few steps and already on the staircase I can smell the woody odour of old paper. Mr Plager tells us to wait, but returns a few minutes later, puffing from exertion and excitement. 'Come! The researcher has already found your grandparents' address!' Even if I don't find anything else in Lviv, it will have been worth coming. Now I'll be able to see my grandparents' house, where my mother grew up.

My heart is pounding as the car noses into Sloneczna Street. And here it is, as sunny as its name, a wide street planted with lime trees, just as my mother always described it. 'This was the best house in the street,' Mr Plager says as we stand outside number forty-three, a handsome three-storey building faced with stone with pediments over the windows and a graceful balcony.

In the entrance my heart is pounding with such excitement that it's hard to focus on the details. I'm actually standing in the house that my mother used to talk about. An old-fashioned black and white tile floor leads to the wooden staircase that I must have climbed so many years ago. These are the stairs that resounded with the boots of the Ukrainian guards when they came to take my grandfather to his death. Inside that flat, a two-year-old called Danusia used to place a warning finger on her nose when she heard someone at the door and whisper, 'Shh. Germs!' It was here that I thrilled my father by naming all the animals in my picture book in Polish and Latin, while my grandparents, Uncle Izio and Aunty Hania, all ran around me, anticipating my every wish. It was the second year of my life and the last year of theirs.

Two doors down, past an entrance wide enough for a truck

to drive through, we stand in a large yard with a long row of sheds on one side. This is where my grandfather had his storeroom. I visualise this gentle man with the shiny bald head, who preferred playing billiards to running a business, hurrying outside to check on deliveries and dispatches. 'It was a big steel business,' recalls Mr Plager. He remembers the place because, as a seventeen-year-old, he was in love with the daughter of my grandfather's partner and used to come here to see her. 'The sheds used to be piled high with sheets and bars of metal, some thin and others weighing half a tonne. Cranes lifted the heavy ones onto heavy waggons pulled by teams of strong horses, carters loaded the others onto their backs,' he reminisces. In one of the downstairs offices, my mother kept the books and extended credit to customers in trouble.

When I mention my mother's first husband Sammy Wechsler, Mr Plager nods excitedly. 'I remember Sammy, he was my brother's friend, a lovely chap.' He racks his brains for details. 'He was solidly built and had receding hair. A good-natured fellow. They were always teasing each other.' Sammy sounds like a dependable fellow, the kind who might have married a young woman to rescue her from an overpossessive boyfriend.

Around the corner from Sloneczna Street we come to the site of the Lwow ghetto where tens of thousands of men, women and children were crowded into tiny dwellings until there was no room for some of them to lie down. Starved, emaciated and ill, they were systematically deported to Belzec and Treblinka. The memorial to the dead is elongated and angular, its tortured shape has one hand raised to the sky for vengeance, the other turned to God in supplication. An inscription underneath from Ezekiel 37 says, 'Here I open your graves and I will lead you my people from your graves and I will give you my spirit and you will become alive again.' Leon

Plager is proud of this memorial which he helped to erect and the present Ukrainian government helped to fund.

Sasha looks at the memorial. 'How many people died here?' he asks.

'136 000,' Leon replies. As usual, Sasha's face gives nothing away but he stands there for a long time.

In the garden beds around the statue, small plaques have been set into the wall in memory of Jewish families who were murdered in this city. These are also Leon's work. I arrange for a plaque to be placed in memory of the Bratter family so that Toni and Bernard, Izio, Hania, Dolek and their nameless baby will be commemorated together with all the other innocent victims of genocide.

That night, while the world is still plunged in darkness, my mind awakes with one thought imprinted on it, each word as. clear as a neon sign on a black highway. I survived when most did not. I survived. It's as if the miracle of my survival has just struck me. In spite of the murder squads, the round-ups, the deportations, the transportations, the cattle trucks, the death camps, the gas chambers and the crematoria, my parents had pitted their strength against the evil raging all around us and they had triumphed. I survived.

It was as if a bolt of lightning had illuminated a darkened room and unexpectedly lit up hidden treasures. I wonder why it took me so long to feel so intensely something that I had always known. Maybe that's how long I needed to stand back from the extraordinary fact of my survival, maybe I had to return to Lviv to grasp its meaning. I fall asleep with another thought emblazoned in my mind. How beautiful and how terrible the world is.

There are few cars on the road to Zolkwa and Sasha pelts

along past toothless women in thick woollen stockings tending their cows by the roadside, and apple-cheeked girls on bicycles with milk churns hanging from the handlebars. Flat fields of wheat stretch across the horizon.

I've come to Zolkwa because my mother's father, Bernard Bratter, was born here. My contact, Zygmunt Lainer, an energetic man in his seventies with a shock of grey hair, ushers us inside his family home, to which he alone returned. As he describes his wartime adventures, which include a succession of daring escapes like tunnelling his way under the electrified perimeter fence of the Janowska Camp, and being brutally beaten by the Germans, Dan and I are on the edge of our chairs. It's not just the story that's so extraordinary, or his indomitable courage, it's the cheerful way he tells it, his eyes twinkling with wonder at his own audacity.

He's proud that, after the war, his evidence helped convict Heinen, the commandant of Janowska Camp who got a life sentence. For once Mr Lanier's face darkens. 'He was a monster. He trained dogs to tear people to pieces and said he couldn't have breakfast if he hadn't seen blood.'

Although Mr Lainer didn't know my relatives, he paints a vivid picture of life in Zolkwa before the war, when 5000 Jews lived in the town. Many of them were furriers, and he recalls one called Bratter who was probably related to my grandfather. 'The Jews here were so poor that at Pesach time American relatives used to send them money for *matzohs*. It was a very devout community. My father would have killed me if I hadn't gone to synagogue every Saturday morning!'

He leads the way to the only synagogue still standing, a solid sixteenth century building which was built like a fortress with metre-thick buttressed walls. Inside, Sasha, Dan and I duck to avoid the pigeons as they flap between the crumbling columns and brush against faded Hebrew letters and fragments of carvings. The synagogue is being restored into a Jewish and Ukrainian museum. Pointing to the blackened paintings on the walls, Mr Lainer recalls the day the Nazis arrived in town. 'They brought kegs of petrol and rounded up the Jews into the synagogue to burn them alive, but some of the Jews spoke German. and bribed them to let them go. But they didn't survive for long. Most of them were deported to Belzec.' Today there are only three Jews left in Zolkwa.

He sighs. 'During the war, when Jews jumped off trains bound for Belzec, locals with staves were waiting to bludgeon them and knock the gold teeth out of their heads. Sometimes a three-year-old orphan would be found wandering among the corn, and the village children would point and call, '*Zhid! Zhid!*' and people would turn the child over to the Germans. Dreadful. But you can't generalise. Don't forget that over 3000 Ukrainians hid Jews, and 1060 were shot for helping them.

'Still, there were 60 000 Ukrainian militia who helped the Germans kill Jews. Life has always shown that there are more evil people than good. Our newspapers reported that after the war some Ukrainian war criminals found refuge in Canada and Australia.'

The current upsurge of militant nationalism and the proliferation of anti-Semitic publications since Ukrainian independence worries him. 'Their lies make my hair stand on end, blaming Jewish conspiracies for everything that's wrong with Ukraine, and denying what happened at Auschwitz. Shocking.'

As he shows us proudly around his historic little town with its ramparts and medieval castle, Mr Lainer gives a potted history lesson about the rulers and feudal lords of Zolkwa. Later, as we stroll around the old town square, I feel that I'm seeing the same shady arcades and dimly-lit narrow buildings where my great-grandparents once walked, where my grandfather Bernard went to *cheder*, and where Jewish craftsmen used to cut and stitch their pelts.

A few minutes' drive from the town centre, Mr Lainer leads us to a simple white monument in a woodland clearing, a memorial to the 3500 Jews of Zolkwa murdered by the Nazis in 1943. As I read the touching inscription, I realise that among the dead were some of my relatives. He designed this memorial himself, had it erected, and planted the bright little garden which he still tends.

Dan, who has said little until now, looks at Zygmunt admiringly. 'I like this man,' he tells me. 'He is very enthusiastic. And he speaks Ukrainian.'

Just before we leave Zolkwa, Mr Lainer fills my arms with knobbly cucumbers and bulbous tomatoes which smell of country sunshine, and a jar of blueberries which he assures me will cure Justine's upset stomach. 'When I'm gone,' he says, 'There will be no-one left who saw what happened here.' He presses a letter into my hands. 'You're writing about the Jews of Lwow. I want you to have my sister's last letter from the Ghetto. She was twenty-nine years old and played the violin so beautifully.'

On the drive back to Lviv, I read Genia's letter.

I didn't intend to leave you a letter but Mama won't leave me alone, I have to write a few words. I know that it will upset you even more because our situation is hopeless and it will make you cry. I never imagined when we parted before you went into the army, that instead of welcoming you back, I'd be saying goodbye.

Our situation is hopeless. We are all condemned to death because we're Jews. The only thing we don't know is when the sentence will be carried out. We expect it any minute, any second. Their persecution doesn't let up.

They push us into graves, with such force and speed, and in some cases, while people are still alive. Can you imagine how terrible it is to live with the knowledge that any moment this will happen to me and those dearest to me, while we so desperately want to live and to see you again? Not long ago, we were so happy to receive news of you.

It must be hard for you to understand why we somehow didn't manage to get out of this predicament, but it was impossible. Only Aryan friends could have helped but as you well know, in times of misfortune, everyone abandoned us and everything failed. And if God has abandoned us, what right do we have to blame our friends who would have to risk their own lives to help us? In other words, there is no way out but to wait for our turn, our turn to die. Death will save us from this emotional torture, of witnessing tragedies every day. Because to see orphaned children wandering around the streets without a roof over their heads, barefoot, ragged and hungry, children who have seen their mother or father or brothers and sisters shot, or parents despairing and mad with grief because they don't know where their children have gone, seeing those trains transporting thousands of Jews to their place of eternal rest. Seeing some jumping out of the train to try and save their lives and being shot on the spot. All this creates such confusion that we start wondering whether there is something wrong with us, whether we've gone insane. Even the strongest individuals collapse emotionally under these conditions.

You know that our father was a remarkably energetic, enterprising, optimistic man, who saw the world through rose-coloured glasses. You wouldn't recognise him. He has grown fearful, depressed, and tired of living. He only wants to die but the poor thing has to keep working hard because things are terribly expensive and we often go hungry, but we're not the only ones.

Mama has had a fight with God, because He refuses to perform any miracles so she is constantly on bad terms with Him. She is upset with him that he makes us suffer like this, and she weeps that maybe she'll never see you again. She weeps about Zunio, too, what will become of him, and goes around in circles.

Zunio [their brother] is also suffering terribly, he's very nervous, but keeps quiet, too proud to complain or make a fool of himself, and anyway he has a very reserved nature. He is so beautiful and so good, you should see how the poor thing works as a glasscutter and gives Mama every cent he earns, my heart breaks when I look at him, so young, so talented, so noble and all this will be wasted. I can't understand why my heart doesn't literally burst with grief. He won't be able to escape death but I'm sure that he will fight for his life, he won't go to the altar like a sacrificial lamb.

I, who had the weakest nerves, am today the most controlled, the most resistant to suffering because I have already suffered so much in my life that death does not frighten me as much as it does others. If only the stones on the road, the blades of grass could talk, what stories you would hear. Well, that's enough of all this.

The most important thing is what I'm going to say now. If we die, which I think is inevitable, I would like you at least to benefit by all these years of our work, so they won't be in vain. I leave you all the most important documents, mortgage papers, our parents' marriage certificate, maybe they'll be useful, as well as an inventory of things which I left with some of our friends, your clothes *among them, which you will certainly need. Olga, God willing, which I fervently pray, will give you exact details, and to her I entrust this mission.*

Apart from that, I have no more to add. I bid you goodbye with sorrow and an aching heart and hope that fate will be kinder to you, that our suffering will save you from all misfortune, and if God forbid, you don't find us, don't grieve, control yourself and try to live the rest of your life in peace. I advise you to sell everything and go far away from this accursed place.

Be well, and don't worry, time heals all wounds of the heart, and your pain will diminish with time. I send you my love,

Genia

Before we leave Lviv, there's one more place I have to visit. When I mention Piaskowa Gora, Sasha and Dan shake their heads. They've never heard of it. But Leon Plager knows. My legs are unsteady as I climb out of the car and walk up the sandy path to a small clearing at the bottom of a squat hill. 'In 1941, they used to bring Jews here by the truckload, shoot them, and either they buried them in shallow pits right here or took the bodies to the Lysienskiego Forest and threw them into mass graves there,' Leon explains.

This is the place my father mentioned in his memoirs. Concealed by trees on one side and the hill on the other, the slope must have been a perfect place for mass killings. I think of my grandfather Bernard standing here while some thug blasted his life away without a qualm. I sit on a tree stump and cry for this gentle man who loved me, whom I never got to know. I'd like Leon to say Kaddish for my grandfather but he shakes his head. 'Not here. Later. At Janowska Camp.'

A few minutes later we are standing outside Janowska Camp which has become a men's prison. A small stone memorial mentions that 200 000 Jews were murdered here. In the annals of man's inhumanity to man, few places match the bestiality of this camp where naked prisoners were wrapped in barbed wire and left outside in barrels of cold water which turned to ice during the night, and where new arrivals had to run the gauntlet of snarling dogs whose razor-sharp teeth were trained to tear off men's genitals and women's breasts. The commandant's favourite sport was throwing Jewish babies up in the air and shooting them like moving targets, to the glee of his three-year-old daughter. When I peer through the gate, I'm shocked to see prison guards training German shepherd dogs inside these grounds.

As we stand beside the torpid stream which once ran red with blood, Leon takes out his handkerchief, knots each corner, places it on his head, and intones the Kaddish prayer for my grandfather. Tears stream down our faces. This is probably the first time that anyone has said Kaddish for my grandfather. He died so brutally and quicklime was his only shroud. No sign marks the place where he fell, no stone marks the place where he lies. It feels important to offer this prayer in gratitude for the gift of his life and to commit his soul to his forefathers.

Back in the centre of Lviv, as we pass the lively flower market where babushkas in patterned kerchiefs gossip beside bright bunches of spicy carnations and yellow roses, Leon Plager points to a manhole beneath my feet. 'This is where a group of Jews survived the war by hiding in the sewers,' he says. Above us rises the bronze cupola of St Bernardine's Church.

I know the extraordinary story of those sewer survivors because one of them later married my second cousin, Marian

Kwasniewski, Hela and Jozek's son. Kristine was nine years old when she emerged from that manhole after fourteen months of hell. Kristine is a cosmetic dentist in Manhattan, an attractive woman in her fifties, who told me her story on a pleasant autumn evening in New York, on her way to a jazz club.

Before she and her family descended into the sewers, they lived in the Lwiw ghetto. During the day, she had to look after her four-year-old brother. 'Whenever I heard the soldiers approaching, I hid him in a suitcase, pushed it under the bed, and hid behind the door, under my mother's dressing gown. I knew how long he could stay in the suitcase before suffocating, and counted the minutes in my head. I held my breath while they looked around. Luckily he never made a sound.' She was seven years old at the time.

Kristine remembered vividly the day when they squeezed into the narrow tunnel her father had helped dig, into the dark, terrifying subterranean world of the sewers. Most of their group died of drowning, starvation or disease, but Kristine's family and eight others survived thanks to a Ukrainian sewer maintenance worker. Leopold Socha had made it his mission to keep them alive.

My cousin will never forget the miraculous day in 1944, after fourteen months of this subhuman existence, when their saviour hoisted her up on his shoulders and carried her out of the sewer. 'At first I couldn't see anything at all,' she says. 'Everything looked crimson. I was blinded by the sun.'

Leon Plager leads us to a cafeteria where a jolly woman in a sky-blue lace cap serves us Ukrainian borscht, cabbage rolls stuffed with *kasha*, potato pancakes with sour cream, and minced meat patties. But I can't get the story of the sewers out of my mind. Every corner of this lovely city holds tragic memories.

That evening the telephone rings in our hotel room. It's

Leon. The researcher has found more documents and we're to go the archive office in the morning. I toss in bed for hours, restless in the warm summer air, too excited to sleep. That night Justine becomes violently ill. Something has upset her system, which seems to be attempting to expel everything she has ingested ever since we arrived. Considering what she has absorbed in the past few days, this isn't surprising. Absorbed in my search and my pain, I haven't paid enough attention to the emotional impact that our search is having on my daughter. It's been draining and harrowing for me, but I realise now that it's been devastating for the sensitive young woman who has been thrust into this maelstrom of hatred and violence.

By early morning, she's still sick, and I'm just about to pick up the receiver to call Michael in Australia for some medical advice when the phone shrills. By an amazing coincidence, it's him. It's comforting to hear his concerned, loving voice and reconnect with normal life for a few minutes.

Leaving Justine to rest, I meet Leon Plager who can hardly wait to thrust a sheaf of documents into my hands. One is an application to the municipal council made by my grandfather in 1932, asking for permission to renovate his apartment in Sloneczna Street. It's signed by him, and contains not only his date of birth but also the names of his parents. I hold this document as if it were a priceless heirloom, and read it over and over again. He was born Berish Bratter, in 1883, to Ester Stalmeister and Izrael Bratter in Zolkwa. I can't believe my luck.

Among these archival treasures is a plan of their apartment which shows how they combined two flats on the right side of the stairs. I remember my mother telling me that while everyone else had gone on holidays she had stayed behind to supervise the renovations. As usual, she was the responsible, unselfish one.

'Wait, there's something else for you!' Leon cries, hardly

able to contain his own excitement. It takes some time for the significance of this document to sink in. It says that Bernard Bratter owned this building together with Mrs Szwagron. I remember my mother mentioning this woman whom she didn't like. Leon points to the stamp of the government archive office. 'This is proof of ownership. If the Ukrainian government ever agrees to compensate the original owners who were dispossessed by the communists, then you'll be able to make a claim,' he explains. I didn't come looking for proof of ownership and I'm not interested in making claims, but I'm thrilled to have this document because it proves something that's far more important to me. It's a sign that my grandparents once lived normal lives here, and it brings them much closer to me.

On Friday night I walk to synagogue with a group of American visitors. The idea of a Shabbat service in Lviv sounds as far-fetched as morning tea on Mars. As we step outside the hotel, Valek, our Jewish guide, warns the men not to wear their *kippahs* until they are almost there. 'It's better not to attract attention. People might shout abuse or even throw stones.'

From the women's gallery, I gaze around. This used to be a progressive synagogue, so maybe my mother had her first wedding here. The restored ceiling is brightly painted with lions, birds and Star of David motifs on an azure background, but the ceiling is perforated by gaping holes made by Nazi bullets, in a stark reminder of the past. This house of prayer escaped the fate of most other synagogues because the Germans used it as their stables.

Downstairs, about thirty men sit on simple wooden chairs in the centre of a big empty space. Most of them have recently come to Lviv from Russia, where religion was outlawed and persecuted, so they're not familiar with the prayers, and Rabbi

Bald walks amongst them, prompting and teaching. Moty Bald is a figure straight out of Isaac Bashevis Singer. Short and portly, with a bushy tar-black beard, he wears a long black satin capote and black circular fur hat which, from this angle, makes him look like a mushroom.

As the service draws to a close, the rabbi links hands with the men who form a circle and sing traditional Sabbath songs. Suddenly everything blurs and I feel overwhelmed by all that I've experienced here. After the service, we walk around the corner to have Shabbat dinner with the rabbi. Two flights up a dark staircase, a door opens and Moty Bald is pumping the men's hands and greeting us with his strong Bronx accent.

This is his first rabbinical post, one that he euphemistically describes as a challenge. This tiny congregation is struggling. There is no kosher meat, no Chevra Kadisha and no consecrated Jewish cemetery. Moty never walks outside without a bodyguard. 'One night, a gang of Ukrainian youths with swastikas on their armbands banged on the synagaogue door and threatened to knock the door down and and kill everyone inside. Luckily we had security guards to deal with them,' he says.

While Moty entertains us with Talmudic stories and anecdotes, his hospitable wife Surele runs to and from the tiny kitchen, plying us with chicken soup, gefillte fish, chopped eggplant, pickled cucumbers, roast chicken, pears, apples, apricots, and strawberry mousse. When we're ready to leave, Valek suggests walking back to the hotel by a different route. 'In case someone saw us enter and is lying in wait,' he says. As we turn into the darkened street, a car parked on the pavement begins to roll towards us and only stops at the last moment as we jump away. Was it deliberate, or are we becoming paranoid?

Just before we leave Lviv, Dan and Sasha come to say goodbye. They've been obliging and caring companions, and we've grown fond of them both. There has been a glimmer of understanding between us, and I'm sorry that we have to leave just as the door has begun to open. When he bends down to kiss my cheek, Dan's eyes are shining with tears.

CHAPTER 42

Back in Poland, Justine and I meet our Polish guide Waclaw who has the revved-up intensity of those consumed by an angry passion. In a secluded corner of south-west Poland, where the trees are barely fifty years old, we stand at the site of the extermination camp of Belzec while Waclaw points to the small memorial erected during the communist regime. 'My God! It makes me furious that this plaque doesn't mention Jews when 600 000 of the 601 500 people murdered here were Jews!' Two of them were Uncle Stasiek and Aunty Karola, who scribbled her last note on the way to this death factory whose stench they must have smelt long before the cattle truck brought them to their final destination.

Although Waclaw is Catholic, he's more passionate about Polish anti-Semitism than most Jews. He became obsessed with the subject twenty years ago when he escorted a group of tourists to Auschwitz. 'I was fascinated to learn about a people who had contributed so much to Poland over the ages, yet had no future in this country. Whenever you want to say something bad about somebody here, you say that he's a Jew. When I wouldn't go to religious classes at school, the other boys called me a Jew!'

Through an idyllic countryside of tawny haystacks rolled into giant wheels, and gently undulating fields where sunflowers turn their smiling faces to the sky, we come to Zamosc where

Jews have lived since 1588. Past the spectacular town square with its vivdly painted facades, we walk down Zamenhof Street, the old Jewish quarter, and Waclaw points out where the synagogue and *mikveh* used to be. Before the war, Jews made up almost half the population of this city, but the Germans killed most of them and the synagogue has become a public library.

In Lublin, which during the sixteenth century was a major centre of Jewish learning, the imposing *yeshiva* with its solid columns is now a medical school. The rabbi who erected it in 1930 had a dream that all over the world Jews should read the same page of the Talmud on the same day, but few of the students who lounge in the spacious lecture hall are aware of its spiritual past. As we drive away, I notice that someone has scrawled the word '*Jude*' inside a Star of David on the ochre-painted wall.

A plaque on a corner building in town commemorates the site of the first Jewish committee organised by survivors in 1944, and I wonder whether my parents came here when we arrived from Piszczac in 1945. All I remember of Lublin was returning home from preschool wearing a pinafore with a big pocket, in which I kept my uneaten liverwurst sandwich.

A young Polish woman has joined our city tour. Magdalena befriended one member of our group that morning and has come to meet the rest of us. Her interest in Jewish topics, and the fact that she used to work in the Jewish museum, prompts me to ask whether anyone in her family was Jewish. After a momentary but telling hesitation, she says, 'Actually, I don't think so. But my grandmother had some Jewish friends.' Centuries of Jewish blood runs silently and secretly through millions of Polish veins and I'm sure that hers are amongst them.

In town after town we learn about the destruction of the

Jews as we visit the unmarked sites where for centuries they prayed, shopped and worked. Waclaw points out marketplaces, kosher stalls, *mikvehs* and synagogues. Justine has been very quiet until now but suddenly she bursts out, 'This only happened fifty years ago but it's like visiting the ruins of some vanished civilisation and being told that once the ancient Babylonians lived here.'

Majdanek concentration camp is a fitting stop on this tour of a vanished people. The ashes of the bodies cindered in its crematoria were intended by the thrifty Nazis as fertiliser to nourish German crops. Under the gigantic dome which crouches like an evil flying saucer over tonnes of human ashes that didn't reach their destination, a sign says, 'Let our fate be a warning to you.' I feel as if I am on a tour of hell.

Next day Justine and I set off for Nowy Sacz in search of information about my great-grandparents, Matus and Rywka Baldinger. Our driver, Stanislaw Stetsko, is a middle-aged man with a ruddy face, knobbly features and a personality which makes the air around him crackle with energy. As we drive past spruce trees whose branches flare out like skirts just above the ground, he wants to know why I am pursuing this family quest. 'Bravo! Oh, bravo!' he exclaims in his booming voice, clapping his hands when I tell him that I'm planning to write a book. 'It's fantastic that you're writing about your people. There is no culture like yours. Whatever we have achieved, it's because of your people. Look at Israel, look what they've done with that strip of desert in fifty short years. We'll never amount to anything in this country unless we learn to think like you.'

This excessive praise makes me feel uncomfortable. It's stereotyping of a positive kind, but stereotyping just the same. I can't resist saying, 'To think like us, you need 2000 years of persecution.'

He drops his voice. 'You're right. So many of you have died right in this country. We Poles should bow our heads in shame. We have blood on our hands. Jewish blood. We sold you out for a few coins. It's not a nice thing to say, dear lady, but what's true is true.' With shaking fingers he pulls out a cigarette from his shirt pocket. 'I'm trying to quit, but I get so upset about these things, I just have to smoke!'

Beside the road, sunflowers tower above a stubbly field, their cheerful faces like good deeds in an evil world. As we pass a village, Stanislaw points to a small house on the curve of the road. 'There used to be a synagogue there,' he says. 'Before the war, Piecz was a typical Jewish town.' By now this is a familiar refrain. I realise that the Jews were annihilated twice in Poland: once by the Nazis, and the second time by their countrymen who covered up their traces, as if they'd never existed.

As we approach Nowy Sacz, the landscape becomes hilly, and simple wooden huts nestle in the valley carved by the Dunajec River. This is the homeland of the Baldingers. In the rundown cottage which houses the state archives, we find the director, Tadeusz Duda, a thin elderly man with one lank strand of grey hair optimistically combed across his bald head. His manner is brusque but his eyes gleam with the thrill of the hunt when I explain my quest. 'We have very few Jewish records left, but let me see,' he barks, and ushers us into a boxlike room which is filled from floor to ceiling with bound records, tomes and population lists, and exudes the sweet, papery smell of old documents. His sharp eyes quickly find what he's looking for and he pulls out three fraying volumes which contain the Jewish population lists for 1870, 1900 and 1910. My heart is beating fast. Surely one of these will record my great-grandparents.

Hands trembling with excitement, Justine and I start scanning the hand-written lists page by page, but although I feel a surge of anticipation each time I come across a Baldinger, to my disappointment I find no mention of Matus, Rywka or their children in any of them. Before I leave, Mr Duda hands me a booklet he has written about the Jews of Nowy Sacz which gives me some insight into the life my antecedents must have led in this pretty little town. Later, walking around the square, I try to visualise it when Jews baked bread, stored flour, sold fabrics, fitted and turned timber, stitched suits and served beer and vodka in the bustling little shops and crowded workrooms.

Before leaving Nowy Sacz, I visit the tomb of the Sanzer Rebbe. To the end of his life, my grandfather Daniel used to go on pilgrimage to the sage's grave on the anniversary of his death, setting out from Krakow and crossing the Tatras on foot. At the end of the overgrown cemetery stands the Ohel, a small cement chapel which contains the tomb of the Sanzer Rebbe. It feels exciting to stand in the place where my grandfather and his own father once prayed and left their *kvitls*, notes requesting the soul of the departed to intercede for them. Standing here, I feel a sense of continuity, but I don't share their faith, so I don't leave a *kvitl* for the Sanzer Rebbe.

Driving away from Nowy Sacz, I feel disheartened that I didn't find any trace of the Baldingers. Next day we are due to visit Szczakowa, the home of my grandmother Lieba's parents, the Spiras, and I'm beginning to wonder whether it's worth going.

My doubts vanish as soon as we arrive in this sleepy township. As we drive along the dusty narrow road that leads to the centre of town, I have a feeling of affinity for this place that I can't explain. Today our driver is Marek, a young man with a chubby face and gentle manner who is delighted to be part of our search for the past. When we see a fruit stall by the roadside, he asks the vendor, a woman with short bleached hair and a sky-blue crocheted top, for information about the Spira family who lived here before the war. 'I don't know anything about them, but Mrs Potocka probably will, she's over seventy,' the woman says and leads us into a building whose floor and walls are a dismal beige.

A frail woman with white hair slowly opens the door. Sensing Mrs Potocka's mistrust, I assure her that we haven't come to claim anything, all we want is information about our family. We sit around a small table in a room where the matrimonial bed almost fills the room and the walls are covered with large religious pictures.

She remembers a Spira who had a hardware shop in town. I know that this was Herman Spira, one of Lieba's brothers, who took over the family business from Abraham. Then she holds up a gnarled hand. 'Wait, there was one *Zhidek* ...' At the sound of this offensive word for Jew, I recoil, and feel Marek's attentive gaze rest on my face.

Then Mrs Potocka says, 'That *Zydoweczka*, Milkowa, she'd know something about those people, wouldn't she?' Again that contemptuous diminutive, this time referring to a Jewess. 'This used to be the Jewish area,' she tells me, 'there was a dairy across the road and all those houses were Jewish.' Then she recalls an old rhyme. 'The Jews used to say, "*Wasze ulice, nasze kamienice*", meaning "You own the streets, but we own the buildings." Well, now the buildings are ours as well!' she chuckles and her eyes gleam with triumph.

All this is fragmentary and frustrating, and I still haven't found any trace of my great-grandparents. 'Why don't you try Jaworzno?' suggests the fruit seller who hasn't left our side. 'You might find out something in the municipal office there.'

In Jaworzno we are sent from the architecture division to the geo-demographic section and on to the survey department.

At each one, the clerks seem keen to help us, but they need time, and each one tells us to come back later in the afternoon. By the time we leave the last office, I'm so confused that I can't remember where I'm supposed to return, what time, or why. Fortunately Marek has it all under control. He remembers which offices we have to return to, the order in which we need to see them, and what time each of them closes for the day. 'While we're waiting, let's go to the court archives,' he says. 'Maybe they'll have records of some legal transactions.'

I look at him with admiration. This young man, who was assigned to us today by chance because his older brother couldn't come, hasn't missed a beat. In his quiet, focused way he has made my quest his own and gone about it with patience and tenacity that exceed mine.

We find the court archives tucked away in an alley beside the small park where clerks and salesgirls are enjoying the sunshine on benches under the trees. The director, in a cream cardigan, white blouse and a businesslike expression, knows exactly where to look. She pulls a thick volume off the shelf in the adjoining room, flicks through the hand-written entries, and pushes it towards me. As I look, the words seem to be jumping off the page. The document concerns my great-grandmother Ryfka Spira who died in a room on Agnieszka Street in Krakow in 1917 after her landlady cast the evil eye on her.

Listed here in painstaking copperplate handwriting are the beneficiaries of her estate, all her sons and daughters, including my grandmother Lieba, who is listed as Leonora Baldinger. As Ryfka's oldest son, Judah, had died by then, the property was divided between her remaining eleven children and six grand-children. From a later entry it appears that after the death of my great-grandfather Abraham in 1931, most of the heirs sold their share of the estate to their brother Herman, whose daughters Lola and Sabina eventually inherited the lot.

On my return to Australia, I find out that my father's cousin Lola Birner, who had migrated to Melbourne after the war, was Herman's daughter who had inherited the estate. It's ironic to think that I travelled to the other side of the globe in search of information which I could have obtained simply by going to Melbourne. Unfortunately, by the time I return to Australia, Lola is dead and her son and daughter can't tell me anything about the house in Szczakowa.

Now it's time to return to the municipal office and Marek checks his notes to make sure we do the rounds of the offices in the right order. In Room 26, the director of the geo-demographic section beckons us inside with an expression that indicates success. I hold my breath while he tells us Ryfka and Abraham Spira's old address.

Running up the stairs to the next office, I learn that Abraham Spira owned Lot 269. The clerk scribbles this information on a piece of paper and we rush to the survey office where old maps are kept. This is like hunting for buried treasure, and the possibility that any minute now I will find the house where my great-grandparents used to live makes it hard to stand still. The researcher takes out a frayed old volume, looks up Lot 269, and then unfurls a more recent map and points. I feel like jumping up and down like a child when she says, 'Here it is!' and points to 11-13 Parkowa Street.

Clutching my great-grandparents' address, we rush back to Szczakowa. A parade of houses in Parkowa Street faces a small park. There's no trace of the pine woods and sand dunes that were once a feature of this little town which still has the leisurely air of forgotten corners where no-one hurries. Number thirteen is still a one-storey building just as it has always been, but it looks dingy with dark green window frames set into a grey cement facade and a small corrugated iron awning over the entrance.

Small boys kicking a ball in the park opposite look curiously in our direction, and an old man stares out of a window. At the back of the house a few women and children are sitting under an overhanging iron roof. As usual, Marek takes the initiative and in his friendly way explains why we are here. The old woman nods. Yes, a family called Spira used to live here. The house is still the same except that it has been divided into four flats. One of the young women toting a baby on her hip invites me inside to have a look.

Beyond the tiny kitchen, a large bright room faces the street. It's a strange feeling, to stand inside the house where my great-grandparents and their twelve children lived so many years ago, where my grandmother Lieba was born and raised. I feel like the descendant of a noble family visiting the ancestral home and finding that it has been taken over by squatters and allowed to moulder and decay.

Someone mentions that the synagogue used to be around the corner. But as we walk under a canopy of chestnut branches in this leafy street, there's no sign that a synagogue ever stood here. I'm almost ready to get back into the car and drive away when a tall man with iron-grey hair and military bearing emerges from a house nearby, strides towards us, introduces himself as Tadeusz Dziekonski, and asks what we are looking for.

The synagogue used to be right here, he says, pointing to his own house, a flat-roofed building faced with knobbly aggregate. It's hard to visualise that this is where my great-grandfather strode that Saturday morning when his son-in-law Daniel was called to the Torah, and where my grandparents Lieba and Daniel stood under the *chuppah* on their wedding day. While Mr Dziekonski was building his house in 1960, he came across the foundations of the synagogue which had been destroyed during the war, and the plumbing of the ritual bathhouse.

Then he says, 'Perhaps you can help me. I've been looking for the sons of a Jew called Bijumin whom I saw being shot by Ukrainians near Lwow in 1942. If they're still alive, they'd want to know where their father was killed. I knew the whole family. While the father was hiding from the Germans, he used to come to us for food. Please come inside for a glass of tea, I have so many stories to tell,' he says and, taking my arm, ushers us inside.

While his wife brings us tea and homemade apricot cake, Tadeusz Dziekonski tells us his story. 'When they started on the Jews, my father told me to watch and remember what was happening to them, so that I would be a witness. And after they'd finished with the Jews, they started on us Poles,' he sighs.

Then he picks up a sheaf of papers he has written and begins to read. He recounts atrocities that befell his own family at the hands of Ukrainians, about children butchered with axes and old people burned alive in their homes. My knuckles are white from gripping the table and Marek's face is the colour of cigarette ash. In his succinct style, Mr Dziekonski describes the outbreak of war in the east in 1939. 'Sad news from the Polish front. Our army retreats under intense Nazi offensive. General mobilisation. Conscription of horses, equipment for the army. Nazi planes fly overhead. Eastern skies glow red in the evening. Poland is burning. Ukrainian nationalists are shouting at the top of their voices, "Death to the Poles, death to the Poles, death to the Jewish communists." Tragedy is approaching.

'In the spring of 1942 they are murdering the Jews of Hoszcza. Some escape to the fields but are caught and killed.

We help, we hide some Jewish families. We help a family called Bijumin from Tuczyn. As he was coming to us for food, he was shot dead near the village of Woskodawa near Czudnica. In our village they killed a Jewish family. An elderly couple, David and his wife, and their daughter, son-in-law, and two small children. They hacked them with axes. The children's mother, badly injured, got away and hanged herself in despair.

'In the spring of 1942 the Germans murdered 16 000 Jews in Rowno. That was so terrible that I can't forget it to this day. The Jews had to dig pits, and then they machine-gunned them. Entire families with their children. Dreadful screams and despair from those poor innocent people. They covered up the pits with all the dead and wounded. People say that long afterwards, the earth heaved, because they'd buried the living along with the dead. I know where this happened. I feel very sorry for the Jewish race and pray for them.

'In 1943 gangs of Ukrainian nationalists murdered and set fire day and night. Night and day, Wolyn burned. Boleslaw Slowinski and his wife were murdered with axes, while their six children aged from one to twelve were speared on rakes and, amid terrible screaming, thrown into a cart. They drove the injured children past the village of Korosciatyn and set them on fire in a wooden hut. The road on which the cart travelled was soaked in blood.

'At the end of July 1943 I was approaching our house one evening when I heard shots and saw skeins of smoke. That day Ukrainian murderers killed my father Stanislaw Dziekonski, forty-three, my mother aged thirty-five, my seventeen-year-old brother Stefan, my ten-year-old sister Adela, my grandmother Jadwiga Dziekonska, and her son Jozef, aged fourteen. From his hiding place in the attic, my grandfather could hear my mother's voice pleading with one of the thugs. "Ivan, we used to be friends, at least spare the children." But after murdering them, they set fire to our house. My grandmother leapt off the roof not to be burned alive and they shot her. My brother Stefan was hiding in the cellar when it went up in flames, and couldn't get out. The neighbours heard his screams coming from our burning house. Only my grandfather survived.

'When Ukrainians dug up the ruins of the house, they found my father's charred pistol and his radio receiver, and handed them in to the Gestapo in Hoszcza. The Gestapo came to arrest me. I was tortured in Rowno jail. The Nazis wanted to know who my father was in contact with. My answer was always the same. I don't know. I was sent to prison in Graz. At the end of 1943 I escaped from the prison to Yugoslavia and fought with a partisan group led by Marshal Tito.

'In the summer of 1944, a gang of Ukrainian thugs murdered my grandfather. They choked him to death with a rope. I don't know to this day where they buried him. Five of these bandits who murdered my family came from our village but I didn't denounce them to the Russian court.

'I have forgiven the murderers. Let God judge them.'

When Mr Dziekonski finishes his harrowing family history, we sit in silence, as if struck on the head by a mallet. My mouth is dry, Marek is staring into space and shakes his head from time to time. He looks shell-shocked.

As far as Szczakowa is concerned, Mr Dziekonski says that in 1942 the Germans hanged about a dozen people from the trees near the Spiras' house. They ordered the residents to watch the execution, and apparently several members of the Spira family were among them. A few days later the Germans deported all the remaining Jews of Szczakowa to an unknown destination from which very few returned.

When we say goodbye on the footpath outside the house that was a synagogue in my great-grandfather's time, Mr Dziekonski takes my hand and says, 'I have a lot of sympathy for Jewish people, for all you have suffered. Don't forget I was a witness.'

In spite of the horror of Mr Dziekonski's story, I feel uplifted by his dignity and forgiving spirit. For centuries this country has been a battleground whose fields, watered by more blood than rain, have nurtured ancient hatreds. Jews have not had a monopoly on suffering, grief and loss.

Before we drive away, I look back at the leafy street where the synagogue and *mikveh* stood, just a short stroll from the house on Parkowa Street. If I close my eyes, I can see a dapper white-haired gentleman in top hat and patent leather shoes like mirrors, striding ahead of his wife in a flowered hat with feathers, her long full skirt rustling as she tries to keep up with him as they walk to the synagogue on Kilinskiego Street for the marriage of their daughter Lieba to Daniel Baldinger. In this forgotten country town, I've found important pieces of the mosaic.

CHAPTER 43

Outside Krakow's Jagellonian University, students have set up makeshift book stalls against the buttresses jutting out onto the pavement. As Marek and I walk along these crooked streets which have been crammed with shops, workrooms and guilds since the Middle Ages, I crane my neck to look at carved reliefs, weathered oak gates, and stone archways, as wide-eyed as a child who has just stepped into the pages of a well-loved storybook.

The Glowny Rynek is a Renaissance square few cities in the world can equal. Dizzy with remembrance of things past, I hardly notice the swarthy gypsies and their tousled children whose wheedling voices beg for coins. Under those long arcades of the medieval cloth hall, the Sukiennice, I used to trot beside my mother so many years ago, licking ice cream flattened between two crisp wafers. In between the vivid flower stalls, children are chasing pigeons which swoop down to pick up crumbs and fly away. Horse *doroskys* with worn upholstery clop across the square while their drivers scan passers-by looking for tourists. Beneath the memorial to Poland's great poet Adam Mickiewicz, young girls and boys in jeans are lolling on the steps, arguing heatedly about the political situation.

High above the square, a tiny window opens in the tower of the Mariacki Church and the bugler blows his cornet. For an instant the high-pitched sound pierces the air. I know that it will stop abruptly, leaving the unfinished note quivering in the summer air, but when it does, I still feel cheated. It's as though some promise hasn't been fulfilled.

At the far end of the square, Marek and I sit at a round table outside the Wierzynek Restaurant, a former nobleman's villa where my parents once celebrated special occasions. Its walls are still adorned with statues, suits of armour, emblems and trophies, and while we sip our coffee, obsequious waiters in tails weave among the tables with silver platters.

Marek's gentle face looks troubled. 'When we were in Szczakowa yesterday, you looked upset when that old woman used the word "Zhidek". Why?' Although he's so perceptive, he can't understand my revulsion at this word for Jew. He doesn't feel its contemptuous connotation. Before we realise it, we're plunged into a discussion about anti-Semitism. He thinks it only started with Hitler during the war, so as delicately as I can, I tell him about official discrimination, university quotas and right-wing attacks on Jews in Poland throughout the 1930s. He's shocked when I tell him about my relatives who were blackmailed or turned over to the Gestapo by fellow Poles during the war. Like most of his generation, he knows very little about the long, sad history of the Jews in Poland.

As he listens, I compliment him on his open-mindedness. It can't be easy to hear this painful history. He's obviously mulling something over while we cross the small cobbled passageway beside the church because he suddenly asks, 'How come there are Jews and Christians anyway? What's the connection between them? When did it happen?' I explain that Jesus was a Jew, as were his apostles and disciples who formed a new sect because most of the Jews didn't accept Jesus as the Messiah. To validate the new religion, their followers began to vilify the old one. Marek is as fascinated as a schoolboy who has suddenly begun to grasp a complex theorem, but the incredulity on his face disturbs me. How can I expect the truth about the Jews to be told in a country where an intelligent man in his thirties has never been told that Jesus was a Jew?

This conversation comes to mind several years later when I read a news item in a Sydney newspaper which astounds and excites me. During his Christmas message in December 1997, the Pope said, 'Whoever meets Jesus Christ meets Judaism.' Karol Wojtyla, who was once Bishop of Krakow and helped Jews during the Holocaust, described Judaism as Christianity's older brother and Christianity as an offshoot of the trunk of King David. He said that it was time that the Catholic Church recognised its responsibility in fostering the anti-Semitism which had made the Holocaust possible, and urged reconciliation between Catholics and Jews. As the first step in this process Catholic bishops lit Chanukkah candles in the Vatican for the first time. One month later, as a result of his directive, special masses were held in Poland to mark the first 'Day of Judaism' ever held. I wonder whether Marek attended this mass, and whether he too remembered our conversation that shimmering summer afternoon in Krakow's Glowny Rynek.

As Marek and I turn into Florianska Street and stroll down this long cobbled street which leads to the city walls, we pass number ten where I used to live. 'Let's go in!' he says and we run up the shallow stairs of the curving staircase I remember so well. A moment later he's explaining to the woman at the door of our old flat why we've come, and she invites us inside.

I stand in a large sunny room with rugs on the floor and tapestries on the wall, so different from the sparsely furnished room I remember. Just here, against this wall, stood my small iron bed where I lay ill with mumps while my father invented stories about benevolent elves who lived inside our tiled stove. I remember sitting at the window on dark winter afternoons, looking down on the red trams clanging along the street below, and reading about unwanted step-children, spoilt princesses and homeless orphans as I escaped into the comforting world of books where mysteries were always solved and people lived happily ever after. It was in that room that I found out I was Jewish.

We wander around the old Kazimierz district where ghosts seem to hover above the marketplace and chant prayers in the recesses of old synagogues and prayer houses. There's Plac Estery, where on market days housewives inspected carp wriggling in wooden barrels, pinched the yellow flesh of the chickens in the poultry stalls and weighed moist farm cheeses in their practised hands.

Instead of bustling merchants, cheeky hawkers and gimlet-eyed housewives, today Kazimierz has the orderly atmosphere of a museum. The unruly technicolour world of the past has faded into a neat pastel print. Ajzyk's Synagogue, where a few years ago I heard those phantasmal voices, has become the headquarters of the Research Centre of Jewish History and Culture. Jewish bookshops, kosher restaurants and nightclubs have mushroomed all over this area. At night, Szeroka Street resounds with sentimental Yiddish folk tunes played by gentile musicians who strike up their fiddles loudly enough to wake my sixteenth century ancestor Nathan Nata Spira, buried in the small cemetery across the road. Kazimierz has become the theme park of a vanished people.

And it isn't just Kazimierz. All over Krakow, as I look into the shops and read the posters, it looks as though the people have become obsessed with Jewish music, Jewish cookery and Jewish literature. Now that there are so few Jews left, everyone is bewitched by Jewish culture. As Justine puts it, it's like our fascination with the dinosaur.

At Aunty Slawa's house for our farewell dinner, I'm thrilled to hear that my cousin Mario has named his second son

Daniel. After his confused religious upbringing, I marvel that he feels the family bond strongly enough to call his son after his Orthodox Jewish grandfather. Slawa is delighted about this, but she thinks that giving the baby David as a second name is overdoing it. 'It's too Jewish,' she says.

It's only recently that she has told her older grandson Tomek about his Jewish background. It happened in summer, when she took Tomek, a lively, bright-eyed ten-year-old, to a holiday camp run by the Lauder Foundation which teaches children about their Jewish heritage. 'That's when I told him,' she tells me. 'When Mario arrived to take us back to Krakow, Tomek said, "Daddy, Grandma is a bit Jewish. What about you?" Mario replied, "Well, what do you think?" Tomek thought about it for a moment and said, "So that means I am too." '

On Saturday morning I attend Shabbat service at the Remu Synagogue. In Sydney, I never walk to *shule*, but here in Krakow it seems important to do things properly. In Miodowa Street, I walk past number nineteen, the handsome corner house where my grandparents lived when they were first married and where Daniel told his apprehensive girl-bride stories from the Talmud to while away the long childless evenings. Aunty Lunia must have stood right here on the pavement as a child, watching wide-eyed as the brides, like fairy princesses, arrived in carriages drawn by horses. A few doors further on, I see graffiti scrawled on a cement wall. The words '*Jude Raus*', 'Jews get out!', inside a Star of David.

Inside the synagogue where visitors far outnumber the locals, I sit with the women behind a white net curtain that separates the sexes. This tiny congregation has no rabbi, and on the *bimah*, men in prayer shawls conduct the service. As their voices chant familiar Hebrew prayers and melodies, tears splash down my face. The young Dutch woman sitting beside me gives me a sympathetic look but she's not Jewish, so how could she understand what I feel when I sit in this synagogue after all that's happened here?

Before leaving Krakow I visit the family memorial once again. As I walk along the silent paths, I notice that the graves have sunk lower; they sag and tilt more than ever, and the spaces in between are overgrown with long grasses and tangled vines. As my eye rests on each name, my heart aches for each of them in turn. Tusiek Selinger. Lieba and Rozia. Jerzy and Rutka. Of them I haven't found a single trace, nor of my mother's brother Izio, nor her sister Hania. Thanks to Justine's influence I realise that Hania is not mentioned by name at all, only as the wife of Adolf Korner who wasn't even related to us. I feel upset that in death this aunt whom my mother adored has been relegated to an appendage, as someone's wife. Karola, too, is only mentioned as Stanislaw Neufeld's wife. Only Tusiek's remains and Daniel's are buried in this ground. The bones and ashes of all the others lie in unmarked, unknown places.

At the top of the memorial Daniel Baldinger's inscription is incised in Hebrew. My grandfather was buried here before the war, in the same grave as Lieba's own grandfather who died in 1872. One day Aunty Slawa will lie here too, next to her beloved father, as she has always wished.

I pull out the feathery grasses that grow around the base and brush away the dead leaves. Then I place four little stones on the base of the memorial, one each for Michael, Justine, Jonathan and me, and walk away from that silent, dark path where the sun seldom shines.

CHAPTER 44

As the car bumps along the country road, I hardly blink for fear of missing a single detail of this landscape. I know I've travelled this way before, seen these tawny haystacks rolled like giant snails on stubbly fields, the cherry orchards soaking up the summer heat and the roadside shrines of suffering Christ garlanded with wild flowers. Even the sunflowers wilting in the blazing sun look familiar, as do the farmers pitching hay onto their wooden carts.

On the last day of our journey, Justine and I are on the way to Piszczac, the remote village on the eastern edge of Poland where, as a tiny girl, I spent three years during the war, years of which I remember nothing. For some reason that I don't understand, at the very last minute something has impelled me to see this place again, so that I might recall something from the time when our life was a thread of gossamer flung across an abyss that gaped wider with each step we took.

As we pass yet another wayside shrine, I recall the mysterious holy picture that Jonathan and Susan found at the back of the wardrobe in my mother's flat shortly after she died. It was a black and white picture of Christ in a narrow walnut frame and on the back someone had written a dedication in a flowing old-fashioned hand. A picture of Christ is an unusual object in a Jewish home, and as I pored over the faded Polish words I wondered why my father had kept it all his life. It said something about God's kindness and mercy shining on Henryk Boguslawski on the occasion of his name day, but I couldn't decipher the name of the donor. Perhaps it was a gift from the priest whom my parents used to mention with affection. Looking out of the car window I sigh. Now that they are both dead, this mystery will never be solved.

Twenty-six kilometres before Piszczac, we come to the bustling little town of Biala Podlaska. Somewhere in this square was the pharmacy where in 1943 my father tried to buy medicine for me when I was so ill that they thought I would die. Somewhere around here was the railway station where he waited for the train back to Piszczac, clutching the precious serum while German soldiers scrutinised his papers.

Biala Podlaska is a friendly little place where women with shopping bags gossip on street corners and no-one seems to hurry. Excited by the prospect of returning to Piszczac, I haven't given any thought to what I hope to find there. Perhaps I could visit the house where we used to live, but I don't know the address. Since this is the administrative centre of the region, it strikes me that they may keep records of my village. If so, I may be able to find the address of Mrs Bogdanowa, our wartime landlady. Seeing the house may jump-start my memory.

Inside the town hall I scrutinise a noticeboard listing the president, chairman, directors and office-bearers by the score. It's midday already, and we have to drive back to Warsaw this afternoon to catch the plane back to Sydney, so I must find someone quickly, but who? Like an arrow aimed at a dartboard, my eye falls on the town president's name. He will know where provincial records are kept.

Up in his office, a young blonde in a crisp white blouse tells me that there are no village records in Biala Podlaska, but as I turn to leave she says casually, 'Actually I'm from

Piszczac myself.' Elated by this revelation, I start reeling off the names of some of the villagers my parents used to mention, but she shakes her head at each one. 'We only arrived after the war, and those people must have left.' I'm almost at the door when she says: 'But we did know the priest there.'

I wheel around. 'The one who was there during the war?' She nods. My heart is beating faster.

'The priest I know lives right here in Biala Podlaska,' she says.

Making a rapid calculation, I shake my head. It couldn't possibly be the same one. 'He'd be very old by now,' I say.

She grins. 'He is!' Pointing out of the window at a church spire, she says, 'Ask for him at St Anne's.'

On the way to the church I can't get over this succession of coincidences, and wonder what guided me to this town, this office, and this woman who seems to be directing me to the past I came to find. Questions and suppositions spin around in my mind. It couldn't possibly be the same priest. But even if it is, at his advanced age, will he remember those times, will he remember my parents, will he remember anything?

Then a bigger question knots my stomach. Should I tell him that we are Jewish or will the shock be too much for him at his age? I wonder whether I'll have the courage to reveal what my parents were forced to conceal. Perhaps he'll be angry at the deception. Maybe after all these years it's better to leave things alone.

A red-faced road worker digging outside the church leans on his spade as he points to a small box-like block of flats across the path. 'The priest from St Anne's lives on the first floor,' he says.

As I bolt up the dark flight of stairs, my heart is banging against the back of my throat and I press the small buzzer with trembling fingers. It's not a priest but a motherly grey-haired woman who opens the door, and she's shaking her head with regret. 'I'm sorry but the priest isn't here,' she says. My shoulders sag with disappointment but Anna, the housekeeper, ushers Justine and me inside, clucking her tongue. 'I'll make you some coffee, please wait, maybe he'll be back soon.'

She sits us down in a cluttered room where the noises of the street float in through the open balcony. There are shelves full of books and papers, a painting of the Virgin Mary, and two carvings of Christ on top of the cupboard. Anna brings us strong coffee and homemade cake, but I can't swallow anything. 'Reverend Father arrived in Piszczac in 1942,' she says. 'He's eighty-three now.' Her eyes dart towards the door at every sound. 'He usually tells me where he's going or leaves me a note to say when he'll be back, but today he didn't say anything, so I don't even know where to look for him,' she laments.

I glance at my watch. There is still no sign of this priest, and if I wait too long, I won't have time to get to Piszczac because we still have to drive all the way back to Warsaw this evening. Anna is wringing her hands. 'Just a few more minutes. Do stay for lunch, he's bound to be back by then. You're welcome to share our potatoes and buttermilk, just wait a little longer,' she pleads. But we have to go on to Piszczac.

All along the way to Piszczac, trucks, vans and trailers are stacked with mattresses fastened with leather straps, rattling bed frames and swaying wardrobes, and many of the farmhouses sport big signs advertising *Meble*. Furniture. Odd, in such an agricultural backwater. 'It's the Russians,' the driver explains. 'They're so short of consumer goods that sharp Ruski operators buy things here to sell over there.' I'd forgotten that we're only about a hundred kilometres from the Russian border, which was one of the reasons why my father thought we'd be safer here, deep in Poland's peaceful eastern countryside.

At the turn-off to Piszczac, sour orange rowanberries hang off the mountain ash trees, and brindle cows graze near a sluggish stream. My nerves rise to fever pitch as I read the road sign to Justine. Piszczac. I can't believe I'm really here.

In the small shady park in the centre of the market square, villagers chat on benches under the tall pine trees. Perhaps someone will remember my parents and their life here during the war. There is something familiar about the little wooden houses around the square which are pressed together like old friends whispering secrets. I approach a man with fine white hair and a singlet who stands outside his cottage talking to a woman with strands of grey hair falling around her plump face.

Aleksander Krynski can't recall a dentist called Boguslawski or a woman called Bogdanowa, but his wife nudges him. 'Take them to see Mrs Kisiel, she may remember,' she says. A moment later he's knocking on the door of a tiny hut that's tilted and sagging, with weathered planks that look as though they're collapsing in slow motion. Peering inside a window covered by a scrap of white net, Mr Krynski presses his nose against the glass but comes away shaking his head. 'She must be out.'

As we stroll around the square, it looks as though little has changed here in the past fifty years. The simple wooden cottages with their net curtains and pots of blood-red geraniums on the windowsills, the untended gardens with spiky sunflowers and spindly tomato plants with their sharp sourish smell, the lean dogs chained up in the yard for security rather than companionship, the horse-drawn carts piled with newly mown grass, all this must have been exactly the same fifty years ago.

In one corner of the square a man in a crumpled suit squats on the heels of his dusty shoes, ready to weigh out his home-grown tomatoes on a set of scales for the stout young woman leaning on a bicycle. 'She's our postmistress,' Mr Krynski explains. As we walk around the perimeter of the square, he points out one little house after another. 'This one belonged to Lejzar the Jewish butcher. Srulek lived over there, he had a hardware shop. Piterman the tailor lived just here. Over there was the haberdasher, another Jew.'

Although we're walking slowly, my breathing is ragged, as if I can't get enough air into my lungs. So Piszczac had a thriving Jewish community with shops, workshops and businesses located around this square. Later I'm surprised to learn that before the war, about one quarter of Piszczac's 2082 inhabitants were Jews.

'And what happened to all those Jews?' I ask.

'First the Germans pushed them all into one part of town, intending to make a ghetto, but then they changed their mind and deported them all to the camps.' I'm sure that Berta, my father's brave cousin whom he saw once after his arrival, had been among them.

When I ask whether any Jews returned, he nods his white head energetically. 'See that house where that man is standing? One fellow returned there. And the house near the lamppost, two women came back there.' He counts out two more. Five survivors out of five hundred people. Even though it's a hot summer's day, a shiver runs down my back.

Two foreign women attract a great deal of attention in a remote Polish village, and several men ride beside us on their beaten-up bicycles, curious to know why we've come. One of them, a man with a bulbous nose, protruding belly and a shirt as yellow as country butter, offers to take us to see someone he knows. 'She remembers everything, she'll tell you what you want to know,' he keeps insisting, but we don't trust him and keep walking.

All this time I'm aware that another man is riding behind us, keeping his distance, saying nothing, just watching. When he comes alongside us, I look into a face whose features seem to be blurred. In a voice that's soft and hesitant, he seems to be asking a question. *'Jude?'* he murmurs.

I stop walking and nod. 'And you?' I ask. 'Are you Jewish?'

An unfathomable expression veils his face. 'Polish,' he says.

I ask his name. It sounds like Zydelko. Zyd means Jew in Polish. Did I just imagine this?

While I'm trying to figure this out, he whispers a word that I hear quite clearly. *'Kim.'* The Yiddish word for come. Is this something remembered from a secret childhood? But when I turn to speak to him again, he has vanished, melted away like a shadow in the summer haze.

By now my spirits are beginning to flag. This excursion is beginning to resemble a wild goose chase. No-one remembers my parents, Mrs Bogdanowa or anything. I no longer see the point of this quest and am ready to give up and drive back to Warsaw when the guy in the yellow shirt reappears and once again urges me to see his neighbour. With nothing to lose, we follow him. Around the corner, a thin woman in a grey cardigan is nodding while he speaks. 'Mrs Bogdanowa used to live at the turn-off to Chotylow,' she says.

A horse and cart heaped with hay rumbles past as we walk towards the crossroads. Before we reach the corner, I catch sight of a handsome gabled farmhouse and grab Justine's arm. 'That's it! That's the house!' Although most of it is hidden by shubbery, I recognise the gabled attic and the little path leading to it that's almost obscured by thick lilac bushes. I have a photograph of myself at the age of four with my mother and Zosia, Mrs Bogdanowa's daughter, taken on this very path. It was a dirt path then, and the bushes were much smaller, but this is definitely the place.

I'm trembling with excitement. This is what I came to find, and here it is, the house that seems to hold the key to a part of my existence which I recall only in tantalising fragments. Seeing that house is a validation. It proves that I really did live here at that time.

As I stand here, memories came flooding back. Chained up to a wooden kennel beside the house was a dog which bit one of my father's patients on the thigh. Zosia and I split pumpkin seeds with our teeth up in the attic while my mother and Mrs Bogdanowa filled barrels with pickled cabbage and pickled apples down in the cellar. At the end of summer our house was filled with the bittersweet fragrance of the cherry vodka my father used to make out of small tart morello cherries. In spring, from my little iron bed by the open window, I drowned in the perfume of lilac blossoms.

My heart is thumping. After fifty years I'll be able to enter that house and see it again and maybe capture more of the memories which have eluded me all these years but which are hovering all around me now, almost close enough to touch and smell. But as I open the wire gate, a furious bull terrier rushes towards us as if catapulted from the house, showing saw-like fangs as he barks. We retreat rapidly, snapping the gate behind us, and wait outside. A burly man in a singlet comes out of the house towards us, but I can't hear a word he's saying above the dog's shrill barking.

When I try to explain why we've come and ask if we could come in for just a moment to refresh my memory, he throws his arms up in the air with an aggressive gesture. 'What do I care?' he snaps. My pleas only make him more truculent and he turns his back on us and strides back to the house.

It doesn't seem possible that I could have come all the way to Piszczac and found the house, yet be barred from going inside. As I stand there, seething with anger and frustration, Justine prods me to action. At least take a photo of the house, she urges. But the man has heard the click of the shutter and rushes towards us like an enraged bull, shouting, 'Who gave you permission to take photographs here, you bloody bitch?' He's gesticulating, yelling obscenities, and I can see that he's capable of breaking my camera, even attacking us. There is nobody around, we are alone. Resigned, we head back to town.

But I don't have time to dwell on my disappointment because before we've reached the square, a short elderly woman with a pale face and hair dyed as black as pitch comes up to us. 'You must be the women who were asking for me,' she says in a friendly way and propels us inside the tiny dwelling where Mr Krynski brought us earlier. As we sit in the small room which is her kitchen, bedroom and living room all in one, she reminisces about the past. 'Of course I remember Mr Boguslawski our village dentist!' she exclaims. 'He was a distinguished-looking man with glasses. He had a pretty wife.' Pointing to a tooth she says with a laugh, 'The filling your father gave me lasted over fifty years!'

Janina Kisiel, who was born in Piszczac, takes us around the village. Pointing to a street behind the square, she says, 'There was a synagogue here, a big one, and every Saturday the Jews prayed there, so devoutly.' There's no trace of it now, no sign that it ever existed. The Germans destroyed it, and the Russians erected an ugly cement box on the site, which became the health unit.

'On Saturdays the Jews used to come and buy *pejsachowka*—plum brandy—from my father. He bought a restaurant before the war from a Jew called Zuckerman. There were a lot of Jews here, but on the whole, we got on quite well,' she recalls. 'Once I remember a drunken brawl where somebody got thumped, but that was unusual.

'Most of the shops belonged to Jews,' she continues. 'In fact there were only four Polish shops. Over there was

Yankel's fruit shop, and his mother, Mrs Mannesowa, had a bakery. A woman called Giza and her sister had a grocery shop nearby. The Koniuchy family sold horses. And over there,' she points at a window with a net curtain, 'was Lejzar's place where they koshered the meat. Lejzar was a tall man with a long beard.' It sounds as though the Jews were well known to their gentile neighbours, with whom they were interdependent. But the memorial to the victims of Nazi atrocities makes no mention of the village Jews who had comprised one quarter of the population and were deported from here en masse.

Past the memorial, Mrs Kisiel leads us to the church. It has a tall tower and a new decorative archway painted cream. Unlike synagogues, the churches of Poland have not been turned into cinemas and health units. Standing in the small garden in front of the church, my mind goes back to the serious little three-year-old with tightly plaited braids who scattered rose petals in religious processions.

Through the iron grille I peer into the church. Above the altar hangs a large painting of Christ, radiating love and compassion. I must have attended Mass here on Sundays, unaware that I was an impostor who belonged to that other religion, the one that was usually mentioned with contempt. I feel a sudden wave of nostalgia for this place, and I long to sit inside and soak up the warmth from the light slanting in through the windows while I try to make some sense of past and present. Maybe then I would recapture something of the child I used to be, instead of remaining an enigma to myself. But the church is locked up.

With a start I realise how late it is. It's already three in the afternoon, and we still have a long drive back to Warsaw. Time is running out, but after seeing Piszczac I feel a new urgency to try the priest's house again. Back in Biala Podlaska

I run up the stairs two at a time, my heart drumming in my ears. Will he be there this time, or will I miss him now and forever? As the bell shrills, I keep thinking over and over, let him be here. Let him be here. And let it be him.

CHAPTER 45

The door opens, and an old man is looking intently into my face. Then he folds his arms around me, he's holding me tightly against him, and he's saying over and over again, 'Little Danusia. My dear little Danusia.'

Tears are pouring down my face; I'm sobbing so hard that I don't think I'll ever stop. Some grief I didn't know I felt is flooding over me as I stand here, a helpless little girl held by this old man who strokes my hair and cups my wet face in his gentle hands. In a soothing voice he murmurs, 'Little Danusia. Cry, my poor child, you have plenty of reason to cry. After all you've gone through, after all the terrible times you've lived through, let it all out now, my child, just cry. My little Danusia. May God keep you, may he always have you in his care.'

When I look up, I see a puckish face, one eye reddened and half closed, but an alert gaze full of compassion. It feels as if he's looking straight into my heart, and I stand in his doorway, sobbing, overwhelmed by feelings I cannot understand.

Seeing him again, feeling his compassion, hearing him use the Polish name which my parents used to call me, releases emotions so deeply lodged that I didn't even know they were there. All the anxiety, tension and sorrow that my childish mind absorbed and suffered in silence fifty years ago are spilling out at this moment.

When I turn around, I see that tears are streaming down Justine's face too. To have my own daughter witness my return to a forgotten childhood, and see her moved to tears by this extraordinary experience, is overwhelming. In that miraculous moment boundaries of time and relationship dissolve. My daughter is looking at the child I used to be, feeling the grief that I've suppressed for so long. She stands beside me in another time and place, supporting me with her empathy and love.

Benevolence shines from Father Soszynski's face. In a voice that's surprisingly strong for a man of eighty-three, he says, 'I was thinking about you just two days ago. I thought about your parents and wondered whether little Danusia was still alive. While I was in town today someone said that people from overseas were looking for me. I thought of you straightaway. Danusia! I thought, and flew home like a bird!'

Why should this telepathy astonish me, when the fact that I am looking into the face of the priest who helped us survive the war in Piszczac is beyond anything I ever dreamed of? To find him as a result of a chance stop in Biala Podlaska, still alive and still living here after fifty years, so alert, and calling me by name as if it all happened yesterday, is a miracle. It has never occurred to me that such a marvellous thing could happen, or that meeting him would be so cathartic.

Smiling into my face with a radiance which dazzles me, he says, 'You were a tiny girl of about three years old, but you prayed so devoutly. So innocent. I was always very moved by you. I can still see you in church before me. You usually sat with your parents, but sometimes with the village children. You were always so docile, so obedient. Mummy or Daddy only had to say "Danusia!" and you left the room at once.'

This image of me as the perfect, invisible child, the child who saw everything, understood everything, yet said nothing, makes my tears flow again. There is enormous power in the language of one's childhood, perhaps because the words have a richer, more intense meaning which evokes the essence of the child within. Without any warning, I'm looking at the child I used to be, plunged into the terrifying times and dark emotions which I suppressed so long.

Although Father Soszynski is no stranger to miracles, he too is overcome by this unexpected encounter. 'To think of you coming here to see me after fifty years!' he marvels, shaking his head. The young priest with the engaging personality who won all the women's hearts in Piszczac fifty years ago is still bright, charismatic and animated in old age. With his twinkling blue eyes and spiky crew-cut grey hair, he reminds me of an elderly leprechaun. 'I remember your father very clearly, better than your mother,' he recalls. 'She was very quiet, very anxious, she seemed frightened. Whenever she spoke, she watched him closely, like a worried pupil before an examiner. Your father was always on his guard. Like a crane watching over its nestlings, he was always vigilant. Whenever she said anything that he didn't like, he just had to look at her and she fell silent.'

I never thought of my mother as fearful, but having experienced my father's sharp glances which could slice through glass, I can well imagine the effect they would have on her when she was already on tenterhooks in case she gave something away. This was not a matter of making a social faux pas, it was a matter of survival, and our lives hung on each word.

'I saw all this,' he says. 'It was very obvious. In fact, the only time your father relaxed was when he sat down to a game of bridge or chess. He played excellent bridge, wiped us out at chess, and enjoyed a glass of vodka. But the moment your mother opened her mouth, he tensed up again.'

In a strong, good-humoured voice that quavers slightly,

Father Soszynski begins to sing a ditty that one of the villagers composed about my father rushing from his patients to his game of chess. He shakes with laughter at the recollection. 'Oh, he demolished us all at chess, he was the village champion! Just once, our game ended in a draw, oh, I was so proud of myself! I never forgot my moment of glory!' And to my amazement, he describes the conclusion of that game, move by move.

Father Soszynski is reminiscing about the first time he met my father, whom he liked immediately. 'He was a distinguished-looking man with a limp and had an aura of nobility about him,' he says. 'Your father was an incomparable raconteur. Sharp witted, knowledgeable, intelligent, he was an extraordinary host. And the jokes he told! Oho! I wouldn't repeat them to you!' He gives a bawdy chuckle just thinking about them. This was a man 'do tanca, i do rozanca' he says, using the rhyming Polish phrase which means 'a man for all seasons'.

Hearing his description of my parents makes me marvel at their courage. My heart aches for my father, the village chess champion, who could drink with the locals and tell bawdy jokes, and for my mother who exchanged recipes and kept up a light-hearted conversation while fear gnawed at her night and day. I feel my mother's anxiety more intensely now than when she told me about those times, because what they tried to keep secret was clearly so obvious to this perceptive man who observed and interpreted their behaviour, yet remained silent.

While he speaks, I keep pushing back the question that is nagging at me. Not yet, I keep thinking. Not yet. Suddenly Father Soszynski stuns me by answering my unspoken question. 'Of course I knew that you were Jewish. We all knew.'

My mind is whirling with confusion. Even after we arrived in Australia, I remember my parents discussing whether they should write and tell him the truth, wondering what he would say if he found out. Only a few minutes ago I'd been figuring out whether it would be too much of a shock. Yet all along he had known the life-threatening secret my parents had tried so hard to conceal.

Father Soszynski continues his reminiscences. 'Not long after I arrived in the village, your father asked the organist to enter his certificate of baptism into the parish records. This seemed a strange request, and I wondered then whether he had bought this certificate somewhere. If so, it was a very smart move because once the information was recorded, he'd be able to obtain authentic copies. Still, in those days it was better not to know too much so I decided not to inquire too closely into it and we entered your names in the parish records.'

Over coffee which he brewed in his small kitchen, the priest chuckles. 'Your father had a gift for extracting information so delicately that people didn't even realise what he was doing. For instance, what could he possibly know about church matters? But he quickly found out what he needed to know, and remembered everything he was told. You were too tiny to be aware of these things, and you probably knew nothing about their secret. It's just as well that you didn't know anything, or the most precious years of your childhood would have been spoiled.'

It's true that I was told nothing, but children are quick to hear the urgency in their parents' voices and read the anxiety in their eyes. I know that I sensed the whirling tensions, saw the agonised glances. Long before my brain knew, my heart understood. Already, at three, I knew that I must never reveal my real name. When Aunty Mania arrived in Piszczac and called herself Wanda Morawska, I knew I must not let on that I recognised her. That need for wariness and secrecy has

577

affected me throughout my life, perhaps it has also affected my children.

'Little Danusia went to church and scattered petals in our processions,' he smiles fondly. While he is speaking, I want to hug myself with joy, I want to stop everything and just have a few quiet moments to revel in this marvellous thing that is happening to me. By helping me recover this solemn little girl I hardly know, Father Soszynski is handing me back the long-lost piece of a jigsaw puzzle, perhaps even the key to the rest of my life. But there is no time for reflection. Time is galloping and I must find out as much as possible in the short time I have left.

The twinkle has gone from Father Soszynski's eyes.

'One day in 1944, Mrs Forycka, the doctor's wife, came to see me and she dropped a bombshell. "Has Reverend Father heard the latest? The whole town is saying that the Boguslawskis are Jews!" I thought to myself, Jesus Maria, can this be true? Then I recalled that business with the baptism certificate, that embittered fellow Mr Jozek who came to work with your father but turned out to be a Jew, your mother's nervousness, your father's constant vigilance . . . But I understood. It was a matter of life and death,' he shakes his head sadly. 'A matter of life and death.'

I'm listening so intently, I hardly breathe. 'I could see that the situation was serious,' he continues. 'Then Mrs Forycka repeated, more vehemently, "All Piszczac is up in arms about it, everyone is saying that the Boguslawskis are Jews, they're saying that they even light Sabbath candles, and that Reverend Father visits them. What are we going to do about it?" she wanted to know. "Well, surely we're not going to condemn them to death," I told her. But she rushed off, too agitated to stay any longer.

'After she left, my sister told me that she too had heard

the same thing, the rumour had spread around the village like wildfire. Next day, your father came to see me. He was not the same person. He had lost all his strength, he was a crushed man. Despair in his eyes. So sad to see.' Father Soszynski shakes his head at the memory, and I can tell that he has my father's distraught face before him. So do I. ' "Catastrophe, Reverend Father!" he told me. "They're saying that we are Jews, and that these rumours started with your sister. How can they make such wicked accusations? To accuse us of being Jews is inhuman." '

My eyes are glued to him as he tells this story which I have already heard from my father and read in his memoirs. 'When your father came to see me that day, I felt like weeping,' he says. 'Such a cultured, witty man, so intelligent and companionable. How could I not extend a helping hand? I said, "Doctor Boguslawski, let's look at it another way. There's no merit being born a Pole any more than there is disgrace being born a Jew. It's not up to us. It's up to God. I can't feel proud of being born a Pole any more than another should feel ashamed of being born a Jew. But the issue is that to accuse someone of being a Jew today is to sentence them to death." ' He leans towards me. 'You know, the Gestapo were stationed only three kilometres down the road in Chotylow.

'So I said to your father, "Doctor, let me figure out how to climb out of this pit. I won't run from house to house, but what I will do is come to your place this afternoon with my sister, and we will walk down the centre of the main street of the town so that everyone will see that we're coming to visit you as if nothing has happened. Let them all see. Will you give us a glass of tea when we come?" '

Father Soszynski is a compelling raconteur. He isn't just relating the past, he is reliving it with every nuance of expression and feeling, his speech slow and rapid in turn, his eyes shining or troubled depending on what he is saying. I'm not just hearing an account of what happened, I'm as close to being there as it's possible to be, with all the terror and despair, hope and humanity, conflicting feelings and divided loyalties. 'I can still see the relief on your father's face when I told him that I'd come over that afternoon and keep coming to visit him,' says Father Soszynski.

As Father Soszynski speaks, I can feel my father's heartfelt gratitude and see his first glimmer of hope that the priest's healing hands will pull us back from plunging into that everwidening abyss. For the first time in my life I realise that our only hope of survival, however slight, rested entirely with Father Soszynski.

'I sat my sister down and told her to zip her lips and to say no more about this matter. I told her to get ready because we were going to pay the Boguslawskis a visit. I took her by the arm and we walked down the main street so everyone could see where we were going. Your parents were overjoyed to see us. They were beginning to feel like outcasts because most people had distanced themselves from them. And remember, we had the Gestapo only three kilometres away. German soldiers often came to Piszczac, drank with their pals, listened in to conversations and spied on people.

'After that visit with my sister, I kept coming more often than usual, to demonstrate my support. When the villagers saw their priest socialising with your parents, they figured out that I must know what I was doing, and decided that they had no business gossiping about them.'

Leaning towards me, Father Soszynski says with great emphasis, 'And no-one in that village denounced you, even though everybody knew that you were Jews. In your case, Piszczac passed with flying colours. We had drunkards, thieves and cheats amongst us, but on that occasion, everyone behaved beyond reproach.'

Although I don't want to argue or diminish the priest's pride in his parishioners, something bothers me. 'If not for you, they would have denounced us even though they knew us so well. How could the fact that we were Jewish outweigh the fact that they were friends and neighbours?'

He sighs. 'My dear, sweet Danusia. Those questions are easier to ask than to answer. Human transgression is a deep and dark mystery. According to our holy books, human nature was corrupted in the Garden of Eden. To some people, money was all that mattered. They just wanted to collect the fifty zlotys which the Germans gave them for turning Jews in. They didn't care about the person they betrayed. Anyway, my child,' he returns to his former theme, 'in this case, the people of Piszczac got full marks, because every single one of them knew, yet no-one gave you away.'

Throughout my life I had been angry that our existence in Piszczac had been so tenuous, that dangerous rumours had proliferated and that, had the war continued, one of our neighbours or acquaintances would have denounced us to the Germans. But Father Soszynski's account of our survival helps me to see it in a different light. During the Holocaust it took only one person to send hundreds to their death, but it sometimes took one hundred people to save a single Jewish life. For the first time I realise that by their silence the people of Piszczac had helped us to survive. Whatever their reasons, the fact was that they did not betray us, and in those inhuman times that was a miracle.

Suddenly I remember the picture of Christ which Jonathan and Susan found in my mother's flat after she died. 'It was I who gave your father that picture,' Father Soszynski replies. 'I believe that it was thanks to Our Lord's loving kindness and intercession that you survived. And your father, may he be praised, accepted my gift in the spirit I gave it.'

Father Soszynski has kept his own mementoes of my parents. From a drawer he takes out two letters my father wrote to him after we left Piszczac, one from Krakow, the other from Brisbane. 'It was sad to say goodbye. Nothing binds people closer together than living through bad times. Like soldiers at the front who have looked death in the eye together.' He explains that he hadn't replied because the communist government persecuted those who had any contact with the west.

Then Father Soszynski gets up, walks over to his bookcase and hands me a history of the village that he has written, called *Piszczac, Once A Royal Town*. He opens it and hands it to me. To my astonishment, I'm reading the story of our stay in Piszczac. What until then was my story has now become recorded history. With a firm hand, Father Soszynski inscribes the book to 'Danusia Boguslawska who lived through a terrible time of terror during which she had to struggle for her own survival and that of her nearest and dearest'.

As we say goodbye, I ask him whether there is anything he needs for himself or his parish. Love shines from his tear-filled eyes. 'Danusia, my darling girl,' he says, 'I need nothing whatsoever. I never thought that such joy would burst into my life. Seeing you here, feeling our common humanity, and knowing that you have such a good soul, that's the best reward I could possibly have.'

As our car speeds away from Biala Podlaska, towards Warsaw, I am so overwhelmed by emotion that it's a long time before I can bring myself to speak. The Talmud, which my grandfather Daniel used to study, says that every good deed tips the balance in favour of humanity, that whoever saves one life, saves the whole world. For the first time, I fully comprehend what that means.

The late afternoon sun pours over orchards, meadows and pastures in shafts of intense golden light and glazes the haystacks and sunflowers in the stubbled wheatfields. A sudden rush of joy swells my throat so that I can hardly swallow. When I return home I will arrange for a grove of trees to be planted in Jerusalem in honour of Father Soszynski, one for every year of my life since he enfolded my parents and me in his sheltering arms.

Tears roll down my face as I realise that I will never be able to tell my parents that I've visited Father Soszynski. 'Nana would have been overjoyed to know that I'd seen him,' I tell Justine.

'Maybe she already knows,' my daughter replies.

EPILOGUE

Standing by my side at the Temple Emanuel Synagogue in Sydney, Jonathan's fiancée Susan slides her slim finger along the page of the Siddur as she follows the Hebrew prayers that I can't read. During the Kaddish prayer, she knows I'm thinking about my mother, and her comforting arm around my shoulders feels light but strong. Jonathan turns towards me with a sympathetic look and my father's sensitivity shines out of his Baldinger blue eyes.

As the rabbi intones the ancient prayers for Rosh Hoshana, my mind goes back to the Shabbat dinner at home three years earlier when Susan told us that she'd decided to become Jewish. Ever since she'd started going out with Jonathan, we'd come to love this spontaneous, warm-hearted young woman with the mischievous smile and delicate strength. Her religion had never been an issue for us or for Jonathan.

'I'm not doing it for you or for Jonathan,' she said. 'I'm doing it for myself. For the first time in my life I feel as if I'm part of a community. I've always liked your traditions and the way that being close as a family is important to you. When I have children, that's what I'd like them to have.' Her next words took my breath away. 'Your religion has continued for thousands of years, and so many Jews have died because of it, including your relatives. I don't want to be the one to break that continuity.'

Jonathan was gazing at her rapturously. 'Nana would have been thrilled, wouldn't she?' he said. My mother adored Susan, whose loving ways and irrepressible sense of fun had been a ray of sunshine in her last bleak years.

Then Susan gave me the most precious gift of all. 'When I convert, I'd like to take on your mother's Hebrew name,' she said. 'I loved Nana, and I'd feel proud to carry on her heritage by taking her name.' This loving tribute to us and to my mother made me feel as though I'd reached up and touched the stars.

Susan walked into my arms and we hugged each other for a long time without speaking. The past few years had been full of stress and sorrow, but looking into her tear-filled eyes, I understood that God takes with one hand but gives with the other.

And now, at the Rosh Hashana service, the New Year prayers focus on repentance, responsibility and redemption, not only for Jews but for all mankind. They remind us that time is fleeting, we are fragile, and our days are scrolls on which we record our lives by actions, not by words. At the conclusion of the service, the tall cantor wrapped in a prayer shawl stands before us like a Biblical prophet. Taking a deep breath, he raises the *shofar* to his lips and blows the ram's horn to usher in the Days of Judgment. At the sound of the stirring fanfare, tears spring to my eyes.

These notes, spiritual in concept but shrill in execution, swirl around and weave me into the mosaic which has been unfurling since time immemorial. In that solemn fanfare, which makes the air around me vibrate with meaning, I hear Daniel Baldinger's voice and feel his firm hand reaching out to me to join the chain.

GLOSSARY

A.K. (Polish):	Initials for Armia Krajowa, Polish right-wing resistance.
Apikojres (Yiddish):	A pagan or heretic. Derived from the Greek philosopher Epicurus.
Apteka (Polish):	Pharmacy.
Bar Mitzvah (Hebrew):	Jewish boy's coming-of-age religious ceremony held at the age of 13.
Bat Mitzvah (Hebrew):	Jewish girl's coming-of-age ceremony held at the age of 12.
Belfer (Yiddish):	Religious teacher.
Bigos (Polish):	Stew made with cabbage and sausage.
Bilineder (Hebrew):	God willing.
Bimah (Hebrew):	The dais in the synagogue.
Bimber (Polish):	Home brew.
Bruderschaft (German):	Means brotherhood. A social ritual in which two people link arms while holding a glass of alcohol and drink with linked arms after which they address each other by first names.
Challah (Hebrew):	Plaited yeast loaf, often glazed with egg yolk or sprinkled with poppy seeds, eaten on the Sabbath and most festivals.
Chanukkah (Hebrew):	Eight-day festival which commemorates the victory of the Maccabeans against the Syrians.
Cheder (Hebrew):	Religious school for children.
Chevra Kadisha (Hebrew):	Jewish burial society.

Cholera psiakrew (Polish):	Swear words. Bloody hell.
Chometz (Hebrew):	Any food which contains leaven and is therefore forbidden in the house during the eight days of Passover.
Chuppah (Hebrew):	Canopy supported by four poles, held above the bride and groom during their wedding ceremony.
Dajsche (Yiddish):	Means German, signifies assimilated Jews.
Dawaj (Russian):	Go on, come on.
Dawaj Stagan (Russian):	Give me a glass.
Dorosky (Polish):	Horse-drawn carriage.
Doven, Dovening (derivation unknown):	To pray, praying.
Dreidl (Yiddish):	Spinning top, given to children for the festival of Chanukkah.
Dreikopf (Yiddish):	Shrewd person.
Dybbuk (Yiddish):	The spirit of a dead person which enters and takes over the soul of the living.
Fleischich (Yiddish):	Refers to dishes which contain meat and according to kosher dietary laws shouldn't be mixed with dishes containing milk or dairy products which are called **Milschich**.
Fufajka (Russian):	A thick padded jacket.
Gamev (Yiddish):	Thief
Gett (Yiddish):	A divorce document which the husband must grant for the divorce to be valid according to Jewish law.
Groschen (German):	A coin.
Histericzka (Polish):	Hysterical woman.
Hoshana Raba (Hebrew):	The seventh day of Sukkoth which has a spiritual significance.
Jude; pl. Juden (German):	Jew, Jews.
Kaddish (Hebrew):	Mourner's prayer which glorifies God and the gift of life.
Kasha (Polish):	Buckwheat.

Kennkarte (German):	ID card.
Kichelech (Yiddish):	Crescent-shaped biscuits.
Kiddush (Hebrew):	Blessing recited over wine on Sabbath and holy days.
Kippah (Hebrew):	Skullcap.
Kitl (Yiddish):	White robe worn by the head of the household during the Seder dinner and Yom Kippur.
Komsomol (Russian):	Communist Party youth group.
Kvitl (Yiddish):	Slip of paper containing a request, left at a sacred site such as the grave of a venerated rebbe.
Maidl (Yiddish):	Young girl.
Malkah (Hebrew):	Queen. Sometimes applied to the mother of the house during the Seder dinner.
Mamuncia (Polish):	Diminutive, mummy.
Manishtana (Hebrew):	Literally, 'Why is this different?' It refers to the four questions traditionally asked by the youngest child at the Seder table, meaning 'Why is this night different from all other nights?'
Matzoh (Hebrew):	Flat, unleavened bread eaten during the eight days of Passover.
Melech (Hebrew):	King. Sometimes applied to the head of the house during the Seder dinner.
Melamed (Hebrew):	Religious teacher.
Menorah (Hebrew):	Candelabra whose candles are lit on eight consecutive nights during Chanukkah.
Mezuzah (Hebrew):	Parchment scroll fixed to the doorposts of orthodox Jewish homes, reminding the residents of the omnipresence of God.
Mikveh (Hebrew):	Pool of natural water for immersion to make people ritually clean, with a secondary purpose of spiritual purification. Mainly used by religious Jewish women before the wedding ceremony and after the menstrual cycle.
Minyan (Hebrew):	A quorum of ten Jewish men required to hold a religious service.

Mohel (Hebrew):	Man trained and authorised to circumcise Jewish boys, usually on the eighth day after birth.
Muktzeh (Yiddish):	Forbidden by Jewish religious law to be used on the Sabbath.
NKVD (Russian):	National Commisariat of Internal Security. Stalin's secret police.
Obwarzanki (Polish):	Twisted breadsticks thickly encrusted with salt, often sold at street stalls.
Panienka (Polish):	Young lady.
Parsha (Hebrew):	Portion of Torah read in the synagogue on Sabbath, often by the Bar Mitzvah boy.
Pejsachowka (Polish):	Plum brandy.
Pesach (Hebrew):	The festival which commemorates the flight of Moses and the Jews from slavery in Egypt.
Peyis (Hebrew):	Uncut side-locks of Chassidic males.
Pierogi (Polish):	Large ravioli-style pockets usually filled with mashed potatoes and served with fried onions.
Proszepana/Proszepani (Polish):	Excuse me, sir/madam.
Rosh Hashana (Hebrew):	The New Year festival which celebrates the birthday of the world. It ushers in a period during which Jews are meant to take stock of themselves, forgive others, and repent for their own sins.
Seder (Hebrew):	Commemorative prayers and readings held on the first and second nights of Passover.
Shivah (Hebrew):	Prescribed seven-day period of mourning by immediate family after funeral.
Shofar (Hebrew):	Ram's horn blown in synagogue on Rosh Hashana to evoke awe of God, humility, and repentance.
Shtetl (Yiddish):	Small Polish village inhabited predominantly by Jews.
Shule (Yiddish):	Synagogue.
Siddu (Hebrew):	Prayer book.

Streiml (Yiddish):	Fur hat worn by Chassidic men on the Sabbath and holy days.
Szczesc Boze (Polish):	Greeting. God bless you.
Szlachta (Polish):	Nobility.
Tallith (Hebrew):	Prayer shawl with fringed ends which Jewish men wrap around their shoulders while praying.
Talmud (Hebrew):	Commentaries made by rabbis and scholars on the Torah.
Talmud-Torah (Hebrew):	Place for religious study.
Tateh (Yiddish):	Father.
Tatunciu (Polish):	Diminutive, daddy.
Tefillin (Hebrew):	Also known as phylacteries. Small leather boxes containing parchment inscribed with scripture passages, strapped onto the forehead and left arm of orthodox Jewish men during certain prayers. This process is called 'laying teffilin'.
Toches (Yiddish):	Backside.
Torah (Hebrew):	First five books of the Old Testament which contain the main tenets of Judaism.
Treif (Hebrew):	Opposite of kosher. Food forbidden by Jewish dietary laws.
Tzimmes (Yiddish):	Carrot casserole.
Tzitzis (Hebrew):	Fringed garment worn by orthodox Jewish males under their coats to remind them to observe the six hundred and thirteen laws.
Tzures (Yiddish):	Worries.
UNRRA (acronym):	United Nations Relief and Rehabilitation Administration.
Yecker (German):	A derogatory term for Jews of German descent, meaning overmeticulous, too literal, humourless.
Yom Kippur (Hebrew):	Day of Atonement. The most solemn festival in the Jewish year.
Zhid (Polish):	Jew.
Zhidek (Polish):	Little Jew (contemptuous).

BIBLIOGRAPHY

Andrzej, K. Paluch (editor), *The Jews In Poland, Vol. I.*, Research Center on Jewish History and Culture in Poland, Jagellonian University, Krakow, 1992.

Arad, Y., Gutman, Y. and Margaliot, A. (eds), *Documents on the Holocaust*, Yad Vashem, Jerusalem, 1993.

Balaban, Prof. M., *Przywodnik Do Zydowskich Zabytkach Krakowa (Guide to Jewish Historical Buildings in Krakow)*, Solidarosc-B'nei-B'rith, Krakow, 1945.

Bieberstein, A., *Zaglada Zydow W Krakowie (The Annihilation of the Jews of Krakow)*, Wydawnictwo Literackie, Krakow, 1985.

Borwicz, M., Rost, N. and Wulf, J. (eds), *Zaglady Ghetta W Krakowie (The Annihilation of the Krakow Ghetto)*, Jewish Historical Institute, Krakow, 1946.

Bronsztejn, S., *The Jewish Population of Poland in 1931*, The World Jewish Congress, 1958.

Davies, N., *God's Playground: A History of Poland*, Clarendon Press, Oxford, 1988.

Dobroszynski, L., Kirschenblatt-Gimblett, B., *Image Before My Eyes: A Photographic History of Jewish Life in Poland 1864–1939*, Schocken Books, New York, 1977.

Duda, E., *Krakowskie Judaica (The Jews of Krakow)*, PTTK KRAJ, Warsaw, 1991.

Edelman, M., *Ghetto Walczy (The Ghetto is Fighting)*, Bund, Warsaw, 1945.

Fishman, J.A. (ed), *Studies on Polish Jewry 1919–1939*, YIVO Institute for Jewish Research, New York, 1974.

Friedman, Dr F., *The Annihilation of the Jews of Lwow*, Jewish Historical Institute, Lodz, 1945.

Gilbert, M., *The Holocaust: The Jewish Tragedy*, Fontana Press, London, 1986.

Gilbert, M., *The Second World War*, Weidenfeld & Nicolson, London, 1989.

Kugelmans, J., Boyarin, J. (ed and trans), *From a Ruined Garden, The Memorial Books of Polish Jewry*, Schocken Books, New York, 1983.

Marshall, R., *In The Sewers of Lvov*, Scribners, New York, 1991.

Shirer, W., *The Rise and Fall of the Third Reich*, Secker & Warburg, London, 1962.

Soszynski, Roman, *Piszczac, Once a Royal Town*, Biala Podlaska, 1992.

Valent, Dr Paul, *Child Survivors*, William Heinemann, Australia, 1994.

Vishniac, R., *A Vanished World*, Allen Lane, London, 1983.

Wood, E.T., Jankowski, S., *Karski: How One Man Tried to Stop the Holocaust*, John Wiley & Sons, New York, 1994.

Zamoyski, A., *The Polish Way*, John Murray, London, 1987.

Ziemian, J., *Papierosiarze Z Placu Trzech Krzyzy (The Little Cigarette Sellers of Warsaw)*, Niezalezna Oficina Wydawnicza, Warsaw, 1989.

ZNAK Publication on Jewish-Catholic Relations, 'Jews in Poland and in the Rest of the World', Krakow, 1983.